Britain, France and Europe, 1945–1975

Britain, France and Europe, 1945–1975

The Elusive Alliance

Anthony Adamthwaite

BLOOMSBURY ACADEMIC
LONDON • NEW YORK • OXFORD • NEW DELHI • SYDNEY

BLOOMSBURY ACADEMIC
Bloomsbury Publishing Plc
50 Bedford Square, London, WC1B 3DP, UK
1385 Broadway, New York, NY 10018, USA
29 Earlsfort Terrace, Dublin 2, Ireland

BLOOMSBURY, BLOOMSBURY ACADEMIC and the Diana logo are trademarks of
Bloomsbury Publishing Plc

First published in Great Britain 2020
This paperback edition published 2022

Copyright © Anthony Adamthwaite, 2020

Anthony Adamthwaite has asserted his right under the Copyright, Designs and Patents Act, 1988,
to be identified as Author of this work.

Cover design by Tjaša Krivec
Cover image: November 1944: British prime minister Winston Churchill walking
with French General Charles de Gaulle whilst on a visit to Paris during World War II.
(© Central Press / Getty Images)

All rights reserved. No part of this publication may be reproduced or transmitted in
any form or by any means, electronic or mechanical, including photocopying,
recording, or any information storage or retrieval system, without prior
permission in writing from the publishers.

Bloomsbury Publishing Plc does not have any control over, or responsibility for,
any third-party websites referred to or in this book. All internet addresses
given in this book were correct at the time of going to press. The author
and publisher regret any inconvenience caused if addresses have
changed or sites have ceased to exist, but can accept no
responsibility for any such changes.

Every effort has been made to trace copyright holders and to obtain their permissions
for the use of copyright material. The publisher apologizes for any errors or
omissions and would be grateful if notified of any corrections that should
be incorporated in future reprints or editions of this book.

A catalogue record for this book is available from the British Library.

Library of Congress Cataloging-in-Publication Data
Names: Adamthwaite, Anthony P., author.
Title: Britain, France and Europe, 1945–1975 : the elusive alliance / by Anthony Adamthwaite.
Other titles: Elusive alliance
Description: London ; New York : Bloomsbury Academic, 2020. |
Includes bibliographical references and index. |
Identifiers: LCCN 2020005653 (print) | LCCN 2020005654 (ebook) | ISBN 9781441156525 (hardback) |
ISBN 9781441100627 (ebook) | ISBN 9781441129178 (epub)
Subjects: LCSH: Great Britain—Foreign relations—France. | France—Foreign relations—Great Britain. |
France—Foreign relations—1945- | Great Britain—Foreign relations—1945- |
Europe—Foreign relations—1945-
Classification: LCC DA47.1 .A63 2020 (print) | LCC DA47.1 (ebook) | DDC 327.4104409/045—dc23
LC record available at https://lccn.loc.gov/2020005653
LC ebook record available at https://lccn.loc.gov/2020005654.

ISBN:	HB:	978-1-4411-5652-5
	PB:	978-1-3503-3861-6
	ePDF:	978-1-4411-0062-7
	eBook:	978-1-4411-2917-8

Typeset by RefineCatch Limited, Bungay, Suffolk

To find out more about our authors and books visit www.bloomsbury.com
and sign up for our newsletters.

To Geraldine

Contents

List of Illustrations	viii
Acknowledgements	ix
List of Abbreviations	xi
Preface: Distrust and Verify	xii
Introduction: A Tale of Two Cities	1

Part I Chosen Peoples

1	Anglo-Saxon Attitudes	13
2	Vive la France	25
3	Strangers	39

Part II Reversal of Fortunes

4	New Look	55
5	De Gaulle Redux	71
6	Unmerrie England	87
7	Running on Empty	101

Part III Bids

8	Unshakable, Constant, Effective	119
9	Supermac	135
10	Another Harold	153
11	Bash on Regardless	167
Conclusion: Endgame		181

Timeline	191
Appendix 1. Britain and French Governments, 1944–75	195
Appendix 2. Foreign Secretaries and Foreign Ministers	197
Appendix 3. Foreign Office and Quai d'Orsay	199
Appendix 4. European Economic Growth, 1950–80	201
Notes	203
Select Bibliography	227
Index	237

Illustrations

4.1	The March of Time: The New France 1946	56
5.1	General de Gaulle walking down the Champs Élysées, Georges Bidault a step behind on left, 25 August 1944.	72
5.2	Foreign Minister Michel Debré with his predecessor Maurice Couve de Murville, 2 June 1968	82
8.1	Winston Churchill in Paris, with his daughter Mary and British ambassador Alfred Duff Cooper, 1945.	120
8.2	French foreign minister Bidault and British foreign secretary Bevin sign Anglo-French alliance in Dunkirk, 4 March 1947	126
8.3	French foreign minister Robert Schuman and German Chancellor Konrad Adenauer, 27 May 1952.	134
9.1	British Prime Minister Harold Macmillan and French Prime Minister Guy Mollet, 9 March 1957	137
9.2	Prime Minister Macmillan and Foreign Secretary Selwyn Lloyd welcomed to Paris by General de Gaulle, 30 June 1958	139
11.1	Probing the Dutch in the Hague, foreign secretary Brown and premier Wilson, 27 February 1967 – note the body language.	168
11.2	Sir Christopher Soames, UK ambassador to France, 22 September 1968	175

Acknowledgements

Britain, France and Europe explores post-Second World War hopes for London–Paris partnership and a Franco–British Europe. There are a number of reasons for writing. It has not been done before, and there is the attraction of doing something for the first time. For sure, there are numerous overviews of interactions between the whale and the elephant from the Sun King on, but no recent book length study of the relationship in the decisive mid-twentieth century decades.[1] Another motive for writing has to do with the bridges between past and present. Spats over post-war European integration may seem like ancient history. Strong continuities persist, however. The rows fuelled Euroscepticism and, ultimately, the UK Brexit referendum of 2016. Shared leadership after 1945 could have fashioned a different and perhaps more satisfying Europe.

In novelist David Lodge's *Changing Places* Professor Morris Zapp has the ambition to kill Jane Austen forever as a subject of criticism and research by dealing with each and every topic that could possibly arise out of reading her novels. I have no ambition to provide saturation coverage of the Franco–British couple. A wide-angle lens contrasts attitudes and cultural baggage, peoples as well as elites. I've profited from French sociologist André Siegfried's experience: 'never have I succeeded in understanding the British and French points of view simultaneously. All I can do is sometimes understand them one after the other.'[2] The two neighbours are profiled in separate chapters.

'The Californian atmosphere is unhelpful for the true comprehension of European affairs', groused a member of the French delegation at the foundation conference of the United Nations in San Francisco, April–June 1945.[3] Readers will judge whether my 'comprehension' is persuasive or not. Distance while not always lending enchantment certainly puts Europe in a global perspective. Location offers special advantages: the archival riches of the Hoover Institution at Stanford University, and the intellectual vibrancy of Berkeley's Institute of European Studies, pulsing with visiting scholars, workshops and colloquia. Pacific Rim colleagues, graduate students and undergraduates share a lively curiosity and enthusiasm about Europe which has nurtured the writing. The book builds on the foundation of earlier research on the cross-channel relationship. Several of the chapters debuted as public lectures, conference presentations and articles. Feedback from audiences and readers helped tremendously.

Thanks are due to the University of California at Berkeley for financial support in funding the archival research, in particular the University Committee on Research; the Institute of European Studies; the Department of History for Shepard Fund grants. A University Humanities Research Fellowship enabled me to spend a study semester in Europe. Grateful acknowledgement is made to the following archives for assistance and for permission to quote material. In the UK: the National Archives; The Bodleian Library, University of Oxford; Churchill College Archive Centre, University of

Cambridge; Trinity College, University of Cambridge; British Library of Political and Economic Science, LSE; The Liddell Hart Centre, King's College London; The Royal Institute of International Affairs; The Brotherton Library, University of Leeds. In France: Archives nationales; Archives d'histoire contemporaine, Fondation nationale des sciences politiques; Archives diplomatiques, Ministère des Affaires étrangères et du Development international; Assemblée nationale, Service des Archives; Fondation Guy Mollet; Ministère de l'Economie, des Finances et de l'Industrie; Comité pour l'histoire économique et financière de la France; Institut Pierre Mendes France; Centre des archives contemporaines, Fontainebleau. In the United States: The Hoover Institution Library and Archives, Stanford University, California; the Lauinger Library, Georgetown University, Washington DC.

Former policy-makers generously talked to me and responded to written queries: Sir Guy Millard; Sir Frank Roberts; Sir Evelyn Shuckburgh; Lord Sherfield; Etienne Burin des Roziers; Etienne de Crouy-Chanel; Jean Donnedieu de Vabres; Louis Joxe; Rene Massigli; Christian Pineau. Special thanks are due to archivists and librarians: the late Yvon Lacaze, Ministère des Affaires étrangères, Paris; Chantal Tourtier de Bonazzi, Archives nationales, France; Colin Harris and Helen Langley, Bodleian Library, Oxford; Odile Gaultier-Voituriez and Dominique Parcollet, Centre d'Histoire de Sciences Po, Paris.

Early drafts of the manuscript benefited from the insightful comments of colleagues John Connelly and Peggy Anderson. I am indebted to my Bloomsbury editors, Rhodri Mogford and Laura Reeves, for advice and encouragement. Over the years the friendship and writings of colleagues have provided inspiration, especially Maurice Vaisse, Robert Frank and Yoichi Kibata. Finally, I can't resist mentioning a schoolmaster ancestor. In the early 1800s the Reverend John Adamthwaite DD of Brough, Cumbria, advertised his school in *The Times*, promising 'no vacations at this school'. Welcome back holidays!

Abbreviations

BBC	British Broadcasting Corporation
BOT	Board of Trade
CAP	Common Agricultural Policy
CND	Campaign for Nuclear Disarmament
CO	Cabinet Office
DEA	Department of Economic Affairs
EC	European Community
ECSC	European Coal and Steel Community
EDC	European Defence Community
EEC	European Economic Community
EFTA	European Free Trade Association
ELDO	European Launcher Development Organisation
ENA	Ecole nationale d'administration
ETC	European Technological Community
EU	European Union
FCO	Foreign and Commonwealth Office (from 1968)
FO	Foreign Office
FTA	Free Trade Area
GATT	General Agreement on Tariffs and Trade
GDP	Gross Domestic Product
IBRD	International Bank for Reconstruction and Development
IMF	International Monetary Fund
NATO	North Atlantic Treaty Organization
OECD	Organization for European Economic Cooperation
Quai	Quai d'Orsay, French foreign ministry
UN	United Nations
WEU	Western European Union

Preface

Distrust and verify

'France is of all European countries', it is claimed, 'the most difficult for any foreigner to write about.'[1] The devotion of the French to their history has made it harder for outsiders to storm the barricades. Nevertheless, they have done so magnificently. Anglophones have made a larger contribution to French history than to the history of any other European country – transforming the way the French think about their past.

Even so, writing about the external policies of the Franco–British couple is no picnic. Though fake online archival sites are not yet a serious hazard, the pitfalls of the paper trail are real enough. The Paris Metro used to have illuminated maps inviting travellers to press a button lighting up connections. Until software engineers design appropriate apps researchers are very much on their own. Mapping Franco–British approaches to the construction of early post-war Europe is a daunting task because of the imbalance between British and French national archives in the twentieth century. At first glance, the rows of published French diplomatic documents – far outnumbering the British sister series – suggest an embarrassment of riches. In fact, qualitatively and quantitatively there is a big disparity between the two archives. Comparing them is like comparing a continental breakfast and a full English.

It's a common misperception that once the voices of witnesses are accessed the rest is plain sailing. 'All knowledge of the past that isn't just supposition derives from people who can say "I was there",' pronounced a distinguished Oxford don. In short, 'if it's not eyewitness testimony then it's a load of hooey'.[2] If only history was so simple! Many questions remain unanswered and may never be satisfactorily resolved. The greatest barrier is the huge inequality of sources – mountainous on some topics, fragmentary or non-existent on others. How to separate the wheat from the chaff? The American loan negotiations of 1945 generated slews of Washington telegrams. 'Foreign Secretary have you got the telegram?' asked the Chancellor of the Exchequer. 'I've got 'undreds', replied Ernest Bevin.[3]

Like Bevin, the researcher's problem is selection. The documentation varies enormously in quantity and quality. The French national archive cannot match the continuous run since 1916 of British cabinet records. As president of the Fifth Republic, de Gaulle decided high policy. Consequently, foreign ministry files track policy execution rather than formulation. Death prevented de Gaulle finishing the second volume of a three-decker memoir about his presidency. His war memoirs registered the deeper springs of action, while staying tight-lipped about day-to-day decision-making. The general curated his reputation with a highly selective and sometimes misleading narrative. Reported conversations tend to be retrospective reconstructions rather than accurate summaries from the archive.⁴ The recollections of the general's familiars – information minister Alain Peyrefitte and Jacques Foccart, chief adviser on African policy – require careful handling, despite claims to be based on diaries and notes written close to events. The presidential archive reveals little about the rough-and-tumble of decision-making and day-to-day perceptions of international affairs.

Continental officials approached record-keeping much more casually than their UK counterparts. Decision-makers tended to treat documents as their own property, and were reluctant to circulate notes of meetings. A British adviser to Belgian statesman and NATO secretary general Paul-Henri Spaak recalled, 'I could not persuade him to keep me informed of his interviews, it had not been his habit to make such records as a minister in the Belgian government'.⁵ Whitehall, by contrast, insisted on the use of note takers and prompt circulation of papers. At a session of the five signatories of the Brussels Treaty of 1948 the French defence minister shocked British officials when he suggested ministers should handle the main business privately without secretaries and interpreters. After much persuasion he agreed to a secretary but no interpreters.⁶ Astonishingly, prime minister Guy Mollet's proposal in September 1956 for a Franco–British union left no trace in the French archives. Mollet does not appear to have consulted colleagues and advisers. Fortunately, Whitehall kept a substantial footprint of the initiative.

There is a world of difference between the reports of the general's views as relayed by visitors and his actual opinions.⁷ The president courted interlocutors, telling the British how bad the Germans were, and vice versa. Much more serious are the substantive differences between versions of the same conversation. Instead of employing note takers or promptly dictating a record the general frequently relied on an interpreter's summary. Interpreting and taking notes do not sit easily together, however. 'I've always had a lot of trouble in getting the general to give me the details of the talks he has', observed Jacques Foccart. 'When asked he (*general*) responded, "You know quite well what it's about, you know the problems".'⁸ Foccart had to insist on the president telling him the main points of a discussion.

Nevertheless, the casualness of the French machine had significant advantages. As well as giving mavericks like Jean Monnet, head of the post-war planning commission, scope to promote their own agendas, it shielded members of leaky and shaky coalitions. Beware documents, counselled French premier Georges Clemenceau, and helped by leaving as few as possible. The Fourth Republic lacked the foreign policy bipartisanship of British politics. Decolonization, German rearmament and European integration whipped up fratricidal strife, and reinforced a minimalist approach to record-keeping. The Vichy state indicted Third Republic leaders in 1942; two years later the Provisional Government arraigned Vichy notables and collaborators in the High Court. In 1946 France's National Assembly established a parliamentary commission of enquiry to investigate political and military elites from 1933 to 1945. Informality had a downside. It enabled an anti-French British FO to turn a potentially game-changing initiative into an international row – l'affaire Soames – wrong-footing both countries.

Whitehall procedures enhanced the quality of the UK national archive. Incoming FO papers went first to desk officers in the appropriate geographical departments. After entering them in a file the official attached a minute listing feedback. With the head of department's approval the folder climbed the ladder collecting further assessments. If judged sufficiently important the file went into one of the foreign secretary's red boxes. In contrast, French foreign ministry papers often circulated without minutes. Officials sometimes annotated documents but it was not standard procedure.

A big culture shock awaited British officials posted in the mid-1970s to the European Commission in Brussels. A French dominated administration assumed 'knowledge is power: the more secret files you have locked in your desk, the more powerful you are ... very little of what went on in some fairly important negotiations ever got written down'.[9] Dossiers were treated as personal property and hoarded in office cupboards. Christopher Soames, Vice-President of the European Commission, countered local customs by circulating records of talks with ministers and ambassadors – 'a British practice hitherto unknown in the Commission'.[10]

Mining more documents does not produce more reliable and authoritative histories. The vast expansion and increasingly multilateral character of post-1945 international politics rule out a definitive narrative. The days are long gone when a historian could aspire to have the last word on anything. Documents have many lives, historians only one. A major segment of national policy like the history of Britain and the European Community defies comprehensive investigation. 'A history confined to policy formulation', wrote historian Alan Milward, 'requires by the mid-1960s, a systematic search through the records of an ever-increasing number of ministries'.[11]

In its own way the archival steeplechase is as perilous as a Tour de France Pyrenean descent. Government papers may trigger a mimetic effect on researchers causing them to regurgitate official slop. A journalist recalled a tip from an old hack: 'You should always ask yourself when talking to a politician: "Why is this lying bastard lying to me?" '[12] This is a sound principle for any investigator. No administration records its deliberations for the enlightenment of posterity. Crucial concerns go unmentioned or unrecorded. No British records survive of an Attlee–Truman summit in Washington in November 1945. For three weeks in 1950 there are gaps in the main Foreign Office file on the Schuman Plan. Missing pieces are par for the course, and records of the same discussion conflict. Differences 'on crucial points in the British and American records' at a Churchill–Truman summit in Washington in 1952 'were so great that they seemed as if they could not apply to the same gathering'.[13] The reasons given for a particular decision may not be the most important. When an action has to be taken for an unavowable reason a specious statement may be supplied for the record. The trail frequently peters out, partly because of government pruning and weeding, and partly because so much went unrecorded.

The fundamental challenge is the uncertainty of all sources. Like witnesses to a street accident, individuals carry away different impressions of the same event. Letters, diaries, oral histories, memoirs and eyewitness testimonies are like the telephone game. Someone whispers a message and by the time it gets to the last person it's completely different. The Bloomsbury luminary Leonard Woolf inquired what had happened to his paper delivery girl Mary. 'Haven't you heard?', replied a neighbour. 'She was machine gunned by a German plane and I saw it happen.' Three months later Woolf met Mary. The story was 'entirely untrue'.[14] Old men forget. A retired ambassador writing a memoir pestered the Foreign Office for 'a letter which, after a time-consuming search ...

proved to exist only in my imagination'.[15] Labour leader Aneurin Bevan mocked Harold Macmillan's taste for reading political autobiographies. 'I have never been able to achieve that level of credulity ... I would rather have my fiction straight.'[16] General de Gaulle's flight to London in June 1940 provoked two quite different narratives.[17] Sinatra-like memoirists insist on 'My Way'. Authors rarely lose an argument, often exaggerating 'constraints' on action – to provide an alibi for passivity or to enhance their initiatives. Vichy head of state Marshal Philippe Pétain excused himself for not writing memoirs, saying he had nothing to hide. Few follow the example of novelist Mary McCarthy whose autobiography alerted readers to the semi-fictional touches.

The grandparents of novelist Julian Barnes entertained themselves by reading out to one another their diary entries for a particular day several years earlier. 'Grandpa: "Friday. Worked in garden. Planted potatoes."'; 'Grandma: "Nonsense. Rained all day. Too wet to work in garden."'[18] As well as inflating the importance of the writer, diaries distort the pressures of the moment, ensuring instant gossip and minimal reflection. 'One defect of diaries and autobiographies', observed writer Simone de Beauvoir, 'is that usually what "goes without saying" goes without being said, and thus one misses the essential'.[19] Missing the essential may mean talking up the nonessential. 'One exaggerates everything,' admitted philosopher Jean-Paul Sartre; 'one is really on the look-out, one continually forces the truth'.[20] Macmillan's diaries for the Suez crisis of 1956 have a crucial gap from 4 October 1956 to 3 February 1957. After claiming to have lost the diary entries, the premier confessed he had destroyed them at the request of his predecessor Anthony Eden.

Much goes unrecorded. Pressures towards concealment intensified after the outbreak of the First World War. War guilt arguments forced governments to publish far more documents than ever before – demolishing the Victorian assumption that almost everything of importance could be committed to paper and locked away indefinitely. After 1945 the British state introduced new procedures to regain control of information. Interwar cabinet minutes attributed expressions of opinion to individual ministers; after 1945 cabinet secretaries were instructed 'to avoid ... recording the opinions expressed by particular ministers'.[21] The record turns bland and opaque. The partial release in recent years of the cabinet secretary's notebooks has enriched the anodyne printed minutes, confirming, for example, the intention to destroy President Nasser as well as repossess the Suez canal. A quick inspection of the kitchen kills the notion that cabinet minutes are a form of holy writ; political advisers may edit the cabinet secretary's record before circulation. While prime minister Margaret Thatcher prepared a favourite dish of shepherds pie, the head of her policy unit 'would sharpen up the somewhat bland typed-up account of proceedings that came over to us from the Cabinet Office'.[22]

The state decrees big gaps in the record – intelligence, royal family and other papers deemed sensitive are shredded or closed indefinitely. Protecting the myth of a resisting France meant locking away Vichy archives about collaboration and Holocaust involvement. The FCO has admitted that it unlawfully hoarded and continues to retain at least half a million files – some dating back to the seventeenth century. The British national archive plays games with researchers – releasing and withdrawing documents without explanation – now you see them, now you don't.

The Eden government tried to destroy any evidence of collusion with Israel in the Suez crisis. A few hours after prime minister Eden denied in the House of Commons any foreknowledge of Israel's invasion of Egypt in October 1956 the Conservative chief whip met cabinet secretary Norman Brook leaving the cabinet room, 'He's (*Eden*) told me to destroy all the relevant documents', Brook said, 'I must go and get it done'.[23] Changes in working procedures make it difficult to discover the whys and wherefores of decisions. Before 1939 the FO consulted with other government departments by correspondence; during the Second World War oral consultation became the norm. The urgency of post-war issues spawned ad hoc informal meetings – 'the chat in the corridor' or the lavatory. Prime minister James Callaghan offered the governorship of Hong Kong to European Commission president Roy Jenkins when they met in the 'Gents' at a European Council meeting in Paris.[24]

To be sure, Britain pioneered official histories based on closed archives. From 1919 the government series focused on the two world wars. In 1966 prime minister Harold Wilson inaugurated a peacetime continuation about episodes of general interest to be written by eminent historians with unrestricted access to relevant material and supplemented by recollections of key players. But the project should carry a health warning. The Official History of Britain and the European Community exemplifies the deficiencies. Publication lagged well behind record releases, and writers interpreted their remit very differently. The author of the first volume was a distinguished academic with a clear idea of what he understood by 'official history'; his in-house successor delivered a shapeless narrative – 'a leading historian asked me what the basic thesis of my book was going to be. The answer is that there is none ... I have thought it best to try to let them [participants] tell their own story as far as possible'. Back to square one – the illusion that history is about letting the actors and documents speak for themselves! Content to toe the line, official authors are short on criticism and tight-lipped about intelligence. MI5 operative Peter Wright claimed that in 1961–3 the agency successfully hacked into top-secret traffic between France's London embassy and Paris – 'every move made by the French ... was monitored'.[25] Not a hint of this in the narrative. Did MI5 continue to read Frog cyphers during Wilson's second EEC membership bid? It's hard to escape the conclusion that the British state has used official histories to curate the past. Early opening of files, not more Whitehall cooks, would benefit researchers and lay readers.

In spite of genuflections to open government, transparency and freedom of information, the cult of secrecy remains intact. Labour minister Tony Benn's call in 1968 for freedom of information legislation went unanswered for decades. The UK Freedom of Information Act of 2000 (FIA) did not open the floodgates. Far from it. Thanks to loopholes and the refinement of bureaucratic procedures, FIA strengthened state restrictions on information. It imposed a general ban on royal family archives. The total of documents retained increases annually. The curating of collective memory goes hand in hand with manipulating the present. The current commemoration craze conceals rather than clarifies issues. In Alan Bennett's play *The History Boys*, history master Irwin warns, 'All this mourning has veiled the truth. It's not so much lest we forget, as lest we remember ... there's no better way of forgetting something than by commemorating it'.

Abandon all hope? 'The moment one begins to investigate the truth of the simplest facts which one has accepted as true', wrote Leonard Woolf, 'it is as though one had stepped off a firm narrow path into a bog or quicksand'.[26] Uncertainty may be a blessing in disguise, however. Minding the evidential gaps points up the potential for alternative outcomes, liberating us from hegemonic narratives. Uncertainty may be closer to reality. As Czesław Miłosz's 'Old Jew of Galicia' put it, 'When someone is honestly 55% right, that's very good and there's no use wrangling. And if someone is 60% right, it's wonderful, it's great luck, and let him thank God. But what's to be said about 75% right? Wise people say this is suspicious. Well, and what about 100% right? Whoever says he's 100% right is a fanatic, a thug, and the worst kind of rascal'.[27]

Introduction

A Tale of Two Cities

'What's it all about?' quipped a taxi driver to philosopher Bertrand Russell – 'and do you know, he couldn't tell me'. This book asks what became of Churchill's promise in 1944 of an 'unshakable, constant and effective' cross-Channel pact. 'If the two countries settled their differences they would be the masters of Europe,' urged French president Vincent Auriol. In June 1962 premier Harold Macmillan stressed 'how a close Anglo–French alliance, really effectively managed from day to day, would have avoided both wars'. A high-wire act for sure, but doable. In the late 1940s a Franco–British Europe came within a whisker of realization, thereafter appearing and disappearing like a Cheshire Cat. Partnership could have revamped Western Europe, empowering London and Paris in the Cold War era.[41]

The impetus for writing originated in a study of the origins of the Second World War. Hitler's empire building in the 1930s thrived on Anglo–French disarray. After 1919 Britain and France shared, and disputed and lost control of Europe. After holding up in the First World War the Entente Cordiale looked the worse for wear by the 1920s. A timely makeover could have prevented the war of 1939. The second conflict reconfigured global politics and opened a nuclear age, enthroning the new behemoths, the United States and the Soviet Union. For over four decades,Moscow and Washington determined the high politics of Europe. Almost forgotten now are the initiatives to reinvent the Entente as a hinge for a Franco–British Europe. The defeat of Germany and its allies left Britain and France the natural leaders of Western Europe. Alliance with France, trumpeted Churchill, was a 'fundamental principle' of British policy. French ministers pushed for bilateral economic planning; foreign secretary Ernest Bevin extolled joint exploitation of African empires to ensure independence from the United States. The rhetoric delivered a mouse – the Dunkirk Treaty of March 1947, a skeletal fifty-year defence pact.

I advance a three-pronged argument. First, partnership offered a second career for redundant imperial powers. Yes, the two neighbours were an odd couple but not so odd as to rule out alliance. Obstacles were surmountable – Franco–German and Anglo–American collaboration overcame substantial hurdles. The synergy of teaming up could have fast tracked London and Paris, making the continent's voice heard in Cold War conclaves and nurturing a different kind of European community. Churchill offered France union in 1940 and the idea stayed in the French playbook – prime minister Guy Mollet resurrected it in 1956. More's the pity. The 1960s offered a second bite of the cherry, a window to reposition Western Europe in world politics that would not reopen until the 1990s. As nuclear states and UN Security Council members, Britain and France in tandem might have accomplished what neither could achieve alone – a more independent Europe, partner rather than client of the United States, with the potential to broker East–West détente.

Second, UK movers and shakers spurned the pooling of resources, alleging conflicting national characters and interests, the priority of an Anglo–American alliance, France's economic and political weakness, and its large Communist party. The pair went their own ways. Surprisingly, despite defeat, occupation and bitter colonial wars, France repackaged itself quickly and successfully. I ask why. Political cultures made a difference. A leaner, casual French style, juiced by modernization and a sense of universal mission, triumphed over a buttoned-up, rule-bound British mode. The architect of modernization, wild card Jean Monnet, epitomized the contrasting approaches. In 1949 he hosted British mandarins at his country house in a bid to promote a Franco–British Europe based on integrated national economic plans.

Third, I argue that de Gaulle, contrary to legend, sought agreement over Europe. His vetoing of British bids for EEC membership in 1963 and 1967 earned him pride of place in the demonology of twentieth-century British political history. The general, concluded an FO official, 'is and always has been the main impediment to ... the resumption of the Entente Cordiale'.[2] Exaggerating France's diplomatic wizardry and calling out its president as a spiteful and intransigent autocrat created a convenient alibi for self-inflicted missteps. Astonishingly, a supplicant UK expected the gatekeeper to give access to the EEC without inducements. Though ministers occasionally dangled carrots – a future European technological community and nuclear cooperation – they played White Queen's rules: 'never jam today'. In fact, the French president – *The Sunday Times* reminded readers – had a 'highly pragmatic and opportunistic' side.[3]

Mainstream narratives have 'misunderestimated' – to use a Bushism – the prospects for Franco–British leadership in Europe. Historians, like international travellers, sometimes miss key developments. Changing trains in the Latvian capital Riga in the 1930s, novelist Graham Greene missed a revolution. The foundation myth of the European Union as a triumph of light and reason squeezed out other scenarios. Cross-channel initiatives left few prints. American–Soviet management of Europe's high politics, coupled with the rise of the legendary 'special relationship', eclipsed earlier dreams of a London–Paris duopoly. Last, but not least, different visions of Europe competed. As late as 1948 French leaders envisioned a neutral 'third force' continent brokering peace terms between the titans; Bevin too talked of a third force – in alliance with the United States. Economic integration supplied another bone of contention. Britain's cautious inter-governmental approach vied with continental sympathy for a supranational solution. The Attlee government rejected France's path-breaking Schuman Plan for a European coal and steel authority, partly because it distrusted France, and partly to protect the Anglo–American alliance, but chiefly to promote UK leadership.

A French historian downplayed the entente's dark side. 'Since 1815, apart from a few clashes between the British and the forces of the Vichy government', wrote François Crouzet, 'the sound of battle has died away', leaving 'a true symbiosis between England and France'.[4] Minimizing the minefields does not help the argument. Crouzet ignored twentieth-century black spots – interwar mésentente, confrontation in Syria and Lebanon 1941–6, and stand-offs over European construction. That said, the 'special relationship' was no lovefest. The UK's subaltern position in the Pax Americana bred resentment and friction. A case can be made for 'a basic incompatibility of outlook' underlying relations 'from the war onward'.[5] In 1971 prime minister Edward Heath assured French president Georges Pompidou, 'there could be no satisfactory partnership' between Britain and the United States when one of them 'was barely a quarter the size of the other'.[6]

What were the options in 1945? War weary and bankrupt neighbours confronted an identical quandary: how to recharge quickly in a fast-moving, upended world. Reactions to the predicament mattered as much as the predicament itself. Magnificently unprepared for the long retreat from empire, political moguls assumed the only show in town was great powerdom. No one questioned whether the assumption made sense in terms of the international order. 'Everyone on both sides of the Atlantic', recalled the Attlee government's chief economic adviser, 'was absurdly optimistic in 1945 about the prospects of recovery'.[7] Economist John Maynard Keynes talked of 'temporary' retirement as a first-class power.[8] The survival of the furniture of rank – armies, empire, moral prestige and a seat at the top table with the superpowers – concealed the price of victory. In 1946 London could still summon Abdullah, ruler of Transjordan, and tell him his country was to be independent and he was to be king.

Historians have lambasted the Attlee government for clinging to grandeur at the expense of the economy and welfare state. The critique is overly simplistic. Downsizing overseas commitments was not practical politics in 1945. Peoples looked forward to the fruits of victory. Like Martin Luther they could do no other. The dream of reclaiming power and glory sustained French morale under German occupation, and fuelled the post–1945 eight-year Indo–China war. Downsizing would have seemed a betrayal of wartime sacrifice. Labour prime minister Clement Attlee broached disengagement from the Middle East, but accepted great power identity. Indian independence in 1947 was considered a one-time fulfilment of wartime promises, leaving empire a going concern.

Power, like Hamlet's father's ghost, quickly dissolved – 'tis here, 'tis gone. The superpowers occupied centre stage. 'There is no solution to our problems over which we ourselves exercise much freedom of choice', confessed one of Attlee's ministers.[9] Hopes of restoring rank faded. Enfeoffed in the American empire Britain and France resorted to make-believe. 'The French are very anxious to go on pretending to be a Great Power', noted foreign secretary Harold Macmillan in 1955. 'They know that we are doing the same. But they tell us that it's no good. The world is bound to be dominated by the new barbarians, in the West and the East.'[10] Was there method in the madness? Political scientist David M. McCourt contends that Britain and France as 'residual great powers' consistently played international roles disproportionate to economic and military resources – 'punching above their weight'.[11] Insistence on great power privilege, McCourt argues, succeeded because it met the expectations of significant others: the United States, major allies, international and domestic constituencies. As America's prefects, London and Paris wielded influence over and above their intrinsic power.

The thesis underwhelms because the terms 'residual great power' and 'disproportionate influence' are undefined. 'Punching above their weight' – when, where and how? The essence of a great power is the ability to make others do what one wants. A UK delegate at the Geneva Conference of 1954 on Indochina considered it 'the last example of an independent British policy exercising significant influence in the resolution of a major international crisis'.[12] The Suez adventure of 1956 demonstrated the incapacity of Britain and France to compel Egypt – a much weaker ex-colony – to return the nationalized canal to international ownership. London and Paris could no longer project world policies at variance with the superpowers. Foreign secretary Selwyn Lloyd's 'Grand Design' of January 1957 admitted the game was up – the UK could not afford the nuclear and conventional forces required for global credibility. The country would have to pool resources with the Six of the EEC, making a 'third Great Power ... within NATO'.[13] The Washington connection brought military security but London lost the respect of American overlords and allies. 'They [British] have a continuing record of stupidity', complained US secretary of state Henry Kissinger in 1974: 'It is a tragedy what is happening in Europe.'[14]

Double harness would have given Britain and France street cred in American and Russian eyes. Post-war reconstruction created uniquely favourable conditions for innovation. An American academic described Europe as a 'living laboratory'.[15] Before he died fighting with Bulgarian partisans in 1944, Major Frank Thompson, brother of historian Edward Thompson, professed faith in a united continent, 'for a United States of Europe I could feel a patriotism far transcending my love for England'.[16] George Orwell advocated a socialist United States of Europe to include parts of North Africa. Dismayed by the dropping of the atomic bomb on Japanese cities, Labour prime minister Clement Attlee urged 'very far-reaching changes in the relationships between states' and a new international order ruling out war as an instrument of state policy.[17] Italian foreign minister Alcide De Gasperi called for a new federal Europe. An FO baron asked, 'Why should not Europe begin to regard itself as an entity with common interests, by which I mean the breaking down of economic barriers ... not ... the destruction of national traditions'.[18]

A new global architecture founded on the Atlantic Charter of 1941 offered traction in a reconfigured world. European regional institutions followed: Brussels Treaty Organization, OEEC, Council of Europe and ECSC. The multilateralism of the revamped international order fostered an interdependence unrealized before 1939. Fledgling institutions forged a collaborative culture, hardwiring habits of cooperation. Yet Franco-British collaboration stalled. Obsolete great power ambitions echoed a Victorian narrative of greatness. The geopolitical revolution demanded a new plot – a reimagining of the nation state. Instead, a narrow focus on regaining 'rank' turned cooperation into a quick fix to speed national recovery.

Over sanguine perceptions of UK economic strength and global ranking put the damper on joint enterprise. In 1945–6 economic and geopolitical fallout appeared reversible, making joint planning seem unnecessary. The realization, however, of the irreversibility of change supplied arguments against partnership in a Cold War climate. A much weaker ally with a large Communist party might turn into a millstone. Going it alone seemed to work best. In *The Future of Socialism* (1956) Labour Party intellectual

Tony Crosland enthused over Britain's pole position in Western Europe, and descried sunny Socialist uplands. In the same year the country scored a first with the opening of Calder Hall, the world's first commercial nuclear power station. Blue Streak, a medium-range ballistic missile, was slated to replace an ageing V-bomber nuclear strike force. A superior British way promised high dividends.

As well as shying away from cooperation London underestimated the French state's powers of renewal. The couple responded differently to crisis and change. From the late 1950s France sprinted ahead while Britain decelerated. In 1945 fire-breathing dragons seemed poised to devour the hexagon. Amazingly, a stricken polity escaped Communist revolution, military coups and civil war, outfoxing a stable and stronger ally. By the mid-1960s European Community members accepted 'Paris as the capital of Europe'.[19] How was it done? Were French diplomats smarter than everyone else? 'Brilliant creatures,' gushed a senior UK ambassador, 'their minds operate with a rapidity and lucidity that is the envy of their colleagues'.[20]

True, the French relished the diplomatic game. During the UK's second membership bid of 1966–7 Britain's ambassador to Paris underscored the finesse with which the French provoked 'doubts and uncertainties among the Five about the consequences of British entry while carefully avoiding any suggestion that they themselves are, in principle, opposed to it'.[21] Style had substance. A modernization cocktail, laced with renewal ideas from wartime resistance, Vichy and the 1930s, rebooted an apparently woebegone state. 'Hope never stopped running', testified wartime diarist Jean Guehenno.[22] Elites proclaimed a messianic mission. 'France will recover a radiance and an influence of the first rank', declared philosopher and political scientist Raymond Aron, creating 'a political and spiritual centre around which will gather the smaller nations . . . The French idea is to protect what is human . . . when all conspire to deliver society to the inhumanity of enslaved masses and the pyramids of steel'.[23]

De Gaulle delivered the cavalry. Sixty years on, the name carries a whiff of Noah's Ark – and perhaps a false memory of him insisting on British cuisine being raised to French standards before UK entry into Europe. 'The only figure in the western world with greatness in him', acknowledged a British ambassador.[24] As a Harvard academic in the 1960s, Kissinger was one of the few Anglo-Saxon commentators with a good word for the general. The future secretary of state likened the French president to Bismarck, praising his originality in recognizing that at a time of superpower détente there was 'little risk and considerable potential gain in political independence'.[25] The general's decision in 1958 to override domestic opposition and stay in the newly launched EEC positioned France as top dog in Western Europe. Surging economic performance gave the Fifth Republic a decided edge over the UK. The general's successors enjoyed cocking a snook at slowcoach *rosbifs*. Opening the Paris–Lille TGV link to the Channel tunnel in May 1993, President François Mitterand declared, 'passengers will race . . . across the plains of northern France, rush through the tunnel on a fast track and then be able to daydream at very low speed, admiring the English countryside.'[26]

While France rebounded, Britain wrestled with a hangover that felt like an endless Pennine tunnel. Greeting King Hussein of Jordan at Victoria Station in July 1966, home secretary Roy Jenkins reflected, 'as the rain poured down around the assembled splendour I could not avoid the thought that this looked like the last act in a dreary imperial charade'.²⁷ Gloom skewed perceptions of Europe and the world. Suez, a sputtering economy and declinism all fed the black dog. Delayed realization of war's degrading effects – voiced in novelist Elizabeth Bowen's *The Heat of the Day* (1948), and the legacy of the culture of crisis from the interwar years, heightened unease.²⁸ A seemingly endless polemic about decline never gelled into a fruitful conversation about the country's prospects. A megadose of introspection gave international change an air of irreversibility. The controversy became self-fulfilling. An effect became a cause, reinforcing the original cause.

What did voters think? Politicians never invited feedback. The gap between government and opinion forms a central theme of this analysis. The reluctance of Conservative and Labour administrations in the 1960s to mobilize public support for their EEC membership bids spawned Euroscepticism and ultimately Brexit. The so-called 'advanced democracies' tolerated large democratic deficits. The obsessively secretive, elitist nature of decision-making impacted severely on insiders and outsiders: restricting information, curtailing debate, narrowing options and sowing distrust. Marxist historian E.P. Thompson sought to rescue the working people he wrote about 'from the enormous condescension of posterity'.²⁹ Older narratives assumed a rooted indifference towards foreign affairs – with Munich and Suez as exceptions. This is a fallacy. Polls in the 1960s recorded sizeable majorities for EEC membership, despite exiguous official publicity. Trained to regard foreign affairs as a spectator sport, ordinary citizens allowed No. 10 and Whitehall to call the shots. Non-governmental networks exerted minimal influence and the sticks did not get a look in. True, on many issues voters perforce knew little, but it would be wrong to conclude they did not care.

The opaque, oligarchical nature of decision-making deliberately kept citizens in the dark. The establishment preferred a passive populace. News management stifled discussion, rationing releases of hard information in the public domain. Until broadcaster Robin Day pioneered the first gloves-off interview with a British prime minister in 1958, interviews went rather like this:

> Q: Sir, would you say that your visit to Timbuktu had been worthwhile? A: Oh, yes, I would definitely say my visit had been worthwhile. Yes, certainly. Q: Ah, good, well, could you say what topics you discussed, sir? A: No, I'm afraid I couldn't do that. These talks were of a highly confidential nature, you understand, and you wouldn't expect me to reveal anything that might prejudice our future relations. Q: No, of course not, sir. Well, sir, you must be very tired after your talks and your journey – may I ask, sir, are you going to take it easy for a while now – a holiday, perhaps?
>
> A: Ah, if only one could. But you know a minister in Her Majesty's Government can never take it easy, never rest, not really, you know. They're waiting for me now.³⁰

Kazuo Ishiguro's novel *The Remains of the Day* catches the reverential tone. Stevens, butler at Darlington Hall, stamping ground of appeasers in the thirties, sets out on a motoring trip to the West country. His car breaks down, forcing him to spend the night at a nearby inn. Looking and sounding like a gentleman he is at first taken for an MP. '"Oh no," I said with a laugh. . . . "In fact, I tended to concern myself with international affairs ..."a sense of awe seemed to descend on them ...' the hushed silence remained for several more seconds'.³¹ 'Hushed silence' speaks to 'the Whig imperialist' tradition of the British state which treated foreign affairs, in Bevin's words, 'as if they were something over the heads of everybody'.³² Only initiates entered the holy of holies. The paternalism of the British and French states excluded democratic republicanism with its emphasis on 'self-government by free and active citizens through open discussion and debate'.³³ Britons vented frustrations in letters to newspapers – the French press rarely published letters to the editor. Dissent and alienation propelled extra-parliamentary protest movements, notably CND and Paris May 1968.

Unlike France, Britain bungled self-marketing. Penny-pinching administrations disinvested in soft power, neglecting Europe and failing to find a distinctive voice. Drastic cuts in the 1950s closed many British Council centres. A generously funded secret FO Cold War propaganda unit, the Information Research Department, in cahoots with the CIA and other American agencies, churned out anti-Communist propaganda. British values hardly got a look in. In contrast, de Gaulle, posing as a European champion, stole a march on London, capturing the moral high ground. 'He talks of Europe, and means France', complained premier Harold Macmillan.³⁴ The French preached 'Europe' as their brainchild, claiming to be kosher Europeans with the right to separate the sheep from the goats. Britain, the Netherlands, Denmark and Norway 'were not true European nations' like France and Germany.³⁵ Impugning Britain's European credentials stretched the truth – French elites had mixed feelings on integration and strong prejudices about fellow Europeans. The general patronizingly lumped 'the poor Germans' with 'the poor Belgians and the poor Dutch'.³⁶ A Gaullist minister arrogantly dismissed Community partners: 'We'll have no trouble with that lot'.³⁷

Information belongs to the jewel box of power. French soft power exploited two motifs: the réclame of 'every man has two countries – his own and France', and the myth of a resisting France. State projection of a unique cultural identity formed the backbone of the international policies of the Fourth and Fifth Republics. Elites identified their values with universal values. Medievalist Marc Bloch, co-founder of the influential *Annales* school of history, considered a 'Frenchman' and a 'civilized man' to be identical.³⁸ Traumatized by Vichy and the German occupation, the French found common cause in humanistic values and a shared belief in a global mission. Shrewd self-promotion kept up appearances. In 1948 in the midst of colonial war in Indo-China, Communist threats at home, food rationing and politicians carrying begging bowls to Washington, the government commemorated the centenary of the 1848 revolutions with a lavishly hosted international conference in Paris. 'In England', recalled a participant, 'we were having one of our financial crises and were not allowed any foreign currency. Fortunately French hospitality was lavish enough'.³⁹

Pivotal to my argument are the shortcomings of UK leaders and government machines. In the 1960s the country went through foreign secretaries like a dose of salts – six in a decade. Politicians behaved like Charlie Chaplin in *The Gold Rush*, bustling about in a shack poised precariously on the edge of a cliff. Was the nation's slide as inexorable as it seemed then and since? Though some diminution was unavoidable, why such a helter-skelter? The Second World War cast long shadows but did not determine the massive haemorrhaging. France, Germany and Italy reinvented themselves. French elites made a better fist of recovery than British counterparts. For sure, Britannia had a poor hand, but why so poorly played?

The effects of stress and sickness on decision-making are easily overlooked because they are difficult to quantify. Six years of war and a huge growth of government drained leaders. Overtired, overwrought and overpromoted ministers strained to make sense of the nation's haemorrhaging. The job, observed foreign secretary Eden on returning to office in 1951, 'had killed Bevin and destroyed Morrison'.[40] Stress and alcohol reduced French foreign minister Georges Bidault to incoherence. As power leached away, the timely reappraisal of ends and means could have widened and refreshed policy options. Seasoned insiders condemned the obsoletism of the FO machine. An aversion to planning stymied strategic thinking. A senior mandarin responded to the idea of regular policy reviews, 'That way lies Bedlam'. Bedlam arrived anyway.

The Titfield Thunderbolt, a 1953 Ealing comedy, captured the amateurish, muddling-through character of British life. Villagers improvise to keep their railway branch line open by borrowing an old steam engine from a local museum. What worked on screen failed in Whitehall. The vast expansion of post-war government and the new international settlement overwhelmed a knackered Victorian policy engine. The gearing of policy-making to the handling of problems as they arose, warned a contemporary analyst, 'rather than to the definition of goals', had become 'a considerable source of weakness'.[41]

Late twentieth-century histories prized integration as an Aladdin's lamp for a new Europe. An updated *1066 and All That* – the classic 1930 parody of school texts – would have included integration on its list of 103 'Good Things'. The reconciliation of former foes after the most destructive war in history had a dark side, though. When young Germans in the 1950s tried to tear down the border gates at the Kehl/Strasbourg bridge over the Rhine they got hit over the head by French guards and bundled into police vans. Unity proved a mixed blessing. In novelist Henry James's short story 'Europe', the idea of the continent holds a family together and destroys it. 'The paradox', as historian Perry Anderson observed, 'is that when Europe was less united, it was in many ways more independent'.[42] The Cold War duopoly reduced Europeans to bit players. The torch passed to the United States, making it 'the last truly sovereign European nation-state'.[43] America preached unity as glue for its informal empire, leaving senior vassals little choice but to support integration. French and British leaders deluded themselves that winning the leadership stakes in Western Europe would ensure a global platform. In fact, both countries needed each other: 'France could keep Britain out of Europe but ... Britain could stop France organizing Europe.'[44] Joined-up, they might have made Western Europe a much better fit for the welfare and aspirations of citizens.

In February 1969 a despondent de Gaulle sought to break the stalemate. In conversation with Britain's ambassador Sir Christopher Soames he floated the idea of secret bilateral talks on Europe's future. The prime minister and foreign secretary squashed the overture. Cabinet colleagues viewed the invitation more sympathetically, condemning 'the infantilism of Harold and Michael Stewart, priggish children who showed moral disapproval of the de Gaulle overture ... they didn't see it as permitting a breakthrough in Anglo-French relations ... another proof of Harold's ineptitude in foreign and external affairs'.[45] Events overtook the affair: de Gaulle's resignation following defeat in the referendum of April 1969, and the Heath government's renewal of entry talks in June 1970.

Genuine bid for rapprochement? It's too easy to dismiss the Soames affair as a storm in a teacup. The envoy believed his government deliberately torpedoed an important offer.[46] Did it matter? After all, the general resigned within weeks. Very much so. It was the president who made the April referendum a resigning issue. His successor Georges Pompidou had no interest in recreating the Entente. A friendly response to the initiative could have silenced the general's black dog, and persuaded him to stay on. 'The beginning of a beautiful friendship'? Who knows? Like Rick and Louis in *Casablanca*, enemies can be reconciled.

Part One

Chosen Peoples

1

Anglo-Saxon Attitudes

'Geography is about maps, History about chaps' runs the adage. Making sense of British and French responses to European unity starts with the consequences of history and geography. An island fostered separateness, providing choices between mainland Europe, North America and the world. Separateness shaped identity just as France's land frontiers and vulnerability to invasion defined Frenchness. A relatively short stretch of water presented more of a barrier than an equivalent swathe of dry land. In pre-Chunnel days London–Paris by train and ferry took most of a day. The channel established a pattern of convergence and divergence, not isolation. Chaucer's fourteenth-century Wife of Bath – 'thries hadde she been at Jerusalem' – travelled extensively in Europe and the Middle East.

History, as much as geography, defined attitudes on both sides of the channel. War united Britain and the United States, overriding old rifts, establishing a model for post-war alliance; it separated Britain and France, leaving misunderstandings over the appeasement of Hitler, conduct of the war in 1939–40, treatment of de Gaulle's Free French movement, and France's exclusion from wartime summits. War appeared to confirm Britain's place in the world, leaving France stripped of rank, reputation and independence. Dogfights between Free French leader General de Gaulle, British prime minister Winston Churchill and US President Franklin Delano Roosevelt left the French leader with a permanent Anglo-Saxon complex.

The war in Europe ended officially on 8 May 1945. A myth-mongering Churchill claimed that VE Day provoked 'the greatest outburst of rejoicing in the history of humanity'.[1] The *Daily Mirror* undressed its comic strip heroine Jane but temperatures and shortage of alcohol discouraged followers. The muted mood contrasted with the saturnalias of Armistice Day November 1918. With Germany's surrender on the cards, for several months relief and a sense of anti-climax prevailed. Six years of continuous conflict left Britons exhausted, apprehensive and sickened by the first pictures from liberated Nazi death and concentration camps. With the Pacific war predicted to last another eighteen months, the future looked bleak.

Britain, a world power in 1939, now rode on Uncle Sam's coattails. 'Big Three (or 2 and a half) at 4', quipped an adviser at the Potsdam summit in July 1945.[2] Germany's defeat shattered the European states system. Going to war in 1939–40 the European great powers took their last fully independent decisions. The United States and the Soviet Union divided and occupied Europe. Loss of power reflected the price of war, and secular trends. Britain's share of world trade fell steadily from 1860. By VE Day the cupboard was bare: export markets lost; overseas portfolios sold; four million homes destroyed or damaged; 28 per cent of the merchant fleet sunk; obsolete industrial equipment. Losing 25 per cent of national wealth left Britannia, in Churchill's words, 'the world's greatest debtor'. In the first nine months of 1945 exports barely reached 42 per cent of pre-war levels. External debt swelled from £476 million in 1939 to £3,355 million in 1945, including debts to sterling area countries like India and Egypt whose wealth had paid for troops and supplies. These debts, together with a large American loan in 1946, contributed to recurrent balance of payments crises. Peace yielded no savings since money had to be found for occupation forces in Germany, Austria and Italy. Policed on the cheap between the wars, the empire now required large garrisons in Palestine, Egypt and India. The onset of the Cold War from 1947 kept the armed forces at almost one million.

Britons mostly had a good war – six years of struggle against Nazism during which the country and empire had for a while fought single-handedly. A London bus conductor greeted the news of the fall of France: 'Well, thank God we're playing the final on the home ground.' A genius for turning defeats into victories transmuted the evacuation of British and French troops at Dunkirk in May 1940, assisted by an armada of small craft from southern ports, into a triumph of island virtues of self-help and grit. 'The Dunkirk spirit' became legendary: 'one of the most magnificent operations in history ... Tired, dirty, hungry, they came back – unbeatable.'[3] For the rest of the century and beyond, the war made headlines – appealing 'to the very heart of Britain's self-perception as a nation'.[4]

Grandeur was a given in 1945. Discussion focused on relations with the new superpowers and the definition of a specifically socialist foreign policy. Possession of the largest empire and Big Three membership made great power rank seem self-evident. Six years of struggle set the seal on perceived national values. Abdicating world power status would have seemed a denial of the purpose and sacrifices of the conflict. Nevertheless, a sense of foreboding clouded the horizon. 'I wish I felt as much confidence about the future as I did at this time last year – when Victory was clearly in sight – and one did not look much beyond it,' confessed politician and diarist Violet Bonham Carter at the end of 1945: 'Now we are facing forces far more incalculable and uncontrollable than the Germans alas!'[5]

Gender, ethnicity, class, religion and region compartmentalized society, inhibiting a national conversation. Not two nations but many. Film-maker Terence Davies's *The Long Day Closes* (1992) captured the conformity of Liverpudlian working-class life in the 1950s. London and the home counties viewed the rest of the country as terra incognita. 'To me, reared on the soft slopes of Salisbury Plain and gently watered at Eton and Oxford,' recalled a visitor to northern England, 'this was a new world ... It is hard to exaggerate how deeply dim and unfashionable anything to do with provincial England had become ... The Manchester Guardian had fled to London out of sheer social embarrassment'.[6]

Huge inequalities fractured the nation. A scholarship winner to Jesus College, Cambridge University, remembered the shock of his working-class parents on seeing the checklist of items to bring, including two damask tablecloths and a china dinner service for twelve. Graduating from the ancient universities was both a rite of passage for the elite and a passport into it for the less advantaged. The political class with its London clubs and country house network was worlds away from Welsh miners or Lancashire mill workers. Apart from a reduction of dinner courses from four to three, wartime austerity barely touched Oxbridge high tables. 'England isn't always going to be divided into officers and other ranks', declared the young wife of Mr Chips in James Hilton's *Goodbye Mr. Chips* (1934). Nothing changed. At an Oxford college dinner economist Sir Roy Harrod identified for a guest the various notables round the table. A young colleague sitting opposite heard the guest ask who he was. Harrod responded audibly, 'Oh, that's nobody'.[7]

Labour's landslide victory in the general election of 1945 alarmed Americans. 'You've had a revolution', US President Harry S. Truman greeted King George VI. 'Oh no', replied the King. 'We don't have those here'.[8] The 'golden triangle' of London and the ancient universities ran the country. Public school and Oxbridge-educated males dominated government, Westminster and Whitehall. Between 1949 and 1952 Oxbridge supplied 74 per cent of successful entrants to the higher levels of the civil service. 'I get the impression of being liked by the little man [Attlee] The truth is – our old school tie is a very strong link . . . Years and years of working-class contacts make him feel entitled to this strong, secret loyalty to Haileybury and Oxford', remarked a colleague.[9] The Foreign Office, apart from one or two token grammar-school entrants, remained an old Etonian playground, for which a sound British name was a prerequisite. Foreign secretary Anthony Eden advised a prospective candidate that without a change of name he would never get anywhere in the diplomatic service.[10] Diplomats looked after their own, covering up the alcoholism and anti-social behaviour of defectors Guy Burgess and Donald MacLean.

Being a Socialist required justification; being a Tory was normal. Attlee's memorial service reminded Labour politician Tony Benn how 'middle class Labour leaders are recaptured by the Establishment when they die and there is no reference to their political work'.[11] Upper class 'vigilantes' enforced boundaries. Sociologist A.H. Halsey recalled how 'my mother, the latest baby, my sister and I rushed into the corridor of a first class carriage seconds before the train drew out . . . a large, florid-faced man in a pinstriped suit flung open the compartment door to demand of my mother whether she had a first class ticket'.[12] A woman's duty was to advance her husband's career. Asked how she spent her days in the Border country the wife of Conservative premier Sir Alec Douglas-Home answered: 'Good heavens I do what every woman in the British Isles does, I spend the morning making sandwiches and then take them down to the men in the butts.'[13] One woman graced Attlee's cabinet; no women held high rank in the civil service; the 600-strong House of Commons had twenty-four women, slipping to twenty one in 1950. Needless to say, the FO confined women to secretarial drudges or Mrs Mops.

Conformity, hierarchy and understatement ranked as cardinal virtues. An American awarded a Nobel Prize while on sabbatical at Oxford University found that, instead of the warm congratulations he would have got at home, British colleagues hardly mentioned it. Family loyalties and deference to age overrode dissent. FO permanent secretary Sir Alexander Cadogan shrank from any remark that might seem critical of his elder brother, having been drilled as a child: 'don't contradict your brother for he is older than you.'[14] The public schools embodied 'classical conservative values . . .

questioning, criticism and dissent were tolerated in only the most anodyne of forms, and were otherwise taboo'.[15] Not everyone kowtowed. Oxford don and former MI5 agent J.C. Masterman, after conforming all his life, finally rebelled in old age against a system that would not allow him to publish the story of how he turned captured German spies into double agents in the Second World War.

Most people knuckled under, however. 'The working-man always feels himself the slave of a more or less mysterious authority', wrote Orwell, noting how when he went to Sheffield Town Hall to ask for some information, two of his local miner friends, 'both of them people of much more forcible character than myself – were nervous, would not come into the office with me, and assumed that the Town Clerk would refuse information. They said: "he might give it to you, but he wouldn't to us"'.[16] Thick-skinned Communists succumbed to the culture of deference. In 1950 lone Communist MP Willie Gallagher stood up to address the House with thumbs hooked in the pockets of unpressed trousers. As Gallagher reached the climax of his speech, Churchill growled sotto voce yet audibly enough: 'Take your hands out of your pockets, man.' Gallagher instantly complied.[17]

The received pronunciation of BBC announcers mimicked the posh tone of the establishment, the voice of officers addressing other ranks, of *them* talking to *us*. This was the waxworks era of plummy voices, double-breasted pinstripes, bowing to royals, bishops and politicians. At a BBC job interview a producer described the dress code of 1954: 'In features they wear sports jackets, and I have to admit that in drama they even wear corduroys. But, as I say, in Talks we like suits.'[18] The golden rule was to say nothing that might be construed as criticism of Crown and Church. People joked that the BBC's idea of a safe lead story on television news would begin: 'The Queen Mother yesterday ...'. Those who spoke their mind got short shrift. In 1957 the BBC – popularly known as Auntie – banned writer and broadcaster Malcolm Muggeridge from the prime-time television news programme Panorama for criticizing the Queen in the American press.

Belief in a common destiny bridged disparate constituencies. Monarchy, church and empire bonded rulers and ruled. Eating spam and being bombed helped restore the monarchy's popularity – dented by the 1936 Abdication Crisis. Cinema and theatre audiences stood respectfully (mostly) for the playing of the national anthem – staying seated became a gesture of teenage rebellion. 'How is the empire?' asked George V on his deathbed. Not everyone's last thoughts were of empire, nevertheless it was a source of pride. Republicans and anti-imperialists were almost invisible. In the countryside the parish church lay at the heart of the community. The Anglicanism of the established Church of England represented for many a happy compromise between the extremes of Catholicism and continental Protestantism. The rescue at Dunkirk in May 1940 of the British Expeditionary Force was 'speedily converted ... into an auspicious deliverance ... civic exertion among miscellaneous and humble Britons had, under Providence, won out against a powerful and malignant enemy'.[19]

A wartime call from *The Times* for a 'revival of national self-confidence' sparked an upsurge of patriotism.[20] Fighter ace Richard Hillary's best-seller *The Last Enemy* (1942), though scathing of traditional patriotism, affirmed Britain's leadership of a crusade for universal values. Lawrence Olivier's Henry V, premiered in November 1944, captured the triumphalist mood. Skilful editing deleted inconvenient textual references to domestic strife, massacre of French prisoners and usurpation. The production 'supported the mythical idea of a wholly integrated British literary culture in which Shakespeare was as meaningful to the masses as the songs of Vera Lynn'.[21]

Historians did their bit for victory. 'In these times of dictatorship abroad, we thank God that we are not as other men are,' pontificated Tudor specialist Professor Sir John Neale. His Ford Lectures in 1942 on the Elizabethan parliaments 'helped to consolidate highbrow national identity'.[22] The runaway success of G.M. Trevelyan's *English Social History* (1944) both reflected and reinforced the sense of the essential soundness and stability of British society. '*Tout va tres bien, Madame l'Angleterre*', quipped one French reviewer.[23] The film *Way to the Stars* (1945), in which John Mills played a schoolmaster who joins the RAF, popularized the myth of an inclusive people's war. Churchill loved this nationalist mood, minuting the Foreign Office on St George's Day 1945: 'I do not consider that names that have been familiar for generations in England should be altered to study the whims of foreigners living in those parts ... Constantinople should never be abandoned, though for stupid people Istanbul may be written in brackets after it ... Foreign names were made for Englishmen, not Englishmen for foreign names.'[24]

Attlee repeatedly referred to Britain having 'stood alone in defence of freedom and civilization'.[25] Bevin praised RAF hero Guy Gibson's *Enemy Coast Ahead* (1945), requesting extra supplies of tightly rationed paper to give it the widest circulation. *The Times* underscored the significance of the victory. Britain and its Empire-Commonwealth had defended civilization alone and for longer than its allies. In resisting tyranny the nation had recovered its traditional grandeur, confirming the values of democracy, patriotism and discipline. God protected his people. The leader writer cited a foreigner who had sought refuge in England: 'You must never forget that you saved civilization and you must never forget that you have not been an occupied country.'[26] Parliamentary democracy, empire, industrial leadership and victory over Nazism gave a sense of uniqueness and superiority. Britons took pride in being the only Allied country which had gone through both world wars from beginning to end. In this perspective the retreats of the 1930s became aberrations, the consequence of the machinations of the appeasers pilloried in the pamphlet *Guilty Men* (1940). The perception of the Second World War as an endorsement of national values survived in the baggage of the neo-liberal Thatcher revolution of the 1980s.

A singular vision of the state distanced Britons from continental Europe. The grand narrative of British history – the Whig interpretation – traced the evolution of institutions from Magna Carta onwards as a teleological progression towards parliamentary democracy and personal freedoms. Churchill's Humble Address to the Sovereign congratulating him on the conclusion of the war in Europe expressed its essence: 'the wisdom of our ancestors has led us to an envied and enviable situation. We have the strongest Parliament in the world. We have the oldest, the most famous, the most secure, and the most serviceable monarchy in the world. King and Parliament both rest safely and solidly upon the will of the people expressed by free and fair election on the basis of universal suffrage ... this system has long worked harmoniously, both in peace and war.'[27] The model assumed a reactive state whose role should not be codified in advance but left to empirical judgement based on particular needs and circumstances. The guiding assumption was one of informal understandings in which a political class acquired the mysteries of statecraft and practised the art of the possible, responding cautiously to changing conditions. The model prized prudence and gradualism over the continental experience of revolution and constitution making.

Distrust of ideology led the British to underestimate the force of continental creeds. Appeasers in the 1930s played down totalitarian pronouncements; policy-makers in the 1950s misjudged the dynamism of the continent's search for unity. The 'White' conservative emigrants from central and eastern Europe, like historian Sir Lewis Namier, viewed England 'as a land built on instinct and custom, free from the ruinous contagion' of ideologies: 'the less man clogs the free play of his mind with political doctrine and dogma the better for his thinking.'[28] Namier's most influential work, *The Structure of Politics at the Accession of George III* (1929), prioritized power struggles over ideas in eighteenth-century politics.

Britons assumed a God-given right to lord it over the world – 'Natives begin at Calais'. The Thanksgiving Service at St Paul's on VE Day included the rarely sung second verse of God Save the King: 'Confound their politics. Frustrate their knavish tricks.' Hungarian exile George Mikes poked fun at British solipsism. His British girlfriend asked him to marry her. 'No', he replied, 'I will not. My mother would never agree to my marrying a foreigner'. 'I a foreigner? What a silly thing to say. I am English, you are the foreigner, and your mother too'.[29] Victory and empire a huge and thriving concern even after the loss of the Indian subcontinent – brought comfort in the immediate post-war years. Maps and media buttressed a sense of specialness. World maps featured 'red for the empire and dull brown for the rest, with Australia and Canada vastly exaggerated in size by Mercator's projection. The Greenwich meridian placed London at the centre of the world'. The influence of H.E. Marshall's *Our Island Story* (1905), mocked by W.C. Sellars and R.J. Yateman in *1066 and All That* (1930), survived into mid-century. The sense of a unique English dream endured. 'What I wish to emphasize most is the universal validity of this our vision', wrote anarchist and avant-garde critic Herbert Read. 'Alone of national ideals, the English ideal transcends nationality'.[30] At a deeper level, the self-image rested on a perception of England as quintessentially Arcadian, untouched by war and revolution. The evocation of an 'over the hills and far away bird tweeting land' guaranteed the popularity of Kenneth Grahame's *The Wind in the Willows* (1908). For an interwar generation, H.V. Morton's *In Search of England* (1927) recycled the bucolic image. It gained a new lease of life as a summation of Englishness in J.R.R. Tolkien's celebration of the inns and gardens of the Shire and hobbits in *The Lord of the Rings* (1954–5).

A smug self-satisfaction with all things British reigned. 'Both my parents ... together with most of our friends and relations took it for granted that the British middle class of the early twentieth century was the triumphant end product of human evolution', recalled a distinguished academic.[31] Attlee attended a conference in France – 'mostly distinguished by the inability to be relevant by all save the Anglo-Saxons'. He closed his autobiography, 'a very happy and fortunate man in having lived so long in the greatest country in the world'.[32] The British, despite knowing little or nothing of others, considered themselves morally superior. Ignorance fuelled stereotypes. A Second World War officer was appalled by his fellow officers' 'lack of curiosity, their complete lack of interest in the people of the countries in which they were stationed'.[33] Historian E.H. Carr remembered his middle-class childhood as 'wholly insular, and uninterested in foreign countries'.[34]

Books and films pandered to insularity and superiority. Film makers released nostalgia-drenched war films, verging on the narcissistic. In *The Bridge on the River Kwai* (1957), a box-office triumph, the perseverance, courage and discipline of Colonel Nicolson [Alec Guinness] conquers the Japanese. *The Italian Job* (1969), released shortly after the failure of the UK's second EEC entry bid, depicted a British gang using a fleet of the then latest Mini Cooper Ss to carry out a successful gold bullion raid on the Turin HQ of automaker Fiat. Clever driving tricks and smart escape manoeuvres showcased the new model – leaving the Italians and, by implication, all continentals looking silly. Thanks to the Cold War, spy fiction topped bestseller lists. The instant success of Ian Fleming's James Bond stories owed much to the updating of the heroic, imperialistic adventure tales of Buchan, Henty, Rider Haggard and Kipling. Bond's world is one in which the British lion calls the shots, outsmarting friends and foes alike. In *Casino Royale* (1953) 007 gets help from 'our French friends' and 'our American colleagues' in his bid to expose the Communist trade unionist, Le Chiffre, a potentially dangerous fifth columnist in France 'in the event of a war with Redland'. In Bondland foreigners are distrusted and scorned: Bulgarians are 'stupid but obedient', Russians 'cold, dedicated and chess playing', Koreans 'the cruelest, most ruthless people on earth'.[35]

The political class took superiority as a given. 'Foreign policy would be OK but for the bloody foreigners', grumbled Labour foreign secretary Herbert Morrison.[36] 'The Arabs', advised Sir John Glubb, British commander of the Transjordanian Arab Legion, 'show all the instability and emotionalism of the adolescent ... Like children they will sometimes be rude, and sometimes plunged in despair ... when things go badly they like to feel that their father [the British] is ... available to be appealed to.'[37] Amid negotiations for EEC membership in December 1962 a former Oxfordshire High Sheriff fired off a broadside of prejudices: France 'the whorehouse of the world', the Dutch 'duller than ditchwater', the Italians 'rather greasy little men ... scum of the earth'.[38] A minister leading the British delegation at a UNESCO international conference, writes Richard Hoggart called in at the conference office to put his name down as a speaker at the opening plenary session. The official in charge told him that he would be the third speaker: 'Third. Who are the others? Mexico and Senegal ... do you mean that the UK is expected to come after those two? He turned to me "We can't have that, can we Hoggart?"'[39]

Britons lived under a state apparatus almost as closed as that of Stalinist Europe. A fetishistic secrecy about anything that might remotely concern national security prevailed. Americans had 'a much looser attitude towards official secrecy', noted an envious British academic, 'a climate we cannot hope to achieve in this country where the trend is all in the opposite direction'.[40] The nearest Britain got to open government was in 1954 when an astonished taxi driver driving down Whitehall heard a cabinet meeting broadcast live over his cab radio. Engineers had revamped the electrics at No. 10 to cope with Churchill's increasing deafness. Today the headquarters of Her Majesty's Secret Intelligence Service (SIS/MI6) is a well-known landmark on the Thames and sports a public website. Transparency has outwardly triumphed over an agency that in the past denied its own existence. Until the 1990s government disclaimed any intelligence activity. Humour trumped secrecy. When MI5 was temporarily headquartered at Wormwood Scrubs in 1939 bus conductors shouted, 'All change for MI5'.

One of the best-kept secrets of the war was the success of Bletchley Park codebreakers in reading Germany's top-level signals intelligence. The state kept the several-thousand-strong operation under wraps until the early 1970s. Ultra staff were forbidden to talk or write about it. Equally hush hush was the post-war development of Britain's atomic bomb. During the war the subject was taboo even within the small War Cabinet – Attlee, deputy prime minister, Service ministers and chiefs of staff knew practically nothing. Once in the know, however, Attlee personified secrecy – excluding the cabinet from atomic energy decision-making. 'A small ring of senior ministers took decisions in a confusing number of ad hoc committees with science fiction titles, which never reported to the Cabinet'.[41]

Bletchley Park was British democracy's dark side. 'Circus dogs', observed Orwell, 'jump when the trainer cracks his whip, but the really well-trained dog is the one that turns his somersault when there is no whip'. Self-censorship worked so well that when a former member of Air Intelligence spilt the beans about Bletchley Park, a wartime colleague was shocked to the point of refusing to read the book. In the Suez affair of 1956 a conservative backbencher responding to accusations of Britain's collusion with France and Israel asked how anyone 'could doubt the veracity of Ministers', since collusion was 'inconceivable'.[42] Uncritical, obsessive secrecy proved a snare and delusion. Spies had the last laugh – Guy Burgess, Donald MacLean, Kim Philby, Anthony Blunt and others betrayed top-secret information and got away with it. M.R.D. Foot, the first historian allowed access to wartime Special Operations Executive (SOE) files, found MI6 archives 'in a fearsome muddle'.[43] After the usual pantomime of vowing not to tell his wife or pet parrot what he was doing, Foot escaped positive vetting because of a turf war between MI6 – which held the SOE files – and MI5 responsible for vetting. The establishment closed ranks against potential challengers. After *The Sunday Times* published the Philby story in 1967 critics accused it of 'undermining the concept of the English gentleman'.[44] Curiously, the five-volume official history of British Intelligence in the Second World War does not mention Philby.

Mid-century Britons knew little about Europe's politics and recent history. Contacts were limited, partly because of post-war austerity, and partly because of insularity. In the 1940s British universities had no posts in the history of ideas and the dismissal of sociology as a non-subject contributed to the impoverishment of related disciplines like history. Academics nowadays live in the 'small world' described by novelist David Lodge – globetrotting from one conference to the next. Before the 1970s they travelled infrequently and knew little about one another. To be sure, specialists kept abreast of international scholarship, but the ever-burgeoning cyberspace networks of research institutes, conferences, colloquia, workshops and journals did not exist.

The academy cold-shouldered contemporary history as too journalistic and contentious for scholarly study. Before the Public Records Act of 1958 introduced a fifty-year access rule, all government files were closed indefinitely. Colleagues excoriated historian A.J.P. Taylor for appearing on TV and writing in the tabloids. Until contemporary historians banded together in 1986 to create the Institute for Contemporary British History (ICBH) they lacked a collective voice. Russianist E.H. Carr claimed that the 'serious study of Soviet history and institutions' was almost entirely neglected. International history privileged First World War origins, sidestepping Munich and appeasement.

The British experience was not read in a global frame. The packaging of the past into 'British', 'European' and 'World History' made it difficult to connect the dots. 'The deeply ingrained and undiminished segregation of "British" – in reality English – history from European history', wrote one critic, created 'a narrowness of vision' and 'a powerfully constricting cultural factor'.[45] Marxist academic Perry Anderson observed that in the 1960s 'there was little sustained literature on the general development of the United Kingdom as a distinct state and society in the twentieth century'.[46] At Oxford University history officially stopped in 1914, barely acknowledging the world beyond Europe except under the rubric 'Expansion of Europe'. After 1945 the university reinstated the humanities curricula of the 1930s 'virtually without revision'. An initiative for a 'European Greats' degree mixing modern history, philosophy, literature and European languages quickly got shot down.[47] Oxford had to wait until the 1970s to establish itself as a leading centre for the study of international relations.

From the 1970s British historians engaged with the histories of the continent and its countries – Richard Cobb on France, Raymond Carr on Spain and Denis Mack Smith on Italy. Their contribution was unique and profound; unique because continental colleagues mostly stayed with their national narrative, profound because UK Europeanists decisively shaped the historiography of their chosen countries. But the renaissance of scholarship on late modern Europe came too late to influence mid-century debates on Britain's European policy. A conservative rearguard struck back. John Kenyon's *The History Men* (1983) denigrated the work of Europeanists, insisting on English political and constitutional history as a core degree requirement.

The new discipline of international politics stayed in its bailiwick. Its intellectual engine, the British Committee on International Relations, founded by historian Herbert Butterfield, targeted specialists, not a wider public. Workshops and publications neglected European integration and Britain's role in the world. The group had the mafia-like features of academia at its worst – ignoring prestigious centres like the London School of Economics and St Antony's College, Oxford, and blackballing leading figures – historian E.H. Carr, physicist and Nobel laureate Patrick Blackett, and historian A.J.P. Taylor 'with his leanings towards the world of journalism'.[48]

A deep schism opened up among philosophers. British philosophers disdained the ideas of continental colleagues. In the 1960s much of Antonio Gramsci, Gregor Lukacs and Karl Marx was unavailable in English. As leaders of the analytic or ordinary language movement, Oxford philosophers marginalized top continental thinkers Jean-Paul Sartre and Gabriel Marcel, and caricatured existentialists as Resistance left-overs. Despite several years of teaching philosophy at Oxford, Mary Warnock had not read Sartre. The first English account of his philosophy – Iris Murdoch's *Sartre: Romantic Rationalist* (1953), seriously misrepresented it. Philosophers, like historians, frowned on efforts to engage lay readers. Warnock's talks on the BBC's Third Programme incurred peer disapproval – 'the very idea of popularizing one's academic subject was anathema'.[49]

Geographical separation nurtured belief in a special destiny – English exceptionalism. Historians Arthur Bryant, G.M. Trevelyan, A.L. Rowse, poet John Betjeman and political scientist Ernest Barker, deliberately distanced the country from the continent. Bryant and fellow 'non-intellectual' writers presented English identity as 'timeless, homogeneous and unique'.⁵⁰ The hermetic, self-sufficient ambience of intellectual life left little appetite for continental delicacies. The intellectual tone was not so much anti-European as ambivalent. Continental culture attracted and repelled Herbert Hart, professor of jurisprudence at Oxford, a shaper of legal theory in the 1950s. He and others suspected that 'continental philosophy had in some way contributed to the rise of fascism'.⁵¹

Received ideas went unexamined because public intellectuals – an endangered species in Britain – were slow to lead. A British thinker wistfully noted, 'France remained ... a country where ideas count and are seriously debated, not merely by a small intellectual elite, but by great bodies of quite ordinary men and women.'⁵² Heavyweights like economist G.D.H. Cole, political theorist Harold J. Laski, philosopher Bertrand Russell and historian R.H. Tawney engaged with public concerns, but they were the exceptions. An act of defiance highlighted the decade's passivity. In 1956 Oxford philosopher Elizabeth Anscombe challenged the University's decision to award an honorary degree to former US President Harry S. Truman, arguing that his authorization of the use of atomic bombs against Hiroshima and Nagasaki made him a mass murderer and unsuitable for an honorary degree. Truman got his degree, of course, but Anscombe's protest signalled a change of climate.

As the 1950s closed the creation of CND, together with scientist and novelist C.P. Snow's 1959 Rede Lecture, published as *The Two Cultures and the Scientific Revolution*, rekindled debate. Supported by Russell, CND's annual protest marches to the Atomic Weapons Research Establishment at Aldermaston in Berkshire started in 1958 and caught world attention. To label the decade, in Perry Anderson's words, as 'parochial and quietist', is to ignore post-Suez debate and ferment; Snow's Rede Lecture began life as a *New Statesman* article in 1956. That said, the dull conformity of much of the decade remains striking. Victory over fascism, full employment, and the welfare state removed the great causes of the 1930s. Unlike France and Italy, no powerful Communist party threatened the status quo.

A class-bound society discouraged dialogue. Martin Pargiter in Virginia Woolf's novel *The Years* 'hated talking to servants, it always made him feel insecure'.⁵³ In the ancient universities communication stalled at times. Dons drawled through the stem of their pipes or affected a cryptic, Delphic style, intimidating all but the most confident undergraduates. The establishment encouraged conformity by annexing leading thinkers. Though giants like Russell and Tawney contested orthodoxy, philosopher Isaiah Berlin truckled to grandees. Marxist and left-wing sympathizers had difficulty finding academic jobs – Berlin successfully opposed the appointment of Marxist Isaac Deutscher to a university chair in Soviet Studies. Intellectuals took for granted the country's moral lead over an unstable France, guilty Germany, fascist Iberia and Communist eastern Europe. 'Great Britain on the whole ... seems to the British intellectual of the mid-1950s to be fundamentally all right', remarked American sociologist Edward Shils; '... never has an intellectual class found its society and its culture so much to its satisfaction'.⁵⁴

Cultural insularity stifled new ideas. Sixteen years after the death of French philosopher Simone Weil in London in 1943 the British journal *The Twentieth Century* published a translation of Weil's essay 'Human Personality'. An apologetic editorial acknowledged that the essay 'involves heavy going for some readers'. American critic Susan Sontag commented, 'It certainly speaks volumes about the philistine level of English intellectual life, if even as good a magazine as the *Twentieth Century* cannot muster an enthusiastic, grateful audience for such a piece'.[55] In a collective letter to *The Times* a group of writers declared their indifference towards Europeanism, asserting that intellectuals should be aloof from a 'blatant commercial arrangement' like the Treaty of Rome.[56]

'It can be fairly said,' Bevin assured the Commons in 1945, 'that we held the fort and preserved the soul of mankind'.[57] The assumption of superior wisdom enshrined in a British way of doing things made it hard to empathize with fellow Europeans. Introducing the National Health Service in 1948, health minister Aneurin Bevan declared, 'there is only one hope for mankind and that hope still remains in this little island'.[58] Philosophers lauded linguistic analysis as a unique British discourse, distinct from continental metaphysics and Marxism; literary critics led by F.R. Leavis in *The Great Tradition* (1948) proclaimed the study of English literature to be the source of life-affirming values, and a supremely civilizing influence; lawyers affirmed British law to be best; political scientists agreed on a 'British' tradition grounded in the belief that the country had 'the wisdom and experience to consider international life with due distance and according to the right principles'.[59]

Persecution, violence and show trials in Communist eastern Europe deepened believe in a separate path. British left wingers criticized the EEC as 'a rich man's club' which would compromise Labour's ideals of waging global war on want. Economist John Vaizey, counting himself 'a good European', warned Labour party leader Hugh Gaitskell, 'the more I hear the more scared I get that it [EEC] becomes a great white plot against Asia and Africa. This I can only feel is both immoral and foolish'.[60] As Labour warmed to the European project in the mid-1960s pro-Europe ministers like foreign secretary George Brown sounded increasingly condescending. 'It is our business', he affirmed, 'to provide political leadership, to provide the stability that for so long has eluded the democracies of the mainland of Europe ... I don't see where else leadership can come from other than from this country'.[61]

And the balance sheet? 'However strong one's native conviction that foreigners are queer', wrote poet and civil servant C.H. Sisson, 'a glance at Europe makes it plain that it is we who are odd'.[62] When in June 1955 the six ECSC states met at Messina in Sicily to discuss extending European integration, Chancellor of the Exchequer R.A. Butler contemptuously dismissed the discussions as 'archaeological excavations'.[63] The political elite found it hard to reimagine Europe. Belgian foreign minister Paul Henri Spaak tried in vain to persuade Butler to support the relaunch of Europe. Afterwards, Spaak asked a British aide, 'Have I been obscene?' 'Why obscene, sir?' 'Well, I don't think I could have shocked him more when I tried to appeal to his imagination than I would have done if I had taken off my trousers.'[64]

2

Vive la France

In the depths of the Second World War, writer Antoine de Saint-Exupéry dedicated *Le Petit Prince* to his friend the Jewish author and art critic Leon Werth: 'He lives in France, where he is cold and hungry. He needs to be comforted.' Paris on VE Day 1945 contrasted starkly with London's self-congratulatory mood. 'People were told to hang out flags', noted philosopher Jean-Paul Sartre; 'they did not do so'.[1] Parisians had no cause for revelry. More people died at the hands of compatriots than by German action. A Franco–French war opened deep wounds. War deaths of 600,000 (UK 400,000) included many civilians killed by Allied air attacks. Devastation exceeded the Great War: Le Havre 82 per cent destroyed; Caen 73 per cent; production down to 40 per cent of 1939; 58 per cent of GNP looted by Germany. In the autumn of 1944 de facto independent republics controlled large areas, with rail, telephone and postal services barely functioning.

The fag-end of the war in Europe found the French feeling more defeated than victorious, with scarcely enough gold and foreign exchange to pay for six months of imports. The winter of 1944–5, one of the coldest on record, forced Parisians to pile on extra layers, reading one-sheet newspapers over breakfast coffee of burned barley before spending the day in long queues for groceries. Food and coal riots broke out in several towns. Cyclists powered hairdryers in the beauty salons. Shortages drove up infant mortality rates. Writer Simone de Beauvoir carried home kilos of groceries from well-stocked station buffets in Spain and Portugal. The click click of wooden heels on pavements provided a constant reminder of daily privations. Bread rationing below occupation levels returned in January 1946. The franc lost two thirds of its value between 1944 and 1947 – three devaluations by 1948. No catalogue of material loss conveys the human tragedy. Hostilities left a million homeless. In 1945 Germany still held captive hundreds of thousands of POWs, captured resisters and drafted workers.

The national psyche suffered most. The war shattered France's self-image as a chosen people. Lucien Febvre, co-founder with Marc Bloch in 1929 of the historical journal *Annales*, equated the prospect of the destruction of France with 'the end of European culture as we have known, loved and served it'.[2] Joachim du Bellay's sixteenth-century sonnet *Les Regrets*, extolling France as 'mother of arts, of warfare, and of laws', framed the pre-1939 self-image. France stood for a fixed middle kingdom, heir to Greece and Rome, acme of Western civilization.

The image of a warrior people found in Julius Caesar's *Commentaries* and confirmed by the wars of Louis XIV and Napoleon I resonated deeply. The French perceived the allied victory of 1918 as a triumph of national arms avenging the defeat of 1871 at the hands of Prussia. The strength of interwar pacifism did not deter the Third Republic from maintaining the largest army in Western Europe and supplying arms and assistance to allies. The French claimed to be guardians of revolution, liberty and human rights. The hyperbole had nuggets of truth. In 1791 the Republic was the first European nation to extend full civil rights to Jews, sheltering dissident Poles in the 1830s and 1860s, followed by Russian exiles after the revolutions of 1917, then German and Spanish refugees after 1933. French leaders, notably Albert Thomas, first director general of the League of Nations International Labour Office, and foreign minister Aristide Briand energized interwar internationalism.

Religion and empire validated specialness. Despite the anti-clericalism that culminated in the church–state separation law of 1905, religious practice remained strong and France took pride in the title 'eldest daughter of the Church'. Government and missionaries cooperated overseas. The empire's sacrifice of blood, sweat and treasure in the Great War stirred popular enthusiasm. The Colonial Exhibition of 1931 attracted seven million visitors. France's appeasement of Nazi Germany in central and eastern Europe refocused attention on empire. War propaganda exploited the colonial myth: '110 million strong, France can stand up to Germany'.

Defeat upended everything. Six weeks sufficed to topple a premier military power and universally acknowledged beacon of civilized values. Sartre captured the trauma. In the thick of the battle for France in June 1940 an army unit became separated from the rest and prepared to surrender or go down fighting:

> 'Odd,' Mathieu mused. 'Yes, quite ridiculous.' He gazed into empty space ... 'I am French.' And for the first time in his life he thought it was an absurd idea ... We were right in it ... It was so natural to be French. It was the simplest, most economical way of feeling universal. There was nothing to explain; let the others explain – the Germans, the British, the Belgians – by what stroke of ill-luck, and through whose fault they were not quite human.... But now France had overturned and was lying flat on her back ... and now we say to ourselves: 'Well, that was it ...'[3]

Vichy, a German vassal state under Marshal Philippe Pétain, replaced the Third Republic of 1870, the most durable regime since the Revolution of 1789. Germany's takeover of the whole of the country in November 1942 intensified the Franco–French war of resisters vs. collaborators. Vichy's national revolution of 'Work, Country, Family' rekindled the post-1789 ideological quarrel between left and right. Most citizens stayed on the sidelines, victims of German reprisals and Allied bombing, and forced to witness compatriots gunning each other down. Events denied them the satisfaction of self-liberation. Resisters sabotaged German communications and helped liberate the capital, but Anglo-Saxon armies defeated the enemy in the field. Many felt like the Frenchman in the film *The Longest Day* – 'wearing a World War I helmet', he 'waves a champagne bottle at the Allied troops rushing past him, shouting "welcome boys". The soldiers laugh but have no time to stop, they cannot feel what he does. He is the one being freed, he is left on his own, in the rubble of his town'.[4]

By the early 1960s France led the pack in Western Europe, overtaking Britain in GNP. How did a down-and-out nation pick itself up? Economic miracle? Baby boom? Gallic brilliance? First and foremost, a revamped and innovative dirigiste state. Between the wars the philosopher Emile Chartier, aka Alain, championed individualism, declaring that resistance to power mattered more than reforming action. Defeat transformed attitudes. Reimagining the nation during 'the dark years' of occupation convinced elites that the state was the essential instrument of modernization. Post-war France benefited from a new contract between state and citizens. An interventionist state offered social welfare, nationalization of core economic sectors and democratization.

Modernization. The state's privileging of innovation and technocracy empowered political economist and diplomat Jean Monnet in creating France's first modernization plan in 1946. The war of 1914 ended with calls for a return to business as usual; the second conflict unleashed calls for a renaissance. 'What was unique about France', writes historian Richard Kuisel, was how 'a collective sense of national decline and disenchantment with the liberal order provided the fundamental impetus for change'.[5] The choice, in Jean Monnet's words, was between 'modernization or decadence'.[6] Technocrats had cut their teeth working with the Third Republic and Vichy. A Communist Party poster caught the get-up-and-go spirit – a worker against a background of factory reconstruction with the slogan 'Let's roll up our sleeves, things will get even better!'

The country reinvented itself. Defeat forced the French to focus on the future. Resisters hailed a 'new springtime'. Defeat, declared philosopher Simone Weil, gave France 'the opportunity of becoming once again among the nations what she was in the past ... an inspiration'.[7] Reformist ideas seeded in the 1930s persuaded elites that the nation was capable of 'a profound transformation on all levels, political, economic, social, cultural'.[8] Confidence in regeneration held up. A Communist resistance group proclaimed: 'France ... will be tomorrow, in spite of its temporary humiliation, the nation capable of making proposals to the world'.[9] Leaders rejected a naïve optimism. 'We will need hard work, much time', cautioned de Gaulle. 'Perhaps within ten or twenty years', speculated a Radical party report in December 1944, 'we will have climbed back up the slope again'.[10]

The myth of a resisting nation personified in de Gaulle recharged morale. True, everyone claimed to have resisted; Marshal Pétain at his trial called himself 'the first of the resisters'. De Gaulle, however, symbolized the fact and spirit of resistance, the refusal to abandon greatness. State and citizens colluded in treating the internal and external resistance movements as a liberation army – with help from allies. The Communist film-makers of the documentary *La Liberation de Paris*, filmed during the rising of August 1944, de-emphasized the infighting between Communist and rival resistance groups, highlighting instead 'a vision of the insurrection that put the city and its population at the heart of events'.[11]

From day one de Gaulle, as head of the Provisional Government, relentlessly pursued recovery of rank, conjuring up a self-liberating resisting France. 'Paris liberated', he proclaimed at the Paris Hôtel de Ville on 25 August 1944, 'liberated by itself, liberated by its people with the help of the French armies'.[12] Third Republic elites shared in the myth-making that rebooted the Republic's profile and moral authority. In *France saved Europe*, Paul Reynaud, prime minister in June 1940, hailed a martyr-like Republic sacrificing itself for Europe; 'most French people responded by taking up arms, or by harassing the enemy or by accepting in their hearts the call of general de Gaulle ... France sacrificed herself and because she sacrificed herself the independence of the world could be saved by the stoicism of the British people, the courage of the Russian army and the colossal power of America'.[13]

The legend cemented the Fourth and Fifth Republics. The state propagated and enforced it by controlling access to Vichy archives, phasing out trials of collaborators, and prioritizing the academic study of the resistance. History was too important to be left to historians. From 1951 a Committee for the History of the Second World War, attached to the prime minister's office and directed by historian Henri Michel, researched testimonies and documents, sponsored conferences and published a quarterly journal. Mythification made it harder to come to terms with the underside of the occupation. Former Vichy officials, notoriously Maurice Papon, who as secretary general for police in Bordeaux helped send Jews to their deaths, held high office in the Fourth and Fifth Republics. Censors delayed the release of Alain Resnais's 1955 documentary *Nuit et Brouillard* (Night and Fog) about Nazi genocide because the film showed the *kepi* of a French policeman in a scene at an internment camp from which French Jews went to their deaths. The authorities banned from state television Marcel Ophuls's 1969 documentary on collaboration *Le Chagrin et la Pitie* (The Sorrow and the Pity), denouncing it as 'anti-patriotic'.

The myth of a resisting nation endured because it embodied a truth. Resistance revealed 'an obscure, secret France, new to her friends, her enemies ... new to herself', with hopes and ambitions for remaking the nation.[14] Vilified by Vichy and the Germans as terrorists, resisters became heroes deliberately defying law and authority – with their own pecking order. Members of de Gaulle's London-based Free French movement in 1940 formed an inner elite, 'Companions of the Liberation', rewarded with top jobs in the Provisional Government of 1944–6 and the Fifth Republic.

Britain made a crucial contribution to the myth of a resisting France. Promising to set Hitler's Europe ablaze, Churchill created the Special Operations Executive (SOE) to work with resistance networks. British resources fuelled the movements. During the long wait for an Allied invasion of the continent, London prioritized resistance. Joseph Kessel's classic resistance novel, *L'Armée des Ombres* (Army of Shadows), underscores the efficiency of the British machine. Shortly after Kessel's arrival in London early in 1943 de Gaulle suggested a story about the resistance. Notwithstanding stringent paper rationing a French edition appeared in Algiers before the end of the year, quickly followed by English translations. An official documentary, *Now It Can Be Told* (1946), followed the careers of SOE agents in occupied France, bolstering the Gaullist myth of a self-liberating France. *Maquis* (1945), the story of SOE agent George Millar, got a 70,000 hardback print run. De Gaulle read it and personally thanked Millar. The British film *Odette* (1950) celebrated the life of Resistance heroine and holder of the George Cross Odette Sampson; Bruce Marshall's *The White Rabbit* (1952) about SOE agent Wing Commander Yeo Thomas came out in a French edition within a year. The memoirs of Colonel Maurice Buckmaster, head of SOE's French section, *Specially*

Employed (1952) and *They Fought Alone* (1958), sustained the momentum. Popular BBC television dramas of the 1970s and 1980s like *Secret Army* and *'Allo, 'Allo!* recycled the myth of a France *resistante*.

Planning the future meant rethinking the past. The retelling of recent history reinforced the image of a reborn Republic. The inquest on 1940 reached back to the First World War. The perceived folly of France's pre-war foreign policy united resisters and Vichyites. The standard explanation of the coming of war in terms of a wicked Hitler, over-indulged by timorous democracies, left the speed of France's collapse unexplained. Perfidious Albion, bogeyman of the Right, supplied a convenient whipping boy. German and Vichy propaganda exploited grievances over Britain's conduct before, during and after the Battle of France. Vichy's Anglophobia, writer Albert Camus pointed out, sprang from 'the ignoble desire to see the person who does stand up to the strength that has overwhelmed you go down himself'.[15]

Scapegoating Anglo-Saxons for interwar pusillanimity towards Germany enhanced the myth of a resisting France and made the French feel better. At the peacemaking in 1919 – ran the script – Anglo-Saxon allies bamboozled France by blocking demands for a separate Rhineland and Saar, offering as a sop a Treaty of Guarantee which collapsed within months, leaving the Republic a lone gendarme of an unpopular peace. British misjudgements led to the retreats of the 1930s and the coming of war. 'The Munich Agreement', affirmed France's former ambassador to Berlin, 'was the logical consequence of the policy practised by Britain and France, but principally inspired by Britain'.[16] Novelist François Mauriac put it more strongly: 'The British', he wrote, were 'responsible, in large part, for the conflict of 1939'.[17] After bullying France into war Britain ensured defeat by holding back RAF fighters in the Battle of France, and prioritizing the evacuation of British troops at Dunkirk. The 3 July 1940 attack on the French fleet at Mers-el-Kébir added insult to injury. Churchill and Roosevelt ganged up against de Gaulle, leader of the Free French, excluded him from allied summits, and plotted to replace him by General Giraud.

The general's war memoirs popularized the myth. Belief in Allied betrayal united the founder of the Fifth Republic and a notable of the despised Third. The general congratulated ex-foreign minister Georges Bonnet on an overview of French foreign policy since 1870, demonstrating how 'after the unforgettable' effort of the First World War France fell victim to the 'downright desertion of the Americans and English ... one of the principal causes of the misfortune of 1940'.[18] The former minister proudly carried the letter in his wallet, displaying it like a testimonial. De Gaulle emphasized the new orthodoxy: 'The Second World War would never have broken out if, in the 1930s, we had not fallen into the habit of relying on the English. Our governments allowed the public to believe that our security depended on what London would do ... We proclaimed that we would not allow Strasbourg to come under German guns. But since the English did not want to do anything, we did nothing. When Chamberlain wanted Munich, we followed'. The general stressed 'the natural propensity of the French to yield to foreigners and become divided ... it was practically an understood thing that France never said "No!"'.[19]

Sans de Gaulle the French would still have resented Anglo–American dominance and their own powerlessness. The Anglo-Saxon hijacking of France's history added salt to the wounds. In Simone de Beauvoir's novel *The Mandarins*, Anne (de Beauvoir) visits her lover Lewis (Nelson Algren) in the United States and listens to him talking with two ex-GI friends. 'They were talking volubly, interrupting each other constantly. There was no doubting their sympathy for France, they were not the least bit complacent about their own country; and yet, listening to them, I felt uncomfortable. It was their war they were talking about, a war in which we had been only the somewhat pitiful excuse. Their scruples concerning us were like those a man could feel toward a weak woman or a passive animal. And already they were making wax legends out of our history'.[20] De Gaulle's accusations of allied betrayal after 1918 resonated with many influencers. Eminent historians accepted Gaullist orthodoxy. 'French statesmen', wrote Jean-Baptiste Duroselle, 'practised appeasement because they needed British help and were subject to constant British pressure'.[21] A.J.P. Taylor's emphasis in *Origins of the Second World War* (1961) on the shared responsibility of London and Paris for the coming of war proved unwelcome. When Taylor personally gave copies of *Origins* to Pierre Renouvin and Maurice Baumont, luminaries of French historiography, 'neither of them acknowledged my gift or spoke to me again'.[22]

National unity, a prerequisite for regaining international rank, dictated a 'softly, softly' transition from Vichy to Provisional Government and Fourth Republic. About 9,000 summary executions occurred in the summer of 1944 before the Provisional Government in Paris imposed its authority. There were no bloodbaths. A general hue and cry would have nullified the myth of a populace united against the German invader. While Pétain, Pierre Laval and assorted Vichy *prominenti* faced High Court trials and execution, lesser fry escaped lightly with sentences of 'national indignity' – loss of civil rights and exclusion from parliament. Amnesties soon restored civil rights. Bonnet's career illustrates the Republic's moderation towards Vichy fellow travellers. Excoriated for abandoning France's ally Czechoslovakia in 1938 and for pro-Vichy sympathies – though never holding office under Vichy – the ex-minister returned from Swiss exile in time to benefit from a 1953 amnesty allowing him to regain his old parliamentary seat and achieve leadership of the radical socialist party. Similarly, right-wing writer Alfred Fabre-Luce, sentenced in 1949 to ten years of 'national indignity', waited only two years for an amnesty. The snail-like progress of the parliamentary commission of enquiry set up in 1946 to investigate the period 1933–45 helped sedate opinion. The commission's mix of politicians and resistance leaders boded ill for impartiality. Over four years Vichy and Third Republic notables testified on oath, but no money could be found to send delegates to the United States to interview Alexis Leger, secretary general of the pre-war foreign ministry, and former premier Camille Chautemps. The investigation never completed a report on the war years. Not that it mattered. By the time hearings concluded in May 1951, parliament and public had long since switched off.

Renowned for food, fashion, wine and culture, the Republic repackaged itself as a leading industrial and scientific power. In 1948 the media acclaimed ZOE, the Republic's first experimental nuclear reactor, 'A great achievement – French and peaceful, which strengthens our role in the defence of civilization.'[23] The emphasis on peaceful applications of nuclear energy inspired a vision of a technological France. Nuclear power stations were marketed as 'contemporary chateaux, symbols of national glory', successors of Versailles and the Eiffel Tower. A 1957 film documentary opened with a picture of the palace of Versailles and Louis XIV's first minister advising him: 'Sire, the grandeur of a state depends on its arts and manufactures'. An overview followed of technological change concluding with nuclear power. In 1964 'Groupe 85', a forum for experts, addressed the future of the nation: 'The first unexpected challenge is the intellectual and cultural survival of an original and individual France ... from now on our presence in the world depends on our ability to imprint our mark on this civilization by means of ... French technology and science.'[24] The challenge was to modernize without losing individuality. As de Gaulle put it, 'the problem is to accomplish this without France ceasing to be France'.[25]

Religion energized the new France. In a laicized Republic with strong anti-clerical traditions the church regained influence. Like Anglicanism in Britain, Catholicism ran deep in the nation's traditions. No other national Christian community rivalled the creativity of mid-twentieth-century French Catholicism. The worker priest movement in the 1950s and the abbé Pierre's crusade for the homeless attracted world interest. Catholic involvement in the resistance realized a reconciliation with the state, generating confidence and cohesion. The church's dynamism boosted the Republic's international prestige. To portray the renewal of the French Church as a short-lived affair in a 'deeply conservative' institution, compromised by collusion with Vichy, is misleading.[26] Religious renewal, like social and economic recovery, began in the interwar years and continued through the 1960s. The initial sympathy which many bishops felt for Petain did not necessarily signify collusion in the regime's racist agenda. Leading prelates condemned Vichy's anti-Jewish legislation. Those who kept silent allowed diocesan facilities and networks to assist Jews. Post-liberation calls for an extensive purge of pro-Vichy bishops yielded only a few forced retirements. The high profile of Catholics in the Resistance offset the hierarchy's mixed record. The church emerged from the war with a renewed presence in public life. Fortnightly meetings between foreign minister Georges Bidault and papal nuncio Mgr Giovanni Roncalli (future Pope Jean XIII) established a modus vivendi. The Provisional Government of 1944-6 was the first administration since the 1870s to be headed by a practising Catholic. In December 1944 the determination of de Gaulle and his foreign minister to attend mass at the little Catholic church in Moscow surprised French diplomats. President René Coty of the Fourth Republic – first head of state to go to mass since Marshal MacMahon in the 1870s – visited Pope Pius XII in May 1957, sealing a church–state reconciliation.

Catholic Action and Christian Democracy shaped post-war politics. The new MRP Christian Democrat party (*Mouvement Republicain Populaire*) averaged 4–5 portfolios in the coalition governments of the Fourth Republic. Led by foreign minister Robert Schuman, Catholics were a driving force in European integration – arousing British suspicions of a Catholic plot. Revival spanned intellectual life and pastoral ministry. The neo-Thomism of philosophers Etienne Gilson and Jacques Maritain influenced the UN Universal Declaration of Human Rights of 1948. The Christian existentialism of Gabriel Marcel and the personalism of Emmanuel Mounier impacted European elites. The Vatican II Council of the 1960s relied on 'the new theology' of Jesuit Henri de Lubac and Dominican Yves Congar. The French Church's traditional title 'eldest daughter of the Church' still resonated. In 1945 Maritain, newly-appointed ambassador to the Holy See, shared with Pius XII his confidence that 'the Church will aid and bless the effort of the nation that prides itself on being called its eldest daughter', affirming that France's ideals for the 'reconstruction of the civilized universe' agreed with Catholic teaching.[27]

The annual parade of French forces down the Champs-Élysées on Bastille Day, 14 July, represented an unparalleled show of strength in Western Europe. Pride in military might survived 1940 and the disasters of colonial war in Indo-China. For one thing, the military record of the Algerian war was one of successful containment of rebellion; for another, the successful testing of A- and H-bombs (1960, 1968) and development of strike capability promised a seat in the first rank of powers. The warrior legend of the original Gallic resister, Vercingetorix, defying Roman invaders melded with the Gaullist *resistantialiste* myth of a united France opposing the occupier, finally from 1959 becoming mass entertainment in the new comic strip character Asterix. The miraculous survival of Asterix's village, thanks to a mix of natural guile and magic, saves it from Roman civilization. History as popular entertainment perpetuated the myth of a unique Gallic destiny. The Fifth Republic added a profitable dimension to the warrior image – the making and marketing of arms, becoming a major world supplier.

The French appeared more imperialist-minded in 1945 than before the conflict. In the dark years of 1940–4 empire offered a pledge for the future – several territories declared for De Gaulle, and Algeria provided a base for the Free French movement. 'Without empire', Gaston Monnerville, deputy for French Guiana and grandson of a slave, told parliament in May 1945, 'France today would be only a liberated country. Thanks to her empire, France is a victorious country'.[28] Those like philosopher Raymond Aron who doubted whether France had the means to retain empire were few and far between.[29] 'No more French Algeria, no more France', chanted supporters of the Algerian war. For many, Algeria was not just another colony but administratively and emotionally part of metropolitan France.

A new story with twin themes of modernization and decolonization replaced the old imperialism. De Gaulle's repackaging of the civilizing mission as a call to modernization caught the imagination. Decolonization became a milestone to modernity, a continuation of French leadership by other means. Grandeur stood for internal modernization, leadership of the European Community, and sponsorship of newly independent Francophone countries. Modernization, argues historian Kristin Ross, was a form of internal colonialism, 'rational administrative techniques developed in the colonies were brought home and put to use side by side with new technological innovations such as advertising in reordering metropolitan, domestic society, the everyday life of its citizens'.[30] In 1960 culture minister André Malraux hired unemployed colonial administrators to run his new ministry of culture 'to help him keep...domestic possessions loyal...by retrofitting *the* unified French culture'.[31] Modernization through decolonization opened up fresh vistas and energies.

Soft power accelerated recovery of influence. A thoroughly elitist project prioritized the marketing of high culture to influential global publics.

The claim to a universal cultural voice commanded respect, and supplied leverage in Franco–American relations. By emphasizing cultural 'specialness' France created a case for preferential treatment from America. Much of the cultural capital amassed since the eighteenth century survived the humiliations of 1940-4. In the late nineteenth century France was the first state to recognize the importance of cultural diplomacy. As the language of diplomacy and educated elites for over two centuries, French retained its reclamé, especially in South America and the Middle East. When writer Romain Gary, chargé d'affaires in La Paz, won the Prix Goncourt in 1956 the city council and Bolivian press lionized him like a Hollywood star. In 1945 the restoration of France as an independent power with a UN Security Council seat strengthened confidence in a global mission. Hosting the United Nations in Paris for five years (1946-51), together with the UN agency UNESCO and the headquarters of the Western military alliance NATO, gave Paris the prestige of a world diplomatic capital. The 1948 Universal Declaration of Human Rights, a landmark of international human rights law, was signed in Paris and drew in part on French inspiration.

The Fourth Republic reopened French institutes and branches of the Alliance française, closed during the war, and established new centres – the Maison française at the University of Oxford (1946). Renewal and expansion meant training language teachers for schools and institutes, restoration of international exchanges in the humanities and social sciences, promotion of high culture through book exhibitions, author lecture tours, film festivals, art shows and tours by flagship theatre companies like the *Comedie française*. Innovations included the creation of a coordinating agency within the Quai d'Orsay: *Direction générale des relations culturelles et des oeuvres a l'étranger*; appointment of cultural advisers at major embassies; bilateral exchanges and agreements. A new emphasis on scientific and technological endeavour alongside language, literature and artistic creation distinguished post-war renewal.

The capital regained its reputation as the world's crossroads – abuzz with the latest ideas, a magnet for creative artists from around the world, including American expats James Baldwin and Allen Ginsburg. Sartre held court at the left bank Café de Flore, expounding existentialism through a Gauloise smokescreen. A burst of exceptional creativity in the country's intellectual life drove soft power. French ideas impacted profoundly worldwide, especially in the humanities. Simone de Beauvoir's *The Second Sex* (1949) became a seminal text of modern feminism. Nobel prizes confirmed primacy in literature – André Gide (1947), François Mauriac (1952), Albert Camus (1957), St. John Perse (1962). Sartre's refusal of a Nobel Prize in 1964 shocked the world and generated extra kudos.

A special relationship between state, culture and public service underpinned the selling of France. No other European state had such a close integration of elites. Like Jewish Old Testament prophets, public intellectuals represented the conscience of society. Raymond Aron, Albert Camus, Jean-Paul Sartre, Simone de Beauvoir and others engaged passionately with the issues of the day. The state treated them as an endangered species. General de Gaulle vetoed Sartre's arrest for civil disobedience: 'You don't arrest Voltaire.'[32] The intelligentsia's front-runners could look forward to election to the French Academy – known as the 'Immortals' – perhaps receiving the ultimate accolade of a state funeral and burial in France's holy of holies, the Pantheon. Savants blended political and public service careers: philosopher Jacques Maritain – ambassador to the Vatican; writer Andre Malraux – minister of culture; philosopher Alexandre

Kojève – an influential economic policy-maker; anthropologist Claude Lévi-Strauss – cultural attaché in Washington DC. Erudition and creative distinction lightly worn had a recognized place in political life. Within days of installing the Provisional Government in August 1944 de Gaulle, master stylist in his own right, wined and dined literary stars starting with François Mauriac, Georges Duhamel, Paul Valéry and Georges Bernanos.

Serious fault lines compromised the marketing of Marianne. In the immediate postwar years French leaders envisioned their country as a third force in world politics. Very quickly, however, the Soviet Union and the United States annexed Europe's high politics. Superpower management of the Cold War excluded a third force. Consequently, medium powers like France and Britain had difficulty finding a distinctive voice. The perception of the Fourth Republic as a crisis-ridden 'sick woman of Europe' undermined its self-projection as a flagship democracy. The army's resort to torture and atrocities in the wars of decolonization in Indo-China and Algeria contradicted France's claim to be the guardian of liberal values and human rights. A cash-strapped state could barely fund its cultural diplomacy. Financial constraints restricted the training of language teachers and capped the number of overseas lecture tours. When novelist Albert Camus undertook a government-sponsored lecture tour of American universities in 1946 he had to travel in an overcrowded freighter sharing a cabin with five others. Actor and director Jean-Louis Barrault, commissioned to present nine plays in South America, sailed in an old boat on its last voyage. Lack of money generated conflict. Some officials prioritized language teaching, others cultural projects. But the language was in full retreat. In mid-twentieth century its primacy as the lingua franca of diplomacy and world elites crumbled. At the foundation conference of the United Nations in San Francisco in 1945 France needed the help of the Soviet Union and Canada to defeat a bid to make English the sole working language.

Film exports exemplified the predicament. A parliamentary enquiry of 1952 into the film industry concluded that the 'eminent role, which France is destined to play in the defence of peace and Western civilization', required a strong film industry, but the contraction of French culture and language reduced the market.[33] Film-makers could no longer assume that the originality and quality of their products would please American audiences. Hollywood's hegemonic position and the universality of English limited the appeal of the low-budget, artisanal French cinema – American audiences disliked subtitles. US distributors delayed and mutilated Robert Bresson's two masterpieces: *Les Anges du Péché* (1943; USA 1950), *Journal d'un curé de campagne* (1950; USA 1954). By the close of the 1950s film-makers capitulated to Hollywood's mass-market criteria. 'Screw the Americans', exclaims postman François in Jacques Tati's comedy *Jour de Fête* (1949). Fascinated by an American Marshall documentary on the speed and efficiency of the US mail service, François tries to imitate it. A hilarious merry-go-round ensues, followed by disillusionment and return to routine. France fought long and hard against Cocacolonization – borrowing some features, rejecting others. In 1949 the government set up a committee to oversee comic strips and books for children. The aim was to block comics coming from America. Restricting American competition helped make Tintin, Herge's Belgian boy reporter, a European hero.[34]

Were the French as clever as they claimed? Historian Tony Judt excoriated Sartre and other idols of the European Left for denouncing the United States while ignoring the evils of Stalinism. Long before Judt's indictment, however, Aron and Camus criticized the attitudes of their peers towards the Cold War. Judt's critique does not detract from the achievement of French thinkers. Combining sympathy for the Soviet Union with vitriolic anti-Americanism was a way of asserting independence. Like the Maginot Line, the Descartes line of French culture has been criticized for breeding introversion, particularly in the social sciences and philosophy. 'For long periods there has been a notable degree of closure, and ignorance of intellectual developments outside the country', observed Marxist historian Perry Anderson, citing slowness to engage with Anglo-Saxon analytic philosophy, the Frankfurt School and British historical sociology.[35] True, when Sartre lectured in the United States in 1946 he did not meet anyone from the Frankfurt School, but no American philosophers contacted him – though existentialism owed much to the pragmatism of C.S. Pierce and the psychologism of William James. Anderson's critique echoed the earlier strictures of cultural historian H. Stuart Hughes. When British historians in the 1970s began to range widely over European and world history French colleagues continued to focus almost exclusively on France.[36]

What worried the French in the 1950s was the lack of international recognition for medicine, science and economics. Of the forty-one Nobel Prizes awarded in physics and chemistry since 1935, headlined the *France Observateur* in 1955, none had gone to France nor had any of the thirty-three prizes awarded in medicine and physiology since 1928. Recognition finally came in 1965 when three French scientists from the Pasteur Institute in Paris – François Jacob, André Lwoff and Jacques Monod – shared the Nobel prize in medicine and physiology for discoveries on genes. French science performed better than critics allowed. The quality of research in the physical sciences and mathematics can easily be underestimated. Before and during the Second World War French scientists contributed significantly to nuclear energy research. Without them, 'neither the British nor the Canadians would have embarked ... on a slow-neutron project, which was to be the indispensable basis for the production of power and plutonium'.[37]

Contradictions bedevilled the self-image of a progressive democracy. Liberty, equality and fraternity, the shibboleth of 1789 commemorated on the Republic's coinage, meant some were more equal than others. The cult of the rational and universal made little allowance for differences of class, gender, ethnicity and region. Women waited for the vote until 1944. Rigid and intolerant centralization suppressed regional languages and cultures – Breton, Langue d'Oc, Basque, Flemish and Alsatian German. Public notices warned: 'It is forbidden to speak Breton and spit on the ground.' Industrial strife embittered the 1940s and 1950s. A wealthy bourgeoisie dominated the prestigious grandes écoles and the higher echelons of public service. The educational system prolonged gross inequalities – a mere 21 per cent of working-class children entered secondary education. Challenges to orthodoxy were sanitized or suppressed. A post-Liberation reform intended to free the press from corruption replaced the venality of the Third Republic with extensive state intervention. Newspapers lost independence and the state had a large stable of journalists on the payroll.

The political elite represented 'a cross-section of the upper bourgeoisie rather than of the population as a whole'. The École nationale d'administration (ENA), founded in

1945, was a nursery for the higher civil service. Its graduates – known as enarques – represented the best and brightest of the civil service. Between 1945 and 1952 barely 3.9 per cent of entrants came from the lower middle class. High rates of tuberculosis and mortality raged in the *bidonvilles* that ringed the elegant quarters of Haussmann's Paris and other large cities. A sociologist accused architects, developers and property companies of having changed Saint-Denis on the northern perimeter of Paris from 'a lively city full of history into a sordid concentration camp for immigrants'.[38]

Guardian of revolution, liberty and human rights? The state insisted that it had lived up to its ideals and had completed in 1945 the fight for liberty begun in September 1939. 'France has throughout the world stood for the ideals of liberty, justice and humanity', affirmed a 1946 edition of *Petit Lavisse*, the standard school history text.[39] An inscription on the huge cross of Lorraine at de Gaulle's village of Colombey-les-Deux-Eglises refers to the ancient pact 'between the greatness of France and the liberty of the world'. True, the Republic accepted more asylum-seekers than any other state in the 1930s, but their reception and treatment was often harsh and insensitive.

Vichy authorities assisted Nazi genocide by deporting 70,000 foreign-born Jews. Compared to other parts of Hitler's Europe the numbers could have been much higher. Seventy-five per cent of the 400,000-strong Jewish community survived, partly because Vichy was not as systematically brutal as alleged, and partly because many Jews found sanctuary in French homes. Saul Friedlander's *Quand Vient Le Souvenir* (1978) and Joseph Joffo's *Un Sac de Billes* (1973) tell of life-saving shelter. The resistance myth, buttressed by tight control of the archives, concealed Vichy's anti-semitism. When the French state's complicity in the Holocaust became widely known in the 1970s the army's use of torture in Algeria had already exploded the myth of France as liberty's champion.

While London talked of Commonwealth partnership and eventual self-rule for tropical Africa, the French Union of 1946 had a centralizing, assimilationist character. Merciless suppression of rebellion in Indo-China and Algeria reflected long-standing state violence against colonial subjects. Twenty thousand Indochinese were forced to work in France between 1939 and 1952. Brutal repression of nationalist movements contradicted the claim to guardianship of human rights. The Setif massacre of 1945, followed by the suppression of the 1947 rebellion in Madagascar, and the atrocities of decolonization wars in Indo-China (1946–54) and Algeria (1954–62) exposed the abyss between image and reality. On the credit side, French voices – Henri Alleg's *La Question* (1958), Pierre Vidal-Naquet's *L'Affaire Audin* (1958) – spoke out early against the army's use of torture in Algeria.

On the face of it, the dizzying carousel of five regimes between 1940 and 1958 confirms the sick woman image. Over twelve years the Fourth Republic averaged a different cabinet every six months. Appearances can deceive. Marianne, unlike Humpty Dumpty, put herself together again. Turbulence masked underlying continuities – comically so at times. 'Vive le Maréchal', cried a befuddled local as de Gaulle arrived in liberated Bayeux. Only marginal differences separated the constitutions of the Third and Fourth Republics. The 'continuous change' of the Fourth Republic, as Richard Vinen argues, is best understood, not as evidence of failure, 'but rather of a bourgeoisie that was innovative and willing to adjust to meet new problems'. Resistance as a symbol of renewal legitimized the post-war polity – 'the prestige conferred on certain sections of the bourgeoisie by their careers in the Resistance strengthened their position'.⁴⁰ The continuity of a large echelon of the political and administrative elite anchored the state. The strong administrative and legal backbone inherited from the Revolution of 1789 and Napoleon I grew stronger. After 1945 the retention of identity cards and the creation of anti-riot police, *Compagnies republicaines de securite* (CRS), strengthened state monopoly of force and surveillance powers.

Modernization offered a unifying vision. France won a vanguard position in technological development – civil and military uses of nuclear power, French communications satellite (1965), then European colour television standard Secam (1967), and supersonic air travel with Concorde (1969). Next came rapid commuter transit – Paris (RER 1977), and high speed intercity (TGV 1980), followed by Minitel (1982–) pre-world-wide web online connection.⁴¹

3

Strangers

'My dear archdeacon... what is the use of always fighting?', Trollope's Mrs Grantly asks her husband.[1] British and French leaders posed the same question. A Franco–British Europe looked a safe bet after 1945. Global upheaval spurred radical thinking. Future French prime minister Michel Debré dismissed national sovereignty as an 'outdated doctrine' that coming generations would associate with a 'semi-savage phase of the life of nations'.[2] The years 1945–50 formed a climacteric for the leading West European democracies, a chance to reinvent themselves as a new force in world politics. The benefits now seem blindingly obvious. Too weak singly to escape the pull of the American and Soviet colossi, together they might have exercised significant leverage. 'The time has arrived for a most momentous decision in British foreign policy', urged a senior ambassador; 'If we now succeed in identifying our interests with those of France, we shall with our two vast empires, be able to remain not only one, but possibly not the least important, of the Big Three'.[3]

Full-bloodied alliance seemed a natural coda to wartime cooperation. Aid for the French resistance counteracted toxic memories of Dunkirk and Mers-el-Kébir. In Kessel's *The Army of Shadows* (1944), the hero returns from a short visit to London, 'because I've been... I'm in danger of becoming the object of a cult... When everything seemed lost, England was the only source of hope and warmth'.[4] Resister and Fourth Republic minister Christian Pineau almost choked with 'emotion and exaltation' on hearing that he would soon be flown to London.[5] 'Our two peoples', affirmed a Free French representative, formed 'in spite of everything a single civilization'.[6] As well as tuning to Radio Londres – the BBC French service – thousands of French people from all walks of life risked denunciation and imprisonment by writing to express their gratitude to Britain for keeping the cause of freedom alive. 'I agree', wrote a Vichy censor on one letter.[7]

Goodwill overflowed. Jubilant crowds welcomed Britain's ambassador Alfred Duff Cooper in September 1944. Escorted by forty-eight Spitfires, his arrival ahead of formal allied recognition of the Provisional Government underscored the specialness of the connection. Pro-British sympathies survived semi-starvation under German occupation and Royal Air Force bombing raids. 'Everywhere... people seemed pleased to see us, saluting and waving,' noted Duff Cooper.[8] The embassy – one of the few heated buildings during the coldest winter on record – hosted nightly free drinks parties. There was a snag. Alcohol and warmth lured collaborators and Vichyites as well as Anglophiles, provoking criticism. 'You understand, my dear', went the current mot, 'it was either Fresnes [Paris prison] or the British embassy'.[9] Sentiment stayed steady, despite a Franco–British military face-off in Syria in May 1945. A French poll registered 79 per cent support for a broad military and political partnership. In May 1947 the capital's Communist Red Belt gratified Churchill with a 'spontaneous and overwhelming' reception when he received the Republic's prestigious *medaille militaire*.[10] The visit of Princess Elizabeth and the Duke of Edinburgh the following year provoked a 'unanimous surge of enthusiasm and interest'.[11] The warm-heartedness of Londoners overwhelmed president Vincent Auriol during a state visit in March 1950: 'people broke through the barriers and knocked on the windows of the car, smiling, laughing and gesticulating.'[12]

Elites bonded. 'Several of us dined together and afterwards ... read Racine out loud', wrote a British liaison officer with the Free French; 'we read the play [Phedre] straight through at a sitting'.[13] At the newly-minted Council of Europe at Strasbourg in August 1949 Conservative leader Harold Macmillan met a 'new kind of Frenchman ... keen, amusing, deeply religious, and patriotic men ... very different from the old French politicians ... I like foreigners; I like listening to their speeches'. Pierre-Henri Teitgen, leader of France's Christian Democrats, gave 'the finest speech which I have ever heard in my life'.[14]

Why, then, so little to show? The Treaty of Dunkirk of 4 March 1947, a fifty-year defensive pact, arrived without bells and whistles and was quickly subsumed into the five-power Brussels Treaty of March 1948, then into the North Atlantic Treaty of April 1950. Partnership never materialized. Narratives indict the usual suspects – clashing great power ambitions, France's perceived weakness and unreliability, and the danger of a communist take-over. The explanation, I contend, ignores the elephant in the room – next door neighbours were comparative strangers.

'I know of no other two peoples which are so impenetrable to each other,' wrote sociologist André Siegfried.[15] Though drilled in Franco–British wars from Joan of Arc to Napoleon Bonaparte, the peoples hardly knew each other. Austerity – especially the Attlee government's miserly sterling allowances in the early post-war years – restricted travel. Many middle-class families hardly knew the continent – Attlee's wife, Vi, first visited Paris in 1956. Town twinning, student exchanges and cuisine were slow to make an impact. Long delays in film releases and book translations curbed interaction. Seminal works like Sartre's *L'Etre et le Néant* (1943) and historian H.R. Kedward's *Resistance in Vichy France* (1978) waited over a decade for French and English editions. The ingredients of Elizabeth David's *A Book of Mediterranean Food* (1950) were hard to find at the time even in London. When cheap holiday packages appeared in the 1960s Britons headed for Spain, and did not buy into the French property market until the 1970s.

Belief in national characteristics created stereotypes. France represented the exotic. The French looked, dressed and behaved differently – hugging and kissing in public, forever shaking hands. A British visitor encountered veteran socialist Leon Blum 'in a curious garb, which I couldn't make out, I didn't like to look too closely, for it was open at the neck and his feet were bare ... later I realized he was in pyjamas and dressing gown, in fact was not dressed at noon!'[16] Art historian Kenneth Clark, member of the *Grand Conseil* of the Louvre, observed his colleagues: 'They came very late, gossiped with each other, interrupted, got up and wandered about in a manner unthinkable among the Trustees of the British Museum, who sit round as solemn as owls.'[17] 'The first thing we did when we got out of bed in the morning', recalled a British teenager boarding at the *Lycée Hoche* in 1947, 'was to shake hands with one another all of us, standing around in our pyjamas'.[18] A party of young Britons went to Paris for the first time in 1952, 'thrilled at everything we saw ... even the pervasive smell of drains and the lavatories that were just a hole in the floor were transfigured by their romantic foreignness.'[19] Instructions warned British D-Day invasion troops against 'a fairly widespread belief among people in Britain that the French are a particularly gay, frivolous people with no morals and few principles'.[20] British cinema reinforced the image of a country where anything goes. In the 1951 Ealing comedy *The Lavender Hill Mob*, the gold bullion stolen by a British bank clerk is exported to France as miniature Eiffel Towers.

Decision-makers took 'national characteristics' for granted: phlegmatic, pragmatic Britons vs. excitable, overly logical Latins. In 1956 Britain denied French prime minister Guy Mollet's request for union – claiming that differences of race, religion and outlook were too great. In the early Cold War the United States funded research by anthropologist Margaret Mead to identify and compare national characters. In the 1990s a trinity of luminaries – Lord Dacre, Norman Stone and Timothy Garton Ash – listed the defining characteristics of the 'German national character' as 'angst, aggressiveness, assertiveness, bullying, egotism, inferiority complex [and] sentimentality'.[21] Opposing post-1945 military cooperation with France, Whitehall instanced 'inherent defects in the French character' – a 'natural garrulous tendency', together with carelessness, and a 'certain decline in moral standards'.[22] The Franco–British commanders in the Suez operation gave the lie to stereotypes. They might have stepped straight out of a Blackadder script: a cool, calm and cerebral French deputy vs. an 'extremely excitable, gesticulating' British land commander deploying a swagger stick 'to make golf strokes with the flower vases and ash trays'.[23]

Language blocked easy interactions. In wartime London Free French officers seemed to know only two words, 'bloody English' – improvising to explain a difficulty, '*Il y avait d'abord un tout petit balls-up*'.[24] Fourth Republic foreign ministers Bidault and Schuman had no English. A handful of senior British ministers spoke competent French. Churchill liked making speeches in the language because he knew so little and did not 'notice nor mind his own mistakes'.[25] Bevin had no French. At the signing of the Dunkirk treaty the delayed arrival of an official carrying the necessary papers left the foreign secretary and Bidault twiddling thumbs in awkward silence. Bevin filled intervals at conferences with songs like *Cockles and Mussels*, interspersed by 'more or less obscene stories' – leaving others to translate.[26] Language influenced interactions in another sense. The Gallic gift of the gab left Britons feeling inadequate: 'There is no doubt the Latins speak as birds fly or fishes swim – and that we speak like people trying to learn to bicycle.'[27]

The ambivalence of leaders contrasted sharply with the warm spontaneity of popular responses. The cocktail of British condescension and French sensitivity proved toxic. 'We are a suspicious and a very sensitive people ... we suspect the worst of others', confided a French insider.[28] The French had a big chip on their shoulder. 'I'm like France,' announces a character in Paul Claudel's play *Le Pain dur*, 'nobody understands me'.[29] Defeat and occupation stoked self-pity. London's defiance of Hitler bred resentment. 'In the space of five years', noted Sartre, 'we have acquired a formidable inferiority complex'.[30] President Vincent Auriol considered the nation was being made to pay twice for 1940: 'Abroad, people are not always kind to us ... blaming us for having been occupied, but if we gave way in 1940 it was because we were alone in the face of an army that took five years to destroy ... occasionally we deserve from our great and powerful allies, if not the respect to which misfortune has a right, at least a little more sympathy and understanding'.[31] In 1959 British and French diplomats, shocked by the backbiting and distrust, agreed the main problem was a continuing inferiority complex because Britain resisted Hitler, and De Gaulle never forgot his difficulties in London – at one time so hard up that he borrowed money from Churchill's liaison officer, General Spears.

The insensitivity of British leaders sowed suspicion. Minor but delicate issues booby-trapped rapprochement: the depiction of French knights on the eve of Agincourt in Lawrence Olivier's 1944 film *Henry V* dismayed the French. The Royal Navy proposed joint naval exercises – closing with a grand finale of British warships escorting a much smaller French fleet into a British port. Memories of British meddling in French politics lingered. UK diplomat Oliver Harvey, observed a French colleague, 'served in the Paris embassy under Lord Tyrrell and copied his chief in believing that it was still possible even in external affairs to play one French politician against another, a dirty business but understandable given the corruption of political life in 1935; Harvey may well have thought it still practicable in 1946, but he soon met resistance, and was astute enough to realize he was now skating on thin ice'.[32]

Alliance in two world wars left minefields of resentment and misunderstanding. An Attlee government discussion on defence touched a raw nerve. An aide mentioned French complaints about London's slowness to do more for the defence of western Europe. 'What the hell right have they got to criticize us?' shouted prime minister Attlee: 'Tell them to go and clear up their own bloody stable. They haven't any decent generals.' De Lattre was dynamic, interjected a minion. 'Dynamic is he?', barked Attlee, 'I know what you mean. Just like General Nivelle [First World War French commander] gets us all killed'.[33] Historian Marc Bloch did not mince words about the Dunkirk evacuation and the behaviour of British troops – the Tommy, 'by nature, a looter and a lecher'.[34] Barely a month after offering political union in June 1940 Churchill ordered the destruction of the French fleet at Mers-el-Kébir. British and Vichy forces clashed in Dakar, Syria and Madagascar. Both countries felt short-changed by events, and more than one generation carried the scars. A schoolboy in the 1960s confessed to hating the English because they killed his uncle in 1940 when the Royal Navy attacked the French fleet.

British hauteur trapped the French in a no-win situation – damned if we do and damned if we don't. Anglophilia and anglophobia both incurred displeasure. Visiting Paris, the Queen Mother 'kept on exclaiming what a bore' French premier Mollet was for saying how much he liked the English.[35] London considered the French fair game for cynical put-downs: Gaillard (prime minister 1957–8) 'probably not a man of high principle or lofty moral stature'; Pinay (prime minister 1952–3) – 'charming manners, honourable and straight – rather naïve'.[36]

Churchill's slighting of French leaders at the Anglo–Franco–American Bermuda conference of December 1953 was a lesson in how to lose friends and influence. Rather than read briefing papers during the flight the prime minister psyched himself up on C.S. Forester's historical novel '*Death to the French*'. 'The French', he declared, 'are going to be very difficult. They will want everything and give nothing'. No *Marseillaise* greeted prime minister Joseph Laniel and foreign minister Bidault on arrival. Laniel had to squeeze into the car for foreign ministers while Churchill and American president Dwight D. Eisenhower travelled separately. Churchill shocked Ike's press secretary by the 'complete and utter disdain' with which he behaved towards an ally – giving the president a drink and snubbing the French leaders. Feeling obliged to offer Laniel a lift home on his plane but not wanting to socialize, Churchill contrived to have the prime minister sent straight to bed on the advice of his own doctor Lord Moran. Heavily sedated, Laniel slept through Churchill's in-flight dinner party.[37]

Despite a curmudgeonly Churchill, the British and French found friendship, and romance: novelist Nancy Mitford and Gaston Palewski, de Gaulle's chef de cabinet; author Louise de Vilmorin, Duff Cooper's mistress, became a family friend and back channel to de Gaulle; Treasury planning chief Edwin Plowden and Jean Monnet enjoyed a life-time friendship; historian Alistair Horne's friendship with diplomat and writer Francis Hure nurtured a lasting love affair with French history. Labour politician Roy Jenkins befriended French diplomats in London – the better to pursue their wives – even taking a holiday house in the Pyrenees to be close to one couple.

The politicians kept their distance. The Atlantic Charter of 1941 proclaimed Anglo–American values, but no singular British vision challenged Hitler's New Order. Influencers such as *The Times* leader writer and historian E.H. Carr – 'the ablest and best-qualified man who has been near the paper for years' – dished up banalities, calling for a new Europe to be achieved through cooperation, not conquest. Privately, Carr talked of an approach 'not through the medium of ideas, but through the concrete medium of economic planning ... we should avoid like the plague all ready made schemes for political organizations'.[38]

Churchill won the prize for vacuity. His rambling 'Morning Thoughts' paper of January 1943 – presented to the Turks after the Allied summit at Casablanca and later copied to Roosevelt and Stalin – proposed an 'instrument of European government' embodying the 'spirit but not ... subject to the weakness of the former League of Nations'. Smaller European states would be herded into 'confederations': Scandinavia, Danubian and Balkan. 'Morning Thoughts' showed Winston at his worst. 'The prime minister', remarked a staffer, 'after obstructing any discussion of such plans brings them out in a paper of his own and hands it to the Turks who are not even fighting for us'.[39] Churchill's aides used an unsafe cypher so Hitler probably got a copy too. The ill-conceived paper prompted an FO spoof, 'Early Morning Thoughts', calling for the fusion of the USA, Britain and Commonwealth-Empire, together with 'the restoration of the ancient glories of Europe, and the construction of a cordon sanitaire extending from the North Cape to Mukden'.[40] By 1944–5 Churchill's confederations had become a Western bloc of European states intended to provide Britain with a platform should great power cooperation break down – ironically a suggestion first put forward by Stalin in December 1941. Churchill and Eden fought tooth and nail at Allied summits for the restoration of an independent France, but kept European projects on the back burner for fear of upsetting Roosevelt and Stalin.

'We have to accept our full share of responsibility for the future of Europe', urged Eden in November 1942; 'If we fail to do that, we shall have fought this war to no purpose'.[41] Ministers ignored exiled European leaders in their midst. 'I have never spoken on these matters ... They have not been encouraged in their various timid advances and they may soon return to their lands ... but then shall we not have missed an exceptional opportunity?', confessed Eden in July 1944.[42] Churchill banned any discussion of a Western group linking France, Belgium and the Netherlands. In April 1944 Paul-Henri Spaak, Belgian foreign minister in exile, warned London against endangering 'the immense prestige' won in western Europe, suggesting an economic bloc of France and Benelux under Anglo–Soviet protection. Embarrassed officials could only say they 'had had no time to study' Spaak's proposal.[43] De Gaulle's presence in London, together with leaders of European governments in exile, offered an unrivalled opportunity to reinvent the Entente and share ideas on the continent's future. Agreeing a broad consensus on first principles could have defanged cross-channel conflict and signposted a new Europe.

Sick of the shilly-shallying, Duff Cooper, Britain's representative to the French Committee of National Liberation in Algiers, proposed alliance with France as a first step towards a federation of West European and Mediterranean powers. Anglo-American interests, he contended, diverged too much for successful cooperation. Britain should pursue a traditional balance of power approach by forming a West European bloc. A federation underpinned by colonial empire would be a guarantee against Germany and the Soviet Union. Eden baulked at the envoy's intervention, insisting that the country's post-war position should be grounded in the United Nations and an Anglo–Soviet alliance against Germany. Churchill objected to the subject being discussed at all – Germany's defeat would be soon enough: 'there is nothing in these countries but hopeless weakness'.[44]

Colleagues were more supportive. Harold Macmillan, resident minister in Algiers, complimented Duff Cooper on expressing 'very clearly and very succinctly the sort of foreign policy which we need, at present ... HMG are groping in the dark'. Dominions Secretary Lord Camborne described Eden's response as 'utterly futile'. The Russians were unlikely to oppose a Western bloc and the Americans would 'mildly dislike anything that increased our importance. But we mustn't allow ourselves to be bullied into the position of a second class power'.[45] The first clues to FO thinking emerged belatedly in a 'Stocktaking' paper of July 1945. It talked patronizingly of 'enrolling' France and lesser European states as 'collaborators' with Britain in Big Three cooperation. Such support would 'compel our two big partners to treat us as an equal'. Britain had to build itself up as '*the* great European Power', cooperation with France would establish London and Paris 'as the leaders of all the Western European Powers'.[46]

Exclusion from Allied conclaves and the threat of extinction as an independent power focused French minds. 'France had ceased to count', announced Field Marshal Jan Smuts, prime minister of South Africa, in November 1943.[47] Smuts anticipated European states joining the British Commonwealth in an Anglo–American–Soviet condominium. In London, Algiers and German occupied Paris French officials debated their country's future. Ideas ranged from a federal United States of Europe to regional unions, including a Latin union. Though the proposals could not be fleshed out without Allied participation, several conclusions emerged.

Powerlessness. 'With a population of 40 million and few resources', wrote Hervé Alphand, director of economic affairs on the French national committee in Algiers, 'France cannot be considered a great power in the world which is emerging. It's as true for England as for us'.[48] Alphand's insight was exceptional. Most of his colleagues perceived weakness as temporary. Marxist philosopher and civil servant Alexandre Kojève grasped the inability of the European nation state to function independently in a superpower era. But his response to the geopolitical revolution – the merging of Latin Catholic states into a French-led Latin empire – lacked credibility.[49] Second conclusion: Anglo–French union à la Churchill 1940 had no appeal. Novelist Maurice Druon, then a young officer with the Free French in London, called for a revival of Churchill's offer, but political commentator Raymond Aron, after initially urging a full strength Franco-British alliance, backpedalled because the disparity of power between the couple would be perceived 'as a subtle form of abdication ... joining Great Britain ... would mean entering an Anglo-Saxon universe'.[50] Third conclusion: Monnet's proposal for a 'completely unified Europe, composed of equal states – Germany could be divided ... European heavy industry under international control, no more custom duties' had few fans.[51] The idea of a West European or Benelux union, underpinned by French or international control of the Ruhr, won broad support. The fourth conclusion expressed agreement on the way forward: recovery of rank, aided by British and Russian alliances, American friendship and economic union with Belgium and Holland.

The Entente was a casualty of the Anglo–American alliance. Wired into a special relationship, British elites lacked an incentive to get to know the French better. The rich web of transatlantic exchanges had no cross-channel equivalent. The war strengthened Atlantic ties: middle-class families sent their children to the safety of American host families, fostering life-long friendships; thousands of GI brides crossed the Atlantic; US food parcels eked out British rations. At Oxford University in the 1950s Americans formed the largest group of foreign students. A US diplomat and former Rhodes scholar posted to London found he knew 'about half of the Labour Cabinet' from Oxford days. Informal and frank consultation on most issues characterized London–Washington exchanges – 'whenever Wilson met with Johnson' (President Lyndon B. Johnson) the London embassy secured a copy of the premier's report to Cabinet 'long before we received any report from Washington'.[52]

No networking events like today's annual Franco–British colloque joined up cross-channel elites. In 1950 a Labour Party pamphlet on European unity privileged the Commonwealth over Europe because so many had families and friends in the White Dominions but few in Europe. A smidgen of Franco–British associations could not compete with programmes like the Ditchley Foundation, Pilgrim Trust, Fulbright, Marshall and Rhodes scholarships. The UK had stronger links with Germany than with France. The annual Anglo–German Konigswinter conference established in 1950 had no Franco–British counterpart. The Franco–British Council of 1972, a spin-off from the Heath government's 1970–2 entry negotiations into Europe, arrived too late.

Given the language hurdle and the dearth of European networks, Britons looked westward. Students took American summer camp jobs, then bought $99 Greyhound bus tickets for route 66 and beyond. Conservative politician William Waldegrave won a scholarship to Harvard University which 'offered ... a seriousness of approach to political philosophy and the teaching of practical politics' unmatched elsewhere.[53] Labour leader Denis Healey holidayed in France and Italy, but recharged intellectually in Boston, New York and Washington DC. Civil servants chose Harvard for sabbatical leaves, not Sciences Po.

Was the Entente a lost cause? Not so. Both the Attlee and Churchill governments of 1945–55 could have rebuilt the relationship. Rather than explore ways to strengthen the Entente, London dispensed royal visits as treats and tranquilizers. Bidault, angered by British airs and graces, refused to meet Princess Elizabeth. In 1956 prime minister Mollet asked for union and got the Queen. The FO sugared rejection of union with a recommendation for a state visit 'in view of the immense popularity of the Royal Family in France'. The invitation 'nearly got ballsed up because no one remembered to consult President Coty'.[54] Paris pulled out all the stops for the visit in April 1957. Cheering Parisians offered distraction from the fractured post-Suez relationship. No sooner had the Queen confessed at a gala dinner in the Louvre that she had never seen Leonardo da Vinci's Mona Lisa than two attendants brought the painting to her. *Le Monde* mischievously hailed the royal circus as proof of 'the vitality of the entente'.

Apart from an Anglo–French economic committee which rarely met, official contacts lacked an institutional infrastructure. In the late 1950s Whitehall attempted to convince the Americans of the need for permanent working groups, but showed no desire to pair off with the French. President Auriol expressed interest in regular summits – to no effect. French officials preparing for Franco–German cooperation recommended monthly meetings of foreign ministers and advisers – 'a common policy had more chance of developing from the habit of living and thinking together'.[55] Exactly what the Entente lacked.

Stinginess strangled cultural contacts. A savage halving of the British Council's French budget torpedoed a March 1948 agreement for educational and cultural cooperation. The Collège Franco–Britannique, part of the Cité universitaire in Paris, became dilapidated because of inadequate funding and falling UK student recruitment. The newly established St Antony's College at the University of Oxford failed to meet the wishes of founder Antonin Besse for a special emphasis on Anglo–French relations. The sole French presence in the British academic world, the Maison française at Oxford, created in 1946, was quite different from today's research hub. Archaeologist Claude Schaeffer wanted a place where French and British scholars could live and study together. The university's veto on a new college or teaching institution left the Maison struggling to survive. Dependent on French foreign ministry funding and with only a trickle of British students, it functioned more as an outpost for French culture than a meeting point.

Academic fashion and prejudice skewed evaluations of France. American economic historians led by David Landes asked why France did not fit the economic model of nineteenth- and early twentieth-century Western Europe. Landes's contention that French culture and values retarded economic development gained wide currency. As a result, the speed of the Fourth Republic's economic take-off in the 1950s caught international observers off guard. A purist academy frowned on the study of contemporary history and politics because government archives remained classified. Unlike American colleagues who craved involvement, British political scientists distanced themselves from practitioners and lay public alike – partly to protect 'neutrality', partly because of Whitehall's insistence on in-house expertise. Oxford University had no history special subject later than the making of the Anglo-French entente of 1904. Many general histories stopped in 1939 leaving lay readers dependent on newspapers and personal memories. The first British studies of the Fourth Republic appeared in the mid-1950s. The low standard of British school texts on European integration published in the 1960s testified to the neglect of contemporary history. In 1959 Henri Michel, a specialist on the Second World War, circulated historians and political scientists in British universities, inviting them to a conference in Liège on European resistance. Only one responded. The bias against recent history influenced appointments: 'In the ten years between 1951 and 1960 the number of new academic appointments in Britain ... to which persons whose main work lay in the field of contemporary history were appointed ... could be counted on the fingers of one hand.'[56]

French historians – with few exceptions – did not welcome foreign colleagues working on France. They assumed they knew their own history best. 'When I first worked alongside US State Department and French historians in the early 1950s on the series *Documents on German Foreign Policy*', recalled a British researcher, 'the leading French scholars, [Pierre] Renouvin, [Maurice] Baumont ... would only with the utmost reluctance and in the deepest privacy accept that any work on France by a product of education systems other than their own was of any interest whatever'.[57]

War and austerity stymied the rebuilding of scholarly connections. Colloquia were few and far between. British historians of France waited until the 1980s before banding together to create the Society for the Study of French History and the journal *French History*. 'Writing about the history of France,' claimed Alistair Horne, has 'the elements of a love affair with an irresistible woman.'[58] French historians found British studies resistible. Eminent early twentieth-century historians of Britain – Elie Halévy, Paul Mantoux and André Siegfried – had no immediate disciples. François Bedarida and François Crouzet started their careers in the 1950s researching Victorian Britain.

The most influential study of Britain's post-war economy – Andrew Schonfield's *British Economic Policy Since the War* – exemplified an institutionalized talking down of France.[59] Schonfield, foreign editor of *The Financial Times*, contrasted Britain's post-Suez 'critical self-examination' with the 'elementary' review in France. The Fourth Republic served as a warning 'of what happens to a nation which ... clings to positions of international prestige, regardless of the fact that the essential structure of its national life is crumbling all around it ... the political decisions imply a heroic readiness for financial sacrifice, which simply is not there – because no one will admit ... France no longer has a natural position of pre-eminence in the world'. French people 'for all the vaunted shrewdness and realism ... in their daily lives', had retreated 'into a world of illusion'. Fortunately, Britain had not lapsed into 'a typically French state of resentment and sulks'. Suez, asserted Schonfield, had stimulated 'fresh thinking on previously accepted assumptions about the UK's position in the world'.

Viewed from London an unknown France appeared mired in permanent crisis. UK coverage of news and issues was sparse. Former *Guardian* journalist Alexander Werth complained that 'apart from the dainty and whimsical "Letters from Paris" in our better-class journals – full of French words in italics, and dealing chiefly with the artistic', the literature offered little sustenance.[60] Slowly British academics began to take an interest. Trailblazing political scientist Philip Williams observed that Britons 'have never had much respect for the political capacity of their nearest neighbor ... official and ministerial circles too often share the view of the man in the street that the French are congenitally incapable of governing themselves properly ... there is so little understanding of the deep differences between the British and French outlook on politics'.[61] The commentariat recycled the image of a diseased polity – hardly noticing French elections. When de Gaulle's prime minister Georges Pompidou visited London for talks in July 1966 he was barely known and the BBC had difficulty finding someone to talk about him.

The runaway success of Werth's *France 1940–1955* – three editions and a French translation in just over a year – confirmed the strength of British curiosity. Overfocused, however, on day-to-day politics Werth imparted little sense of underlying trends. In a preface former prime minister Pierre Mendès France chided Werth for his 'pessimistic view of our future'. In contrast, Swiss historian and journalist Herbert Lüthy, one of the few to recognize the successes of the Fourth Republic, congratulated French diplomacy on 'an audacious attempt' to take 'American foreign policy in tow'. Lüthy identified 'a deep sense of renewed vigour' as modernization and population growth gained traction.[62]

How well did the diplomats size up the French? Labour politician George Brown denounced the Paris embassy for being 'totally out of touch with what was really going on ... when I used to visit there I seemed to arrive just as they were trying to get the dust-sheets off the furniture ... Embassy didn't seem to know anybody outside the normal channels of the Quai d'Orsay'.[63] He blamed staff for not anticipating the general's return to power in 1958. Separating smoke and substance in a moving target isn't easy. Britain's Paris embassy mostly did a good job, but London-based officials were slow to pick up on the speed of economic take-off, and even slower to realize the implications for Britain and Europe. The embassy flagged economic recovery, but HQ wanted only bad news. The favourite pastime was running down French leaders – arguing that trying to change French politicians would have as much effect as the campaign of premier Mendès France to persuade the French to drink milk instead of wine.

Ambassador Oliver Harvey fought his corner, insisting that French political crises 'should not be taken too tragically' and had 'little real effect on the workings of the French state'.[64] A disgruntled HQ requested a comprehensive assessment, attacking over-optimistic embassy references to 'the great and unexpected strides' made on all fronts. How could a nation, asked London mandarins, 'which nine short years ago had sunk so low ... have undergone a rebirth so utterly transforming? ... French public life remains corrupt and self-seeking'. Permanent secretary William Strang believed that 'the slaughter of the First World War and the occupation during the Second have broken France's spirit'. London bypassed the embassy and circulated its own appraisal – 'In building on France are we not building on sand?' After conceding 'a great change for the better – agriculture, industry and finance have largely recovered [from the war] the political situation is relatively healthy' but, continued the report, 'there remain still grave causes to doubt France's capacity to play her proper role in the defence of western Europe ... political instability is endemic ... there is a widespread lack of moral fibre in the country'.

Could the diplomats have done more for rapprochement? There was no stable of white knights. Multilateralism eroded the position of resident envoys, and their influence waned quickly after 1945. Early post-war representatives in London and Paris – Duff Cooper, Harvey and Massigli – wanted to re-energize the Entente. But the days of panjandrums like Stratford de Redcliffe in Constantinople and Francis Bertie in Paris were long gone. In 1956 Britain and France excluded their ambassadors from Suez decision-making. By the 1960s some analysts considered resident ambassadors an anachronism.

Other factors compounded the loss of diplomatic clout. Nudging retirement by the late 1950s both Jean Chauvel in London and Gladwyn Jebb in Paris were disinclined to rock the boat. Prudence tempered Chauvel's anglophile sympathies. The sacking of his predecessor and kindred spirit Massigli from the secretary generalship demonstrated the perils of Fourth Republic politics. De Gaulle's return to power in 1958 imposed extreme caution. As secretary general from 1944 Chauvel had endured a difficult relationship with the head of the provisional government. Similarly, in Paris Jebb toed the official line and made no special pleas for a strengthened Entente. Arrogance and prolixity curbed his effectiveness. Telegrams from Paris began 'The Prime Minister must insist'. Long-winded, convoluted dispatches left the reader struggling for the sense. Paying tribute to French personalities at a farewell dinner in his honour, Jebb singled out ex-premier Pierre Mendès France – ignoring foreign minister Couve de Murville sitting nearby. This and other gaffes clouded his departure.[65] The suggestion that in summer 1960 Jebb significantly shaped Macmillan's thinking on EEC membership is unconvincing.[66] In retirement he bombarded ministers with accounts of interviews with de Gaulle which largely retailed his own views. No. 10 switched off: 'The PM wishes neither to see Lord Gladwyn nor to read his report.'[67]

Chauvel's successor in London, Geoffroy de Courcel (1962–72), was the general's faithful sidekick, more Gaullist than de Gaulle. Totally his master's voice he accompanied the general to London in June 1940, and served as Élysée secretary general from 1958 to 1962. Apart from putting the embassy on the capital's gastronomic map, the envoy had little to show for a decade-long posting. He avoided, observed an obituarist, 'giving even the slightest impression that he could be influenced by any British attitude that ran counter to de Gaulle's policy or that the French embassy could ever be used as a place from which a discreet influence could be exerted in Paris ... his support for non-political Anglo–French initiatives, such as those of the Franco–British Society, though friendly, did not always seem as enthusiastic as it might have been'.[68] Courcel's negativism as ambassador, then as Quai secretary general, annoyed British officials. 'Courcel found it necessary to find something to complain about whenever one saw him', noted British colleague Nicholas Henderson. As Quai secretary general from 1972 Courcel became a standing joke – smoothing over awkward moments between British and French leaders. 'Courcel put him thoroughly on edge, so when he wanted a peaceful evening, he just refused to see him at all', confided foreign minister Michel Jobert to Heath.[69]

Politicians squandered the talents of Paris ambassadors, Pierson Dixon (1960–5) and Patrick Reilly (1965–8). Dixon's rapport with de Gaulle earned him an impossible balancing act – running the embassy while negotiating the UK's membership bid in Brussels in 1961–3. Reilly, best remembered for vetoing Soviet spy Kim Philby's appointment as head of MI6, lasted barely three years in Paris before being fired. He blamed a London-based whispering campaign for undermining him. Foreign secretary George Brown bullied the envoy and his wife appallingly.

A smart think tank might have reset the relationship but Chatham House (The Royal Institute of International Affairs) was unfit for purpose. Funded in part by the FO and American foundations, it drew media fire for perceived amateurishness, snobbishness and lack of impact. The summary of a study group discussion on French policy in March 1955 conveys the level of analysis: 'Mendès-France was a hopeless politician, but was a good leader if someone did the organizing for him. There might be a new coalition of the Left. All had different schemes for constitutional reform; none were likely to go through ... The Gaullist movement seemed to have collapsed ... The army might revive in the next few years.'[70] Liaising with its Paris counterpart, the Centre d'Etudes de Politique étrangère, Chatham House organized an Anglo–French relations study group. After meetings in Oxford and Paris in 1957, the British think tank withdrew, pleading lack of money. 'We in Chatham House', explained director C.M. Woodhouse, 'have only been able to take part ... because the initiative was taken, and some funds were found, by Professor Beloff in Oxford ... we were never in a position nor is it likely that we shall be to act as hosts in London'. In twenty years it commissioned only one substantial publication on Anglo–French relations.[71]

A dying Churchill administration was incapable of bold new initiatives towards France. In 1954 an unenthusiastic Eden presided over the Entente's muted fiftieth birthday celebrations. Gladwyn Jebb, newly appointed ambassador to France, sought guidance. 'Long conversations' with permanent secretary Sir Ivone Kirkpatrick 'did not disclose what he believed should be the general objectives of our policy towards the French'. After consulting prime minister Churchill, the envoy concluded, 'his main function was to go out and prevent the French from being so tiresome'.[72] The ambassador – rarely backward in coming forward – had no suggestions of his own. How had things come to such a pass? The ambassador was part of the problem. He personified the superciliousness separating the Franco–British couple. On one occasion, he 'swept' into the FO private secretary's room, 'looked around and commented to his companion "No, there's no one here"' – ignoring a colleague sitting there.[73] Early in 1956 Eden excoriated the French as 'our enemies in the Middle East'.[74] The Paris embassy reminded him that ministers shared responsibility for the mesentente because they kept the French at a distance and offered only pretend consultation. Government had no clear idea what it wanted from France and Europe. Premier and foreign secretary seemed satisfied acting as offshore policemen – keeping the Germans in order and saving France from the consequences of her follies. Was a real entente possible? The FO consistently exaggerated the obstacles to a closer relationship – the British and French 'like each other about as well as cat and dog'.[75] The career of German ex-paratrooper Bert Trautmann demonstrated how quickly attitudes can soften. Twice awarded the iron cross for bravery, he overcame great hostility and played for Manchester City from 1949. In 1955 the Attlees took a German maid with them on holiday – 'a very nice girl who has done something to mitigate my prejudice against that people'.[76] UK governments neglected a groundswell of cross-channel goodwill. The welcomes received by the Queen in Paris and de Gaulle in London confirmed a fund of friendship.

De Gaulle's expressions of friendship for Britain reflected changes in French perceptions. The Paris embassy in July 1966 reported 'undoubtedly much popular support now ... for British entry into the EEC'. Anglophile sentiment strengthened, diluting the old ambivalence – respect for the British lion coupled with resentment at poor relation status. The depth of pro-British feeling surprised professional observers. Commemorations in 1966 of the Norman Conquest and the anniversaries of the Battle of the Somme and D-Day 'evoked much goodwill for Britain', reported the Paris embassy. Between 1964 and 1966 public support for Britain's EEC membership rose from 41 per cent (October 1964) to 48 per cent (December 1966). The 'swinging sixties' softened stereotypes and provoked a desire to get to know the other. Rapid change diluted prejudice, especially among young people. Economic modernization changed the power relationship and renewed French confidence – in 1963 France's GDP overtook Britain's.[77]

Fascination triumphed as London set the pace in fashion, entertainment and avant garde lifestyle. Beatles, Minis, mini-skirts, tweed jackets, and Vidal Sassoon hairstyles became Parisian chic. 'Whereas in England one feels that the diplomatic war in which we have been engaged for some five years now with the French Government has left its mark and created a good deal of hostility', ambassador Christopher Soames informed the Queen, 'here on the other hand one gets an impression of people having a bad conscience over the anti-British attitudes of their government ... Even the most fervent Gaullists are anxious to say how deeply they resent the General's attitude to Britain ... The reception which Mary and I got in Lille from crowds gathered in the streets ... was, to us, quite remarkable and most warming'. Marketing an alliance as passport to the Community would not have over-taxed the skills of Downing Street spin doctors. Indeed, premier Harold Wilson claimed, there was 'virtually unanimous public support, in Parliament and in the country', for resuming friendly relations with France.[78]

Part Two

Reversal of Fortunes

4

New Look

In February 1947 couturier Christian Dior regained world fashion leadership, unveiling a calf-length hemline known as 'The New Look'. France too got a new look. In Sartre's *Les jeux sont faits* (1943) Pierre and Eve, recently deceased, return to Paris for 24 hours to try to find love together, having never met in life (despite being made for each other) due to 'administrative oversight'. France, like Pierre and Eve, got a second chance; a longing for redemption drove an astonishing make-over. By 1950 plans for European economic and military integration replaced earlier opposition to German rearmament and claims for German territory. By the mid-1960s the destitute 'non-power' of the late 1940s replaced Britain as political leader of Western Europe.[1]

How did a country in 'perpetual crisis' revive?[2] Resistance and liberation generated dreams of renewal. Before the Germans executed him as a hostage in December 1941 Communist deputy Gabriel Peri testified: 'I should like my fellow-countrymen to know that I am dying so that France may live ... In a few minutes I am going out to prepare a future full of song.'[3] Wartime study groups debated the nation's future; ex-Vichy civil servants and technocrats shared ideas and expertise. The roller-coaster Fourth Republic took defining decisions on economic modernization, European integration, technology and nuclear energy that empowered de Gaulle's Fifth Republic. 'Despite weakness of government, and foreign policy follies, all foreign observers consider that what France has done for its economy over ten years is extraordinary', declared Aron in 1957.[4] Rapid economic recovery and smart statecraft enabled Paris to seize the initiative and shape 'the outcome of the major diplomatic and security debates between 1944 and 1954, especially concerning the occupation of Germany, the Marshall Plan, and the shaping of the NATO alliance'.[5]

The cards looked heavily stacked against recovery. The early post-war years felt only marginally better than the German occupation: devastated infrastructure; Mother Hubbard economy; ideological strife; colonial war in Indo-China; dysfunctional regime. Over twelve years the Republic caromed from one calamity to the next, swallowing up twenty-five coalition cabinets, seventeen heads of government and six foreign ministers. In November 1947 political and economic storms aroused fear of civil war: 'We are again in a state of appalling anxiety', wrote de Gaulle's personal secretary, 'close to that experienced during the worst days of the occupation; the other night neither my father [François Mauriac] nor Brisson [Pierre Brisson, director of Le Figaro] slept at home'.[6]

Figure 4.1 The March of Time: The New France 1946, showing Maurice Thorez, Léon Blum, Bidault and Roger Dannes. Credit: Everett Collection Inc. / Alamy Stock Photo.

A weak executive flawed the regime. Ministers treated the premier as first among equals, running their departments like personal fiefdoms. Pressure of domestic business, the presence of Communist ministers until 1947, lack of expertise, and a culture of leaks, all stifled cabinet discussion of external policies. Politicians prioritized party and personal ambition, leaking secrets and circulating in advance what they proposed to say in cabinet. The quotidian treadmill of balancing a fragile parliamentary coalition while battling domestic and international hazards left premiers prostrate and often physically lighter. Edgar Faure claimed to have lost four kilos during his brief premiership of 1952: In 'forty days, including five spent in Lisbon, I had three major parliamentary debates: cost of living, European army, the budget. I still had Tunisia on my hands. In practice I constantly had to do two things at the same time: write a speech while receiving an ambassador, solve a financial problem while in a political discussion.'[7] Ministerial musical chairs rotated the same small pool of players at the expense of continuity and expertise. Coalitions privileged party solidarity over cabinet cohesion. Getting the party balance right mattered more than building effective teams. Fine-tuning imposed caution, compromise and inertia.

The head of state did not play ringmaster. The Fourth Republic's constitution authorized the President to sign treaties, to be kept informed of negotiations and receive copies of important diplomatic papers. Vincent Auriol and René Coty sought to escape from the wreath-laying ceremonial prison of Third Republic presidents. Chairing cabinet meetings certainly gave them more scope than British monarchs, but access to official papers could not be assumed. Auriol protested that he had not seen a single document from a three-power conference in New York. The president found allies among top officials and diplomats, especially Henri Bonnet, ambassador in Washington, and Rene Massigli, ambassador in London. After inauguration the president sent for Quai secretary-general Chauvel, asking to be informed at once if national interests appeared to be endangered: 'I'm permanent, you are permanent'.[8] Coty, as well as intervening vigorously in Tunisian and Moroccan affairs, staunchly advocated European integration, urging prime minister Guy Mollet in 1956 to appoint a pro-European foreign minister. Nevertheless, Auriol and Coty did not decisively shape policies.

Algerian and Indo-Chinese decolonization wars, each twice as long as the First World War, splintered opinion, producing a virtual breakdown of cabinet government. Memories of 1940 were still fresh when the communist Vietminh inflicted a humiliating defeat on French forces at Dien Bien Phu in 1954. The Mollet government's use of conscripts in Algeria and condoning of torture opened up a debate between domestic critics who widened their protest into a general condemnation of the war, and the military and politicians who blamed the opposition for the war's continuation. The kidnapping by French forces in October 1956 of the Algerian nationalist leader Ahmed Ben Bella during cease-fire talks exposed a dysfunctional regime, which had lost control of soldiers and officials. En route to Tunis, Ben Bella's aircraft was diverted and forced to land. Though Mollet had not authorized the action, he felt obliged to defend the fait accompli. The minister for Tunisian and Moroccan affairs resigned in protest. The bombing of the Tunisian border village of Sakiet in February 1958, without the approval of premier Félix Gaillard, confirmed a malfunctioning state. The threat of civil war posed by the revolt of settlers and generals in Algeria toppled the Republic in May 1958.

France's large Communist party panicked British leaders. Nearly a third of the electorate voted communist in 1947; a quarter in 1956. In 1955 Communists called a general strike paralysing the country for nearly a month. They adopted a fierce anti-American stance, attacking Washington's Marshall Plan of 1948 as political and economic vassalage. Anglo-American promotion of West German rearmament touched a raw nerve, alienating many non-communists. The arrival of United States Supreme Commander in Europe General Matthew B. Ridgway in May 1952 touched off some of the country's worst post-war riots. Premier René Plevin's advocacy of a European Defence Community (EDC) integrating French and German forces split elite and popular opinion. The regime's apparent inability to sustain a coherent strategy exasperated allies. In December 1953 US secretary of state John Foster Dulles threatened an 'agonizing reappraisal' of commitments in Europe. The political and administrative machine seemed close to meltdown. Politicians routinely breached conventions of secrecy and ministerial solidarity – torpedoing by premature disclosure the projects of colleagues. Foreign leaders advised French envoys, 'This is for your personal information only, don't pass it on to Paris'.[9]

Regaining rank resembled an obstacle race. Post-war multilateralism fazed the French because defeat and occupation excluded them from Allied planning. Other hurdles compounded the pain of a new rulebook: insularity, education and a broken foreign service. France's delegation at the foundation conference of the United Nations in San Francisco in May 1945 provided a 'sorry spectacle... nervous, diffuse, unused to these kinds of meeting'.[10] 'Russians and English lead the discussion,' acknowledged a French official at the London foreign ministers conference in September 1945, 'we follow with difficulty... our services have not recovered their old working methods'.[11] Soviet foreign minister Vyacheslav Molotov ran rings round the inexperienced foreign minister Georges Bidault. More worrying was French distrust of the UN. 'The Security Council', observed French delegate Alexander Parodi, 'is more the place where world rivalries are photographed than the place where they are settled'.[12] Bidault admitted having no taste for 'the publicity, and endless repetitions'.[13] Scepticism about the organization hardened into animosity and resentment because of UN criticism of France's Algerian war.

A late eighteenth-century French traveller in Italy amazed German writer Johann Wolfgang Goethe because he journeyed 'without noticing anything in the world outside himself'.[14] Insularity and a fondness for abstraction delayed adaptation to the superpower era. The occupation years scaled back exchanges, reinforcing an isolation derived partly from an assumption of cultural superiority, partly from the strength of local and regional identities. Before 1939 notables like Emile Moreau, governor of the Bank of France, and Pierre Brisson, director of the newspaper *Le Figaro*, had no English and travelled little. In the heyday of newspaper reading in the 1930s no French newspaper had a permanent representative in Moscow, only one had a correspondent in the USA. The French had international connections but close overseas friendships were rare. America, in de Gaulle's words, represented 'another world'.[15] Transatlantic go-between Jean Monnet, banker, civil servant and friend of Washington insiders, was an exception. Americanization in the 1950s furnished an added reason for staying at home. 'This nation', declared François Mauriac, 'is more foreign to me than any other. I've never been there ... what is the point? It has done more than just visit us; it has transformed us'.[16]

An educational formation emphasizing philosophy and rhetoric delayed adaptation to the post-war world. 'The French', observed anthropologist Claude Lévi-Strauss, had 'the stubborn conviction that it is enough to solve problems on paper to be immediately rid of them'.[17] Careful cultivation of the written and spoken word became a substitute for action. A Paris 1968 slogan ran: 'I take my wishes to be realities because I believe in the reality of my wishes'.[18] Logic and verbalism, allied to Catholicism, rendered the French doubly suspect. 'If there are two things on earth that John Bull hates', remarked Victorian statesman William Ewart Gladstone, 'they are an abstract proposition and the Pope'.[19] Excessive abstraction clogged communication between different groups in French society as well as between France and the world. A senior mandarin criticized the 'consistently doctrinaire point of view which our inexperienced legislators adopt towards all difficulties ... they take liberties with reality'.[20]

The grandiloquence of French political rhetoric disadvantaged policy-makers. Until the introduction in the late 1940s of simultaneous interpretation the slowness of consecutive interpretation privileged the clear expository style of English-speaking delegations. Language conditioned the chemistry of international gatherings. Anglo-Saxon dominance of international organizations enabled English to displace French as the traditional language of diplomacy. Bidault had no English, and foreign minister Robert Schuman barely any. For American Secretary of State Dean Acheson, Ernest Bevin was 'Ernie', Robert Schuman 'Monsieur Schuman'.[21] Chatting with the British after dealing with continental Europeans, remarked an American official, was like putting on a comfortable old shoe.

Antiquated telephone services snarled the new diplomacy – with comic effects. The Canadian delegation at the foreign ministers conference in Paris in 1946 found food and service excellent at the Hôtel de Crillon, but the telephone service functioned erratically, at times isolating the delegation from others, and cutting it off from Ottawa. An exasperated delegate went to find out why the system did not work:

> I expected to encounter an array of overworked telephone operators; instead, I found one plump blonde lady placidly reading a magazine, with a box of chocolates at her side, facing a board in which light signals were frantically flashing from the different floors of the hotel. To these she seemed sublimely indifferent. 'Where', I asked, 'are your colleagues?'. 'I am alone', she replied, giving me a glance of pathos, as though she languished for company, even my own.[22]

What ensured renewal? Two things: de Gaulle; and faith in renewal. At a crucial moment de Gaulle stabilized a ravaged country awaiting a constitution and an elected parliament. As head of the Provisional Government the general provided security and reassurance amid fears of civil war and Communist revolution in the autumn and winter of 1944–5. Notwithstanding exclusion from the Yalta and Potsdam summits in 1945, France notched up substantial gains: an occupation zone in Germany; membership of the five-power Security Council of the United Nations; membership of the European Consultative Commission; participation in the Consultative Committee for Italy; admission to the conference of foreign ministers. Germany's formal surrender on French soil at Rheims on 8 May 1945 and General Leclerc's presence at Japan's surrender on 2 September 1945 supplied further signs of great power ranking. Victories had a downside. De Gaulle's insistence on prior satisfaction of France's German and Middle Eastern claims blocked a general European settlement. There was no likelihood of such terms being fulfilled. The general's resignation in January 1946 freed up policy-making.

Resistance and liberation charged up France, fuelling hope in renewal. 'To be twenty or twenty-five in September 1944', recalled Simone de Beauvoir, 'seemed a great stroke of good luck: all roads opened up. Journalists, writers, budding filmmakers, discussed, planned, made decisions with passion, as if their future depended only on them'.[23] Ahead of the Liberation de Gaulle's Free French movement asserted a world role: 'France is international ... by her geographic situation, by the radiation of her genius, by her catholicity, by her revolutionary generosity'.[24] Jubilation and stoicism marked the mood. Francis Gruber's sensation-making painting 'Job', unveiled at the Salon of the Liberation only a few weeks after the Germans left Paris, framed the stoicism. The biblical figure of Job symbolized oppressed Parisians enduring great suffering without forfeiting hope and faith. A gaunt male nude, like Rodin's Thinker, resting head on hand, looks at an inscription from the Book of Job: 'Now, once more my cry is a revolt, and yet my hand suppresses my sobs'. In the early days ambition, food and romance boosted morale. Within weeks of VE Day officials who during the winter of 1944–5 downed grogs and burnt furniture to keep warm, hosted a dinner for over 100 in honour of the Sultan of Morocco. 'It was all beautifully done – the flowers were pretty, the service was quick and the food was good,' acknowledged ambassador Duff Cooper.[25] As he and foreign minister Bidault padded through spacious salons the envoy spotted de Gaulle's chef de cabinet Palewski making love on a sofa to the wife of Alphand, Quai director for economic affairs.

France's hosting of the peace conference in July to October 1946 simulated greatness. Delegates attending a reception at the Palace of Versailles marvelled at 'a scene of amazing magnificence and beauty'.[26] Abroad, the French put on a good face: 'We had a tremendous feast', noted a guest at France's London embassy; 'the food was exquisite – consommé, lobster and rice, chicken and (really green) peas, ices'.[27] Keeping up appearances encouraged the French to think restoration of rank was just round the corner. As powerlessness became apparent, people remained in denial, partly from a feeling that after so much suffering things just had to get better, partly from pride in empire and its resources as pledge for future power, and partly because of an inclination to take rhetoric for reality. Vichy and the resistance had enthused so much about renewal that liberation seemed 'the day of resurrection' promised by premier Paul Reynaud in June 1940, when the world would defer to France 'as the leader of civilization'.[28]

By 1946 the euphoria was too painful to recall. 'The French no longer have the strength to react,' lamented de Gaulle in March 1946. Raymond Aron identified 'a form of indifference to the destiny of France' born of a sense of national powerlessness.[29] 'We had this dream', wrote François Mauriac, 'that France, the cloth barely snatched from her face, would propose to the world the formula for the new age'.[30] A down-at-heel Paris with dirty buildings and tatty public spaces made gloom and doom almost palpable. Tiredness and stress affected public behaviour. A UK exchange student encountered 'repressed aggression, bristling hostility ... everywhere'.[31]

Cinema caught the mood swing. The pessimism of René Clement's film *Au-Dela des Grilles* (1949) signalled 'a rapid moving away from the enthusiasms, which had now become illusions, of the Liberation'.[32] Withdrawal from Indo-China in 1954, after the disaster of Dien Bien Phu, closed an Asian empire. 'As in 1940,' noted Simone de Beauvoir, 'the future lost all perceptible shape, and I vegetated without living; the subjection of France was almost as painful to me as it had been then'. The nation's main ambition, wrote Sartre, seemed to be 'dying in peace'.[33] The public clutched at sporting success – Yvon Petra's victory in the Wimbledon singles in 1946, middleweight Marcel Cerdan's world title triumph in the United States in September 1948.

Influencers scarcely attempted to inform opinion. Rookie deputies in the newly elected Assembly of 1946 lacked experience in international affairs, and political parties said little about foreign policy. There was plenty to be pessimistic about. The wherewithal to assure independence, never mind influence, was conspicuously absent. The coming of the Cold War with the threat of a third world war collapsed the ambitions of the Liberation. Britain and the United States advocated German rearmament, and London paid court to Washington, not Paris. American aid came with a price tag – German rearmament and membership of a Western alliance. Revolts in Algeria in May 1945, riots in the Cameroons, disturbances in Tunisia, and uprisings in Madagascar and Indo-China, turned empire into a costly liability. The independence of Syria and Lebanon in 1945 terminated a Middle East presence. The general staff confessed impotence: 'the state of our military power ... ruled out a French mobilization and prevented France from taking part in ... a war without the help of a foreign power'.

Modernization, spurred by a booming global economy, was the chief energizer. More than an upgrading of economy and infrastructure, it crafted a new social compact between government and society, including a welfare state. France's modernization plan, in it's own words, was 'not a state of affairs but a state of mind'.[34] A huge migration from countryside to town propelled change. In the last pre-war census of 1936 the population was divided almost equally between town and country; by 1966 only 18 per cent of the population worked on the land and depopulation continued apace. The Republic was the first liberal democratic state to commit permanently to planning. With a tradition of state intervention France followed the developmental pattern set by post-1945 Japan. Economist André Philip expressed the conviction of decision-makers that 'only great industrial states count in the modern world'.[35] The *economie concertée*, emphasizing close cooperation between government and large private sector companies, supplied the growth model. The Commissariat general du plan (CGP) targeted transportation, telecommunications, public finances and nuclear power.

Decent housing, indoor loos and consumer durables transformed the quality of life. An American investigator researched two villages – Roussillon in the Vaucluse and Chanzeaux near Angers – and discovered a startling contrast. In 1951 the Roussillonais 'seemed haunted by despair ... *Pauvre France, on est foutu* [We're done for]'. Ten years on, a new confidence 'in the ability of themselves and their children to face the future' had taken hold.³⁶ A local farmer who in 1950 possessed only a mule and a twenty-year-old car now boasted a new car, a tractor and a television set. Roussillon's experience reflected a national metamorphosis. Even a remote backwater like the Breton commune of Plozevet changed dramatically from late nineteenth-century rustic to consumer take-off.³⁷ The availability of consumer goods improved rapidly. In 1950 razor blades were rationed and of poor quality. Returning to Paris after two years absence abroad a diplomat stocked up on them in New York only to find the same brand readily obtainable in Paris.

Modernization included the harnessing of nuclear power for peaceful and military purposes. The first five-year plan of 1952 for atomic energy marked a decisive stage in the development of France's Atomic Agency. 'It depends on us, today,' declared the Plan's preamble, 'whether France will still be a great modern country in ten years'. Pursuit of rank and independence drove the project. 'A nation without the A-bomb', warned a defence chief, 'is a second rank military power, without much influence on the international stage'.³⁸ The military programme advanced so well that in April 1958 a date could be set for the first atomic test.

Renewal of the state machine delivered a supercharged engine that outpaced Whitehall, a fossil of the mid-Victorian Northcote-Trevelyan reforms. Until 1945 France's higher civil service was a ramshackle, lethargic body, lacking up-to-date reference tools and quantitative data for informed decision-making. Government departments operated and recruited independently without common standards and central fiscal controls. The war delayed the consolidation of the general secretariat of government created in 1935. By the mid-1950s a revamped machine had the edge on European rivals. The ability and open-mindedness of French officials impressed an IMF colleague, particularly 'their willingness to expound and then controvert the official line'.³⁹ Of the central administration's four main branches – Conseil d'Etat, Cour des Comptes, Inspection des Finances and Foreign Service – the first three recruited the ablest candidates and ranked as the most prestigious. A 1946 statute for functionaries created a unified rationalized service. The ENA, a fast-track school of public administration, opened its doors in 1945. Its graduates – énarques – constituted a meritocracy that rejuvenated the civil service. Entering students represented the best products of the highly selective system of the Grandes Ecoles – Polytechnique, Normale and Sciences Po, with a strong bias towards mathematics, engineering, science, law or economics. Fierce competition governed ENA admission and order of graduation. Enarques supplied the cadres for modernization.

A fundamental makeover of social science research retooled a reformed bureaucracy. Alongside the Centre d'etudes sociologiques (CES) created in 1946, specialist agencies focused on demographic renewal and recruiting immigrant workers – Institut national de la statistique et des études économiques (INSEE), Institut national d'études démographiques (INED), and L'office national de l'immigration (ONI). The rapid growth of research centres – twenty in 1955, 300 by 1965 – confirmed the reinvention of French social science. The Centre national de la recherche scientifique (CNRS), the largest government-sponsored research organization, funded scientific and technology projects. Founded in October 1939, the war delayed the agency's opening. The state machine benefited from the restructuring and expansion of the general secretariat of government. France had lagged in the development of central coordinating machinery. The country gained a more integrated, informed and effective higher civil service, though not a more democratic one. Rather than diversifying recruitment across social strata, reform confirmed middle-class domination of the administrative elite.

The high public esteem enjoyed by government service undergirded the Fourth and Fifth Republics. In its golden years from 1945 to 74 state service recruited the best and brightest and exercised unprecedented influence. 'I chose to serve one master and only one: the State', declared chief mandarin François Bloch-Laine, architect of the modernization of public finances, 'a master whose servants enjoy an independence and a liberty that one finds in few other occupations'.[40] The cross-fertilization and continuity of political, administrative and business elites maximized talent and skills. Civil servants enjoyed a significant advantage over foreign counterparts: a two-way flow between central administration and top jobs in the public and private sectors, including politics. An official could stand for parliament without resigning. Defeated, he returned to the administration; elected, he kept pension rights and the option to return. The French did not live in a bubble. From the late 1950s *Le Club Jean Moulin* gathered functionaries, business leaders, technocrats and politicians in an informal think tank. By contrast, British mandarins had to wait until retirement to enter academe and business. They were also more isolated from other elites.

The reinvented administration had the flexibility to allow mavericks like Monnet to operate across ministerial boundaries. Canonized in the hagiography of European unity as 'Saint Europe', the author of France's first modernization plan, he was first and foremost an architect of a reborn France. The success of his 1946 plan secured the backing of foreign minister Robert Schuman for the first step in economic integration, the ECSC. The Anglo-American decision to rearm West Germany forced a fundamental reappraisal of national strategy. Monnet's advocacy of Franco-German entente and supranational control of iron and steel allowed France to contain and profit from Germany's recovery. The workaholic policy wonk bombarded ministers and officials with notes, telephone calls and visits, jumping hierarchies and shaking up routines – leaving his secretary with a perpetual twitch.

The French engine sported an extra cylinder – 'mission control', a gold standard policy–coordination mechanism. Created in 1948 to organize Marshall Plan credits within the OEEC, the general secretariat of the interministerial committee for European economic cooperation questions (SGCI) coordinated policy. Chaired by the prime minister, the committee harmonized inputs from two principal agencies: the Quai's *direction des affaires économiques et financières* (DAEF); and the *direction des relations économiques extérieures* (DREE) in the ministry of finance. Its remit covered all aspects of European policy – organizing agreed positions across the gamut of European institutions; preparing and overseeing Cabinet decision-making. From July 1956 the SGCI played a central role in the negotiation of the Treaty of Rome. Whitehall took the hint. 'When we did join the Community,' acknowledged the head of the FCO, 'we set up a similar committee in the Cabinet Office because we had been very impressed by the extent to which French policy was pulled together ... very characteristically French but very efficient'.[41]

The revamped civil service anchored a weak executive. Surprisingly, the atrophy of state authority did not produce grey eminences. Though mandarins shaped policy choices, they were not an unstoppable mafia. To talk of 'a Republic of officials' overlooks two considerations. First, despite high turnover, ministers occupied strong ground. Their private office – *cabinet* – enabled them to make the running when they chose to do so. Functioning independently from the civil service the cabinet gave ministers extra control levers in their departments as well as a channel for personal policy initiatives. Second, determined premiers and foreign ministers overrode colleagues and officials. The full cabinet only learnt of the Republic's most important post-war international initiative, the Schuman Plan of 1950 for a European Coal and Steel Community, hours before the public announcement.

In the Suez crisis of 1956 ministers marginalized senior advisers and took France to war with Egypt. Premier Mollet 'drove through France's membership of the common market in face of considerable bureaucratic resistance'.[42] Prime ministers who stayed in the saddle long enough were well positioned to take a lead. The premier's office oversaw top agencies: the secretariats of national defence and European economic cooperation; the general commissariats for the Plan and for atomic energy. Parliament had no significant say in foreign policy-making. In theory, legislators could exert control through debates, questions and foreign affairs committees; in practice, the executive blocked them with a mix of prevarication and faits accomplis. Foreign minister Schuman delayed until the end of May 1950 parliamentary discussion of the ECSC announced on 9 May. After 1958 de Gaulle trimmed back the powers of the foreign affairs and defence committees.

The post-war makeover of the foreign ministry honed French diplomacy. The skill of French diplomats awed British politicians: 'God, the French are clever diplomats', remarked a minister; 'we are very foolish in allowing them to dominate the Common Market'.[43] The success of French diplomacy was all the more remarkable because the service had to be rebuilt almost from scratch. In August 1944 staff returned to scenes of devastation: a wrecked tank in the courtyard, a fire-damaged wing, burnt archives and debris everywhere. A severe winter tested morale. 'Life is hard in Paris', recorded a diplomat, 'without heating and food. In my Quai office, my fingers and my head are numbed. The whole country is paralysed.'[44] The doyen of early twentieth-century French ambassadors, André François Poncet, observed that the British Foreign Office was wonderfully organized while the Quai d'Orsay was chaotic, and for this reason it was possible for a British diplomat of modest attainment to become a successful ambassador while to be a successful French ambassador required a superb intellect. He was wrong about the efficiency of the Foreign Office and right about the Quai's disorganization – in the early post-war years. A three-way split between Vichy staff, Free French representatives in London and Algiers, and Jean Chauvel's Paris group guaranteed bitter feuds. Getting the ministry up and running again seemed a Herculean task. Against the odds, the Quai clawed back reputation and influence.

A shortage of experienced staff impeded recovery. 'I am scared by the work of the Quai', noted France's ambassador in London. 'They are mostly inexperienced young people. They have forgotten that finance and economics bulk large in the concerns of a diplomat.'[45] Free French officials were too few to compensate for purged Vichy diplomats. Resistance groups demanded the Quai's democratization and the firing of Vichyites. Purges hit ambassadorial ranks hardest – ten fired out of fifteen. After the fall of France secretary general Alexis Leger, aka poet Saint-John Perse, went to the United States and did not return. Bidault refused to rehire pre-war heavyweights Charles Corbin and André François-Poncet, former ambassadors to London and Berlin, branding them museum pieces. With files scattered, destroyed or captured by Germany, institutional memory barely survived. On the plus side, the purges fast-tracked young highfliers – Maurice Couve de Murville and Hervé Alphand, appointed director general of political affairs and director of economic affairs respectively.

The mixed provenance of new hires – internal resistance, Free French, reinstated Vichy staff, and newly graduated énarques – bred rivalries and missteps. Mismanaged travel arrangements and a frosty welcome from France's local representatives bugged Albert Camus's lecture tour of South America in 1949.[46] An internal investigation into low morale identified three issues – mediocre quality of interwar recruitment, high living costs in Paris making overseas posts more attractive than central administration, and an over-severe and sometimes inequitable purge of Vichy staff.

As secretary general from late 1954, Massigli diagnosed an organizational crisis, compounded by low morale – 'not only is there no esprit de corps ... there is no longer any team spirit'.[47] He blamed overloaded staff – some had not taken holidays for two years – a bureaucratic structure ill-adapted to the shift of world power from Europe to the United States, and the decline of the secretary general's authority. Massigli tried to shore up his authority, insisting on being kept in the loop. American secretary of state Dean Acheson blamed the infighting on 'strong personalities', and the conspiratorial habits of wartime resistance.[48] This was only part of the story. Front-line issues – EDC, Cold War, German rearmament, European integration, Algerian war and Suez crisis – proved far more incendiary than personality conflicts and career rivalries. France's ambassador to the United Nations collapsed under the strain of Suez. From mid-1952, testified Massigli, '"Europeans" and "anti-Europeans" confronted each other'.[49]

The row in 1954–5 over the Tokyo ambassadorship of 'super-European' Alphand highlighted the idiosyncrasies of Fourth Republic decision-making. In early November 1954, after the National Assembly's rejection of the EDC, prime minister and foreign minister Pierre Mendes-France announced assignments – Massigli: secretary general; Alphand – ally of Monnet and partisan of the EDC: ambassador to Japan. Eight months later the ambassador designate remained in Paris and Antoine Pinay was premier. The media debated whether the envoy should go to Tokyo or be reassigned. Pro-Mendes newspapers accused Alphand of trying to persuade Pinay to pursue full European integration. The envoy's diary completes the story: 'Pinay abruptly decides to take me with him to San Francisco for the tenth anniversary conference of the United Nations. Massigli, furious, tries to resist the minister's will. He tells me: "You are making a fool of yourself" ... he fears the reactions of Hoppenot our delegate at the United Nations ... At Idlewild [New York airport] Hoppenot receives me with these words "I thought it was a joke".'[50] Within a year Alphand had pocketed Hoppenot's job.

Notwithstanding vendettas, the lack of a policy planning section, and charges of being ill-adapted to 'contemporary realities', the Quai recovered its pre-war reputation as a leading player.[51] By late 1951 British ambassador Harvey considered that the department had fully recovered from wartime woes and become 'a very efficient instrument'.[52] The Quai kept its legendary panache. In 1953 Soviet Counsellor Nicolai Korukine made a 'vigorous protest' to Guy de la Tournelle, political director, about a bomb that had been left in one of the Soviet Embassy's buildings in Paris. In La Tournelle's office he pulled a bomb from his pocket and placed it on the desk: 'La Tournelle said he hoped that it had been disconnected ... Korukine said it had been "partially disconnected". Tournelle then said [that] what seemed to him abnormal in the whole affair was that the Russians had taken over a month to bring the matter to the notice of the French ... as the Russians had waited so long the matter was clearly of no importance, and then ... threw the bomb into the waste paper basket.'[53]

The Quai mastered multilateralism – helped by the presence of the UN in Paris until 1951, together with UNESCO and NATO. In November 1949 the ministry hosted so many meetings that organizers no longer bothered with the names of different organizations but called out the numbers of states in the different groupings: 'Today the Nineteen, tomorrow the Twelve, followed by the Five, concluding with the Three.'[54] Short on economic and military muscle, France maximized geopolitical assets. Most important by far was the country's indispensability in America's Cold War alliance. The position and size of the hexagon ensured that it had to be accommodated, not bypassed. Geography supplied the resources to integrate Western Europe under French leadership. Effective integration required French participation. France exploited soft power in the form of cultural diplomacy much more effectively than Britain. Ambitious officials competed for management of the Quai's cultural affairs service – 'persons in comparable positions in London would sooner die than take any kind of cultural post', admitted a British ambassador.[55] A core group of pre-war officials ensured continuity of ideas, in particular the belief that morally and historically France was a great power.

Reforms raised the profile and autonomy of economic services by consolidating them in one division – Direction générale des Affaires économiques, financières et techniques. Recruitment from other branches of the civil service infused new blood. As well as presenting a progressive face – the only European foreign service with a woman (Suzanne Borel) in a senior post – the Quai ran a much leaner operation than its competitors – smaller embassy staffing levels gave early and mid-career officials more experience than their peers in other foreign services. Paris profited from stability of personnel in key embassies – postings tended to be considerably longer than American and British appointments. Top diplomats enjoyed a longer leash than British counterparts. Preparing for the Brussels Treaty of March 1948, secretary general Chauvel went to London without specific instructions from Bidault. After consulting foreign secretary Bevin, the French official, accompanied by a senior British adviser, travelled to the Hague and Brussels. While his companion spent much of the time telephoning London for approval of the numerous treaty drafts and redrafts, Chauvel returned to Paris without once contacting his minister or department. De Gaulle's oversight of external policy-making after 1958 ended this freedom.

The Quai raised the nation's overseas profile, but globalization and multilateralism undermined the ministry's ascendancy in national policy-making. Foreign policy, formerly a semi-autonomous enclave, became part of general government policy. Foreign ministers had to defend their corner against colleagues, military chiefs, parliamentary deputies and foreign affairs committees. The interdependence of internal and external issues spawned specialist agencies with overlapping interests in international affairs – three in 1913; fifteen in 1938; sixty-six in 1954. An external trade ministry opened its doors in 1951; a ministry of overseas cooperation from 1959. The first secretary general of the influential SGCI came from the ministry of finance, not the foreign ministry. Large fiefdoms escaped Quai oversight: German and Austrian occupation authorities, Algeria, Indo-China, Tunisia and Morocco. The leisured caste depicted in Abel Hermant's *La Carrière* (1894), devoted to foreign affairs in a romantic sense, had long gone. Technology and multilateralism undermined the ambassador's role and the allure of diplomacy. Olivier Wormser, director of financial and economic affairs, 'had no use for a modern Ambassadorship ... it meant endless waste of time drinking, traveling to and from airports and conveying messages to governments'.[56] In the 1960s the Quai, like the FO, absorbed staff from disbanded agencies – Moroccan and Tunisian affairs, and the ministry of overseas cooperation. Multilateralism cranked up the workload, multiplying missions, meetings and conferences – twenty international conferences in 1940 became 290 a year by the 1970s. Monsieur de Norpois – Marcel Proust's diplomat – would have struggled in the new environment.

Post-war secretary generals – five in twenty years (1944–64) – lacked the stature of interwar predecessors Philippe Berthelot and Alexis Leger. In 1950 Alexandre Parodi knew nothing of the Schuman Plan until the eve of its announcement. His efforts to defuse the polemic between supporters and critics of the EDC compromised his authority. Massigli barely lasted eighteen months, allegedly crushed between two factions: 'on the one hand the resentment of those whom I call the "super-Europeans" who never forgave me for having opposed the EDC and for having collaborated effectively with Pierre Mendes France for the creation of WEU ... on the other hand the clan of those who for various reasons identify France's interest with that of Israel'.[57] The expansion of the minister's office into a pivotal coordinating agency undermined the authority of the secretary general. Schuman's office, not the department, arranged Monnet's contacts with the minister. The presence of outsiders in lead positions confirmed the Quai as one voice among several. In 1949 officials from other branches of the mandarinate filled four of the Quai's top posts. Chef de protocole Jacques Dumaine deplored the appointment of outsider Parodi [*Conseil d'Etat*] to the secretary generalship: 'It is a sign of the present lack of distinction among the staff of our foreign office that it cannot provide men of sufficient stature to fill this position'.[58]

Whatever the virtuosity of individual players and the charisma of French diplomacy, ministerial vision came first. Among the Republic's longest-serving foreign ministers, only Schuman had the genius to reshape national strategy. He and Bidault belonged to the same Christian Democrat party, but Bidault lacked strong European convictions – expressing support only when the United States made integration a condition of economic reconstruction. By spring 1954, reported a British observer, a 'worn out, garrulous' Bidault 'scarcely making any sense at all ... said that he was casting himself to the wolves, into the waves, under the train', but the audience 'could not quite make out which wolves, waves, train'.[59]

Schuman had the ambition and will to redefine France's place in the world. Inspired by his Catholicism – the only foreign minister in modern times whose cause for beatification has been reviewed by the Catholic Church – he sought to act on philosopher Jacques Maritain's belief that a European federation would inaugurate a new Christendom. Fluent German and a German education made him a born ambassador for Franco–German reconciliation. His ascetic private life seemed as dull as Bidault's was bohemian. Monk-like, he shunned the glitz of the capital, returning as frequently as possible to his home near Metz in the Moselle. Piety and modesty exposed him to ridicule and suspicion. A British politician found him 'too much of the mystic ... very much under the influence of the priests'.[60] Cartoons showed him clasping a prostitute with the caption: '*Monsieur Schuman et sa poule*' – mischievous word play on the French word for a prostitute and the Franco–German coal and steel pool. Spurning razzmatazz, he preferred to catch a bus rather than use an official car with outriders. The challenge was to devise a European solution to a resurgent Germany. Given the tug of war within the Quai on German rearmament, Schuman turned to outsiders led by Monnet, head of France's modernization programme and main author of the ECSC. When Massigli, ambassador in London, telephoned the Quai for details of the Schuman Plan the secretary-general responded, 'The administration has been virtually excluded from this business'.[61]

What made France special? Benelux, Britain, Italy and West Germany all experienced high growth and modernization. Not by bread alone – wartime dreams persisted. Gabriel Peri's promise of a reborn nation piloting a resurrected Europe, 'a future full of song', lived on. The motif of effort and redemption ran through the best-sellers of the mid-1950s – still dominated by narratives of the Resistance. Commentators talked of a Sleeping Beauty with an influential role to play. 'The day would come', avowed historian Charles Moraze, 'when enlightened opinion will look towards France for the ideas with which to guide ... commercial, industrial and human progress'.[62] Moraze's best seller *Les Français et la République* (1956) concluded that the nation would 'blossom forth slowly and splendidly in the new era of world history'.[63] Sheer will power, argued Raymond Aron, would power recovery, 'a resolute nation will in the end find a way to survive' – confirming the 'virtues of our race'.[64] Mauriac commemorated the Liberation's tenth anniversary with an upbeat assessment, stressing a profound desire for political reform, concluding: 'Let us rejoice ... because this anniversary ... is celebrated in hope ... We suffered from sleeping sickness but not terminally ... now we are awake ... nothing is ever lost for France'.[65] The Algerian-born French runner Alain Mimoun symbolized recovery, dazzling the world by beating the Czech Emil Zatopek to win the 1956 Olympic marathon. In 1957 politician and journalist Jean-Jacques Servan-Schreiber expressed confidence that his memoir of national service in Algeria would 'persuade ... people ... that my country retains a faith and energy which will yet permit her to surmount her present sea of troubles'.[66]

Servan-Schreiber's testimony explains why a regime riding an economic roller-coaster unravelled in May 1958. Anglo-Saxon critics viewed the crisis as proof of a diseased polity and torn nation. In fact, the force of frustrated post-Liberation hopes helped topple the Fourth Republic. 'Faith and energy', born of resistance and liberation, lost patience with political uncertainty. Making a go of some things does not guarantee overall success. The 'rejection of the Republic', William Hitchcock argues, 'was made possible by its very success'.[67] The confidence that came with prosperity demanded a new political settlement. The constitutional compromise of 1946 proved unequal to the strains of almost continuous colonial war. Miscalculation, hesitation and drift destabilized the regime. Arguably, the legacy of wartime clandestinity shaped outcomes more than was realized. Beset by multiple risks and choices during the occupation, resisters adopted a wait and see approach. Bidault's Christian Democrat colleague, Francisque Gay, chided him that the temporization of resistance life had become a settled principle of government, producing a 'fear of effectiveness which is largely responsible for the *immobilisme* that has engulfed our political life for nearly ten years'.[68] Nevertheless, the Republic successfully constructed an economic platform for the next decade. The launch in 1955 of the Citroen DS with its aerodynamic futuristic body and innovative technology, and the Caravelle, France's first commercial medium range jet airliner – internationally one of the most successful of the decade – showcased a rebooted economy. De Gaulle's Fifth Republic reaped the harvest.

5

De Gaulle Redux

Winston Churchill stays sexy – Kiplingesque imperialist, Second World War hero and Cold War peace-maker. Why, then, does the dinosaur-like General Charles de Gaulle still attract interest? Unlike Russian President Valdimir Putin, he wasn't a scuba-diving, Siberian bear-hunting, bare-chested equestrian. The most celebrated of de Gaulle's ministers, author André Malraux, remarked that only three people in France would outlive the twentieth century: de Gaulle, Picasso and Chanel. In 2009 France's *baccalaureat* syllabus listed a volume of the general's memoirs – assigned for literature, not history. No other twentieth-century head of state continues to be discussed for what he wrote rather than what he did. The devil's own luck in escaping assassination enhanced his fame – the towering, uniformed, képi-wearing figure marching amid sniper fire into Notre-Dame cathedral for a solemn *Te Deum* in August 1944. Ambushed at Petit-Clamart in suburban Paris in August 1962 he cheated death by centimetres. Part of the fascination is that the general said 'Non', and got away with it – Adolf Hitler 1940, British premier Harold Macmillan 1963, and Parisian students 1968. Saving his country three times – 1940, 1944 and 1958 – gives the French leader a stronger claim to renown than Churchill. Without his presence in 1944 the Liberation might have turned nasty. Over sixty years on, de Gaulle's Fifth Republic stands firm.

Gaullism's mainsprings predated 1940: passion for the greatness of France, confidence that its interests overrode all others, a quasi-mystical self-selection as a saviour on the model of Joan of Arc and Clémenceau, allied to a belief that rulers, to be effective, had to be aloof. The war added the conviction that a leader should have a direct relationship with the people.

Leadership of the Free French movement and the Provisional Government of 1944 formed the general's outlook on the Western alliance and European unity. Labelling him a political dinosaur misses an essential truth – his wide domestic and international support. Even British Labour Party members had 'a sneaking admiration … They would have liked to see Britain also putting national interests first'.[1] The pursuit of greatness was profoundly realistic, designed to bind together a riven nation, emphasizing 'what Frenchmen had in common by bringing them into confrontation with the "foreigner"'.[2]

In June 1940 de Gaulle's claim to represent the French state and the continuation of the war sounded totally bizarre. An obscure junior general with a stage army defied France's ruler Marshal Philippe Pétain, senior statesman, hero of Verdun, endorsed by most of France's political and military elite. A Gaullist aide observed: 'if Hitler was looking through the keyhole at ... this temporary general claiming: we are France, he would surely think that we were ready for the padded cell'.³ Against all the odds a refugee without resources operated successfully in an alien culture, in a language that he spoke imperfectly, with Allied leaders eager to oust him. 'Extreme weakness', remarked his legal adviser René Cassin, 'imposes extreme intransigence'.⁴

What was de Gaulle like? A disconcerting habit of referring to himself in the third person as 'de Gaulle' discouraged intimacy. A bullying streak turned highly strung foreign minister Bidault into a terrified rabbit. Angry with his information minister the general 'grabbed him by the shoulders and literally threw him out' – at 2 in the morning.⁵ A loner from childhood he thought highly of himself – writing at fifteen a school essay about a nation saved from military humiliation by 'General de Gaulle'. He liked to surprise others but took exception when US President John F. Kennedy telephoned him unexpectedly. The White House was informed that in future the general required at least an hour's notice. Resistance to wearing spectacles in public brought comic relief. 'Good day, vicar', he said, shaking hands in a crowd. 'But, General, I'm one of the gorillas [bodyguards].' 'Then Good Day, Mr Gorilla!'.⁶ Myopia forced him to memorize speeches. On a state visit to Britain in 1960 his classical political

Figure 5.1 General de Gaulle walking down the Champs Élysées, Georges Bidault a step behind on left, 25 August 1944.

oratory – every phrase carefully picked and polished – held a capacity audience from both houses of parliament spellbound.

An unsmiling public face concealed a prankster with a wry sense of humour. On Monnet: 'he makes a very good cognac. Alas, that doesn't satisfy him!' – a dig at the family cognac business. In January 1963 elder statesman Paul Reynaud, the general's patron in the 1930s, condemned the veto of Britain's EEC application. Shortly after, a letter arrived, addressed to Reynaud in the general's handwriting, but the envelope was empty. On the back it said: 'If away, forward to Agincourt or Waterloo.'[7] In wartime London he starred in a Free French group which mimicked Vichy leaders. In the run-up to the 1965 presidential election advisers urged him to personalize his TV appearances –'you really want me to stick myself in front of the screen and say: my name is Charles de Gaulle and I am seventy-five years old! I'd be a laughing stock!'[8] The general did not party. At the end of a cheerless reception a guest observed, 'Things dreaded were not usually as bad as one expected but this had been even worse'. He ran a tight ship. On a private cruise to the Pacific in 1956, a young journalist invited an Australian girl to his cabin. Within minutes the General's aide de camp knocked loudly on the door, 'Jean, you are part of the general's suite – no girls ever please'.[9]

The wilderness years from 1946 to 58 confirmed de Gaulle's belief that the hexagon needed a strong executive under a new constitution. Rejecting superpower hegemony, supranationality and federalism, he insisted on the primacy of the nation state, envisioning French leadership of a confederal Western Europe. Consequently, he opposed the ECSC, EDC and EEC. For six years from the end of the Algerian war in July 1962 to the barricades of May 1968 de Gaulle was master of the house. Making France top nation in Western Europe required vision and a firm grasp of economic issues. His genie and indispensability as the one person capable of uniting army and nation gave him a strong hand. No other contemporary European leader had such allure. In his valedictory dispatch Britain's Paris ambassador Sir Pierson Dixon paid tribute: 'During 1964 de Gaulle dominated the political scene, like Pharaoh on a frieze of the Temple of Luxor, enjoying a secure base of national prosperity and personal popularity.'[10]

De Gaulle and grandeur are almost synonymous. 'France', he declared in 1961, 'must fulfill her mission as a world power. We are everywhere in the world. There is no corner of the earth, where, at a given time, men do not look to us and ask what France says. It is a great responsibility to be France, the humanizing power par excellence'.[11] In *The Choice for Europe* (1998) Andrew Moravcsik argued that economics more than grandeur drove the general's statecraft. But the argument was a bit of a red herring. Gaullist statecraft blended grain and grandeur – the visionary was also a realist. Disentangling the strands defies definitive analysis. In 1958 the general confounded critics by abandoning opposition to the EEC. Arguably, without de Gaulle's support for the Community, deeply protectionist French business interests would have resisted the liberalization measures of the Treaty of Rome. A beefed-up executive imposed the economic and fiscal measures required for Community membership.

The honeymoon years with Brussels between 1958 and 1962 helped validate a claim to leadership. Similarly, following the Algerian war de Gaulle built up friendly relations with the newly independent state. Pursuing reconciliation with Germany in 1958 after three German wars represented a hard-headed bid for a strong continental ally. The creation of a global Francophonie community of newly decolonized francophone states brilliantly repackaged retreat from empire. Flexibility in day-to-day diplomacy belied dogmatic pronouncements. Approaches to the Community, for example, exposed a significant gap between what de Gaulle said and what his representatives did in Brussels. 'French policy in practice' accepted 'a level of supranationality that had been verbally rejected by the General'.[12] Officials made the best deals they could to maximize national interests.

Modernization and economic expansion fired primacy. Population jumped 12.3 per cent from 44.8 million in 1958 to 50.3 in 1969. Between 1949 and 1959 GNP grew at 4.5 per cent – Britain averaged only 2.4 per cent in the same period. An annual 5.8 per cent economic growth rate after 1960 made the economy one of the fastest growing in the EEC. The resistance myth cemented domestic cohesion. The apotheosis of de Gaulle's takeover of the myth came in 1964 with the transfer of the remains of hero Jean Moulin to the Pantheon. Parachuted into occupied France Moulin unified resistance groups under de Gaulle's authority until captured and killed by the Gestapo. At the ceremony de Gaulle positioned himself on the steps of the Pantheon by the casket 'so that the parade could "salute in one single motion both the mortal remains of Jean Moulin and the President of the Republic."'[13]

'What an immense advantage de Gaulle has over me', bemoaned Macmillan in May 1961. 'No parliament and a press that carries little influence'.[14] The Fifth Republic's constitution of October 1958 provided for the direct election of the head of state, and gave the executive extensive powers over the National Assembly – control of agendas, and ways of ensuring the adoption of legislation without discussion. The government determined the policy of the nation; in practice foreign and defence issues constituted a reserved presidential domain. The Élysée palace interpreted this liberally – annexing the hot button issue of the moment. The general wrote his own speeches and decided what he said to the press. He retreated from his micromanagement of 1944–6, allowing foreign minister Couve a longer leash than Bidault. Unlike his successors, he did not indulge in a parallel Élysée diplomacy.

'All goes well for France', boasted de Gaulle in April 1963, claiming that only the United States, the Soviet Union and France counted.[15] The general made a special claim for France's moral leadership in the developing world. France stood for racial equality and the rights of man and nations. 'France's vocation', he claimed, was 'more disinterested and more universal than any other country's'. Other states tried to impose their interests, but France, 'the light of the world', worked 'for the interest of all'. De Gaulle, declared novelist François Mauriac, reminded France of her greatness – 'to serve France, "the irreplaceable nation", is to serve the world'.[16]

The hiring of ministers based on technical competence rather than political clout made for stability. Ministers did not have to be members of the legislature. Embedded in their specialties they shied away from larger concerns. Louis Joxe, justice minister in 1968, described himself and colleagues as 'simply executants. They did their jobs, but ... had no possibility of independent thought on major issues'.[17] One third came from the senior civil service, compared to 12 per cent under the Fourth Republic. Freedom from parliamentary and constituency cares meant more time for their departments.

When giving instructions to ministers the general avoided smiling for fear of suggesting a collegiality between them. The obsequiousness of the prime minister and foreign minister amazed American secretary of state Dean Rusk: 'I watched ... as the prime minister walked up to de Gaulle, gave a little schoolboy bow, clicked his heels and presented himself much like a cadet at St. Cyr. The foreign minister did the same'.[18] Bootlicking had limits. Jean-Bedel Bokassa, president of the Central African Republic, went too far, clicking his heels, and saying 'Good Day, Father'. A vexed de Gaulle told him not to say father. Bokassa replied, 'Yes, papa'.

An authoritarian regime, but not autocratic. Prime minister Georges Pompidou had a mind of his own. Well-connected in avant-garde society and a collector of abstract painting, his banking background and lack of wartime resistance credentials distanced him from career politicians. Threatening to resign, Pompidou successfully opposed the execution of General Edmond Jouhaud of the OAS, the ultra right terrorist organization fighting to keep Algeria French. Reluctantly, de Gaulle exercised clemency. The premier's firm handling of the May '68 troubles enhanced his authority and popularity while the president's approval ratings slumped.

Decision-making operated on three levels: weekly cabinets chaired jointly by the president and prime minister; ad hoc committees of ministers and officials (*conseils restreints*) convened by the Élysée secretary general or the prime minister's office; standing interministerial committees with permanent secretariats. The weekly cabinet was a starchy affair in which a frown from the general daunted all but the bravest. Admonished for expressing opinions on matters outside his departmental remit, finance minister Antoine Pinay protested that there was nowhere else he could air them. Pre-cabinet one-on-one discussions usually settled agenda items in advance of meetings. 'It was always extremely difficult to penetrate General de Gaulle's mind', confided agriculture minister Edgar Faure; 'the general would summon him and ask for his views on a problem ... but if he then asked for the general's views on another question ... the general would give no clear answer'.[19]

Cabinets followed a set ritual. The agenda invariably listed 'Communication of the foreign minister on the international situation'. A barely audible, monotone summary of current issues by Couve would be immediately followed by the next item of business. No discussion took place. Ministers with items on the agenda spoke to them, replying briefly to comments, then prime minister and president wound up. At a cabinet two days after de Gaulle's 14 January 1963 press conference vetoing British membership, Couve's summary of international events ignored the veto. As ministers prepared to leave de Gaulle spoke – almost as an afterthought, 'It's a strange age, gentlemen, when one cannot say without provoking an uproar that England is an island,[20] and America is not Europe'. For political hot potatoes like British entry into the EEC de Gaulle went round the table soliciting opinions, but avoiding general discussion. However, the cabinet was not consulted about the decision to withdraw from NATO's military command, and the president kept his own counsel on most matters.

American ambassador Chips Bohlen quizzed at least ten ministers about the veto on UK entry; 'I received widely different interpretations and concluded that de Gaulle kept them in ignorance of what he was doing'.[21] In January 1962 Premier Michel Debré protested that the Élysée summoned ministers and sent instructions to his own staff without his knowledge: 'I reproach you', he told de Gaulle, 'for summoning a minister to see you behind my back about a problem which I have not discussed with you.'²² After imposing ministerial solidarity, the general switched position without notice. The practice came to a head in 1962 when de Gaulle at his 15 May press conference poured scorn on supranationalism: 'The only Europe possible is that of states.' Six Christian Democrat ministers (MRP) resigned in protest – invoking a presidential commitment that the cabinet would have an opportunity to debate the issue. By contrast, the relative informality of ad hoc committees and one-on-one consultation allowed for give and take. At a meeting in October 1967 about Britain's second membership bid, de Gaulle suggested making an offer to review the position in 1970. He retreated when three senior ministers advised that the offer might be perceived as an advance commitment to enlargement.

Presidential oversight of defence and foreign affairs went unchallenged. The power to call referendums and the introduction of direct presidential election by universal suffrage from October 1962 buttressed the Élysée. Strong referendum majorities strengthened the presidency: new constitution 79.2 per cent; Algerian self-determination 75.2 per cent; direct election of the president 61.7 per cent. Even the April 1969 referendum which triggered resignation gave the general 46.8 per cent of the vote. The stately presidential tours of the Third and Fourth Republics became intensive regional crowd baths. The general was the last head of state to draw large crowds.

How did the general's day go? A list of appointments and a selection of foreign ministry telegrams and press summaries awaited him on entering his office shortly before 10am. Compacting appointments into two afternoons in the week maximized reflection time. The schedule included twice-weekly consultations with the prime minister, weekly with the foreign minister. About 6pm the general conferred in turn with top advisers – Élysée secretary general, the chief of his private office, secretary general for African and Madagascan affairs, and the head of military staff. Shortly before the prime time 8pm TV news – France's 'High Mass' – de Gaulle picked up his black leather briefcase, rang for the duty ADC, and shook hands, telling him to make sure all the lights were switched off. The president guarded his privacy and rest. 'Don't disturb the president except in the event of a world war' ran one version of night duty instructions. Lavish entertainment was not on the menu. Minimalism reigned. At presidential receptions guests arrived around 9.30–10pm and left at 11.30. Weekends and holidays were spent at the family house of La Boisserie, Colombey-les-Deux-Eglises, about 160 miles east of Paris in the Haute Marne – walking, solitaire and reading Westerns formed the main relaxations.

De Gaulle made his own decisions. Occasionally, he asked, 'So, what are they saying?' Sometimes to form an opinion he provoked a response by taking an extreme position on a particular issue. Even the secretary general hesitated to challenge a decision once made. Insistence on written notes gave the president more thinking time and greater control. The procedure, however, allowed top advisers to screen out inputs and limit informal exchanges. As well as determining the broad lines of policy the president kept an eye on detail. Newly appointed ambassadors received precise instructions which Couve confirmed in a follow-up interview.

The president cultivated an image of Olympian detachment while keeping an ear close to the ground. 'Keep me informed', he instructed Élysée secretary general Bernard Tricot. Polls, fan mail, media comment, police reports and wiretaps could not replace live contacts, however. Accordingly, afternoon audiences targeted a wide cross section of elites. Gruelling four- to six-day roadshows replaced the presidential tours of the past, enabling him to keep a finger on the popular pulse.

With a far smaller staff than leading foreign embassies in the capital, the Élysée Palace lacked the resources to function as a second government. A handful of foreign policy advisers depended on the Quai for information and guidance. At the Hotel Matignon the prime minister and secretary general of the government kept a firm grip on the administrative backbone – the interministerial committees. About seventy officials ran the presidential secretariat, private office and secretariat for African and Madagascan affairs. Bonded by wartime comradeship in the general's Free French movement they were loyal to a fault. Pierre Lefranc, one of the nabobs of Gaullism, as well as adopting de Gaulle's views on most subjects actually dressed and talked like him. The secretary general convened committees, and liaised with ministers and the government secretary general. He was not a super cabinet secretary on the lines of the legendary Sir Humphrey (Nigel Hawthorne) of the BBC's satirical sitcom *Yes, Prime Minister*. De Gaulle played master puppeteer: hiring, firing and reassigning collaborators. Secretary generals advised, but did not control policy.

Ministers clung to fig leaves of independence. When secretary general Tricot responded optimistically to a journalist's question about prospects for a renewal of UK entry negotiations, an angry Couve telephoned: 'Who is foreign minister, you or me?' Premier Georges Pompidou insisted, 'I'm the first adviser of the general, the secretary general should not have ideas'. Tricot demurred, pointing out that while the secretary general should not have his own policy he had to have ideas and be able to discuss them with the president.[23]

State media turbocharged the Citroën. Skilful tuning of radio and television constructed a supportive public. 'I cannot accept', proclaimed the general in 1964, 'that French radio and television be put at the disposal of a critic or an author taking de Gaulle as his subject without my consent'.[24] The head of television news expressed it more succinctly: 'a journalist should be French first, objective second'.[25] RTF (*Radiodiffusion-Television-Française*) and its successor from 1964 ORTF (*Office de radiodiffusion-television française*) had a virtual broadcasting monopoly. Government influence on the media was an established feature of the Third and Fourth Republics.

As minister of information in 1947, socialist François Mitterand called for broadcasting to undertake a 'national policy of defending the interests of France' – as determined by the government.[26] During the strike wave of 1947 the government instructed RTF to label workers as demonstrators, not strikers, and to target Communist union leaders. A 'black notebook' in the RTF newsroom 'listed off-limit subjects' and prescribed appropriate language for the handling of politically sensitive topics.[27] In 1956 Socialist premier Mollet recommended the employment of party faithful to vet radio and TV news bulletins. From the founding in 1947 of the Gaullist party RPF (*Rassemblement du people français*) the Fourth Republic kept de Gaulle off the air, refusing to relay his speeches.

The general's grip on the media, reinforced by radio chats and televised press conferences, gave him the advantage over British leaders. News channels suppressed anti-Gaullist criticism. Electoral campaigns had to be covered, but choice of camera angles disadvantaged opposition candidates – television pictures of the Socialist mayor of Marseilles, Gaston Defferre, showed him only from behind. During the president's visit to the United States in April 1960 a radio news bulletin announced: 'In the absence of General de Gaulle there is no political news in France today.'[28] News bulletins were a mishmash of official ceremonies, interviews with ministers, tendentious political reporting, dog shows and beauty contests.

Information minister Alain Peyrefitte oversaw radio and television. His predecessor advised him to telephone every day 'about 5pm to decide the main lines of the evening news ... Don't leave your office before ... 8.30pm. After the television news, your colleagues will call to blame you for what has displeased them'.[29] Minister and state broadcasting co-habited. Civil servants occupied the upper floor and the minister's desk had a row of buttons to summon senior RTF management. Peyrefitte described state radio and television as 'the government in every Frenchman's dining-room'.[30] Prime minister Pompidou reminded him that he served two masters: 'You are the spokesman of the government, that means both of the general and of me. When the Cabinet is over he'll give you his instructions ... You will see me every morning and I'll give you mine. You'll be between a rock and a hard place'.[31] Peyrefitte initiated off the record press briefings – conferring privately with de Gaulle before the briefing. As information minister and government spokesperson he was authorized to take notes of cabinet discussions.

Media management fell far short of totalitarian ruthlessness. Peyrefitte waited until 1963 before setting up a coordinating agency for government information services – SLII (*Service de liaison interministeriel pour l'information*). It organized daily meetings with representatives from the main ministries but encountered resistance from some officials and agencies.[32]

Peyrefitte's biographer claimed that the minister would have preferred a more liberal Anglo-Saxon model – citing the transformation in 1964 of the state-owned RTF into a seemingly more independent ORTF.[33] But ORTF's independence was more nominal than real. Media baron Christian Chavanon's career illustrates the tightness of the state–media embrace: secretary general for information 1958; director general RTF 1958–60; president of state news agency, Havas, 1960–73. Premier Debré recommended him to de Gaulle as a safe pair of hands for the Havas presidency: 'he has been very loyal during this time ... I consider that [he] will be loyal to you.'[34]

Gaullist censorship met its match in the grande dame of British politics, octogenarian Violet Bonham Carter, friend of Winston Churchill and daughter of Liberal prime minister Herbert Asquith. In December 1967 ORTF invited her to join a panel of French academics for a television discussion about the making of the Entente Cordiale. A few weeks earlier the general's second veto registered a new low in the Franco-British diplomatic war. Bonham Carter pleaded for the renewal of the Entente, reminding viewers of Churchill's offer of union in 1940 and attacking de Gaulle's narrow and 'dying' nationalism. The producer tried to take her off the air – telephoning the presenter 'on a little black telephone under the table'. Cocking a snook at the general brought her a large fan mail – mostly French. Britain's ambassador congratulated her: 'you made a tremendous impression ... it is of course quite exceptional for the French public to hear frank speaking of this kind'.[35]

The Quai frequently cracked the whip: preventing ORTF from commemorating the tenth anniversary of the Suez affair and the Soviet Union's suppression of the Hungarian rising; blocking a documentary on President Nasser of Egypt for fear of compromising Franco–Arab relations; banning an interview with Soviet Communist Party Secretary Nikita Khrushchev about the Battle of Stalingrad because it clashed with the signing of the Franco–German treaty of January 1963. The government blacklisted films and documentaries perceived as endangering policies and official myths, chiefly Gillo Pontecorvo's *Battle of Algiers* (1966) and Marcel Ophuls's television documentary *Le Chagrin et la Pitie* (1969). The first response of state media to the May '68 student protest was to ignore it. A BBC Panorama programme of 10 May about the troubles was suppressed. Government propaganda achieved a major triumph in priming opinion for the recognition of the People's Republic of China in January 1964.

Television was the great success story. 'The press is against me,' the general declared, 'television is mine'.[36] The press lost its centrality in political life, in part because the presidential regime diluted traditional links between newspapers and deputies. Readership did not keep pace with a 12 per cent population rise in the decade 1959–69, falling well below British and American levels. Between 1946 and 1952 the number of daily newspapers dropped sharply from 203 to 131 and circulation fell from 15 million to 9.5. Television's rapid expansion in the 1960s – from 13 per cent of homes in 1960 to 70 per cent in 1970 – gave the president an unprecedented opportunity. Dubbed the 'first viewer of France', the general introduced two innovations: televised presidential press conferences (eighteen in ten years); and regular broadcast talks. In a pre-teleprompter age his first appearances had a comic appeal. The general read on camera from a script as in a radio address, caricaturing himself in the process – head, hands and arms thrashing about as in a seizure. The president quickly learnt how to make the most effective use of the new medium: memorizing lines, applying make-up and appropriate body language – coached in all probability by a Comédie-Française actor. Though politicians had for many years briefed the press and made broadcasts, de Gaulle transformed press conferences into cleverly choreographed performances, ostensibly retaining a question/answer format while actually constituting de Gaulle's conference *to* the press. Questions had to be submitted in advance, with answers sometimes running to twenty-five minutes. Wonderfully crafted political theatre attracted a world-wide audience of millions. A thousand guests assembled in the banqueting hall of the Élysée Palace; at 3pm precisely a drawn red curtain revealed the general at a desk on a raised platform, flanked on one side at a lower level by the whole cabinet seated according to seniority, on the other by presidential officials. Script and setting radiated authority, assurance and hierarchy. All State channels repeated the event.

Ex cathedra-style pronouncements on the international scene – two-thirds of the conferences concerned foreign policy – gave de Gaulle the persona of a prime mover in world politics. Momentarily, France monopolized global attention. Conferences launched new policy initiatives – new not only to the public but to ministers, notably the veto on British membership of the Community. The tone of presidential discourse expressed a sense of finality and closure of public debate. Over a decade the general delivered fifty-two radio talks – more than most heads of state. At a time of rapid cultural change with demotic language in vogue the general's classical oratorical style evoked continuity and greatness. 'Nobody has spoken like that in France since Louis XIV', quipped an anti-Gaullist. Success flowed from an artful blend of body language – expressive movement of arms and hands – and personal appeals: 'I need, Yes I need! to know what is in your hearts and minds', and repetition of emotive core words: France, country, state, world, people, nation, progress, peace.[37] Statements could be sardonic and entertaining. Alluding to Britain's second bid of November 1967 the president 'denied that he had ever wanted to see Britain "stripped naked". "For a beautiful creature", he said, "nakedness is natural enough. For those around her, it is satisfying enough. But I have never said that of England"'.[38]

More influential than press conferences and state media management was the marketing of French culture. The 1960s marked the Indian summer of France's cultural ascendancy. Cleaning the façades of the capital's sooty public buildings in the early 1960s attracted global interest and enhanced the legendary 'city of light'. Avant-garde artists and intellectuals confirmed creative leadership – philosopher Louis Althusser, semiotician Roland Barthes, cultural theorist Jean Baudrillard, philosopher Jacques Derrida, sociologist Michel Foucault, and fledgling movements like Oulipo. New wave film-makers Jean Luc Godard, François Truffaut and disciples, together with *nouveau roman* authors Marguerite Duras, Alain Robbe-Grillet and others, shaped global fashions.

Selling France soaked up half of the foreign ministry's budget. The most important innovation was the grouping together of newly independent French-speaking countries in la Francophonie (OIF). Expanded cultural and technical programmes established fifty-nine institutes, 150 cultural centres, nearly 180 French schools and over 800 *Alliance française* committees in eighty-four countries. Grand gestures like the loaning for the first time of the Louvre's Mona Lisa to the United States in 1963 made world news. Patronage of the arts grew by leaps and bounds, starting with de Gaulle's appointment of writer and resistance leader André Malraux as France's first minister for cultural affairs (1959–69). Malraux proposed to make France a 'cultural third force' between the Soviet and American giants. But the attempted democratization of culture through the creation of *maisons de la culture* in France ran out of money, leaving only seven constructed in ten years.

Campaigning for the leadership of the EEC the French artfully presented themselves as quintessential Europeans, embodying the best of European values. The French-led European Community of the 1960s and 1970s supplied a last redoubt for the defence of the language. French was the first language at the Community's Brussels headquarters. Declining numbers of French speakers outside francophone countries threatened to marginalize the language. The vulnerability of the language strengthened France's resistance to enlargement. Britain's ambassador to the Community felt that it was 'becoming increasingly a major reason for our exclusion … seldom referred to in public; but it loomed and swelled in the background'.[39]

Defending the language had comic effects. The film *Death on the Nile* (1978), based on Agatha Christie's novel, had subtitles for francophone countries. At one point Peter

Ustinov [playing Hercule Poirot] broke into French, quoting Molière, upon which David Niven, playing an English colonel, protested, 'My God, can't you speak some civilized language?' The subtitle read: 'Would you please translate?'

Americanization, globalization and the clash of Cold War empires compromised the notion of a unique and universal cultural mission. Flying home from a South American lecture tour in 1949, Camus glimpsed a shrinking world; 'the faster the airplane flies, the less important are France, Spain, and Italy. They were nations, now they are provinces ... the future is not ours.'[40] Loaning the Mona Lisa to America in 1963 brought praise from President John F. Kennedy for 'the leading artistic power in the world'.[41] In reality, New York had dethroned Paris as world art capital. American-led globalization and the relentless advance of the English language presented policy-makers with an insoluble problem – how to sustain a credible cultural presence in a superpower-dominated show? The tight budgets of the 1950s prioritized language over culture. But global relevance was no longer a given – the *Alliance française* now had to make a case for the beauty and utility of French as a living universal language.

The retreat of the language and culture brought whistling in the dark. 'If English is becoming more and more the language of business,' asserted international relations specialist Jacques Vernant, 'French remains the language of culture'.[42] Some officials gave up the fight – considering it chic to speak English. In 1988 Maurice Allais won France's first Nobel Prize in economics. The long-delayed recognition reflected the laureate's reluctance to use English until quite late in his career. An encounter between French mountaineers and Nepalese villagers in 1950 illustrates what the French were up against. In June 1950, after conquering the Himalayan peak Annapurna, the mountaineers met local villagers: 'American?' 'No, French'. Villagers nodded approval: 'American!' 'No, there are Americans, and there are Englishmen, but we are French'. 'Oh Yes! But you're Americans all the same!'[43]

Seismic shocks demolished the Gaullist model. The convulsions of the 1960s brought a crisis of legitimacy for the language, the regime and its version of high culture. The British musical skit *Oh What A Lovely War* (1963) satirized France's self-representation, 'La belle France, the seat of reason, and the centre of world civilization, culture and l'amour'. The student explosion of Paris May 1968 threatened to overturn the Republic. The counter-culture with its emphasis on individualism, authenticity and diversity mocked the 'one size fits all' export model of high culture. As early as 1946 the elitist absurdity of a South American lecture tour shocked the writer Jean Guehenno – speaking only to the 'happy few'.[44] For *soixante-huitards* the state's version of high culture was as dead as a dodo. The vogue for self-realization, multiple cultural sites and regional identities torpedoed the cultural monolith.

Culture wars erupted. Rejecting the universality of moral and political values, postmodernists contested the state's cultural construct. The changing face of the nation as a result of Muslim immigration, together with the revival of regional identities and local languages such as Breton, fuelled polemic about French identity. Defining the cultural patrimony provoked passionate debate. Historian Pierre Nora's ground-breaking *Les Lieux de memoire (1984-1992)* mirrored the controversy. A highly centralized and homogenized state culture which had always targeted French-speaking global elites struggled to come to terms with a pluralist multicultural world.

The Quai housed the main arsenal of soft power. The pick of its diplomats more than matched Britain's brightest. Of the French forwards the fastest was Olivier Wormser, director of financial and economic affairs. After a talk with Wormser, Treasury mandarin Frank Lee observed: 'I have rarely seen a more consummate display of playing all the bowling with a dead bat.'[45] Super-smart, subtle and tenacious, scion of a wealthy banking dynasty, Wormser joined de Gaulle in 1940. In wartime London he had an affair with Iris Murdoch. A pipe smoker with a soft spot for his Cairn terrier, he spoke excellent English, bought his suits in Savile Row and had family in London. Awed British diplomats treated the economic policy czar as a grey eminence, and his colleagues delighted in offering conflicting advice on how best to handle him. Though the Paris embassy labelled him an Anglophobe, others defended him, praising his chairing of international meetings. His donation to the National Gallery of an Edouard Vuillard painting of himself and his sister as children suggested some affection for Britain.

Figure 5.2 Foreign Minister Michel Debré with his predecessor Maurice Couve de Murville, 2 June 1968. Credit: Interfoto / Alamy Stock Photo.

Lengthy stints for senior diplomats in major capitals maximized experience and skills. London had three ambassadors in twenty-eight years: René Massigli (1944–55); Jean Chauvel (1955–62); Geoffroy de Courcel (1962–72). Over the same period six British ambassadors in Paris averaged a tad over four years each. No Whitehall permanent secretaries got close to Alphand's seven-year term as Quai secretary-general (1965–72). Wormser's twelve-year innings as director of economic and financial affairs (1954–66), followed by the nine-year stint of successor Jean-Pierre Brunet (1966–75), gave outstanding continuity. The long service of two top officials contributed decisively to France's ascendancy in the European Community: Jean-Marc Boegner, permanent representative in Brussels (1961–72); Emile Noël, secretary general of the European Commission (1958–87). By contrast, the UK went through foreign secretaries like football managers: six in all during Couve de Marville's reign at the Quai – three of them in fifteen months (1964–5) – a higher ministerial turnover than in the maligned Fourth Republic. That said, long postings could bring boredom and burnout. Wormser confessed to being bored stiff with his work and having no deep convictions on Europe and international politics, comparing himself to a barrister making the best case for a client.[46]

Couve, the general's ace, was the longest serving French foreign minister since the eighteenth-century ancien régime. His loyalty and skill upheld French influence worldwide. The minister claimed 'a kind of spontaneous and instinctive agreement' with the president.[47] Only one important issue caused dissension – how best to withdraw from NATO. An *inspecteur des finances*, the cream of the *grands corps*, Couve played his master's voice to perfection. Cold in manner, calm and poker-faced, he served Vichy as director of external finances and negotiated the financial clauses of the Franco-German armistice in 1940. Switching allegiance to de Gaulle in 1943 fast tracked him – Quai political director 1945, then ambassadorships to Egypt, the United States and West Germany. 'How little like a Frenchman Couve is,' mused a Canadian diplomat, 'with his reserved, cool manner and his English clothes, but perhaps the difference is only skin deep or perhaps it is because he is a Protestant'.[48]

Savile Row tailoring and British-like phlegm did not make an Anglophile. Couve's experience as a young man tutoring the sons of diplomat and writer Harold Nicolson may have influenced his attitude towards Britain. Dining with ambassador Massigli, Nicolson recalled how in 1928 twenty-one-year old Couve, 'a shy youth, brittle as a biscuit, dressed in midsummer tweeds ... came to Long Barn expecting the grandeur of Chatsworth and the intellectual stimulus of Madame Geoffrin's salon, to find that he had to act as tutor to two schoolboys in a cottage. It was a misunderstanding'. 'Oh, that explains', replied Massigli, 'why Couve is always so anti-British'.[49]

The tutor is unlikely to have earned the devotion of his young charges. Most found the minister a cold fish – arrogant, off-putting and serving up icy discourtesies. Armed with a pipe and 'installed comfortably in his armchair, he lit up with a prudent slowness. A cloud of smoke formed a second screen behind which he reflected. Many were put out by his silences and caustic remarks'.[50] A workhorse hardly ever taking holidays, even writing his own speeches, Couve brilliantly defended French theses. Command of the Quai's resources saved him from being a complete cipher. The first career official to lead the ministry for over a century, he knew the house inside out and concentrated 100 per cent on the job. The minister took France's Community commitment seriously, spending two days a week in Brussels with the French delegation. In the early 1960s he vigorously defended his corner against premier Debré who wanted a stronger say in policy-making.

Couve deployed smokescreens to keep opponents guessing. Shortly before the veto of Britain's first bid he spoke in reassuring terms to UK chief negotiator Edward Heath and US Under-Secretary of State for Economic Affairs George Ball. Close to the second veto in November 1967, he confirmed to foreign secretary George Brown that Britain was bound to enter the Community. Asked when talks might begin he answered, 'certainly before the end of the year'.[51] Although the minister does not seem to have resented playing second fiddle, Parisians joked about a smart dinner party where everybody lamented the alarming state of France's international relations, upon which Couve exclaimed, 'Ah, if only I were foreign minister!'

Until May 1968 France's prestige stood higher than at any time since 1919. The Quai basked in the radiance. An ambassador to the United States recalled the respectful silence that greeted his arrival at Washington parties: 'I was a celebrity'.[52] Strength was also weakness. The general's control of external policy accelerated the Quai's loss of autonomy – already undermined by globalization, technology and multilateralism. Dissenters were marginalized. Presidential advisers meddled in the ministry's affairs. Jacques Foccart, secretary general for Africa and Madagascar, operated as an uber minister, plotting the removal of the Quai's director for Africa and Madagascar, and rumoured to have had Couve followed.

While president and foreign minister strutted their stuff, secretary general Alphand minded the shop: 'I feel rather useless ... I stay at home ... but for what?'.[53] Leisure, perhaps, to polish his superb mimicry – a hilarious send-up of a conversation between former secretary general Chauvel and ambassador Massigli topped Alphand's repertoire. Chauvel mumbled inaudibly into his tie while Massigli's machine gun delivery made him difficult to follow. Alphand felt marginalized by the imperialist ways of the minister's private office chief, Jean-Yves Haberer. Diplomacy's dethronement as number one public career impacted on recruitment. Public service under the Fifth Republic offered attractive career opportunities at home without the stress on family and personal life of lengthy absences overseas.

Gamesmanship was a poor substitute for the Quai's eroded autonomy. In Frederick Raphael's novel *A Double Life* a French diplomat recalls the Franco–British guessing game of the 1960s: 'The purpose of our duplicity was not so much to confuse the British as to leave evidence that, whatever the eventual outcome, it was a triumph for French diplomacy'.[54] Clever footwork kept the Tricolore flying in Brussels and elsewhere – at the cost of strategic reflection and independence. In 1960 a survey of great power diplomacy criticized the Quai for 'excessive formalism ... when the desire to play the diplomatic game correctly becomes a substitute for hard thought'.[55] An official acknowledged that 'There was a complete vacuum whenever de Gaulle's wishes and intentions were unknown'.[56] One of the most talented and resourceful foreign services in the world was under-used. In June 1962 the Quai's director of European affairs, Jean-Marie Soutou, advised the new prime minister Pompidou that Britain's membership of the Community was inevitable and desirable. The premier accepted the argument but suppressed the paper, instructing Soutou not to speak to de Gaulle.

Did de Gaulle speak for France? Anglo-Saxon critics treated French external policy as a solo performance – implying that sans general the Western powers might have lived happily ever after. In reality, de Gaulle enjoyed substantial popular and elite support. But support was nuanced. Historians have simplistically assumed voter indifference towards international affairs. Polls, despite shortcomings, tell a different story. Should France be 'a leading world power' or accept 'a more modest role?', asked a 1964 poll. Respondents divided equally: 42 per cent wanted a world role, 42 per cent a more modest role. But the terms 'leading world power' and 'more modest role' were undefined and ambiguous.[57] Nearly two-thirds of the electorate in a poll of March 1968 expressed satisfaction 'with France's role in the world'.[58] Far from being a blast from the past, the notion of a world role still resonated.

Opinion fluctuated over time. Responding in September 1965 to the question 'What is the most important problem for France at this time?', 'The Common Market, Europe' topped the list (18 per cent), then 'salaries, standard of living' (14 per cent). Five months later, in February 1966, 'Peace, international relations' came first (12.2 per cent) above 'stability of prices' (10.5 per cent) and 'housing' (6.4 per cent). There was no blanket approval for foreign policy decisions. In January 1963 approval ratings for policies towards the USA, West Germany and Britain varied appreciably: United States: 47 per cent; West Germany: 54 per cent; Great Britain: 40 per cent. Despite official reticence, public interest in international affairs grew. The Six-Day War in 1967 unleashed an intense public debate about France's Middle East stance in which domestic and international concerns were closely meshed.[59]

The state sought endorsement for its policies, not citizen engagement. Fencing off the presidential domains of foreign affairs and defence deliberately distanced citizens. A December 1964 poll went to the heart of the matter. 'Regarding foreign policy,' it asked, 'in your opinion, how is it generally determined – essentially by governments without too much public influence or with a good deal of public involvement?' It elicited the following replies: government decision without public influence: 58 per cent; government decision with a good deal of public influence: 27 per cent; no opinion: 15 per cent.[60] Discouraging public involvement sowed distrust and alienation. A state radio and television poll in 1963 found that only 9 per cent of the public trusted radio and TV news.[61] 'I listen to the news every night, true or false, good or bad,' declared a Toulouse metal worker, 'without believing what they say just to know what they are trying to make us believe'.[62] The iconic May 1968 poster of a helmeted policeman in silhouette with the caption 'L'ORTF – it's the police talking to you [*c'est la police qui vous parle*]' epitomized the distrust.

The pace and scale of global change disoriented rulers and people. Globalization rendered hard and fast distinctions between internal and external issues redundant. France's burgeoning arms trade integrated foreign and domestic concerns. Making and selling arms world-wide reconciled 'security and welfare [domestic] imperatives by stimulating ... socio-economic and political modernization'.[63] Determined to preserve control over external policies, governments of the Fourth and Fifth Republics made no attempt to create an informed public. The United Nations was a case in point. Making sense of an expanding and complex international organization required top-down initiatives. Government failed the challenge. Asked in 1960 what they thought of the

UN, 36 per cent of respondents had no opinion. In a January 1965 poll, 64 per cent did not know the United Nations was headquartered in New York.[64]

The game finally vanquished the president. From the summer of 1967 presidential ratings slipped. Students clipped de Gaulle's wings. Panicked by the bedlam of May 1968 into a secret helicopter dash from the capital to seek support from general Jacques Massu, commander of French forces in West Germany, the president departed without informing his prime minister. 'The government', he complained, 'does not follow my directives ... I've practically lost control of the executive'.[65] Fresh elections brought a vote of confidence and an apparent return to normality. In reality, the quake left the country badly shaken. Strong aftershocks followed – pressure on the franc, renewed student agitation spreading to lycées, and the Warsaw Pact invasion of Czechoslovakia in August.

Dismayed by the regime's loss of momentum, foreign minister Debré shared anxieties with Élysée secretary general Tricot.[66] The general was part of the problem. Symptoms of ageing multiplied from 1965 – deteriorating eyesight, shorter working days, time increasingly spent with the family or watching television. The septuagenarian allowed his prime minister a larger discretionary role; the secretary general held back lengthy and complex items of business until sure of the general's full attention. Deceleration induced depression – deepened by the belief that American, British and Israeli intelligence services had exploited student disturbances in order to hasten his departure. The outcome was a long overdue rethinking of international policy resulting in an offer to Britain of secret talks – the Soames affair of 1969.

What had the general achieved? His astute exploitation of geopolitics and prosperity won kudos. France tailored the Pax Americana to its advantage. America's European hegemony was an empire by invitation, offering a consensual relationship. Washington's need for a stable Paris–London–Bonn triangle allowed European allies sufficient wiggle room to fashion a comfortable connection. The originality lay in de Gaulle's ability to reset the nation's sense of identity and purpose.[67] The verdict of UK technology minister Tony Benn on the 1967 Paris International Air Show would have given de Gaulle a sense of mission accomplished: 'the French do these things in a fantastic way – far better than we do. The Farnborough Air Show is just a pre-First World War country cricket match compared to Paris ... Of course the French planes and French technology dominated. The F-111 came over, folding its wings ... Concorde was presented as a French plane – it was a marvelous example of the glory of France being exploited.'[68] An old man in a hurry attempted too much. In the film *Sleeper* (1973), doctors wake up Woody Allen 200 years after a hospital mishap. They show him mid-twentieth century celebrity photos: Charles de Gaulle? Allen: 'Oh, he was a very famous French chef, had his own television show – making soufflés.' Like soufflés, the general's foreign policy confections had a short life.

6

Unmerrie England

Of the forces shaping attitudes to Europe, the great British hangover has gone almost unnoticed. It contributed hugely to the country's underperformance. Melancholia inhibited a rethinking of national strategy, encouraging policy-makers to rely on an obsolete great power plot. Disheartened elites bemoaned challenges rather than projecting a vision of the nation's future. Underperformance reflected an identity crisis. Britain, declared former US secretary of state Dean Acheson in 1962, had lost an empire, but had not yet found a role. The comment was wide of the mark. It was the attempt to play too many roles after 1945 that triggered a self-reinforcing crisis of confidence. By the early 1960s the hangover had become the 'British disease'. Reports of the Union Jack on the Tower of London flying upside down during the Suez crisis shocked *News Chronicle* readers. By the late 1960s Lord Feversham confessed to fellow peers that, while 'vaguely aware of being a Yorkshireman', he did not have 'a clue what Britain is or where it is going, if it has not gone already'.

The Pyrrhic nature of the 1945 victory, compounded by the exhaustion of two back-breaking conflicts and a lot of misery in between, largely explains the hangover. Peace did not bring sunlit uplands. On the contrary, post-war austerity exacerbated the consequences of the war. The nation suffered from a megadose of the universal anxiety about a shifting universe voiced in W.H. Auden's six-part poem 'The Age of Anxiety' (1947). There was plenty to be anxious about. The 'People's War' had not democratized the country – many, like novelist David Lodge, found the experience of national service an eye-opener. The dawn of the atomic age stoked anxiety. 'Europe is finished, possibly parts of North and South America may survive', declared Labour MP Evan Durbin after the destruction of Hiroshima and Nagasaki. 'How sad it is that I shall see a third world war in my lifetime', reflected former diplomat Harold Nicolson.[1]

Loss of empire dismayed the political elite. From South Africa in 1947 Conservative politician Harold Macmillan mourned, 'I sorrow for Britain now rapidly moving to a grave crisis, of which people are dimly aware ... Much of the empire is in liquidation'.[2] Bomb sites, run down cities, shabby furnishings and dreary clothes thickened the gloom. At No. 10 a visitor had 'the odd feeling ... of everything rather broken-down'; at the Foreign Office, 'intimations of decay everywhere ... chairs threadbare ... porters in their long frock coats also somehow threadbare'.[3]

Philosopher Isaiah Berlin pronounced apocalyptically, 'the ultimate end ... is that we shall be absorbed – at least the Commonwealth will be – in the American orbit. We can never recover ... People here will never work ... they have become too civilized to do so'. Author Cyril Connolly contrasted Britain and America: 'Here [London] the ego is at half-pressure; most of us are not men and women but members of a vast, seedy, overworked, over-legislated neuter class, with our drab clothes, our ration books and murder stories, our envious, strict, old-world apathies – a care-worn people'. Living for years on a weekly egg and microscopic meat ration made emigration attractive. A 1948 poll recorded 42 per cent of the population wished to emigrate. As war receded, rations contracted – bread in 1946, meat in 1952. American food parcels underscored the transatlantic power balance. The breakneck velocity of international change fazed rulers and ruled. The Soviet Union's explosion of an atom bomb in 1949 – three years before Britain and much sooner than expected – exposed the nation's vulnerability. Chief scientific adviser Sir Henry Tizzard was so shocked that he 'could only believe that the Russians had stolen some plutonium'.[4]

France shook off post-Liberation blues; Britain's hangover seemed permanent. Morale boosters made matters worse. In 1946 a V&A museum exhibition, 'Britain Can Make it', popularly known as 'Britain Can't Have It', featured designs and manufactures mostly unavailable in UK shops. The vaunted 'New Elizabethan Age' arrived stillborn. Benjamin Britten's Coronation opera *Gloriana* – an interweaving of the private and public lives of Elizabeth I – flopped disastrously. Historian Peter Hennessy asserts that spectaculars like the London Olympic Games (1948), Festival of Britain (1951), Coronation of Elizabeth II (1953) and Edmund Hillary's conquest of Everest (1953) created the feeling 'that one really did belong to a success-story nation'. The milestone events may have worked magic for some, but they could not remedy the attrition of what *The Times* in its Coronation Day leader called 'the recent thirty years war' and 'the barrenness of the victory so far'. The fact that everyone over the age of thirty had either experienced two world wars or lived in their shadow filled many with a sense of 'the tragic outpouring of the life of two generations and the dissipation of a century's work, thrift and investment'.[5]

In the campus novel *Lucky Jim* author Kingsley Amis satirized the establishment's crude PR exercise about a new Elizabethan age. Professor Welch asks junior lecturer Jim Dixon to give a public lecture for the College's Open Week: 'I thought something like "Merrie England" might do as a subject. Not too academic, and not too ... not too'. A tipsy Dixon botches the lecture and his academic career: 'The point about Merrie England is that it was about the most un-Merrie period in our history.' The fifties were as un-merrie as the first Elizabethan age.[6]

The frustrations of peacemaking disheartened many. The *Manchester Guardian* compared the 1946 Paris peace conference to Sartre's play *Huis-Clos*. 'Like the characters in Sartre's Hell, the nations are trapped by their own past actions and cannot escape. The situation is frozen.'[7] A senior UN official observed, 'It is very difficult to make an interesting report on the proceedings and atmosphere of such a dull conference – there is no enthusiasm anywhere, because everybody knows beforehand what the results will be, which is no results whatever'.[8]

Multilateralism added to the ennui. Labour MP Hugh Gaitskell, impatient for a new Jerusalem, lamented 'the extraordinary slowness' of international conferences: 'it is depressing to see how slowly the Democracies work'. Superpower rivalry subverted conventional notions of independent sovereignty, breeding more anxiety. 'There is no solution to our problems over which we ourselves exercise much freedom of choice', acknowledged a minister. The massive 30 per cent devaluation of sterling in September 1949 traumatized a veteran backbencher: 'How hopeless it all is ... a truly desperate state of affairs and I for one cannot see any way out of the mess so long as we don't face the facts – we are living above our means'. A year later, he wrote of his sadness 'to see the end of an epoch when England meant so much to the rest of the world and when one felt such pride in being an Englishman'.[9]

Sport barely lifted spirits. Roger Bannister's four-minute mile (1954) hardly compensated for humiliating defeats in the 1950 World Cup in Brazil and a thrashing by a West Indies cricket team at Lords. In 1953 Hungary's national team, 'the Magical Magyars', became the first Continental team to beat the English 6–3 at their own game on their own soil. Ealing comedies and spy fiction offered escape. *Passport to Pimlico* (1949), *Kind Hearts and Coronets* (1949) and *The Lavender Hill Mob* (1951) each grossed more than *Scott of the Antarctic* (1948), apotheosizing self-sacrifice, physical endurance and stiff-upper lip; spy fiction suggested that British brains might compensate for lack of brawn in a superpower era. Ian Fleming's James Bond, Agent 007, played a pretend game in which Britannia still ruled the waves.

A devil's kitchen of refractory issues besieged the Churchill government of 1951–5, leaving premier and aides 'depressed and bewildered':

> It is foolish to continue living with illusions ... the facts are stark, wrote the premier's secretary. What can we do? Increasing production is only a palliative in the face of foreign competition. We cannot till sufficient soil to feed 50 million people. We cannot emigrate fast enough to meet the danger, even if we were willing to face the consequent abdication of our position as a great power ... Lord Cherwell [Paymaster General] sees hope in the union of the English Speaking World ... But now England, and Europe, distrust, dislike and despise the United States. Some pin their faith on the development of the Empire as a great economic unit ... We have left it too late.[10]

Labour's elder statesman Hugh Dalton lamented the prospect of 'Europe going by default ... Germany will be forging ahead; with all their gifts of efficiency. And we, in our mismanaged, mixed economy, overpopulated little island, shall become a second rate power, with no influence and continuing crises ... I should advise all younger people to migrate to Canada or Australia'. In *Corridors of Power* (1964) novelist C.P. Snow captured Whitehall despair. A tabloid leader, 'Are they throwing away our independence?', roused mandarin Hector Rose: 'Good God alive, what kind of world are they living in? Do they think that if there were a single way in heaven or earth, which could keep this damned country a great power, some of us wouldn't have killed ourselves to find it?'[11]

Decolonization deepened depression. Graceful British farewells are sometimes contrasted with French colonialism's death agonies. The comparison ignores the psychological effects of flight from empire. Historian A.L. Rowse, having grown up 'with intense pride' in the empire and 'an unquestioned assumption ... that England and the Empire were the greatest thing in the world', could hardly believe that it had vanished. 'The young officers think we are on the decline as a great power,' reported the British embassy in Cairo, 'they have a real hatred politically for us ... No amount of concession or evacuation on our part will evoke the slightest gratitude in return. Whoever Egypt may want in the future as an ally, it will not be us'. From Aleppo, traveller Freya Stark described how 'a pale young *effendi* ... made me a long speech about the wicked British colonial empire – a crowd all clustering round ... I am never thought to be English, but when I said that I was, "You love the Jews" said another *effendi*'. Egyptian university students provided much-needed light relief, apologizing to their instructor, 'we all honor you Sir, you are our teacher. But we cannot work today – it is Down with Britain day – if you will excuse it, Sir'.[12]

Suspicions that the Americans were 'out to take our place' and 'to run the world' made retreat harder to stomach. Citing a conversation with the director of the CIA, a former cabinet secretary warned Churchill that once Britain left the Canal Zone America would move in. Eden's private secretary 'slept badly and became very depressed about the world in general. Our economic situation, German and Japanese competition, destruction of British influence in the Mediterranean and Middle East ... The Americans are not backing us anywhere. In fact, having destroyed the Dutch empire, the United States are now engaged in undermining the French and British empires as hard as they can.'[13]

How had the country got into such a state? The literati pondered the state of affairs. Novelist and civil servant C.P. Snow 'probed ... a failure of national will, the incapacity of an ageing society to adapt itself to the challenge of the new'. Anthony Hartley, deputy editor of the *Spectator*, accused intellectuals of a betrayal. Shrinking power and the Welfare State had brought 'a narrowing of horizons and a sense of frustration', leaving individuals and governments feeling they had 'little freedom of manoeuvre'. Historian G.R. Elton lashed out at socialist intellectual R.H. Tawney, condemning his *Religion and the Rise of Capitalism* (1926) for 'the whole collapse of self-confidence which we have encountered in this present generation'. Adversity had its uses. Interviewed in 1963, writer Doris Lessing found England 'a paradise' for writing because it 'is a backwater and it doesn't make much difference what happens here, or what decisions are made here'.[14]

Westward the land looked bright. Comparisons with the United States cranked up gloom. The UK could not compete with stellar American analysts Herman Kahn, Henry Kissinger and Thomas Schelling on defence and foreign policy. Labour backbencher Denis Healey regularly visited the Boston area, his 'intellectual paradise'. A young historian migrated to the University of Wisconsin: 'made the more attractive by my gloomy assessment of the state of British society in the late 1950s. Although the austerities of post-war Britain had gone and there was much trumpeting about affluence and assurances that "you never had it so good", too many of the old class divisions and inequalities remained for my liking'.[15]

Exclusion from the Space Age added to despondency. Hope lingered that a country which had invented radar and the Spitfire would move into rockets and eventually moon shots. *Eagle* comic's Dan Dare conquered the solar system wearing something that looked very much like an RAF uniform; Sir Hubert called the shots in the international space force, with bit-parts for 'Hank' and 'Pierre'.[16] From 1954 Britain's contribution to joint missile research with the United States was an intermediate range ballistic missile (IRBM) called Blue Streak. By 1960 escalating costs forced cancellation and dependence on American technology. Britain's pride and joy, Jodrell Bank, the largest radio telescope in the world in 1957, began live tracking American and Soviet moon probes.

Anxiety for the nation's future provoked a questioning of assumptions. The Campaign for Nuclear Disarmament (CND) rallied young and old. The film comedy *I'm All Right Jack* (1959) satirized the class system and labour relations. TV shows like *Beyond the Fringe* (1961), *That Was The Week That Was* (1962), and the film *Dr Strangelove* (1964) targeted the establishment, giving political satire mass appeal. Philip Larkin's poetry evoked a climate of fatalism, uncertainty and sense of overwhelmingly hostile circumstances. The nation was no longer sure of what it was, or wanted to be. Of those polled by *New Society* in 1963, 73 per cent considered 'individual happiness' much more important than 'national greatness'. Historian Arthur Bryant, whose writings crafted wartime patriotism, lamented: 'there is no unifying faith to bind us together.'[17]

'The Angry Young Men' writers pulled and pummelled identity and values in an ironic, sceptical and mocking tone. As consumer durables multiplied, international clout contracted. Why so much self-doubt when Britons had 'never had it so good'? The mid-1950s surge in living standards came too late to wipe out memories of the Great Depression in the 1930s. Affluence does not equal contentment. On the contrary, as historian Avner Offer argues, it 'breeds impatience, and impatience undermines well-being'.[18] Mixed messages about the nation's ranking sowed confusion. 'His Majesty's Government do not accept the view ... that we have ceased to be a Great Power', Bevin reassured the Commons in 1947. Privately, chief scientific adviser Sir Henry Tizard conceded, 'We are not a Great Power and never will be again. We are a great nation but if we continue to behave like a Great Power we shall soon cease to be a great nation.'[19]

Conflicting pronouncements from on high continued. In 1950 Bevin confessed, 'the day when we, as Great Britain, can declare a policy independently of our allies, has gone'. Greatness returned four years later. In 1954 Whitehall's grand vizier, Sir Oliver Franks, delivered the annual Reith Lectures, the BBC's crown jewels. Under the title 'Britain and the tide of world affairs', Franks talked up British power, and avoided an 'exact definition of a Great Power'. After citing American opinion that Britain no longer counted, he asserted: 'Britain is going to continue to be what she has been, a Great Power'. Two years later in May 1956 readers, sedated by establishment pap, read in the *News Chronicle*: 'The Days of GREAT Britain are over.'[20]

Within months a frenzy of recrimination over the Suez débâcle outed the issue. 'Britain at this moment is no longer a great Power', announced Labour's *Daily Herald*. 'Is Britain now a Second-Class Power?' asked the Conservative *Daily Mail*. Macmillan's first television broadcast after becoming prime minister in January 1957 unequivocally rejected dethronement: 'I've heard people say: "is not Britain only a second or third-class Power now?" What nonsense! It's not just material resources that make a nation great. It's character and leadership ... So don't let's have any more defeatist talk of second-class Power'.[21]

The monarchy joined in the post-Suez gnashing of teeth. 'Just at this moment we are suffering a national defeat comparable to any lost military campaign', chided Prince Philip, Duke of Edinburgh; 'it is about time we pulled our fingers out'. In different language *The Times* rounded up the usual suspects to explain 'the present malaise' – 'the pointlessness' of life felt by many young people, 'confusion' about economic problems, 'bewilderment' caused by the sudden sharp contraction of imperial and international power, especially painful for a people that had always looked for external outlets, and a conviction that 'material ease is not enough'. Uncertainty about the country's domestic and international future ran counter to a profound belief 'that we should do admirable things and that we should do them better than anyone else'. The leader writer invested hope in the Common Market: 'if and when Britain enters the Common Market, she may have opened another and a new field in which to employ her outward looking impulses in a constructive manner.'[22]

'The British are still quite capable of surrendering to facts provided they are told them,' argued one analyst, 'but the institutions and the men who work them have ... become dangerously out of touch with the public, insensitive to change, and wrapped up in their private rituals'. This gap between people and decision-makers sustained and deepened the malaise. Citizens had no say in external policy-making. In the general election of 1945 a Conservative candidate refused even to answer questions: 'It is not my policy during elections.' A self-styled mature democracy asserting global moral leadership allowed almost no space outside Whitehall and Westminster for international affairs. Parliamentary foreign affairs debates were comparatively rare; MPs and influencers were kept away from the holy of holies. One of the problems in international relations is to ensure that a sufficient quantity and variety of information circulates not only between governments but through the whole spectrum of decision-makers, opinion formers and citizens, then feeds back into government, supplementing the flow through official channels. Whitehall made no effort to connect with metropolitan elites, let alone voters.[23]

An Anglo–American exchange crystallized conflicting outlooks on policy-making. Livingstone Merchant, assistant secretary in the State Department, astonished Evelyn Shuckburgh, Eden's secretary, with stories of how he had 'to appear before Congressional Committees' to explain policy issues, 'and even to be "quizzed by Senators on the TV for hours on end"'. Merchant continued: 'Foreign Policy could no longer be a matter handled by experts in secret, but must be the subject of continuous scrutiny by the masses. Even the English would have to give up the "old-fashioned" idea of entrusting vital secrets to experts.' Shuckburgh 'feared that democracy could not survive if *issues*, as opposed to personalities, were to be put before the public. This was the fascist referendum idea. You can fool the public about issues, but not ... about the character and quality of leaders'.[24]

Why so little debate about foreign policy? No Cobdens and Brights energized Westminster. Parliamentary groups – Keep Left Group, Bevanites, Tory Suez Group and Conservative Monday Club – though mettlesome at times, lacked the muscle to shape policy decisively. The European Movement and Federalist associations did not target a wide public. In his 1955 Ford Lectures historian A.J.P. Taylor charted the dissenting tradition in British foreign policy, but stopped the story in 1939, ignoring the near invisibility of opposition after 1945. Strong extra-parliamentary lobbies like CND and the Anti-Apartheid Movement did not appear until almost the end of the 1950s.

An older historiography assumed indifference to international affairs. 'Where foreign affairs are concerned,' wrote one analyst, 'the bulk of the population knows little and cares less'. In fact, the supposedly silent majority held decided opinions on the Cold War, nuclear weapons, Egypt, Korea and German rearmament. George Kennan, a prime mover in America's Cold War strategy, became its critic. Invited by the BBC to give the 1957 Reith Lectures, Kennan – rehearsing for one of the talks – caught sight of 'one of the technicians, a wiry, little Cockney woman', who he later learned was the wife of a London bobby, 'pounding the table vehemently with her fist in enthusiasm and approval'. Voter indifference on overseas interests has been greatly exaggerated. Though polls registered big fluctuations of interest in world affairs, they showed consistently strong support for a summit. Asked in December 1951 what was 'the most urgent problem the government must solve in the next few months', a majority replied 'foreign affairs'. Five months later 'the cost of living' pushed international affairs into fourth place – by June 1953 international problems again topped the list. The public knew quite a lot about Europe. In 1949 67 per cent of respondents had heard of the Council of Europe and 44 per cent approved; in 1950 77 per cent of those asked knew of the Schuman Plan. Between July 1960 and January 1963 a consistent majority favoured British membership of the EEC. Support for membership peaked at 71 per cent in August 1966.[25]

Why, then, so little involvement? Quite simply, citizens were unwanted. 'Keep off the grass' signs abounded. A secretive, paternalistic state insisted on people knowing their place and deferring to government. Occasionally, one of the political elite broke ranks. A junior minister in the Attlee government believed ministers should give more information: 'the Government ought to issue a statement explaining exactly to the country the nature of the danger threatening us and the inevitability of sacrifice'. The dearth of think tanks and the absence of a strong community of experts outside Whitehall made 'the public ... much more dependent upon the version of events which the government chooses to give it'. Government managed information, discouraging discussion of defence, security and overseas issues. Before the Public Records Act of 1958 the state locked up official files indefinitely. The foreign secretary refused to allow a prominent backbencher from his own party to consult fifty-year-old FO papers about the Entente Cordiale of 1904.[26]

The convention that questions involving 'the national interest' should not be raised served as a catch-all. Anything nasty in the woodshed had to stay there. 'I have heard it maintained, in all seriousness,' wrote historian Geoffrey Barraclough apropos the Suez affair, 'that no attempt should be made to discover the actual course of events, lest something be revealed which might be detrimental to Anglo–US relations'. 'I think our spokesmen talk too much', foreign secretary Selwyn Lloyd advised Macmillan. 'I am instructing the Department ... to say flatly they have no statement to make. We want to have the output reduced and News Department confined as far as possible to statements which it is really in our interest to have published'. Briefing BBC chiefs about civil defence and the H-bomb, Macmillan confided: 'They [ministers] did not desire to keep the public in entire ignorance; on the other hand they did not want to stimulate the feeling so easily accepted by the British people because it agreed with their natural laziness in these matters, that because of the terrible nature of the hydrogen bomb there was no need for them to take any part in home defense measures.'²⁷

Apparent indifference to international issues reflected inanition, not apathy. British Blue Books and French Yellow Books kept Victorians better informed on foreign policy than their mid-twentieth-century descendants. Globalization and the new communications technology of the sixties released floods of information, but quality suffered. The rise of television forced the downsizing of newspaper offices overseas, leaving coverage patchy. Foreign news had to be of the 'Gee Whiz!' variety to win space and attention. The BBC, familiarly known as Auntie or the Beeb, trumpeted its 'educational role' in a democracy, providing the public 'with a service of information' on foreign affairs 'so that the public should take an enlightened interest in, and form a balanced view of, current world events'.²⁸ But government had the whip hand because the Corporation's Royal Charter gave ministers the power to revoke the licence. Ministers appointed the Board of Governors and set the annual licence fee, ensuring opportunities for further interference. The BBC, like the press, was subject to the Official Secrets Act and censorship via Defence Notices (D-Notices). A D-Notice of February 1958 instructed the BBC not to disclose any details of ballistic missile deployment in the United Kingdom. MI5 vetted newly appointed staff and candidates for promotion.

The BBC–Whitehall marriage deprived listeners of an effective forum. The war reinforced deference. 'The war-time habits of authority on the side of the Government and of subordination on the side of the BBC', noted a BBC producer, 'have been transmitted as acquired characteristics to their peace-time descendants'. The popular discussion programme 'The Brains Trust' was told to avoid 'all questions' involving religion and political philosophy. Questions rejected included: 'What does "The Brains Trust" think should be the future of the British Empire? Reason for rejection: "risky".' In its anxiety to run with the establishment the Beeb shied away from controversy and analysis of overseas news and world affairs. BBC Governor Arthur Mann, former editor of the *Yorkshire Post*, called for an expansion of news services – all evidence indicated 'a growing public interest in what is happening of importance at home and abroad'.²⁹

The Corporation gagged itself with the Fourteen Day Rule – excluding any issues currently being discussed in Parliament, or for two weeks before parliamentary debates. The announcement of parliamentary business only one week in advance put discussion of topical issues off limits. Another self-denying ordinance forbade anything controversial between the dissolution of parliament and general elections, and during parliamentary sittings. In the 1950 general election only the BBC and Radio Moscow ignored 'the headline news of an "atom talks" proposal for the Big Three made by Churchill'. Commented one observer, 'this was neutrality carried to the lengths of castration'.³⁰ Deeply fractured opinion during the Suez crisis pointed up the absurdity of the Fourteen Day Rule, forcing government to concede its indefinite suspension. As a result, the general election of 1959 was the first to be reported on television and radio like any other news.

'Coverage of elections and international affairs', wrote broadcaster Robin Day, 'was ludicrously unworthy of a mature democracy'. The house-trained Corporation took the initiative in securing Whitehall clearance for potentially controversial broadcasts. In

April 1957 foreign secretary Lloyd in a talk on 'Woman's Hour' blamed Communists for instigating an anti-H Bomb tests movement. The smear provoked hundreds of critical letters and the comment from Labour MP Barbara Castle that Lloyd 'must have thought he was talking on Children's Hour'. A producer went cap in hand to the Foreign Office to ask permission to broadcast some of the feedback. A.J.P. Taylor's challenge to the government's Cold War policy got him banned from the Third Programme. His advocacy of alliance with Russia provoked questions in Parliament – mischievous as ever, he promised not to say 'anything that will make a Member of Parliament of limited intelligence ask questions in the House of Commons'.[31]

Insiders spoke out. Third Programme talks producer Peter Laslett protested against the impact of self-censorship:

> We deliberately confine ourselves to discussion of foreign affairs, that is, of events and personalities, and meticulously avoid discussion of foreign policy ... In my view we should make every effort to rehabilitate its reputation as an organ for the discussion of British foreign policy, and of the attitude of people in foreign countries to us and our allies. I realize that there is a possibility of embarrassing the Foreign Office if we go too far in this direction. But I feel that the Foreign Office is ... inordinately sensitive.[32]

Auntie's self-censorship ensured that hot button issues escaped effective scrutiny. Taboo subjects included nuclear weapons and pacifism. A ban on unscripted discussions made it easy to filter and monitor output. Scripts about nuclear energy had to be cleared with the prime minister personally. A twenty-minute feature on the peaceful uses of atomic energy took six months to get clearance. The film *War Game* (1965) was suppressed and not broadcast until 1986. Only two broadcasts about pacifism took place in nearly a decade.

Despite a doubling of weekly television news time in 1954–5, critical discussion of news had to wait until the 1960s and 1970s. The Beeb made little effort to assess continental political developments, barely mentioning French and West German general elections – extensive live coverage went to American politics. Until commercial television arrived in 1955 no one attempted the probing interview. Politicians chose the questions they would answer. Interviewing foreign secretary Lloyd in December 1955 BBC Radio submitted questions in advance: 'his officials arrived at Broadcasting House ... with the questions beautifully typed on thick grey paper which would not crackle and so give the game away when we read our parts from this script'. The sixties helped to liberalize the Corporation, but it had a long way to go. In 1968 technology minister Tony Benn spoke out: 'in my view, the BBC absolutely failed in its function because it ... always edited things and it always wanted to squeeze people into ... programmes instead of providing facilities for people to say what they wanted to say'.[33]

The press offered no comfort to those turned off by Auntie's sycophantic twaddle. The 'Yes Sir, No Sir, three bags full' relationship between lobby correspondents and politicians bred mistrust. Journalists focused on projecting the decisions and views of politicians rather than nurturing a critical understanding of the political process. Downing Street's press adviser found the Westminster lobby correspondents remarkably easy to manipulate: 'it is amazing to see how much of one's lightest guidance over the phone appears in the papers next day from the Political Correspondents.' Lobby management worked smoothly, 'by its control of the sources of information, with the implied threat that criticism of policies would lead to a less full flow to that correspondent, by co-opting all of us diplomatic correspondents into a cosy club of those in the know, I fear that the government ... did manage the news of our foreign policy.' In the *Spectator* Bernard Levin sided with voters and popularized a new iconoclastic style of parliamentary reporting – treated the Commons as theatre. Journalist John Freeman's television interrogations in the BBC series *Face to Face* (1959–62) ended the era of kid-glove treatment. The breakthrough came too late. Sociologist Richard Hoggart claimed that 'a generation had grown up expert at explaining away, insulated from thinking that there is ever likely to be a cause for genuine enthusiasm or a freely good act ... the catch phrase is the brittle and negative, "So what"'.[34]

The inventor of the term 'soft power', Harvard academic Joseph S. Nye, defined it as 'the ability to get what you want through attraction rather than coercion or payments'. Politicians disarmed themselves, imposing draconian financial cuts on the main arsenals of British soft power. True, a travelling circus of royalty, Old Vic, Sadler's Wells and Spurs could not replace hard power, but a determined bid to project language and values would have revived brand Britain. The main agencies for publicity – FO, BBC and British Council – liaised closely with Whitehall. Though British propaganda in both world wars scored highly – winning Hitler's praise – self-marketing in peacetime did not come easily. Churchill's response to ministerial protests against the Treasury's unprecedented cuts in overseas publicity illustrates the limitations of his leadership in the early 1950s: 'As for information that we send abroad, surely that task is accomplished by the newspapers at their own expense. We might help them circulate, but ... they say a lot of nasty things about us.'[35]

Selling Britannia went awry in a Monty Python-like way. Shaped like a medieval tent, the British pavilion at the Expo 58 Brussels World Fair seemed to point backwards in time. The British Council in Asia had lost touch with younger audiences. A Council lecturer invited at short notice to speak in a South East Asian village was surprised to find an audience of mostly small children already dressed for bed. He delivered a set piece on British universities – illustrated by a film on Oxbridge 'notable for its portrayal of a don in action, giving a tutorial to his pipe. At the end the children had to be woken up just sufficiently to get them into bed'. For some time the United States Information Service had offered a weekly evening of old cartoon films, Mickey Mouse and Donald Duck, and the audience assumed they would get the same.[36]

UK propaganda neglected mainland Europe and failed to find a voice. From 1951 the BBC's external services, together with overseas information agencies, suffered savage cuts. Total weekly programme hours sank from 648 hours in 1950 to 540 in 1952 at a time when the Soviet Union trebled its own external broadcasting. BBC offices in Latin America closed down. The widely read *Arabic Listener* ceased publication. Capital equipment like transmitters could not be replaced. The British Council fell under the Treasury axe, losing 40 per cent of funding between 1949 and 1954. Cuts of this size blighted most activities in Western Europe and Latin America.

'Our European friends and clients', recalled a Council representative, 'were astonished ... the whole of Europe had become almost everywhere Anglophile'.³⁷

Officials demanded an intensification of propaganda, leaving their masters in no doubt about its importance. 'We are already accused of not being serious about the European "idea". If we were to pull out of cultural activity in Europe our critics would have an unanswerable case against us'. Vincent Tewson, General Secretary of the Trades Union Council (TUC), protested: 'I am not anti-American ... But it would be just as well if we faced the fact that the Americans are pouring people into the countries of Asia and Africa who are making contacts with organized workers and are putting over American ideas.... In many instances Trade Unionists in certain countries would be glad to turn to the British for advice if there was someone with whom they were in contact ... the diplomacy of the West is not to be thought of in terms of what the Americans are doing ... there is a British angle to be advanced'.³⁸

In the mid-50s Britain lost the initiative in Europe and the Middle East. 'We are at present being "talked" out of the Middle East. Vicious and wholly mendacious propaganda continues against us, unchecked and unanswered,' bewailed a leading Conservative. 'The overriding lesson of the Suez operation', the commander of the Anglo-French military intervention at Suez insisted, 'is that world opinion is now an absolute principle of war ... However successful the pure military operations may be they will fail ... unless national, Commonwealth and Western world opinion is sufficiently on our side'.³⁹

Soft power demanded values and engagement. A penniless Britannia could only appeal to fading moral leadership: 'it is for us to show that the British way of life with its freedom and democracy, can in peace as in war be an example to the whole world', proclaimed Attlee. The constant parading of war service invited mockery. 'How ready they showed themselves to claim the world's moral leadership in and out of season, or to rub in the debt of admiration owed to them for their steadfastness in their finest hour by endlessly intoning the old theme song "we stood alone"', jeered a Dutch journalist. The Cold War focus on 'Free World' values made it harder to project a distinctive post-imperial British voice. 'All our propaganda', noted junior minister Anthony Nutting, 'is planned against the background of the Soviet threat – no longer just "projecting Britain"'. 'Our need', Commonwealth Secretary Lord Swinton urged Cabinet colleagues, 'is to sell Britain as a great industrial country with great assets, moral, physical and scientific'. A country forced to abandon its Blue Streak missile for American technology could hardly boast of scientific leadership, however. Labour leader Harold Wilson's electioneering talk in 1964 of 'the white heat' of scientific revolution swayed party faithful but not the world. Propaganda lacked a sense of the country's future.⁴⁰

The state's reluctance to reach out to citizens imposed a huge handicap in the race to stay competitive. 'I doubt if we can really ... continue to play a dominant part in world affairs', warned a Treasury official in 1945, 'unless the average man or woman in the UK realizes just how we stand, and the colossal effort which is necessary if we are to remain an important and even a leading country'. The 'nanny knows best' ethos shunned a national conversation, focusing instead on constructing a Cold War consensus to underpin an Anglo-American alliance and an Atlanticist approach to

European unity. Could Britain have rediscovered a sense of purpose? Belief in a 'British way' was robust but undefined – 'our people' have 'never had it so good' an election slogan, no more. Macmillan's 'Let us, if we can, be the Greeks of the new Roman Empire' was a non-starter. Nothing sounded less sexy than playing sage uncle to American cousins.[41]

Diagnosing the need for a vision was one thing, defining it another. David Eccles, President of the Board of Trade in the Macmillan government, mused: 'North America and Russia have that mysterious dynamic which makes a people grow. If we are losing it this is because the nature and direction of the next advance in our strength has to be in ways which offend our tradition of greatness ... as incentives we have discarded imperialism and religion.' Diplomat and moral rearmament crusader Archie Mackenzie vented frustration: 'We desperately need an ideology to guide our trade, a titanic effort to re-organize and redirect the resources of the Free World – something so big that it will call for sacrifices from us all but will also turn the tide in the key under-developed areas'.[42]

Macmillan's efforts to galvanize backbenchers backfired. The ending of 'the great dominant period of British power and wealth', he declared, 'was no reason for defeatism ... We now had to struggle to keep the sterling area alive ... Yet that was nothing new in our experience. The first Elizabethan age was a period of struggle to play off Spain against France, and even at the time of Marlborough's wars we had to contend with similar difficulties'. The 'history for dummies' ploy fooled no one, least of all ministerial colleagues: 'Harold's conversation was littered as usual with historical analogies: "Of course the situation is really like the Augustan Age" etc. Anthony [Eden] said this analogy was inaccurate and anyway unfortunate. On another occasion Bobbety [Robert Cecil, Marquess of Salisbury] had lost his patience in Cabinet and said to Harold, "I really don't see any resemblance between us and Queen Elizabeth I".'[43]

Radical protest arrived too late to correct the democratic deficit or shake off the national depression. The sixties subversion of taboos and authority exacerbated the sense of a collective nervous breakdown. Reminders of 'national values and enterprise' provoked mockery. Disillusioned with ageing home models, young Britons hero-worshipped a dynamic and youthful-looking American President. In his *English History 1914–1945*, A.J.P. Taylor, one of the country's most popular historians, attempted to restore a sense of national pride, praising Britons as 'the only people who went through both world wars from beginning to end. Yet ... remained a peaceful and civilized people, tolerant, patient, and generous'. Northern Ireland Catholics, prisoners of Kenya's Hola detention camp and the Nyasaland 'police state', and expelled Diego Garcia islanders, would have vigorously dissented.[44]

The British state defied a quick fix. The hegemony of governing elites made outsider criticisms seem naïve and ill-informed. In 1959 historian Hugh Thomas edited *The Establishment*, a collection of essays on the theme of the master class's redundancy. 'The assumption was that once that class was swept away, proud old England would reassert herself as a society both humane and industrially efficient and capable of exercising by her example a moral force for good in the world'. By 1968 Thomas had retreated: 'well-established and broad national attitudes rather than those of an elite are making it rather difficult for either a Labour or a Conservative administration to resolve "the English question".'⁴⁵

Revelations of political mendacity in the Suez affair and the Profumo scandal of 1961 quickened the corrosion of trust in government, making it much harder to reset the national mood. Hugh Thomas's *The Suez Affair* (1966), the first non-partisan history of the episode, rekindled indignation and humiliation. Many sitting Labour MPs had been in the Commons in 1956 and several tried to introduce legislation establishing an inquiry into the episode. Two best-sellers – Anthony Nutting's *No End of a Lesson: The Story of Suez* (1967) and J.C. Masterman's *The Double Cross System in the War of 1939–1945* (1972) signalled changing attitudes within and towards the governing elite. Masterman fought for years to publish an internal MI5 study of Britain's double agents which he had written while working for the agency. Nutting, junior minister in the Eden government of 1955–7, resigned over Suez, losing his parliamentary seat. He waited ten years before spilling the beans.

Nutting debunked denials of Anglo–French collusion with Israel in the attack on Egypt. The perseverance of Nutting and Masterman achieved a significant victory. The state's guardians no longer preached as an article of faith that policy-making and the existence of the security services were off-limits. Masterman reflected: 'how strange it was that I, who all my life had been a supporter of the Establishment, should become, at eighty, a successful rebel ... But ... sometimes in life you feel that there is something which you *must* do and in which you must trust your own judgment and not that of any other person'.⁴⁶

7

Running on Empty

In his war memoirs General de Gaulle rated the Whitehall engine 'the finest ... in the world'. 'To resist the British machine', he wrote, 'when it set itself in motion to impose something was a severe test. Without having experienced it oneself, it is impossible to imagine what a concentration of effort, what a variety of procedures, what insistence, by turns gracious, pressing, and threatening, the English were capable of deploying in order to obtain satisfaction'. Nevertheless, the general resisted. By 1963 he had turned the tables, and slammed the door on UK membership of the European Community. A revolution in international affairs overwhelmed UK policy-makers. Two prime ministers, Clement Attlee and Winston Churchill, and foreign secretary Ernest Bevin, occupied top place in the British pantheon. Yet they seriously underperformed on overseas policy – disabled by war weariness, sickness and lack of reflection. The Plowden Report on Representational Services Overseas (1964) concluded, that 'some of the most intractable international issues in which we have been involved in the last two decades could, in our view, have been handled better if their implications had been more fully explored in advance'.[1]

The geopolitical revolution presented the biggest headache: how to recover a world role with greatly diminished resources in a predatory, swiftly changing environment? The pain and bewilderment of policy-makers as they struggled to make sense of the post-war world is almost palpable. 'The problems in front of us', warned a top diplomat, 'are manifold and awful'. 'In the worst of the war I could always see how to do it', confided Churchill; 'today's problems are elusive and intangible'. The war brought a sea change in international affairs. The second conflict was much more destructive for the European powers than the first. The American–Soviet monopoly of high politics disempowered Europe. The superpowers grew more intimidating both in absolute terms and in relation to others. The polarization of power blocs around the United States and the Soviet Union reduced elbow room for lesser powers. The proliferation of states, agents and subjects of negotiation transformed the international order. Multilateralism radically reconfigured diplomacy.[2]

Bilateral diplomacy conducted by representatives in the field was the pre-1939 norm. Apart from occasional jaunts to the League of Nations at Geneva, ministers stayed at home. The urgency of recovery enforced cooperation at all levels. The Atlantic Charter of 1941 and the Bretton Woods Agreement of 1944 introduced global institutions – UN, IMF and GATT. By the late 1940s ministers formed a flying circus. Eighteen-hour transatlantic flights in ear-splitting piston-engined aircraft left everyone worse for wear. When a budget-conscious minister booked commercial flights for short-haul European trips, fellow passengers tried to read paperwork over his shoulder. Getting there was only half the battle. Hotels might be uncomfortable in more ways than one. At the Geneva Conference on Vietnam in 1954 foreign secretary Eden was 'unable to sleep owing to the traffic outside his window' and unable to speak 'without being overheard by Chinks'. Frequent travel multiplied the potential for gaffes. 'Peking, Alec, Peking, Peking', whispered the wife of foreign secretary Alec Douglas-Home as she followed her husband out of the plane. The hours lost to overseas visits slowed down No. 10: 'jobs were continually frustrated, particularly when it was impossible to get more direct advice and instructions from the Prime Minister.'[3]

Multilateralism spewed out an 'alarming growth of international committees and commissions of every sort and kind', prolonging negotiating times, and making it harder to keep overall objectives in sight. Meetings, paperwork and travel expanded. Worst of all, decision-makers had to adjust to a complex institutional web 'in which the same issues were discussed by the same people on different occasions and in different places'. The Council of Ministers of the Council of Europe assembled foreign ministers; NATO Council meetings gathered fourteen foreign and defence ministers. Foreign ministers of the three Western occupying powers in Germany met regularly for discussion of German and European questions. London and Paris maintained permanent delegations at the UN, NATO, OEEC, ECSC, Council of Europe, WEU and EEC. The 'great care taken to avoid anything in the nature of a row or argument developing – anything contentious referred to officials' – increased the tedium of proceedings. At UN meetings in Paris a show-off black cat would stroll across the stage disconcerting podium speakers and amusing bored delegates. From 1958 the European Community added more layers to the onion – weekly and monthly meetings of Community members in world capitals. 'The amount of time now spent on co-ordination', groaned an official, 'is horrendous, bloody inefficient'.[4]

Two other aspects of the revolution in world politics stymied decision-making: the terrifying speed and simultaneity of change; the fusing of foreign and domestic issues. Fresh eruptions remade the landscape: Cold War, Korean War, Afro–Asian nationalism, Communist victory in China, wars of decolonization. 'All the world is in trouble', said Bevin, 'and I have to deal with all the troubles at once'. Soviet representatives set up road blocks. At the 1946 Paris peace conference Vyacheslav Molotov, Soviet commissar for foreign affairs – 'Mr. Nyet' – stonewalled American secretary of state James Byrnes and British foreign secretary Bevin. Overlapping issues grew like Topsy. 'At every Cabinet today', noted Churchill, 'there are discussed at least two or three problems which would have filled a whole session before the first war'. Weary ministers and advisers strove to make sense of the merry-go-round. 'I see nothing intimate of UNO', wrote traveller Freya Stark from the United Nations in Paris; 'the fact is that everyone is hectically busy, away all day on committees ... the leisurely feel of the old days in Geneva has gone ... there is a desperate feeling of trying to cope with the floods of people – UNO, European Defence, Atlantic Pact, American Aid, a huge octopus organization'.[5]

The old distinction between foreign and domestic issues no longer held. The terms of American loans determined domestic living standards – essential imports from the United States had to be paid for in scarce dollars. Multilateralism broke the unity of external representation. Before 1939 the Quai and the FO were the ringmasters of overseas policy; after 1945 home ministries established external affairs sections and delegations. Councils of Ministers directing international bodies bypassed foreign ministries. Council members and staffs communicated directly with each other and took final decisions. Diplomats could no longer count on leading negotiations. Interdepartmental coordination became the norm – often making for lengthy delays.

Language and technology added to the frustrations of multilateral diplomacy. Consecutive interpretation functioned with mind-numbing slowness, every sentence repeated in all working languages. Historian Arnold Toynbee compared his experience of the Paris peace conferences of 1919 and 1946: 'In 1919 the principal representatives of the powers had been in a human enough relation with each other to be able to quarrel; and they had commanded the necessary means of linguistic communication for quarrelling vocally, thanks to Clémenceau's being able to speak English ... In 1946 all interchanges between the principal delegates were channeled through interpreters. The life was taken out of the proceedings by the lengthiness and boringness of the process of translation.'[6]

The success of simultaneous interpretation at the Nuremberg war crimes trials led to its adoption by the United Nations. It saved time, but prolix speeches delivered in a monotone without the inflexions and nuances of the original emerged worse in translation. An 'Oh, my God' from the British representative – spoken when the chair of the UN Council called upon a long-winded delegate – 'was heard all over America'. Politicians perfected escape strategies. At a Paris conference the UK minister for education and science Patrick Gordon Walker 'missed a lot of the morning session because he was looking at the tapestries, this afternoon he was viewing the Impressionists, he read the papers most of the time, wore earphones unplugged, did crossword puzzles ... laziest man I have ever known ... ought to be dismissed'.[7]

The meshing of domestic and international issues quickened public interest in foreign affairs, and compounded the complexities of policymaking. Disoriented policy-makers struggled to define the role of their country and Europe in a Cold War era; world and domestic opinion interacted as never before. Total war added a new dimension to pre-1914 diplomacy. Allied propaganda in the First World War projected 'a war to end wars'. American President Woodrow Wilson's Fourteen Points of January 1918 embedded international affairs in mass politics. The League of Nations and the League of Nations Union fostered an informed public. After 1945 the United Nations championed a revived internationalism calling for recognition of human rights and condemning European colonialism.

The rush of fledgling states and spiralling superpower competition turned the United Nations into a platform for Cold War confrontation. As a result, a non-aligned movement gained traction. Yet citizens still expected governments to play God. 'What is the most important problem the government must solve over the next few months' was the perennial Gallup question. Wartime summits stimulated wildly unrealistic expectations that conferences would solve world problems. 'The technique of modern government becomes almost intolerably difficult', complained one minister; 'key ministers are hopelessly overworked. Stafford [Stafford Cripps, Chancellor of the Exchequer] spends his time dashing between Paris, Brussels and London, thinking out and arguing most frightfully complicated questions of international trade and payments, and somehow all this has got to be explained to the general public sometime'. Electorates of the 1940s and 1950s still trusted politicians and the state. The exposure of Anglo-French collusion and mendacity in the Suez crisis ended an age of innocence. Deference died hard. *Guardian* editor Alistair Hetherington recalled that years after Suez the belief lingered that the paper had 'behaved discreditably in doubting the word of Ministers'.[8]

Rearmament after the outbreak of the Korean War in June 1950 sharply defined the limits of British power, overstraining the economy and imposing a heavier burden of spending per capita than the United States. By 1953 defence spending totalled 28.5 per cent of government expenditure. The testing of an atom bomb in 1952 could not disguise the British Cinderella – in the same year the United States exploded a hydrogen bomb, followed a year later by the Soviet Union. Though Britain caught up by 1957, it lacked effective delivery capacity and the money to maintain adequate conventional and nuclear arms. 'We really cannot fight any war *except* a nuclear war', confessed defence minister Harold Macmillan in 1954. 'It is quite impossible to arm our forces with *two* sets of weapons – conventional and unconventional'.[9]

Given the huge unprecedented challenges, the quality of leadership and the relationship between prime minister and foreign secretary were decisive. Good chemistry smoothed the way, but the make or break factor was whether the premier wanted both jobs. The Attlee–Bevin partnership was less fruitful than commonly supposed. Attlee allowed Bevin too long a leash. Unfettered by a cabinet foreign affairs committee, Bevin was authorized to chair ministerial meetings of overseas departments without constituting a committee reporting to the cabinet. As a result, policies escaped close scrutiny. Magnificent on the home front, Attlee faltered overseas. He got off to a good start, envisaging the downsizing of empire and a rethinking of international relations in a nuclear era, but would not fight his corner. Bevin and the Chiefs of Staff baulked at the suggestion of withdrawal from the Middle East and Mediterranean.

The unparalleled challenges demanded strong teamwork between premier and foreign secretary. Small and unprepossessing, Clem the clam – as King George VI nicknamed him – never wasted a word where none would do. A news clip shows him being interviewed in 1950 – so laconic that a despairing interviewer asks, 'Have you anything to add, prime minister?' To which Attlee replied 'No, I don't think so'. Truncated speech turned off dialogue. A telephone call to Frank Pakenham, minister for British zones in Germany and Austria, gave Pakenham a chance to pre-empt the use of the 'retort monosyllabic' by adopting it himself:

Clem Is that you, Frank?

Frank Yes.

Clem I've spoken to Ernie about the point you raised.

Frank Yes

Clem It's all part of a very big picture he's discussing with the Americans. It's one of a number of things.

Frank   Yes

Clem   He's going to get in touch with you before the end of the week

Frank   Yes – thank you very much.

Clem   Right. Good-bye

Frank   Right [*rings off*]¹⁰

In cabinet Attlee doodled but never dawdled. He would start by praising the paper under discussion, then say, turning to the minister who proposed it, that he presumed he did not wish to add anything to so excellent a presentation of the case. That usually silenced him. The next step was to move rapidly to a conclusion, by saying, 'Well, if no one has any objection, we'll let that go'. 'His summing-up was often blurred and incomplete and he rarely produced any constructive ideas of his own'.¹¹ Attlee knew how to take care of himself. With sterling on the rocks he escaped to 'Lords on Saturday morning and Wimbledon on Saturday afternoon, and went down to Chequers for the weekend' – rereading Gibbon.¹²

Ernie, unlike Clem, loved to do the talking – rambling, repetitive and tactless, telling Molotov that he sounded like Hitler. Though vexed by lack of cabinet response to foreign policy questions – 'none of them seemed interested' – he did not welcome advice from junior ministers, 'That young man, 'e worries me'. His jokes and anecdotes tended to strangle serious reflection. Advisers translated 'often rambling and rather chaotic discussions' into a coherent document, but were kept on a tight leash. For all the feisty talk of a new Palmerston, inexperienced junior ministers increasingly covered for an ailing foreign secretary.¹³

Churchill's clinging to office and determination to control overseas policy in his government of 1951–5 fuelled a bitchy, acrimonious relationship with Crown Prince Eden. Consciousness of failing powers made the seventy-six-year-old the more determined in 1951 to concentrate on his hobbyhorses: defence and foreign policy. Whenever Eden went away, including honeymooning in 1952, Churchill jumped into the driving seat.

The foreign secretary's glamour boy image of the 1930s concealed a vain, irascible, overstrung make-up. His 'Anthony Eden', a black Homburg hat the symbol of pre-war popularity, sat on a side table in the office where charladies dusted it reverently. In a temper he was almost uncontrollable. In Lisbon his taxi driver ignored instructions to go to the French embassy, setting off instead for the American. Halfway there Eden, realizing the mistake, went berserk. 'It developed', wrote his secretary 'into a physical struggle between me trying to shut the window between us and the driver ... and A.E. leaning forward to wind it down so that he might call them bloody fools!'¹⁴

Living on his nerves, unwell, and compulsively interfering, Eden was temperamentally unsuited to the premiership. Too long in the giant's shadow, he lacked the killer instinct to challenge Churchill's party leadership after the 1945 election defeat. Macmillan barely lasted nine months as Eden's foreign secretary. Differing approaches to Europe and the Middle East, combined with the prime minister's micro-management, created friction. Macmillan's successor Lloyd was rung up thirty times over a Christmas weekend.

Appointed in 1951 as a junior foreign office minister Lloyd's sense of inadequacy is best conveyed in his own words, 'I think there must be some mistake. I do not speak any foreign language ... I do not like foreigners ... I have never spoken in a Foreign Affairs debate ... I have never listened to one'. From December 1955 an 'over-promoted' Lloyd became foreign secretary, compounding Eden's micro-management. 'It becomes daily more apparent', complained an under-secretary, 'that we have no secretary of state'. 'WEU dinner', noted Lloyd, 'very long discussions about Six – Seven after dinner – my trouble is that I am so tired by the end of the day that I am incapable of remembering next day what took place the day before'.[15]

'We have all been too long in office', confessed a senior Labour leader. Tiredness and illness meant poor decisions. By the summer of 1945 Churchill and Eden were so fagged out that they 'could no longer look at the problems properly and read the papers about them. It had become mere improvisation.' Bevin's health deteriorated fast – coronary thrombosis in 1946, increasingly severe angina. Sailing to New York in October 1946 he 'collapsed as soon as he relaxed on the boat ... spent each of the 3 days we have been at sea in bed till tea-time'. His junior minister noted: 'EB is not doing well at the Council of Foreign Ministers. There is a lack of leadership, initiative and even clear thinking in our delegation. Ernest knows he is below par.'[16]

Serious illness ravaged Churchill's peacetime administration of 1951–5, incapacitating premier and foreign secretary for weeks and months. Almost constant ill-health (itself ill-treated) plagued Eden until the end of 1953. A black tin box of medicines accompanied the red boxes. A severe infection and the misuse of sleeping pills and amphetamines almost certainly impaired the premier's judgement in the Suez imbroglio. Overwork killed forward thinking.[17]

Wartime treadmill became post-war norm. The American loan negotiations in the autumn of 1945 required late night meetings virtually every weekday evening from mid-September to mid-December. Frequent and lengthy ministerial absences abroad tightened the screw. Bevin complained that 'he had no minister in the FO' since his junior ministers had arranged independently of one another, and of him', to be in New York. Overload became part of Whitehall culture – enhancing institutional and individual self-esteem. In the 1960s Labour frontbenchers like Barbara Castle turned overload into a political virility symbol.[18]

A broken-backed Churchill administration was incapable of forceful and imaginative management of external policy: 'I feel like an aeroplane at the end of its flight, in the dusk, with the petrol running out, in search of a safe landing', confessed Churchill. 'It's a pity we are governed by crocks', commented a senior official. Despite the urgency of new machinery and policy options, the giant in decay had no appetite for modernizing Whitehall. Even before a major stroke in June 1953, a colleague described the old man as 'terribly drooling ... fast losing his grip'. 'Things have gotten ten or fifteen times more complicated', Churchill confessed; 'the problems I now face are much greater in number and complexity than they used to be'. 'He is, of course', concluded Macmillan, 'physically and mentally incapable of a serious negotiation'. Stiffened with champagne and piloted by the cabinet secretary the warlord managed routine business but lacked the will and energy to follow up ideas and descry the whole field of policy. Early in 1954 two senior ministers informed him he was unfit to be prime minister; by the summer Macmillan and others considered him mentally unbalanced.[19]

Horror stories about overstretch abounded. 'One has got used during these past three years to apparently insoluble programmes of work', recorded one of Bevin's secretaries, 'but at the beginning of last week I really thought our machine would crack under it. S of S [Secretary of State] himself was unwell, we were one short and there was never a clear run in which to make our preparations for New York ... The pressure is becoming appalling, and Niko [Nicholas Henderson] and I are really finding it hard to keep our heads above water.' A permanent secretary tracked the pressures: 'The mind revolted against the reading of discourses and articles that had no immediate bearing on day-to-day problems. The next resistance erected would be against aimless discussions at large about foreign affairs ... the mind was attempting to shed all but the inescapable task of dealing with essential interviews or with the flow of papers.' An FO junior minister found the job overwhelming: 'I have been busier than ever before in my life, not only is it too tiring, but it prevents one ever reading the press properly or talking to one's friends or fellow members [MPs]. Already I feel out of touch with everything but the FO which is thoroughly bad for my judgment.'[20]

Parliament and cabinet contributed little to policy-making. Decision-making preceded parliamentary discussion and was rarely influenced by it. Backbench ginger groups – Tory Suez Group, Labour's Little Englanders and Bevanites – were lucky if they managed to squeeze tactical concessions from ministers. Parliamentary Questions were designed to embarrass ministers rather than elicit information. They were 'taken seriously only if it was thought that the Member who tabled a question already knew the answer so that he could put an embarrassing supplementary'. Unlike committees of the United States Congress, defence and foreign affairs committees had no power to subpoena ministers and officials. Labour Party left winger Aneurin Bevan reprimanded the wartime coalition for evasiveness on external policy: 'The ordinary man ... has been spending his life for the last couple of generations in this will-o'-the wisp pursuit of power, trying to get his hands on the levers of big policy, and trying to find out where it is, and how it was that his life was shaped for him by somebody else. We were convinced by our institutions and representative democracy that the House of Commons itself was that instrument ... but these debates ... have convinced me that the House of Commons is becoming almost irrelevant.'[21]

In theory, the cabinet was a forum for review and discussion; in practice, it had 'no common basis to its thinking ... quite unequal to big decisions'. Power lay with ad hoc committees which did not report to cabinet – their existence unknown to many cabinet members. Too engrossed in their own patch, ministers could not keep up with international affairs, and pressure of business left no time for discussion. 'Foreign affairs statements' were 'the least invigorating part of Cabinet business' and a really good foreign affairs debate in the cabinet was a rare event. This suited senior ministers. Chancellor Hugh Dalton preferred not to initiate discussions on foreign affairs in the cabinet 'where so many knew so little and, if you gave them an opening, talked so much'. Various ploys discouraged debate. Attlee's fire-extinguisher style closed down issues: 'it is no good your coming here so ill-prepared and wasting everyone's time.' Restricted distribution of FO telegrams blocked informed debate. In his premiership of

1951–5 Churchill could count on affection and loyalty for an elder statesman inhibiting unwelcome discussion. A professed liking for free ranging debate usually meant lengthy Churchillian monologues, with colleagues slipping away as lunchtime approached; another ploy was to send for Eden and talk him out of circulating papers.[22]

Even the Cuban missile crisis of 1962, the most important international crisis since the war, did not engage the whole cabinet: 'I told the Cabinet about Cuba,' recorded Macmillan, 'which they are quite happy to leave to me and Alec Home' [foreign secretary]. Labour premier Harold Wilson sought to concentrate all decisions in his own hands. The decline of the full cabinet can be measured in the frequency of meetings and papers circulated. The Attlee government averaged 87 meetings annually with 340 papers; by the early 1970s the average was 60 and 140 memoranda. The tendency to settle everything in committee ensured perfunctory discussion on core items. By centralizing decision-making in specialist committees Wilson bypassed the cabinet. The full cabinet was encouraged to talk itself out. 'We shall go into Europe on a wave of exhaustion', noted one minister. 'Just boring our way in', a colleague scribbled back. In 1967 Richard Crossman, Lord President, urged a committee on devaluation unaware that one already existed. Wilson conceded that it was 'increasingly difficult for a minister to play a constructive role in the collective business of the government as a whole'.[23]

Foreign policy was not formulated in committee. Attlee and Churchill did not revive the pre-war foreign affairs committee, and the defence committee met infrequently. The merging of external affairs departments in the 1960s strengthened prime ministerial influence. In 1945 overseas policy had seven cabinet representatives: foreign, commonwealth and colonial secretaries, together with three secretaries of state for the army, navy and air force, and a minister for defence; by 1968 there were only two cabinet ministers for external affairs, the foreign secretary and the defence secretary: 'the external departments had little prospect of winning their case unless the prime minister himself threw his weight behind them.'[24]

After lauding Attlee's engine room as 'the acme of efficiency', a historian of British government recanted, acknowledging that 'administrative elephantiasis' better describes it. 'The coincidence of the end of the war with the beginning of the new Labour government', observed a cabinet office economist, 'has put a strain of work on the central Whitehall machine such as I cannot remember since I came to Whitehall in 1940'. Ministers were alerted that 'the increasing volume of international work was already in danger of imposing intolerable strains on the machinery of national government'. In 1954 a senior politician sounded the alarm: 'The civil service gives us loyal, devoted and competent service; but the chief officers ... like the ministers, are so encumbered with a host of problems that very few have time or energy left to sit back and think'. Lord Hailsham, Lord President in the Macmillan government, warned 'the present system' was 'breaking down'. Cabinet secretary Norman Brook confided that he would not be able 'to carry on ... without having a physical and mental breakdown'.[25]

The mandarinate was part of the problem. Public school and Oxbridge-educated officials distrusted outsiders. Strict enforcement of the Official Secrets Act strengthened inwardness, minimizing interaction with non-governmental communities and inhibiting the exploration of alternatives. Entrants learned on the job without formal training. The institutional ethos prized generalists rather than specialists, privileging conformity, hierarchy and cooperation rather than creativity, originality and imagination. The emphasis on hierarchy and conformity made it more difficult to speak the truth to those in power. By the 1950s the higher civil service, virtually unchanged since the mid-Victorian reforms implementing the 1854 Northcote-Trevelyan Report, urgently required a make-over. The absence of specialist training comparable to France's ENA presented a glaring deficiency. 'By general European standards', concluded civil servant and poet Charles Sisson, 'the education of our administrators is inadequate and their training slipshod'.[26]

The Whitehall bubble isolated senior officials. A cabinet office official 'felt uncomfortable' about the 'strange restricted world with narrow frontiers of convention' that bounded the lives of the mandarinate, noting: 'most of them move and have their daily being in a sort of intellectual camp, bounded by the House of Parliament, the Embankment ... Charing Cross, Northumberland Avenue, Trafalgar Square, Pall Mall, St. James's Park, Storey's Gate and so back to Parliament Square, a narrow world indeed where the only outsiders were banner carrying deputations ... and where most of the pubs were clubs'. In the 1930s upper echelons lived in central London, enjoying a social life that enabled them to see the world 'through other than Whitehall eyes'; by the 1950s few could afford to do so and found it hard to maintain social contacts outside official life. An Olympian-like conviction that the mandarinate had a monopoly of wisdom produced 'a certain disregard of the world of ideas, on the one hand, and what might be called common opinion on the other'.[27]

Whitehall asserted superior knowledge and wisdom. A discussion of defence issues between a scientific adviser and a distinguished cabinet secretary 'was at cross-purposes' until the adviser discovered that the cabinet secretary believed Aden was an island. A hermetic machine blurred issues, making it more difficult to assess their unique features. From wartime Washington DC Isaiah Berlin described the process: 'I have talked to no labor leaders or intellectuals, nobody but officials now for so long that I am beginning to acquire that frosted glass view of events ... dim contours each very much like the other – which I realize is the typical officials' normal panorama and not a cynical defeatist vision at all'. Whitehallese, especially Foreign Office speak, reinforced the bubble, blocking effective communication. In Churchill's words, 'If you want a line of policy from an F.O. memorandum you must send either the paragraphs with even numbers or those with odd numbers. Every alternate paragraph begins "On the other hand..."'[28]

Civil service reform stayed on the back burner. Critics inveighed against amateurishness, a dearth of economic and scientific expertise, and the social exclusiveness of the top tier administrative class. Anthony Sampson's best-selling broadside against the establishment, *Anatomy of Britain* (1962), targeted dilettantism and the old boy network. Several years passed before the publication of the deeply flawed Fulton Report of 1968. In the meantime, Labour's restructuring of government stretched the service to its limits.[29] Why did the modernizing Labour government of 1964–70 miss the opportunity for a fundamental rethink? Whitehall's culture of complacency and secrecy deterred root and branch reform: 'The gentleman in Whitehall knows best ... and the gentleman who dares to question Whitehall is no gentleman'. The service's reputation as 'the best in the world' shielded it from investigation. The Fulton Report, wrote the official historian of the civil service, 'might have been modified by strong, external political leadership', but Wilson and his allies were 'uninterested in serious reform'. By the mid-1960s the public viewed the higher civil service as 'overmanned' and 'overpaid' – incoming Labour ministers in 1964 were said to be suspicious of their permanent advisers. Thereafter Whitehall was 'subjected to a decade of vilification … as a principal cause of Britain's relative decline and ungovernability'.

The FO, the main engine of overseas policy, occupied Giles Gilbert Scott's citadel-like Victorian palazzo. The department was unfit for purpose. 'It needs the most drastic overhaul, physically and morally,' warned a senior diplomat in 1945, 'it's not that the average ability isn't high enough, but the whole machine is slow, cumbrous and obsolete; and there is still too much of the anointment with holy oil.' Nevertheless, the FO had to wrestle with more challenges than at any other point in its history: its own obsoletism, the modernizing Eden–Bevin reforms of 1943; Cold War defections of senior diplomats; the Suez affair; two major external investigations of the service within a decade; amalgamation in 1968 with the Commonwealth Relations Office to form the Foreign and Commonwealth Office (FCO). Having the worst public image of all Whitehall departments did nothing for morale. The FO was the favourite whipping boy of politicians, press and Treasury. The antics of Terry-Thomas and Peter Sellers in Roy Boulting's film *Carlton-Browne of the FO* (1959) traded on the popular perception of diplomats as an effete, effeminate enclave of striped suits, rolled umbrellas and rolled-up minds. Labour's foreign secretary George Brown, denounced 'cynical, long-haired young gentlemen toddling from one cocktail party to another, never meeting ordinary people, and proclaiming a belief in nothing at all'.[30]

Isolated within Whitehall as well as from the general public, the department skirmished regularly with Treasury knights, MPs and press barons. From their trenches diplomats repelled critics, oversaw internal reform and tried to rebuild morale shattered by spy scandals and fall-out from the Suez affair. Former foreign secretary Douglas Hurd recalled a 'defensive mood' when he joined in the 1950s; 'people were trying to take things away from us or to hit us, or to change things in a way which we thought unreasonable'. In the early post-war years the implementation of the 1943 Foreign Service Act, the 'Eden–Bevin reforms', liberalizing recruitment and creating for the first time a unified foreign service, had priority. Westminster and the press kept close tabs on the modernization. The exclusion of women until 1946 – apart from Mrs Mops and 'typewriter ladies' – represented an incalculable loss of talent. The service admitted only four women between 1946 and 1948, none occupied senior positions in the 1950s and the first woman ambassador was only appointed in 1976. All entrants were thrown in at the deep end, learning on the job – by contrast, Quai d'Orsay candidates spent over two years at the ENA, while State Department recruits followed a training programme at the Foreign Service Institute (FSI).[31]

The Treasury harried the FO mercilessly. A 1955 report censured diplomats for leisurely habits of work, overly rigid divisions between departments and a negative attitude to criticism. The Treasury, supported by the Board of Trade, succeeded in the mid-1950s in dominating policy-making on Europe. From the early 1960s the department regained ground, only to lose it to Downing Street after 1964. Treasury knights decisively shaped ministerial approaches to Europe in two instances: from June to December 1955, as the ECSC Six launched new integration initiatives, the Treasury led the definition of policy; in 1960–1 Sir Frank Lee, joint permanent secretary at the Treasury, and Freddie Bishop, deputy secretary of the cabinet, initiated significant changes in official attitudes towards the EEC.

Obsolescence was the biggest obstacle to coherent policymaking. 'Exasperation amounting to demoralization (and I mean it) at the obsoletism of the FO machine,' complained an official. Attlee protested repeatedly about 'the dilatory practice of the Foreign Office' – on one occasion waiting four days for an answer to a request for information. FO departments inhabited 'a little world of their own', putting up 'suggestions which are clearly in conflict with the government's domestic policy and even with our own foreign policy in some other part of the globe'. Multiplication of staff and paper gave 'little time to think, to look ahead and to make wise long-term plans'. Overseas postings offered more leisure – future Conservative foreign secretary Douglas Hurd found time in the 1950s to write novels. Economics was the department's Achilles heel. An entrant in 1945 was 'struck by the fact that hardly any of the career members knew any economics'. Only political jobs carried prestige – 'consular, economic and commercial jobs were considered demeaning'. Not until 1944 did the Foreign Office acquire its own set of economic advisers. Economic work had less appeal because it was more intellectually demanding – no short cuts, no skimming or skipping. The downgrading of economic expertise represented a huge disability at a time when it mattered more than ever. Treasury permanent secretary Sir Frank Lee conceded that relations with Europe had suffered 'by reason of the comparative indifference with which FO ministers have tended in the past to regard the economic issues involved in the problem of the Six and the Seven'.[32]

Permanent secretaries mostly functioned as office managers, not policy-makers. Alexander Cadogan kept a detailed diary but offered no suggestions on how things might be better ordered. 'Moley' Orme Sargent, his Cassandra-like successor, did not push his views. Bereft of political skills he resembled 'a philosopher strayed into Whitehall. He knew all the answers; when politicians did not want them he went out to lunch'. Reserved, tactful, cautious to a fault, William Strang was 'not a policy-maker such as one might expect from a Permanent Under-Secretary'. A grammar-school entrant, he was 'constantly exhibited like a prize heifer as a proof of our profound democracy'. The bustling and combative Ivone Kirkpatrick 'did not like meetings or advice, acted on his own' and 'had little use for research or analysis or for prolonged discussion'. Frederick Hoyer Millar brought a touch of the old grandee style. A private fortune enabled him to take time off to attend Ascot or a parade of the Scots Guards, and to distribute grouse from his Perthshire estate. Rarely intervening in policy matters, the restoration of office morale after Suez preoccupied him. Brisk, energetic and hardworking Harold Caccia 'immersed himself in policy' and made frequent interventions. In the autumn of 1964 he initiated the first daily conferences of senior officials. Paul Gore-Booth appeared overwhelmed by events and personalities – Duncan enquiry (1969), merger of the FO and CRO (1968), and not least foreign secretary George Brown. Gore-Booth lacked empathy – never extending a 'timely word of thanks and praise' to the many forced to take early retirement as a result of office reorganization. Nor did he battle for his staff – allowing Brown to sack the ambassador in Paris, Sir Patrick Reilly. 'The particular manner', noted an obituarist, 'of his unswerving loyalty to his master was not ... fully intelligible to his younger colleagues'.[33]

Divided control presented a huge handicap in formulating a coherent policy. In 1945 nine separate ministries with different communication systems shared responsibility for overseas policy. By 1964 the main stakeholders were the FO, CRO and CO. Bevin and Eden had to argue and agree policy with the Commonwealth and Colonial Secretaries. Multilateralism cut across ministerial and departmental boundaries. The urgency of economic, financial and strategic issues brought incessant consultation and bargaining with core Whitehall players via interdepartmental committees on which the FO was one voice among many. Until the late 1950s the economic ministries drove foreign economic policy – a key committee on European integration had only one FO representative. The reconciling of conflicting viewpoints absorbed energies, lengthening lead times. Excessive coordination, complained a Labour politician, meant that the workload on a minister was much greater in the mid-1960s than during the Second World War. What took three hours to decide in 1944 often took three months in 1965.[34]

Did leadership deficiencies and a ramshackle engine spell relegation? Not necessarily. Thinking in time would have sparked innovative ideas. Foreign secretaries and grandees nursed a deep aversion to forward thinking. Sans think tanks and effective coordinating machinery, the highly compartmentalized conduct of day-to-day business proved a liability. Prime resources – the library and research department – were tucked away in a dingy block south of the Thames. By spring 1949 when Bevin authorized a permanent under-secretary's committee (PUSC) 'to identify the longer-term trends in international affairs' the defining decisions for the coming decade were already taken. Eden allowed the committee to wither.

Six years on the FO established a planning section – staffed by *one* middle-ranking diplomat. Responding to recommendations in the Plowden Report of 1964 the department rustled up more staff, but the unit did not play a mainstream role until the early 1970s. The history of structured reflection, confessed a permanent secretary, was 'one of much trial and a good deal of error ... work suffered from papers being submitted to detailed scrutiny by senior people who had not the time to supervise them properly'. Planners 'did not proceed from an assessment of British interests but ... from the fact of Britain's strained economic situation ... rarely did the policy thinkers try to start from the bottom up ... to define in some detail where British interests lay and then decide what the priorities were.'[35]

Bevin claimed to be 'following a plan which had been carefully worked out, and which would take at least five years before it assumed its final shape', but there was little sense of a defined current policy, let alone a five-year plan. 'One of my first actions', recalled one of Bevin's junior ministers, 'was to approach a certain very shrewd and experienced official to ask innocently for some document which would tell me just what the current foreign policy ... was'. The answer was 'not merely that no such document existed' but 'that it was really rather doubtful whether we had a foreign policy in the proper sense at all'.[36]

Two big external inquiries within a decade – Plowden (1964), Duncan (1969) – and a merger with the Commonwealth Office demoralized diplomats. 'Since 1962', protested permanent secretary Paul Gore-Booth, 'we have been under examination, amalgamation, merging, re-organizing and now we are under examination again'. Rated 'weak and ineffective', Gore-Booth had his work cut out to keep the ship afloat. Policy-makers lacked an effective planning unit. In the 1950s a one-man section in the Western Organizations department oversaw a global waterfront. Tipped off about the recommendations of the Plowden Report the department scrambled to create an independent unit under Michael Palliser. Palliser fought for several months to secure an office close to the Secretary of State's room. Lacking resources and access to ministers, planners had to sell their ideas to operational departments. The expanded section produced little on France and Europe: 'We ... kept off the European issue because there were so many people working on it, our job was really to act as a catalyst, and the European issue was already at the top of the agenda.'[37]

De Gaulle's second veto highlighted troubling gaps in policy research. Defence minister Denis Healey requested urgently 'three contingency studies': a study of how free we would be 'over the next three years to change our policies ... to our own advantage'; an investigation of areas like technology where it might be an advantage to keep good relations with the Community; a review of alternative relationships between West European states, including a collective relationship between EFTA and the EEC. Reappointed foreign secretary in March 1968, Stewart set up 'quarterly talks' with planning staff, making known his preference for big, open-ended questions: 'I ... suggest that they should consider the question of how an affluent argumentative society – such as the West – can keep in condition to resist Communism's Spartan attitude.'[38]

The lack of a wider non-governmental international affairs community impoverished policy-making. Retreat from power did not spark a national conversation or interaction between government and lay opinion. Gold star international networks like the Bilderberg and Königswinter conferences gave the political elite opportunities to talk to foreign counterparts but not fellow citizens. By the early 1950s the principal think tank, Chatham House (Royal Institute of International Affairs), looked decidedly staid. Denis Healey found the American Council on Foreign Relations in New York 'much more effective ... in engaging the interest of key figures from the city outside'. In 1954 the *Observer* and the *Manchester Guardian* berated the think tank for 'lack of purpose ... and a certain failure to make a proper impact on the public mind ... There are numerous discussion groups, frequent conferences, a massive list of publications ... But there is little or no guidance to distinguish between what really matters and what is of only marginal importance ... It is by fostering vigorous controversy on key problems that Chatham House can best fulfill its role'. As the FO emerged from its carapace, Chatham House retreated. From 1958 the FO Research Department made several overtures, inviting feedback on its papers; 'we have felt for some time that some of these papers would have benefited from the advice of experts outside the Foreign Service'. Wary of working with Whitehall because of the press onslaught and the receipt of FO funding, director Kenneth Younger repelled advances: 'although our relations with the FO are quite close we are in no way part of the official machine. I think if we were to join this group, people would draw the contrary conclusion.'[39]

Policy-makers not only failed to think in time, they neglected a prime resource – the usable past. The governing elite seemed indifferent to the national experience and institutional memory. Drawing on a multi-decade career as official historian of the UK Atomic Energy Authority (UKAEA), Professor Margaret Gowing criticized government for 'neglecting history'. Historians, she pointed out, were just as necessary to government as economists. Frequent changes of people, policies and machinery obliterated institutional memory: 'In my 33 years as an official historian, working on thousands of recent files in many government departments ... I have found that the recording even of high policy has often been inadequate and that when the record exists, subsequent policy formation has often taken no account of it or has misunderstood it.'[40]

'If you want to reform a great institution', remarked a cabinet secretary of the 1990s, 'you must understand it; and if you want to understand it, you need to understand its past'. Cabinet secretary Norman Brook's 'funding experience' initiative of 1957 attempted to change attitudes and encourage Whitehall in-house narratives but soon ran into the sands. In practice, 'the historical dimension was more frequently ignored than used by policymakers'. The initiative foundered because no provision was made for monitoring and review. Government had no interest in keeping up reform momentum. Historical memory building initiatives were considered soft targets for spending cuts. Two fundamental questions went unexamined: the integration of in-house histories into current policy-making; making Whitehall history part of mainstream academic history, and bringing academics and practitioners into conversation.[41]

Ex-diplomat Harold Nicolson eulogized British diplomacy 'as almost miraculously effective – continental critics are united in the awe with which they regard ... our masterly handling of the balance of power'. Zeal for his old profession got the better of Nicolson. The FO was unfit for purpose. 'The root of the trouble', observed an official, 'is that we are, no doubt inevitably, trying to deal with problems which are the direct product of new conditions and circumstances by applying completely worn-out standards'. Instead of thinking through issues the FO attempted 'to recreate those conditions which produced the kind of status which it believed was Britain's right, rather than adapting to the new power-political conditions existing at the end of the Second World War'.[42]

The Attlee government had an opportunity to revaluate national strategy and devise appropriate initiatives. *The Times* considered that 'If Mr Attlee and his chief colleagues have both the will and the capacity to seize the chance offered to them, they can transform the quality of government almost over-night. Their opportunity is nothing less than the salvation of Britain: it is in direct proportion to the magnitude of the difficulties with which they are confronted'. The mix of obsolescent engine and exhausted leaders produced inadequate responses. The American loan talks in the autumn of 1945 that helped lock Britain into a dependency culture did not have to take the form they did. Ministers 'had not seriously studied alternatives, such as consultations with other West European countries'. Commenting on the Macmillan government's rethinking of attitudes towards Europe in the late 1950s, the editor of *Documents on British Policy Overseas* remarked: 'in the typical British manner this reversal of policy came several years after the initial policy had begun to crumble.'[43]

An episode of the TV sitcom *Dad's Army* epitomized the prevailing back-of-an envelope, muddling-through culture: German invasion forces in 1940 enjoy a large HQ and detailed maps – Captain Mainwaring, commander of the Walmington-on-Sea Home Guard, relies on the village hall and an AA road map. Muddling through occasionally worked and officials cheered: 'There was an amazing process of muddling through but it came out quite well', enthused a Ministry of Defence official on the Wilson government's decision of 1967 to withdraw from east of Suez. Mostly it didn't. Thinking in time was no panacea but with so few cards in hand it was essential to play them with the utmost skill and deliberation. At the end of the day Bevin relaxed and let his mind 'expand' with Harvey's Bristol Cream sherry. Alas, liberal servings of sherry and the foreign secretary's "edgerows of experience' were not enough.[44]

Part Three

Bids

8

Unshakable, Constant, Effective

Parisians chanted 'Chur-chill' as the premier walked down the Champs-Elysees at de Gaulle's side on Armistice Day 11 November 1944. 'The alliance with France', promised Churchill, 'should be unshakable, constant, and effective'. Rapprochement seemed the natural expression of post-Liberation euphoria. 'Unforgettable days and nights,' recalled a British observer, 'when the toughest French and British hearts were fit to burst with love, and it seemed the whole world must be warmed by so much cheering.' In April 1945 79 per cent of French people polled wanted an alliance with Britain. Time was of the essence. 'Never have circumstances so favoured a Franco–British rapprochement. We have three months of euphoria to realize it; perhaps less; afterwards it may be too late', urged a French adviser. Three years later, after talks with French premier Paul Ramadier, Bevin claimed: 'We've made the union of England and France this morning'. 'If there was a window for the development of a special Anglo–French relationship', writes historian Andrew Knapp, 'it was surely in 1944–47.'[1]

Alliance-shy divas decided otherwise. The prime minister flew home empty-handed, having banned in advance any negotiations. The Treaty of Dunkirk of March 1947 was a far cry from the close relationship trumpeted in 1944. Minefields separated London and Paris: Middle East rivalry, France's German claims, and the design of a West European bloc. French delays in granting independence to mandated Syria and the Lebanon brought London and Paris to the brink of war in June 1945. French troops, de Gaulle warned, had orders to fire on Syrian and British soldiers if force was used against them. Minefields can be cleared, however. A Syrian settlement came in 1946, and mutual goodwill could have defused other disputes, including Germany. Great power ambitions, personality conflicts and defective policy engines combined to scupper an alliance.

Cooperation offered a fulcrum for a Franco–British Europe, and London had the initiative. 'France has not – and will not have for several years – the material resources of a great power', Raymond Aron told a Chatham House audience in 1945. Two decades later France's assertion of primacy in Western Europe provoked British politicians and commentators to ask what went wrong. Anthony Nutting's *Europe Will Not Wait* claimed Britain 'could have had the leadership of Europe on any terms which she cared to name'. Debating 'lost opportunities' became a stamping ground for historians. Bevin is said to have 'spurned' leadership. 'It is not true', wrote Alan Milward, 'that the United Kingdom had a fund of goodwill in Europe on which it could have traded to lead Europe in support of shared common interests. Europe was not asking to be led'. John

Young opined: 'The fact is that Britain could not have had the leadership of Europe on its own terms because Britain saw no need to abandon its sovereignty to common institutions'.[2]

As the strongest West European state and member of the 'Big Three' wartime alliance, Britain in 1945 possessed both primacy and a large fund of goodwill. Approval ratings had never stood higher. The director of the British Institute in Prague described how 'people, hearing us talking in English, ran after us, sometimes with tears in their eyes, to tell us how glad they were that we had come; as if "we" were the precursors of a relieving army for which they had been waiting'. Nobel novelist Thomas Mann, observed Harold Nicholson, 'really believes that the English are the hope of the world ... Only we can establish "humanistic socialism."'[3] So what happened? The timeline is crucial. Britain wanted to take the initiative but what seemed desirable in 1945 quickly looked unrealistic. Britain lacked the wherewithal to build a European bloc. By the close of 1950 an Anglo–American-sponsored Atlanticist Europe had replaced Bevin's Western Union proposal for a Franco–British Europe.

Initially, prospects for a British-led Europe appeared promising. In a 'Stocktaking' exercise of July 1945 planners advised the Attlee government that influence should be increased by encouraging 'cooperation between the three World Powers', and by leadership of the Dominions, France and smaller West European powers – 'only so shall we be able to compel our two big partners to treat us as an equal.' Ministers accepted that rapprochement with France should underpin a wider West European

Figure 8.1 Winston Churchill in Paris, with his daughter Mary and British ambassador Alfred Duff Cooper, 1945.

grouping, giving London extra muscle in Washington and Moscow. 'There was a tendency in the United States', counselled an adviser, 'to consider the UK as an exhausted and rather second rate Power, the USSR treated us with scant consideration. If we became the recognized and vigorous leader of a group of Western Powers with large dependent territories we could gain weight in the counsels of the Big Three ... the obvious starting point for such a grouping was a close association with France'.[4] The mission statement left the shape of a Franco–British Europe undefined.

Early in 1947 mandarins checked the temperature. Drafted in the middle of one of the worst winters on record the document made grim reading. The main assumption of 1945, Big Three cooperation, had dissolved. The necessity for an independent British foreign policy was judged 'still valid', but in the light of the nation's weakness and Soviet threats, 'too great an independence of the United States would be a dangerous luxury'. The goal of leading Western democratic states held good but Britain could not play an active role in solving European economic problems because 'we do not seem to have any economic resources available for political purposes'. Britain could offer only the model of a successful Labour government as a 'workable alternative to Communism'.[5] A sea of troubles engulfed Britons: dollar drain, food and fuel shortages, fears of Soviet expansion, civil war in Greece, rebellion in Palestine, withdrawal from India, the soaring cost of the British zone of occupation in Germany, and 'General Winter'. Huddled in overcoats the cabinet met by candlelight. Bevin's charwoman asked to start work in the mornings at 6am instead of 7 so that she could be away by 10am to make sure of a place in food queues for her family.

By 1948 VE-Day prestige had lost its fizz. Britain's reluctance to commit to European supranational ideals corroded continental goodwill. In 1945 journalist and politician Pierre Maillaud from the BBC's wartime French service warned that half-heartedness towards Europe would 'alienate the Continent'. The deepening Cold War and rapid contraction of power eroded the ascendancy of 1945. The haemorrhaging encouraged France and the Benelux countries to pursue their own agendas, lengthening the odds against a Franco–British Europe. London's Atlanticist, intergovernmental vision aroused continental fears of reversion to a traditional divide and rule strategy in Europe. Belgian foreign minister Paul-Henri Spaak later confided his disappointment at the fall from grace, 'You had no idea just how much Britain meant to all of us ... during the years immediately after the war ... she represented something pure and untarnished ... and we looked for ... moral leadership'.[6]

Was a Franco–British Europe a mirage? Not necessarily. Understandably, the French had no desire to recreate the old entente discordiale of the interwar years. But the experience of working together from 1944–5 could have generated trust and momentum for the future. Crucially, leaders were unwilling to reimagine the relationship. Personality conflicts and the neglect of forward thinking prevented a duumvirate. The Churchill government's wartime ban on discussion of post-war Europe, despite the presence of de Gaulle and European governments in exile, stymied the building of an understanding and disadvantaged the incoming Attlee cabinet. The prima donnas, Churchill and de Gaulle, opposed rapprochement on their watches, while shrinking from the opprobrium of openly obstructing it. From London, ambassador Massigli vented his frustration, deploring his country's ingratitude to

Britain and intransigence in Syria: 'England passionately wished for an entente in 1944 and even into the middle of 1945 ... you [Chauvel] know how [de Gaulle] by his words and deeds responded'.⁷

Churchill matched de Gaulle's obduracy. Self-styled victim of a megalomaniac – his 'heaviest cross ... the Cross of Lorraine', the prime minister relished infantilizing his adversary: de Gaulle had come back from Washington 'in a most mischievous mood'; 'We should be most unwise to appear to be suppliants. This would give de Gaulle every opportunity for misbehaviour'. The premier sought to outgeneral the general, censuring his ambassador for advocating alliance, 'Why on earth cannot he remain passive and be wooed, instead of always playing into de Gaulle's hands'. The envoy's diary captured the seesaw between the divas: 5 January 1945: 'He [de Gaulle] is not keen on one [alliance] and doesn't wish to appear so. Nor is the prime minister'; April 1945: de Gaulle 'most friendly and most anxious for an Anglo-French treaty while saying "there was no hurry"'. Foreign minister Bidault and Chauvel favoured agreement before the opening of the United Nations foundation conference in San Francisco in late April. Reassured, the ambassador departed on a provincial tour only to find on return that nothing had happened. Churchill, primed for a French initiative, sulked.⁸

Realpolitik ruled. Notwithstanding a soft spot for France, Churchill followed his head, not his heart. At wartime summits prime minister and foreign secretary fought for an independent France as a barrier to Germany, but had no desire to jeopardize Big Three membership by going to bed with a weak and demanding ally. Before going to Paris Churchill flew to Moscow in October 1944 to carve out spheres of influence in Eastern Europe – the percentages agreement with Stalin. Ministers ignored Duff Cooper's warning in June 1945 that without a British lead on a customs union Europe would develop independently. Kowtowing to the United States and the Soviet Union paralysed initiatives on Europe. Committed to Roosevelt's vision of Big Three cooperation, the prime minister feared lest alliance with France might be interpreted as endorsement of de Gaulle's German claims. Regrets about his offer of union in 1940 may have influenced Churchill – he was 'never sure' it was 'a good idea'. Churchill rebuffed President Auriol's request in March 1950 for France's inclusion in East–West summit talks: 'if you took part we would have to bring in Italy'. 'France', he told President Truman in 1953, 'has lived in ignominy ever since the war and enjoyed every moment of it'.⁹

In September 1945 De Gaulle proposed a remodelled Entente pursuing common policies world-wide, including support for French plans to create Rhineland client states while placing the Ruhr under international mandate and giving the Saar autonomy. But the general was in no hurry to tie the knot – fearing France was too weak to get the best terms. Accordingly, in early December 1944, he wooed Stalin, in the hope of enlisting Soviet sympathy for France's German claims and pleasing Communist ministers in his government. Russians were indifferent to the French visit – Londoners would have greeted de Gaulle much more warmly. In the Moscow subway people jostled the general, treading on his large feet as they tried to enter and exit overcrowded carriages. Stalin also trod on the French leader – refusing to underwrite German claims and voting to exclude France from the Yalta Conference in February 1945.

Once bitten, twice shy. The general's belief that Britain bounced France into the Second World War made him chary of an instant pact. No one wanted to rehire the English governess and repeat the Alice in Wonderland world of the 1930s – with London the capital of Paris. The only way to get support for German claims, de Gaulle believed, was to play hard to get. Other concerns impacted. The urgency of mobilizing Anglophobe ex-Vichyites for unity and reconstruction meant avoiding any suggestion of British tutelage. Wishful thinking played a part. A rapid withdrawal of Anglo–American forces from Germany would enable French troops, with Soviet backing, to enforce territorial claims. Deteriorating Anglo–Soviet relations in 1946 applied a further brake – a pact might force France to take sides. Leading Anglophiles like Chauvel and Massigli stood no chance of influencing de Gaulle. Headship of the provisional government put him in the driving seat. An irate general scrawled across one of Massigli's telegrams, 'Idiot'. The efforts of Churchill and Roosevelt to dump him induced paranoia about Anglo-Saxon machinations. 'The Allies! They are betraying us', he thundered in September 1944, 'as they are betraying Europe, the bastards, but I'll make them pay for it'![10]

De Gaulle's low opinion of the French – 'the natural propensity ... to yield to foreigners and become divided' – applied especially to diplomats because of the Quai's pre-war appeasement record. Officials were scolded for truckling to London in the 1930s: 'for many of the men in charge of our foreign relations, concord with England was a kind of principle'. While Bidault honeymooned, the general lambasted the Quai: 'The foreign ministry, led by Massigli and Chauvel, has engaged us in a so-called agreement with the English, which is turning into a swindle ... All that I've said to Bidault on this subject has been wasted.... I insist that no new decisions on this important matter are taken in my absence'.[11]

A tough and experienced foreign minister would have had a hard fight on his hands. For the goblin-like, highly-strung Bidault – 'Georges Bidet', as *Le Canard Enchaîné* dubbed him – there was no contest. Jesuit-educated like his master, looking younger than his 45 years, a fiery opponent of pre-war appeasement, and a founder of the Christian Democrat party *Mouvement republicain populaire* (*MRP*), Bidault became president of the council of the resistance following the Gestapo's execution of Free French representative Jean Moulin in July 1943. His inexperience recommended him to de Gaulle. From day one the general put the former history professor in his place. At the parade celebrating the liberation of Paris the minister started to walk alongside the general only to be told: 'Monsieur, a little further back please'.[12]

The foreign minister's decision to live over the shop gave Chauvel a tutoring opportunity:

> The round table was covered with breakfast leftovers next to all kinds of papers. In the corner of the fireplace grog was heating. On the floor, piles of documents of all kinds were spread out in an order not immediately obvious to the uninitiated ... Bidault, in lambskin slippers, padded about with a cat-like agility, grabbing on the way a salted almond, drinking a mouthful of grog, prodding a book ... I arrived with a big pile of dossiers, inserted myself edgeways into the ministerial monologue ... people came and went, my interlocutor went to shave, dressing himself bit by bit.[13]

Bidault probably learnt little from the crash course – Chauvel's habit of mumbling into his tie and finishing sentences with a hissing noise made him barely audible.

The general bullied and bypassed his foreign minister. On the eve of the London conference of foreign ministers in September 1945 de Gaulle called for a new Franco-British alliance. Bidault learned of it at the conference. Gaullist micromanagement fooled no one. 'The French delegation, unable to express even the worst platitude without prior authorization from General de Gaulle, remained entirely in the background', recorded an American observer at the 1945 UN foundation conference in San Francisco. Serving de Gaulle after playing hide and seek with the Gestapo shattered Bidault's nerves. After eating almost nothing during the day a couple of glasses of wine knocked him out. In December 1944 during the parliamentary debate on the Franco-Soviet Alliance the minister staggered to the podium, hardly able to speak: 'We will do what we say and we will say what we will do', he repeated fifteen times. 'That pig has had one glass too many', barked de Gaulle. Returning to his seat Bidault gasped: 'Have I been too awful?' 'You haven't had the time', snapped his master.[14]

De Gaulle's wedding present to Bidault was a Cartier gold cigarette case left over from gifts taken to Moscow in December 1944. When Bidault became head of government in June 1946 Cartier billed him for the cigarette case – none of the gifts had been paid for. Much worse followed in the early 1960s. Bidault's decision to lead the underground far right OAS (*organization armée secrète*) paramilitary movement against de Gaulle's policy of Algerian independence finished him politically. Having fled to Brazil to escape vengeance he waited until 1968 for an amnesty.

The Churchill–de Gaulle feud made policy rifts harder to settle. Dogfights over Germany, the Middle East and European construction spoke to the unpreparedness of policy-makers and creaky machinery. In the last months of war ministers floundered. 'Altogether our foreign policy seems a sad wreck', bemoaned Eden in March 1945. 'He [Eden] never has time to read our papers now', an aide complained, 'so his handling has become very superficial'.[15] Churchill banned discussions of Europe's future.

The new Labour government had good intentions. 'Without Anglo–French cooperation', affirmed a Labour party pamphlet, 'it is difficult to see how she [Britain] could make her proper contribution to the alliance [Big Three] or be an effective partner rather than a subordinate'.[16] Flawed assumptions, ignorance and stereotypes lamed policy-making. The sudden ending of Lend-Lease in August 1945 could have been anticipated. No one pointed out the need to secure an American loan before the war in Europe ended. UK negotiator John Maynard Keynes lived in cloud cuckoo land, confident of getting most of the loan interest free or as a gift.

Bevin lauded the Entente and called for an 'Anglo–French Monnet Plan', but rebuffed a French appeal for a five-year Anglo–French cooperation plan: 'We don't do things like that in our country'. Bidault expressed astonishment that British and French recovery plans might be shaped or implemented without consultation. UK economic ministries anathematized planning and customs unions. When The *Times* called for a plan to integrate plans, Whitehall riposted: 'It would be better to review the immediate day to day problems as they come'. An Anglo–French economic committee set up by Bevin in 1946 had its remit redefined as one of preventing 'conflicts' rather than harmonizing national economic plans.[17]

Bevin and Bidault were like chalk and cheese. Bevin's patronizing 'such a dear little man' epitomized the relationship. The foreign secretary's respect for former Popular Front leader Leon Blum did not extend to Blum's more doctrinaire colleagues. At a Paris embassy dinner Bevin was 'barely polite' towards socialist ministers. Bevin and his jokes did not travel well. The bayonet-sharp snapshots of interactions with Parisian elites catch the forced jollity. 'Socially he [Bevin] is a bore. Whisky improved his temper and caused him to tell endless stories about drunkards and churchmen. He unbent so far as to sing some songs ... while Mrs. Bevin kept clucking: "Sing us some more Ernest" ... vastly amused, Lady Diana Cooper [ambassadress] beamed on the scene ... with a fond eye'. She was less pleased when Ernie groped her in the embassy lift, urging her to join him in bed. Conviviality was more apparent than real. 'The Embassy staff of elegant young and not so young Etonians ... had obviously fortified themselves for the evening with every drop of alcohol they could lay their hands on'. 'Ernie turned to me,' recalled an aide: 'Now let's tell Monsieur Schuman my story about the bull in an English pub'. This was a story which might have gone down well enough in an English pub, but translated into French in a salon of the Quai d'Orsay 'was not a great success'.[18]

Over two years went by before the signature of a no-frills utility pact in March 1947. Why so long for so little? France seemed a poor bet. 'Looks like civil war within a year', observed Bevin in early 1946, adding, 'the Channel ports will virtually be in Russian hands'. Without the cash and coal France needed, a treaty seemed problematical. Lingering hopes of Big Three cooperation, coupled with the desire to keep in step with the United States, and fear of the international communist movement in France and Western Europe, imposed extreme caution. Without a Whitehall nerve centre, and beset by firestorms in Germany, Greece, India and the Middle East, ministers stumbled from one ill-defined policy to the next. Edward Bridges, permanent secretary to the Treasury, asked the FO to explain to him and other senior colleagues the meaning of Western Union. Alas, the FO was equally at a loss.[19]

In December 1946 an increasingly bumpy ride with the Soviet Union prompted fresh talk of a French alliance to shore up a democratic ally and rally Western Europe. This was music to the ears of Duff Cooper who had campaigned for it since 1944. The ambassador seized the moment and recruited premier Leon Blum. Even without cash and coal an alliance would buttress the Republic. A sense of time running out for Britain's European ambitions spurred FO thinking. The longer the delay in taking an initiative towards Western Europe the less chance of Britain becoming the great European power envisioned in July 1945. 'If we make every move ... contingent on American prior approval,' argued permanent secretary Orme Sargent, 'our prospects of being able to give a lead to western Europe will vanish and we shall never attain ... our primary objective ... to create a European group which will enable us to deal on a footing of equality with our two gigantic neighbours, the USA and the USSR'.[20] Even so, the British constantly looked over their shoulders lest the United States made the Dunkirk Treaty a pretext for pulling out of Europe.

London offered a basic fifty-year defence pact against German aggression, rejecting Duff Cooper's preference for a two-stage arrangement – general treaty followed by detailed agreements on defence, colonial and economic matters. The choice of Dunkirk for the signing evoked unwelcome memories for everyone. Freezing winds and pouring rain assaulted a town in ruins. An old Citroën carrying an official with the treaty text broke down – holding up the ceremony in the Sous-Prefecture – the only rebuilt building. An aide spotted Bevin venting frustration in the courtyard, 'raising his hands to heaven amidst the pouring rain and crying with gusto "I love the French! I love the French!"'. As Bidault headed back to the station fans waylaid him with a song to Jean Bart, the local corsair who savaged English shipping in the Anglo–French conflicts of the 1690s.[21]

Within days officialdom sounded an alert: 'little reliance can be placed in a country whose largest party, dominating the trades unions and controlling half the life of the country, takes its orders from a foreign capital.' Whitehall vetoed economic and military cooperation: 'we have no confidence in French security'. Military weakness and Communist participation in ruling coalitions until May 1947 panicked defence chiefs. Britain, Monnet noted, 'has no confidence that France and the other countries of Europe have the ability or even the will effectively to resist a possible Russian invasion'. The *Observer* newspaper mirrored changing perceptions. Eighteen months after calling for an Anglo–French economic plan the paper warned, 'France is an ally on which we cannot count'.[22]

Britain shrugged off wartime debts to French nuclear know-how, and denied requests for help, citing Anglo–American agreements prohibiting third country

Figure 8.2 French foreign minister Bidault and British foreign secretary Bevin sign Anglo-French alliance in Dunkirk, 4 March 1947. Credit: J. Walforf / INP / AFP / Getty Images.

sharing of nuclear information. Sure, security was an issue. Soviet agents infiltrated French state agencies. Moscow, it is claimed, may have read 'much of the cypher traffic between the Quai d'Orsay and French embassies abroad'. The operative word is 'may'. The quality of secret material accessed is unknown. The Russians hit the jackpot in London, not Paris. British spies – Burgess, Maclean, Fuchs, Philby, Blunt, Vassall – quarried a rich seam for Moscow. Blackballing the French from the nuclear secrets club strengthened their determination to build an independent deterrent. American covert assistance to France in the 1970s made nonsense of earlier Anglo–American negativity.[23]

The Treasury and Board of Trade opposed a customs union, citing adverse trade patterns. France's top trading partner until 1930, Britain lost ground to Germany and the United States. Its main market became North America and the Commonwealth. More to the point, American and German coal replaced British. Within months of loaning France £100 million in March 1945 Britain went bankrupt. Cross-channel trade picked up in 1949–50, but not enough to tempt London. Both countries increasingly competed for the same markets.

But the main stumbling block was Britain's 'one-world strategy', a return to a pre-1931 multilateral free trade regime. The aim was to re-establish the country as a premier commercial and financial player alongside the United States, ending trade discrimination and retaining sterling as a leading reserve currency. Between 1945 and 1950 Britain applied strict import controls as a transitional regime for launching the system. There was no room for a struggling neighbour. Too weak to compete in a global free trade economy without endangering post-Liberation social reforms, France sought shelter in a customs union with access to Britain's imperial trade and preferences.

Dunkirk proved a damp squib – a sop to the French instead of the coal they begged. A leading French historian, J.-B. Duroselle, scathingly dismissed the treaty as 'only a platonic and sentimental gesture – Britain's real policy was to place Anglo–American cooperation above everything else'. This is far too harsh a verdict. No one bought a pig in a poke. Both sides knew the treaty was a sop. Yet it could have jump-started real cooperation – Bevin, despite Whitehall reservations, remained committed to working with France.[24]

Stalled by Whitehall resistance to a customs union, Bevin played his imperial card – collaboration in Africa. Fearful of a Big Three plot to confiscate her colonies, France welcomed Euro-Africa as insurance against predators and nationalist movements. 'We must free ourselves of financial dependence on the United States as soon as possible,' Bevin announced in September 1947; 'we shall never be able to pull our weight in foreign affairs until we do so.' Harnessing empires would keep London and Paris safe from superpower hugs. 'The British Commonwealth', announced Bevin, 'had a separate contribution to make in world leadership, which it would be unable to make if the UK became dependent on the US.' Britain and France 'with their populations of 47 millions and 40 millions respectively and with their vast colonial possessions,' Bevin assured French premier Paul Ramadier in September 1947, 'could if they acted together be as powerful as either the Soviet Union or the United States.' A wildly over-sanguine foreign secretary fantasized about American dependency on Britain: 'if only we pushed on and developed Africa we would have the US dependent on us and eating out of our hands in four or five years ... the US was very barren of essential minerals ... in Africa we have them all.' African partnership was a non-starter because it put the cart before the horse – cooperation had to begin in Europe. There was no money for imperial development. The 30 per cent sterling devaluation of September 1949 demonstrated Britain's plight, and established a unique dollar–sterling link, persuading ministers that Euro-Africa was 'unworkable'.[25]

Feet firmly in Europe, Duff Cooper in December 1947 pleaded for the treaty's consummation. If the Entente had a hero it was the ambassador. 'You may think that I am making a lot of fuss about nothing, and that it matters little whether staff conversations start in January, or in June, or in the year after next. But, to my mind, this is just one of those many small matters upon the settlement of which depends the fate of great nations.' Approaching retirement, the envoy pulled no punches – comparing the Attlee government's procrastination with Britain's interwar foreign policy. 'I watched the process in operation during the twenty years that separated the wars ... The attitude of the Government at every turn was always defensible, logical, and supported by sound arguments, but it lacked one thing – a guiding policy behind it – and so, in the end, it landed us in a ghastly war'.[26]

Bevin moved on: 'Western Union', a Franco–British-led West European bloc, to include Africa and a customs union. Launched in January 1948 Western Union proposed to mobilize the resources of Africa, enabling Europe to 'equal the Western hemisphere and Soviet blocs in terms of productive capacity and manpower'. The 'terribly vague' proposal required, as writer and diplomat Harold Nicolson mischievously observed, half a dozen different and equally imprecise expressions to define it. Nevertheless, a flurry of cooperation on new economic and security architecture suggested a Franco–British Europe taking shape: the signing of the Brussels Treaty of March 1948; the coordination of American Marshal Aid through the OEEC; partnering the United States in establishing a West German state; joining Brussels Pact powers in talks with the United States on an Atlantic Pact, leading to the North Atlantic Treaty of April 1949 establishing NATO.[27]

Cracks appeared in the façade. In May 1948 the federalist inspired Hague Congress called for a European parliament with powers over a political union. Notwithstanding Franco–Belgian backing for the proposal, Bevin objected: 'Never 'eard such bloody rubbish.' Tussles over the creation of a Council of Europe exposed the conflict between the UK's intergovernmental approach and France's willingness to make supranational concessions. A neutered Council of Europe emerged as a consultative body limited to short annual meetings and chaperoned by a ministerial committee. By the end of 1949 the foreign secretary had a new script, prioritizing the USA and Canada because 'in the last resort we cannot rely upon the European countries'.[28]

Why the about-face? True, the Cold War and fears of a third world war magnified Europe's vulnerability and ramped up American dominance – but East–West enmity had not deterred Bevin from launching Western Union. His methods of working and the paucity of personal papers rule out any certainty about intentions. To be sure, he was no federalist. 'If you open that Pandora's Box [European federalism] you never know what Trojan 'orses will jump out.' Bidault accused him of 'playing with Europe'. *The Economist* expressed doubts: 'If he is not fully committed to the idea of Western

Union, then let him not talk as though he were. Britain's European neighbours will be watching suspiciously for every sign that the British are not really in earnest but are once again ... using a European alliance as a temporary measure to be abandoned when the need is past'.[29]

Vanishing power, accelerating Cold War, life-threatening illness and no think tank, all imposed a sticking-plaster approach. In the spring of 1950, 'half-alive' and 'too ill to speak' at a NATO Council, Bevin 'could barely read out the agenda, let alone take charge'. Until the creation of a Central Economic Planning Staff (CEPS) in mid-1947 there was no machinery to implement economic cooperation with France. An assessment of Bevin's January 1947 customs union proposal had to be outsourced to Cambridge dons who did not report until late October. Whitehall acknowledged 'our lack of a foreign economic policy'. The director of the cabinet's economic section conceded, 'We had done little work on what we mean by European Cooperation'. The FO's first think tank, the PUSC, only came online in mid-1949. As a result, immediate post-war initiatives lacked clarity and coherence. Bevin improvised, confessing 'he had to bluff his way through in foreign policy, given the financial weakness of this country'.[30]

What drove the foreign secretary? Affection for France and Europe? Not by a long chalk. The problem, in his own words, was how to keep the 'little bit of dignity we have left'. In a topsy-turvy world Bevin reached for grab bars – Big Three partnership, Anglo–French cooperation, then an Anglo–American duumvirate – to bind Western Europe 'more closely to the United Kingdom'. Regional leadership would give the UK extra clout in Washington – 'a question of saving Europe rather than joining it'. Once assured of an American military commitment, Bevin wanted 'to get away from talk about Europe. We must think in terms of the west ... the "Free World"'.[31]

The intensity of the Cold War – Communist coup in Czechoslovakia in February 1948, and Berlin Blockade in June, together with strong doubts about the ability of the French economy to deliver its targets, pulled the plug on Western Union. On 25 November 1948 the Cabinet's Economic Policy Committee decided against joint economic planning. Less than a year later, in September 1949, Britain devalued sterling by 30 per cent without consulting European allies – forcing France's third devaluation in eleven months.

The decision to abandon joint economic planning is said to have 'consigned' a Franco–British bloc 'to the realm of might-have-beens'. This is too hasty a conclusion. A Franco–British Europe remained an option through 1950. Monnet, head of the French planning commissariat, tried twice in 1949 to initiate cooperation, suggesting talks to integrate national economic plans for 1950–2. Hosting British negotiators at his country house he proposed a dramatic gesture – British coal for French beef. Monnet envisaged 'an Anglo–French nucleus around which a European Community could be built'. The FO fired a warning shot. The 'special relationship' took precedence and nothing should be agreed 'which would render us incapable of sustaining an independent resistance if France were overrun'. Towards the end of 1949 Monnet tried again, only to be told 'there is at present little basis for an arrangement of the kind you suggest outside the ordinary commercial exchanges'.[32]

As Bevin backpedalled, foreign minister Robert Schuman advanced, inviting others to join France and Germany in pooling coal and steel production under a common authority (ECSC) as a first step towards European federation. His press conference of 9 May 1950 was almost a non-event. Journalists received such short notice that many did not attend and those who did had difficulty following it because of the minister's mumbling, elliptical speech. Angered by lack of prior consultation, and a request on 1 June for a response within twenty-four hours, British ministers suspected a plot to exclude them. They missed the irony of an allegedly super leaky neighbour keeping a mainspring post-war initiative secret.

UK membership of the Schuman Plan would have opened a new European future, powering the partnership which had eluded the couple since 1944. UK decision-making on the Plan – sometimes portrayed as a knee-jerk reaction – was more open-ended than was supposed. There was no wicked French plot to keep Britain out. The lack of advance consultation was not payback for London's failure to consult on sterling's devaluation in September 1949. Schuman's announcement surprised colleagues as much as UK politicians. France needed Britain to balance Germany and provide a bridge to the United States. Shutting out a major ally made no sense to French policy-makers.

First reactions to Schuman's invitation were welcoming. 'We must be in from the beginning', Attlee insisted. Paris ambassador Harvey enthused about 'a never-to-be-repeated opportunity of getting a real move on in Europe ... We really have the ball at our feet'. There was nothing cut and dried about Schuman's proposal – it was a statement of intentions, no more. On 18 May Bevin and Schuman conceded they had not had time to consider its implications thoroughly. With Bevin in the London Clinic and many ministers away because of the Whit holiday, junior FO minister Kenneth Younger coordinated responses. Though credited with urging Bevin to accept the Plan, his diary confirms the timidity and indecisiveness of the political elite.[33]

What motivated the decision to stay out? Was it, in Eden's words, something which 'we know, in our bones, we cannot do'? According to historian Tony Judt, non-participation reflected an existential crisis, standing aside 'was above all an instinctive, psychological and even emotional' decision – 'a product of the utter peculiarity of recent British experience'. This reads too much into an essentially pragmatic and opportunist decision. The FO permanent secretary claimed that 'a cool appraisement of the national interest' drove rejection – joining Schuman risked jeopardizing the nation's ability to maintain independence should Western Europe be overwhelmed. It's far from obvious, however, why participation would have threatened the nation's independence in war. The project had yet to be fleshed out and Britain would have wielded a substantial say in its design.[34]

Three considerations decided the outcome: commitment to a one-world economic strategy; determination to assert British leadership; and complacency. The one-world economic strategy supplied the chief reason for the decision to steer clear of the Plan and later the EEC. The strategy precluded alignment with a protectionist France and Western Europe. Far from cold-shouldering European allies, Britain was poised to insert new proposals. Franco–German talks 'would inevitably break down ... we would then have a chance of coming in as deus ex machina with a solution of our own'. Whitehall considered 'the whole thing nonsense ... a French attempt to evade realities'. The issue of sovereignty played a minor role. For one thing, it had not stopped Churchill offering France union in 1940; for another, the concept of supranationality baffled officials. In 1952 the FO had difficulty deciding whether the ECSC was supranational or intergovernmental. Once the community bedded down the UK pragmatically negotiated associated status. Lastly, complacency. The afterglow of world power induced an 'I'm all right, Jack' attitude – British ways were best and London would roll out its own proposals.[35]

At Messina, Sicily, in June 1955, ECSC foreign ministers agreed on further integration. The initiative created a quandary for a Britain intent on exercising leadership in its own way. Joining the Messina powers ran counter to the UK's one-world economic strategy and perceived global interests; ignoring a customs union threatened exclusion from a potentially dominant economic bloc. London adopted a two-pronged response: sending Board of Trade official Russell Bretherton as a representative to Messina; devising its own proposals for a free trade area. Both actions were self-harming. Émile Noël, future grey eminence of the EEC, an adviser of socialist premier Guy Mollet, recalled Bretherton playing 'hookie from the receptions and out-of-conference discussions, skipping even some formal sessions', indulging his passion as an entomologist chasing moths and butterflies in the Sicilian countryside.[36]

UK proposals for a free trade area to counter a customs union of the Six coincided with the eruption of the Suez crisis. Egyptian president Gamal Abdel Nasser's nationalization of the Franco–British-owned Suez canal company on 26 July 1956 sparked the biggest international scare since the Korean War. On 31 October Britain and France, in cahoots with Israel, intervened militarily – ostensibly to stop an Israeli invasion of Egypt, in fact to repossess the canal and topple Nasser. Superpower and UN disapproval imposed a cease-fire and ignominious withdrawal, a last hurrah for Britain and France as independent world powers.

One train may hide another. The Suez fiasco destroyed a bid for a Franco–British Europe. Out of the blue on 10 September premier Mollet, soccer-loving anglophile and former English teacher, asked British prime minister Eden for union. The main narratives barely acknowledge a request that could have transformed Western Europe. London and Paris kept the approach secret. In 1976 Mollet's foreign minister, Christian Pineau, revealed the proposal – dismissing it as a quickly scuttled spur of the moment idea. Franco–British media claimed in 2007 to have 'discovered' the union request story, despite the UK's release of the file in the mid-1980s.[37]

Excellent rapport between the two premiers encouraged Mollet to ask for union. Eden claimed he had never enjoyed 'a more completely loyal understanding with any man'. The request caught No. 10 on the hop: 'The French have been proposing Anglo–French union again, we feel it is impossible at present because of the Commonwealth.' After sitting on the idea for three days Downing Street took it on board. The request was much more than a ploy to beef up action against Egypt and win help for France's Algerian war. It reflected the radical rethinking generated by post-war reconstruction. Nation state unions and a Euro-Commonwealth were buzzwords in European political elites. Veteran Pan-Europeanist Richard Coudenhove-Kalergi lobbied for closer Commonwealth–Europe links, including a Franco–German Republic associated with the Commonwealth. In January 1956 a British minister suggested bribing France with Commonwealth membership in order to block the project for a common market.[38]

Why propose marriage in the middle of a gale? The lack of French files rules out any certainty, but a speech by Pineau supplies a clue. The fact that neither Britain nor France could stand alone in the storm, argued Pineau, made it urgent to create Europe with Britain. Current European integration negotiations, not Suez, motivated the French leader. In early September 1956 six-power talks on a common market reached a critical stage. The pros and cons of a common market and a British free trade area splintered French opinion. Mollet gambled on winning a British concession package as an alternative to both a common market and UK free trade area, including perhaps a lasting political connection, and Sterling Area membership. Support for the French empire and the Algerian war would have put icing on the cake. The premier had a strong negotiating position. The hexagon had the ability to exercise a stranglehold on both a common market and a free trade area. The size of its economy ensured that partners would be unlikely to proceed without France. Entering the market would enable France to bar member states from a free trade area.[39]

As a bolt from the blue the union idea stood no chance. Whitehall was intent on finalizing its free trade area plan G. The absence of a French archival footprint underscores the personal character of the request and the casualness of Mollet's policy-making. Even his chef de cabinet Emile Noël 'had not worked on it'. Did Mollet act on impulse? Almost certainly. There was no consultation with advisers and colleagues. Distrust of the Quai, old habits of wartime clandestinity, and the secrecy of Suez planning, supply a partial explanation of the premier's solo style. More importantly, the clustering of hard-hat ventures – intervention in Egypt, collusion with Israel, Algerian war and common market negotiations, overwhelmed a dysfunctional government, forcing Mollet to bypass the machine.[40]

The French leader over-valued his relationship with Eden. The prime minister grasped the importance of the union request, but lacked time, energy and imagination to explore it. Sickness and obsession with Nasser narrowed his vision. When cabinet discussion of a free trade area resumed on 18 September, Eden damned union with faint praise: 'There might prove to be scope for a closer association in military, financial and economic affairs which would make the two countries a powerful partnership.' Eden had in mind Bevin's idea of a 'Commonwealth union' to include Belgium, the Netherlands and Scandinavia which would break up the Six and leave Britain and France running Western Europe. Opening the Commonwealth to France, however, would mean including Belgium and the Netherlands – raising difficulties with Germany and Italy: 'against these, there should be weighed the additional strength which the adhesion of some European countries would give to offset the weakness of the Asian members of the Commonwealth.'[41]

A strong pro-French constituency did not exist. Grandees like FO permanent secretary Kirkpatrick distrusted the French – 'they would be certain to let us down'. The UK's one-world free trade strategy excluded union and common market. To protect their pet project, captious mandarins pulled out all the stops. France's 'weakness and ineffectiveness' presented 'one of the gravest problems' facing 'the Western Alliance'. Differences 'of race, religion and above all outlook' militated against union. A shotgun marriage would upset everyone, especially the United States and the Commonwealth. The rise of multilateralism had outdated Churchill's wartime offer of 1940. Partnership would endanger Britain's global stance, especially the special relationship. Apparently unaware of France's growth rate, the Treasury refused to partner a sluggish, protectionist economy. Association would bring 'a large number of new problems' because France's economic axis lay with Germany and the Benelux countries. As a sop, advisers suggested 'it might please Mollet to be told of an impending new British initiative [Plan G] for a European free trade area'. The machine spat out yet more negatives in response to the French premier's appeal on 26 September for Commonwealth membership and common citizenship. Membership 'could not be offered to France alone', but the inclusion of other countries would rock the boat dangerously.[42]

During the Suez adventure France's ambassador in London read Agatha Christie's *Death on the Nile*. The title catches the ironies of the affair. Joint action against Egypt closed off any prospect of partnership. The misconceived and badly planned intervention put paid to a fragile Entente. The first major Franco–British military intervention since 1940 left a legacy of misunderstanding and distrust. Mollet's one-off union gamble in September was tied to the flow of the Brussels common market talks. Within days of accepting the UN ceasefire of 6 November 1956, disillusioned French officials conducted a reality check. The two leading Western European powers lacked the strength to impose their will, leaving France's security dependent on America. Officials accused Britain of timid and clumsy conduct throughout the crisis, and concluded that making Europe was now more urgent than ever. Paris, London and Washington, advised the Quai, should patch up differences and resist Soviet penetration of the Middle East.[43]

France scored, gaining a Franco–German entente and a strengthening of French pro-common market opinion. Angered by international censure and threats of Soviet rockets, the French closed ranks behind Mollet and the common market. When Eden on 6 November called Mollet about a cease fire in Egypt, a Franco–German summit had reached agreement on the EEC and Euratom. West German chancellor Konrad Adenauer affirmed the need 'to make Europe'.

Nothing solid emerged from the heady post-Liberation days. What would it have taken to reboot the connection? A Harry Potter-like Ministry of Magic? A race of supermen? In a Nietzschean moment a British diplomat reported that the authors of the Schuman Plan regarded a 'supra-national authority controlled by supermen as essential to success'. Simply, the magic of an imaginative leap inspired by recognition that collaboration could bring decisive benefits. In 1950 English soccer suffered its first defeat in a World Cup. 'If there was a time when English football should have ... taken a long hard look at itself', opined star Stanley Matthews, 'it was in the aftermath of the 1950 World Cup'. Far more than soccer, overseas policy needed a long hard look. A post-Schuman review of UK responses to European integration ambled along for nearly two years.[44] Nor did the UK make a better fist of attempts at association with the ECSC. 'The history of the attempt at association between summer 1950 and April 1954', concluded Alan Milward, 'is a model of how policy should not be formulated.'

Leaders and government machines decisively shaped outcomes. Bevin's 'ignorance of and contempt for the realities' of Fourth Republic politics, concluded historian Geoffrey Warner, prevented him 'from seeing that successive French governments were no more eager to surrender their sovereignty to some federal entity than he was', and 'shared his objective of an independent Europe'. With goodwill, understanding and a

Figure 8.3 French foreign minister Robert Schuman and German Chancellor Konrad Adenauer, 27 May 1952. Credit: World History Archive / Alamy Stock Photo.

fair wind, 'a European community might have grown up around an Anglo–French instead of a Franco–German axis'. Disillusioned by Bevin's efforts to emasculate the Council of Europe, a senior member of the UK delegation resigned because government tactics called into question its sincerity. 'What was needed was ... an act of faith.'[45]

UK policy-makers lacked the faith to follow Schuman's 'leap in the dark'. They underestimated the continent's growing desire for integration, and Britain's loss of moral authority. The one-world strategy was fatally flawed because the economy was better suited to EEC protectionism than to the government's free trade vision. Deputy premier Herbert Morrison's response to Schuman – 'It's no good. We cannot do it; the Durham miners won't wear it' – illustrates a central trope of this book, the democratic deficit of a 'mature' democracy. No one asked the people what they thought. Government did not consult the electorate about the likely harsh consequences of its commitment to a one-world free trade strategy. If there was a moment of truth when Britain might have reset the relationship with France and Europe it was between 1950 and 1952. 'Courageous leadership', wrote official historian Alan Milward, 'would have ... set out these ... facts about the national future to the population ... They had faced worse in 1940. They were left in ignorance'. Trollope deserves the last word: 'the cross-grainedness of men is so great that things will often be forced to go wrong, even when they have the strongest possible natural tendency of their own to go right.'[46]

9

Supermac

Among mid-twentieth-century prime ministers, Harold Macmillan ranks below demigods Attlee and Churchill, sharing third place with Wilson, and ahead of Eden and Home. 'Supermac ... the Super Statesman', headlined the *Daily Mail* on his death in 1986. The superlatives now sound distinctly overblown. Even in 1963 journalist Nora Beloff argued that the prime minister 'also had his part in the final rupture' with de Gaulle. Biographers disagree on the merits of Macmillan's European initiatives. 'The Common Market application', writes Francis Beckett, 'was an achievement'. Without the premier's 'groundwork on British public opinion, on the British political class, and on the leaders of Europe ... membership would have taken longer', D.R. Thorpe dissents. Britain 'made the worst of both worlds – missing the opportunities afforded by Messina ... Macmillan must take his portion of the blame for the lack of clarity and commitment in the British approach to European membership'.[1]

'All our policies ... are in ruins,' lamented Macmillan after de Gaulle harpooned his EEC membership bid.[2] Nevertheless, the image of a humane, courageous and witty one-nation conservative outlasted the shambles of his European projects. The premier organized immortality in six doorstopper tomes of autobiography, portraying a Jekyll and Hyde de Gaulle – by turns friendly, charming, obstinate and inscrutable. In short, a plausible alibi for the failure to reach an understanding on Europe. Alistair Horne's two-decker official biography published shortly after the premier's death gave the icon a final burnish.

Macmillan over-egged the pudding. Sesquipedalian prose, freighted with detail and self-justification, obfuscated crucial questions. What happened to the Macmillan who in 1949 enthused about collaborating with a new cohort of continental politicians in the rebirth of Europe? Or, the apparent Francophile who in June 1962 reminded de Gaulle 'how a close Anglo–French alliance, really effectively managed from day to day, would have avoided both wars'. Ambition drove out any real sympathy for France and Europe. Climbing the greasy pole demanded ruthlessness. The public persona of an urbane Edwardian gentleman concealed a killer politician. In the 'Night of the Long Knives' in July 1962 Macmillan sacked seven ministers on the trot. Curiously, his European strategy lacked urgency and boldness. It evoked Labour politician Nye Bevan's characterization of wartime Allied Command's approach to the conquest of Italy – 'like an old man approaching a young bride – fascinated, sluggish and apprehensive'.[3]

There was nothing sluggish about the way British commentators blackened the French. Nora Beloff led the charge: 'Is there still ... hidden somewhere inside this incredible artifact [de Gaulle], a real person with pity for his fellow men ... no one will ever know.' On British and French advisers: 'the British team ... headed by Sir Roderick Barclay ... a gentle, persuasive British diplomat with ... a disarming smile. Opposite him ... M Olivier Wormser – redoubtable dialectician, tall, elegant, crushingly sarcastic'. Official historian and former diplomat Stephen Wall compares the Franco-British stand-off of the 1960s to the hostility of the Napoleonic wars. Britain gave the 1961 entry bid its best shot in the teeth of Gallic bloody-mindedness. Whitehall worried how 'to get round' the French 'or defeat them or convert them'. British leaders 'all realized that ... accession would only be possible if an accommodation could be reached with the French'. De Gaulle wrecked everything, belittling and excluding Britain.[4]

What more can be said? Plenty. To assert that ministers 'realized' entry depended on an accommodation with the French misleads – No. 10 dropped hints of future collaboration but made no offers. In the classic Irish tale a tourist asks a local for directions to Dublin: 'Well, sir, if I were you, I wouldn't start from here,' replies the Irishman. He might have added, first catch your general. After wasted years pursuing a Six/Seven compromise, Macmillan announced in July 1961 an application to join the EEC – giving Paris just three days' notice. Downing Street viewed French support as desirable but not essential. There was no seduction – mostly sticks and a few post-dated carrots. The prime minister assumed the general would not risk a veto. Macmillan, as biographer D.R. Thorpe concluded, shares responsibility for the failure of the UK's European ambitions. The French president was no ogre. In vetoing British bids he defended French interests as obdurately as the British defended theirs.

Denigrating de Gaulle diverted attention from British singularities – tired premier, obsolescent machine and gloom-ridden political class. In exaggerating Macmillan's incipiently doddering manner, satirists and others did him a disservice. Health, not age, was the issue. Years before the prostate operation of October 1963 ended his political career, severe stress debilitated the premier. Symptoms that today would be diagnosed as indicative of chronic fatigue syndrome (CFS) surfaced from the mid-1950s. No fresh thinking on Europe inspired Macmillan. The memoirs attempted to establish an alibi by invoking 'old friendship' with de Gaulle and the restoration of 'old relations' with France. The premier assumed the role of injured party, victim of the general's antipathy. The ploy underwhelms – the diaries provide ample evidence of mutual dislike. As minister resident at Allied headquarters in wartime Algiers, Macmillan liaised with the general. 'Ramrod' de Gaulle, recalled the premier, had 'all the rigidity of a poker without its occasional warmth'. A beach afternoon says it all. The minister skinny-dipped while a uniformed general looked on.[5]

Macmillan showed scant sympathy for mainland Europeans. Condescending towards the French, apprehensive of Germans, he shared the nation's ambivalence towards continental neighbours. 'Don't you think', suggested a colleague, 'that in our country we have a special aptitude for not seeing the other country's point of view?'. Cranford's Miss Pole, denouncing 'that wicked Paris, where they are always having Revolutions', was alive and well. Cross-channel elites, like Dover Mail passengers, suspected each other. The premier's condemnation of de Gaulle's veto of 1963 accused president and people: 'French duplicity has defeated us all ... there is the return of the old feeling "the French always betray you in the end."'[6]

Like Churchill, Macmillan flirted with Europeanism. At Zurich in September 1946 Churchill called for a United States of Europe and founded the British United Europe Movement. With fellow Conservatives, Macmillan joined the UK delegation to the Council of Europe at Strasbourg, briefly bonding with continental colleagues. Churchill's indifference to the European cause after returning to power in 1951 made Macmillan as housing minister wary of going out on a limb. Delivery of the government's promised 300,000 new-builds a year claimed energies. In a last flourish of European sentiments in March 1952 he criticized cabinet proposals for the Council's reorganization. As foreign secretary in the Eden government he steered clear of the Messina conference's integration initiative in June 1955. Spaak pleaded with him to seize the initiative in creating a united Europe. By 1958 the sympathetic Strasbourg colleagues of yesteryear had become pushy continentals exploiting, in Macmillan's words, 'our natural good manners and reticence. We are apt not to press our points too strongly in the early stages of a negotiation, and then when a crisis arises and we have to take a definite position we are accused of perfidy'.[7]

'Perfidy' was the word. Macmillan's refusal to give a strong lead on integration seemed a betrayal of the European loyalties he and Churchill espoused in the early post-war years. As premier from January 1957, Macmillan had the authority to craft a post-Suez London–Paris rapprochement capable of shoehorning Britain into the Community. The UK had an economic and political edge over a beleaguered France, nascent EEC and uncertain West Germany. Fourth Republic notables sought an

Figure 9.1 British Prime Minister Harold Macmillan and French Prime Minister Guy Mollet, 9 March 1957. Credit: Everett Collection Inc. / Alamy Stock Photo.

understanding. Instead, Macmillan prioritized the repairing of the special relationship. Hostility overflowed on a visit to Paris in March 1957. The premier indulged in 'a very long, and rather unpleasant argument' about money-saving British force reductions in Europe. Were it not for the two hours of wasted argument about force reductions, he 'would have attacked the French' for their management of the last stages of the common market negotiations. Rather than concert approaches to the United States, Macmillan elbowed France aside in the race to mend fences. At Bermuda on 20 March he cosied up to President Eisenhower to win help for a British nuclear deterrent. Bermuda 'makes all the difference to us ... I was afraid the French would be hurt; or, worse still, want to make it a Tripartite meeting'.[8]

Undismayed, French ministers in June 1957 hinted at acceptance of a British free trade area in return for support in the Middle East. 'Times had changed very much recently', declared premier Bourges Maunoury: 'old-fashioned rivalries which still seemed to preoccupy our representatives on the spot were entirely out of date ... the additional constitution of a Free Trade Area on the lines suggested by London was vital.' Downing Street spurned the advance: 'it is far more important to achieve a meeting of minds with the Americans.'[9]

The shock of the military–settler Algiers coup of 13 May 1958 catapulted de Gaulle back to power – heading a transitional government charged with devising a new constitution. Macmillan had the advantage over a crisis-riven general, juggling with the Algerian war, the creation of a new Republic and EEC membership. He approached their first meeting since the Second World War with gladiatorial swagger. Ahead of the 29–30 June 1958 encounter, a macho premier emphasized duelling, not dialogue:

> If little Europe is formed without a parallel development of the Free Trade area we will have to reconsider the whole of our political and economic attitude towards Europe. I doubt if we could remain in NATO. We should certainly put on highly protective tariffs and quotas ... adopt a policy of isolationism ... surround ourselves with rockets ... say to the Germans, the French and all the rest ... 'Look after yourselves with your own forces. Look after yourselves when the Russians overrun your countries.'[10]

Cheering crowds at Orly airport and lining the route into the capital surprised and delighted Macmillan. 'All affability and charm', the general apologized for being 'so tiresome' during the war. Unmoved, Macmillan adopted a minatory tone: 'If the negotiations [free trade talks] broke down', it would be 'a great effort for us to keep four divisions on the continent ... we would be driven back on ourselves and would have to seek our friends elsewhere ... Europe would break up'. De Gaulle's reminder that France could not go faster in the trade talks because of Treaty of Rome obligations triggered an ultimatum – failure to reach agreement by 1 January 1959 'might even spell the end of NATO'.[11]

The ultimatum was no tantrum. The prime minister handed his host 'a very strong letter' confirming the verbal warning. De Gaulle's mellowness went untested – Macmillan's 'willing to wound, and yet afraid to strike' language excluded amity. He stayed on the warpath, redoubling efforts to muster American support for Britain's FTA

Figure 9.2 Prime Minister Macmillan and Foreign Secretary Selwyn Lloyd welcomed to Paris by General de Gaulle, 30 June 1958. Credit: Keystone Press / Alamy Stock Photo.

project. Infuriated by what he perceived as procrastination, the premier let rip, 'it looks as if the whole of this great effort will break down, foiled by the selfishness and insularity of the French'. In November de Gaulle confirmed opposition to the FTA. *The Times*, dancing to Macmillan's tune, denounced 'France the Wrecker'.[12]

The electoral triumph of October 1959 made Macmillan 'one of the most powerful prime ministers in British history ... All options were open to him'. De Gaulle's prime minister, Michel Debré, hastened to congratulate Macmillan, looking forward to regular contacts and 'the closest cooperation'. An opportunity came in mid-December. Hosting preparatory Anglo–Franco–American talks for an upcoming East–West summit, de Gaulle, president of France since December 1958, invited Macmillan to join him for tea after the formal talks ended. The impromptu one-on-one at the Élysée Palace exuded pre-Christmas cheer. The general spoke 'very freely and in a most friendly and even affectionate mood – *Cher ami* and all that'.[13]

Trapped in a Six/Seven box of his own making Macmillan saw no further than 'the chance of getting some European economic compromise with the only man who is capable of making it today'. A refurbished Anglo–American alliance 'must never be abandoned', the premier strategized. Paris would get a limited settlement. In return for UK sponsorship of France's re-entry into 'the ranks of the Great Powers', de Gaulle would have to give 'the greatest practical accommodation that he can on the economic front'.[14]

Clearly a revamped Entente was not on the premier's wish list. Nevertheless, two meetings with de Gaulle in the spring of 1960 gave him every opportunity to rethink the relationship. A meeting at the Chateau de Rambouillet on 12–13 March 1960 to finalize arrangements for the general's state visit to the UK set the scene for a game-changing initiative. The prime minister's arrival in the latest Citroën DS seemed a good omen. The president radiated bonhomie – which Macmillan ascribed to the successful testing of France's first atom bomb the previous month. Alas, not the faintest wisp of white smoke escaped the chimneys. Fixated by the will-o'-the-wisp of a Six/Seven compromise, Macmillan again missed the bus. His demand for an immediate French commitment to resist an acceleration of EEC tariff reductions sat uncomfortably with calls for frequent get-togethers and 'a real renewal' of friendship. Nuclear cooperation surfaced: 'I put the idea in his mind that we might be able to help him, either with American agreement or connivance.' De Gaulle pricked up his ears – declaring that a Six/Seven agreement should be possible. Macmillan's call for tri-monthly meetings went unanswered – his interlocutor prudently awaited delivery of nuclear know-how.[15]

Flying home empty-handed, the premier put a good face on failure – discussions revitalized 'our old friendship'. Macmillan drew a blank because he sought only limited cooperation on his terms. Old friends from wartime Algiers were old adversaries. De Gaulle's request for one-on-one conversations in French without interpreters did not make for smooth exchanges. Shared melancholic temperaments and elliptical speech frustrated full understanding at the best of times. The weekend left the premier with a severe headache. 'The strain of talking French ... and trying not to fall into any major error of judgement' exhausted him. Why did he accept a procedure guaranteed to sow confusion? The image of a born world leader cultivating friendship with peers tickled his vanity. More importantly, conversations without interpreters allowed both leaders maximum wiggle room.[16]

The disproportion between the razzmatazz of the French president's 5–7 April 1960 state visit and the exiguous political results would have supplied a skit for the comedy stage revue *Beyond The Fringe* which premiered later that year. Ministers spared no expense. Huge Crosses of Lorraine lit by fireworks decorated the façade of Buckingham Palace and the general enjoyed the rare privilege of addressing both Houses of Parliament in the Palace of Westminster. Even the Queen, 'with appropriate humility', asked the general 'what he thought her role ought to be'. Instead of strengthening the Entente, leaders speculated about the intentions of Nikita Khrushchev, general secretary of the Soviet communist party. The Soviet leader had just ended a visit to France and an East–West summit loomed the following month. The preoccupation with Khrushchev and Cold War politics pointed up the poverty of ideas for a post-colonial global order and how Britain and France might shape it.[17]

Wasted pyrotechnics? Unexpectedly, during an exchange about Sixes and Sevens de Gaulle offered a cue, 'Why didn't England enter the Common Market?' – the very question engaging Macmillan. Caught on the hop he responded brusquely in one word, 'Impossible', reiterating the urgency of a Six/Seven alignment. A chance missed? After the 1963 veto American president John F. Kennedy observed: 'If you had applied one year earlier – before Algeria was settled, de Gaulle couldn't have stopped you'. In fact, this was what the premier attempted in mid-July 1960 – to secure cabinet approval for an application.[18]

Several pressures pushed an application upfront. The Six/Seven impasse heightened a sense of time running out. The electoral victory of October 1959 was losing its shine, and voters expected big initiatives at home and abroad. Delaying decisions on Europe lengthened the odds against acceptable entry terms. Applying for entry would enhance Britain's standing with a new American president after the November 1960 presidential election. The collapse of the four-power East–West Paris summit in May dashed the premier's hopes of playing world statesman, making movement on Europe essential to keep up momentum. From late 1959 the premier's consigliere, deputy cabinet secretary Freddie Bishop, advocated the importance of courting France and Western Europe. In early July 1960 he proposed 'developing a special bilateral relationship' with joint control over nuclear capability. Macmillan conceded that 'what he [de Gaulle] says, counts – and nothing else'. The public success of de Gaulle's April 1960 state visit invited closer links. Delay reinforced continental suspicions of British motives. An exchange between Macmillan and a dance partner circulated in Brussels: '"Oh! Prime Minister. Are we going to join the Common Market? It's awful!" ... he squeezed her in his arms and replied: "Don't worry my dear, we shall embrace them destructively!"'

In politics as in comedy, timing is everything. Macmillan made a costly misjudgement. Ignoring warnings from aides, he took the issue of EEC membership to the full cabinet on 13 July 1960 without first exploring a cross-channel understanding. The misstep derailed the initiative for another year. Bizarrely, after ruminating for months the premier rushed his fences, and provoked heavy flak. It was an avoidable defeat. Softening up individual ministers and small group retreats at Chequers could have won early support for entry.

Why lose another year before announcing a bid? Mismanaged exploratory talks with France heightened cross-channel suspicions. Launched with a clear mandate the conversations might have created a pathway for an application. Instead, noted a participant, 'We did little more than state the problems ... because we were not allowed to show most of the cards in our hand.' The French spent a good deal of time 'in telling us that we would have to move from this or that position when in fact we knew perfectly well ... we would have to go a good long way further to meet the Six'.[19]

Macmillan fretted about 'getting nearer to the French without losing the Americans'. Panic attacks about breaking transatlantic ties provoked 'an unrealistic search for the best of all possible worlds'. The premier's 'Grand Design' of December 1960 presented Britain 'as one of the great forces of the Free World' *beside* Europe and America. It did not occur to Macmillan that America might welcome a Franco–British Europe. Advice came from the Paris embassy. 'The key to the whole business', wrote ambassador Sir Pierson Dixon, 'may in fact lie in somehow conveying to de Gaulle that the French are as important to us as the Americans.' Britain, the envoy urged, would have to take 'some significant step ... in the nuclear field'. Dixon proposed offering a deal, 'provided that we did not too obviously appear to be trying to get the best of both worlds, European and American ... [though] what we are after is precisely the best of both worlds'.[20]

De Gaulle remained friendly, despite Macmillan's unresponsiveness. For a Rambouillet summit on 29–30 January 1961 he upgraded his guests – better plumbing, warmer bedrooms, plentiful bed clothes, and an after dinner treat – a French documentary about a priapic New Guinea tribe. At the very start of conversations de Gaulle emphasized the urgency of a genuinely close alliance. Evading a direct response the premier went off at a tangent on a different topic – the Cold War and the West's economic strength.

Preferring stealth to trumpets, No. 10 announced a UK membership application on 31 July – just before the parliamentary summer recess. The bare-bones Commons statement had all the passion of a train station announcement. No one explained why ministers had changed their minds since the formation of the EEC. *The Times* deplored the Scottish mist, and censured the lord privy seal Edward Heath for claiming the decision had been taken 'after searching debate', concluding: 'the best way to breed confidence is to show the greatest possible candour'. France was not consulted. The FO advised the government to confine itself 'to telling him [De Gaulle] what we propose to do and do not invite him to declare his attitude in advance'. The veto of 14 January 1963 locked Britain out of the Community for another decade.[21]

The rest is history – or, is it? Politicians, civil servants and commentators pilloried de Gaulle for the deadlock. The exception was Sir Eric Roll on the UK's Brussels negotiating team. Instead of castigating the general, Roll criticized his country's performance. The breakdown, he informed colleagues in February 1963, was 'not so much a failure of negotiations per se, but a failure of a major aspect of our foreign policy'. London and Paris shared responsibility for an avoidable outcome.[22]

Would the general have lowered the drawbridge? 'From the start and continuously,' concluded a leading French scholar, 'de Gaulle opposed British entry into the common market'. How, then, should we interpret the general's friendliness? Until mid-1962 de Gaulle, I contend, anticipated a marriage proposal. For sure, he had mixed feelings about British membership, but as a pragmatist he sought the best outcome for his country. London's reluctance to negotiate a comprehensive deal, and the frustrations of the Brussels multi-dimensional chess game, determined the veto.[23]

Caveats are necessary. The fragmentary and circumstantial nature of the evidence excludes definitive judgements about the French president's intentions. We know much more about Macmillan's thinking than de Gaulle's. No presidential secret diaries have surfaced – fake or real. The president considered the secrecy of policy-making part of the mystique of power. Governing without kitchen cabinet or think tank he played his cards close, forcing historians to lean heavily on information minister Alain Peyrefitte's notes of meetings. The thirty-year gap between events and publication of Peyrefitte's memoir imposes caution. The records of Franco–British swordplay carry a special health warning. There was no agreed record of discussions – both sides made separate versions to allow for editing and fudging. The general's aversion to interpreters for one-on-one conversations forced Macmillan to speak French. Private secretaries took notes but the premier's secretary believed that at Rambouillet in December 1962 de Gaulle had not 'entirely understood everything that was said'. One unrecorded conversation took place on that occasion.[24]

The president was not a one-man band. Advisers, people and Community partners fretted about a destructive British embrace merging the Community into an Atlanticist free trade area shorn of supranational ideals. Britain's EFTA grouping suggested a traditional divide and rule approach in Europe. Washington's overly zealous lobbying for the UK might portend an American Trojan Horse. The virtually simultaneous applications of Britain's escorts – Ireland (31 July) and Denmark (10 August) – added to the Six's unease. Enlargement negotiations sharpened the Community's sense of identity. To jump from six to nine seemed more threat than blessing. An ambassador's gaffe captured the anxieties of the time. Presenting the UK application to the president of the European Commission, a nervous British envoy made a Freudian slip – implying the EEC might join the Commonwealth.[25]

Pigeonholing de Gaulle as an unreconstructed nationalist playing king of the castle undervalues his pragmatism. The ideologue concealed an opportunist. Grain and grandeur motivated the president. His abandonment of earlier opposition to the EEC forced French protectionist interests to accept the liberalization measures of the Treaty of Rome. The Community supplied an economic and political armoury for leadership in Europe. The measured response to Macmillan's bid illustrates the balancing of principle and pragmatism. For de Gaulle, Britain's quest for EEC entry had a plus side, opening up vistas of a Paris–London–Bonn troika leading Western Europe. The willingness to pay upfront for French sponsorship would provide a litmus test of commitment to the Six and shared direction of a European Europe.

The Gaullist rulebook prized secrecy, surprise and avoiding the opening move in negotiations. 'He [de Gaulle] knows nothing of the gentle art whereby an opponent's face can be saved', remarked a French diplomat, 'so the problem lies in being prepared to make all the advances before starting talks with him'. There was no stooping to conquer – presidential hospitality at Rambouillet featured a pheasant shoot with the general standing behind – he did not participate – commenting loudly each time guests missed. They paid for their cartridges. Likewise, de Gaulle expected Macmillan as an applicant would do his sums and make an offer.[26]

True, the general had red lines – rejecting Britain's FTA and EFTA initiatives because they jeopardized the new-born EEC. Nevertheless, Élysée cordiality flagged a desire for rapprochement. At Rambouillet in January 1961 the general appealed for a Franco-British alliance – a big step for a leader chary of making the first move. To dismiss charm as a delaying device until the president felt strong enough to slam the door is simplistic. The adage, 'keep your friends close, but your enemies closer', guided Gaullist realpolitik. Affability telegraphed readiness for rapprochement while protecting France's world image. UK admission under French aegis would balance West Germany and advance a European Europe.

De Gaulle walked a tightrope. Too negative a posture risked upsetting Brussels partners, endangering agreement on CAP and France's Fouchet Plan of 1961–2 for an intergovernmental EEC. Any weakening of the Community would hinder the hexagon's economic modernization. Too welcoming a stance would encourage Britain to believe it could enter on the cheap without a quid pro quo. The high risks make it unlikely that de Gaulle decided from the outset to veto the bid. France had worries enough without adding to them. Threats of civil war rumbled on. The Algiers military putsch in April 1961 highlighted the fragility of the new Republic and the urgency of peace-making in North Africa. The UK's choice of a two-stage application format – exploratory talks to clarify admission terms, then confirmation or withdrawal, reassured the general. The likelihood of Britain becoming ensnared in prolonged bargaining promised a breathing space to finalize CAP and stabilize the Fifth Republic. Protracted discussions might persuade Macmillan to settle on France's terms or withdraw.

The divas pirouetted but would not dance together, despite professing amity. Early agreement would have fast-tracked the bid before Macmillan's domestic critics woke up. Apart from inviting the general to play concierge and leave the Brussels door open, No. 10 made no overtures. Whispers of nuclear treats remained whispers. The premier vowed not to go to Paris 'as if we are a supplicant' and had no plans for a new Entente. Macmillan acknowledged French mistrust but believed de Gaulle would not dare pull up the drawbridge. Shortly after France's veto a Whitehall intelligence chief blamed the premier for trying to run two hares at the same time – America and Europe. Like novelist William Golding's *Pincher Martin*, Macmillan clung to a mid-Atlantic rock.[27]

Why did No. 10 make a dog's dinner of the bid? Great power assumptions, reluctance to leave the Anglo-American comfort zone, and lack of sympathy for the EEC and its ideals, are only part of the answer. More specifically, three influences – often overlooked – hobbled the handling of the application: the prime minister's health, character and decision-making style. Tiredness plagued performance – action and lethargy alternated. The premier presented symptoms of chronic fatigue syndrome (CFS), then unrecognized as an illness. Long before the prostate operation of September 1963 Macmillan's health seesawed, blighting many working days. A gallstone operation in May 1954 left him 'very tired ... the truth is that my work is getting rather too much for me, with all the speaking engagements which I have unwisely accepted'. Promotion to foreign secretary cranked up the stress: 'One sees people all day and we work from one morning till the early hours of the next ... I am beginning to feel the strain'. No. 10 workloads knocked him for six: 'very tired and overdone' (4 December 1958); 'retired to Chequers for four days as I am completely exhausted. I am alone and staying in bed' (30 October 1959). Age was not an issue – sixty in 1954, he lived into his nineties.[28]

On Eden's resignation in January 1957 Churchill recommended Macmillan for the succession, believing him to be more decisive than rival R.A. Butler. In fact, indecisiveness and inconsistency flawed the premier's handling of Sixes/Sevens and the UK bid. The would-be world statesman cultivated the image of an unflappable wonder working leader reading Trollope while acolytes slaved. In reality, lassitude strengthened a natural melancholy that magnified difficulties – 'problems crowd in upon us. I do not see how to deal with them'. Aides fretted over a slowing down: 'he seems unable to sustain the same intensity of concentration and effort over prolonged periods.' In private, Macmillan confessed bafflement at the 'intractability' of everything. Overdosing on historian Arnold Toynbee's *A Study of History* fed a natural pessimism. The slowly shrinking power of 'the civilized world in the face of the barbarians', the premier confessed, dwarfed the common market and everything else.[29]

A rigid top-down style starved policy-making of fresh ideas and thinking. Slow, solitary reflections authored several 'Grand Designs', but no one master design. The much touted 'Grand Design' of December 1960 primarily addressed external policy aims for 1961, not long-range strategy. Its genesis illustrates the limitations of the premier's style: leisurely ruminations, then bouncing ideas off intimates, followed by feedback meetings with a chosen few, finally circulation among boss mandarins.

Craving centre stage the premier selected a mediocre FO ministerial team – keeping Selwyn Lloyd, Eden's foreign secretary, in post until July 1960, despite rubbishing him as 'one of Eden's stooges'. Lloyd dismissed the EEC as 'much ado about nothing'. From July 1960 a duo operated – Alec Douglas-Home, Earl of Home, as foreign secretary in the Lords, Lord Privy Seal Edward Heath as deputy foreign secretary in the Commons with responsibility for Europe. The premier picked Heath because he would follow instructions – describing him as 'a first class staff officer, but no army commander'. Macmillan's premiership reveals the extent to which a powerful prime minister and advisers could sideline cabinet, parliament and people and initiate major policy changes. That ministers finally fought back and stipulated the terms of the EEC application does not weaken the significance of the marginalization. Greater decisiveness and better management would have enabled Macmillan to see off critics and launch a bid in 1960. Prime minister Harold Wilson's handling of the second bid demonstrated how a savvy leader tamed his cabinet.[30]

An efficient and sophisticated machine would have energized and buttressed Macmillan. Whitehall had nothing to rival France's superb SGCI with its own secretariat and research committees. A visiting US President joked nervously about whether the floors in No. 10 would stand the extra weight of TV cameras. In the summer of 1960 the premier moved to Admiralty House before No. 10 collapsed. Policy-making, like No 10, was structurally flawed. 'It's a strange thing,' remarked Macmillan on becoming prime minister, 'I have now got the biggest job I ever had and less help in doing it than I have ever known'. A sclerotic engine supplied patchy support at best. Once the envy of the world, the Rolls-Royce Phantom IV only fired on two cylinders. The Treasury, Macmillan groused, could produce 'a perfectly adequate short-term policy to cope with an existing situation, but could not put it into a long-term context'. The premier did not install a policy unit in No. 10, despite a warning from a senior minister that 'The present system' was 'breaking down'.[31] Snail-pace interdepartmental committees, weakly coordinated and riddled with turf wars, conducted ad hoc policy reviews. A major post-war 'horizon scanning' exercise, 'Future Policy for 1960–1970', chugged along for nearly a year until shelved without its recommendations going to cabinet. The lead economic policy committee had a three-month gap in its meetings schedule. Plagued by inertia, policy drift and poor coordination, mandarins shrank from confronting the implications of changing geopolitics.

The pudding had no theme. As foreign secretary, Macmillan searched in vain for a sequel to the island story about imperial glory. 'There is a vision and (or) a theme – if ever we can get away from negotiations on the future of eggs and pig meat – it is the march to the unity of the whole world – United Europe with Commonwealth, USA.' The premier diagnosed world-wide unease, 'a malaise which is beginning to show itself everywhere'. The malaise began nearer home – a crisis of confidence in the political class that rubbed off on the premier. Fresh from a round of gold star international conferences, economist Roy Harrod alerted Macmillan to negative perceptions of the UK – 'now universally recognized as a country of very low growth ... we are on our way out as a country of leadership'.

Crumbling power fostered self-doubt. Labour's Roy Jenkins warned the Commons of 'a real danger ... we shall go into a drab decline'. Suez shredded the moral leadership inherited from the war. The British, wrote journalist Peregrine Worsthorne, 'never have ... been so completely in the dark about what, as a nation, they are trying to do'. The premier lacked the fire to enthuse parliament and nation. A friend heard him speak at a WEU meeting, 'It was the old, old story, nothing he could say or do would make it [European unity] grew any faster. Then came the old stuff about the Commonwealth, our EFTA partners, British agriculture. There was one dreadful passage, "Let us count our blessings."' Inconsistent pronouncements about the nation's ranking undermined trust. Paris ambassadress Cynthia Gladwyn dismissed Macmillan's insistence on Britain still being a great power as 'further proof of the sickening hypocrisy of politicians. Only a few weeks ago ... he was giving us a long tirade on how European civilization had come to an end, that England was finished'.[32]

A sense of amputated identity and loss of purpose impacted policy-making, and generated ennui with European issues. Asked why the government had not fully committed to the Six at Messina in 1955 the then chancellor of the exchequer answered – 'boredom'. Labour leader Hugh Gaitskell belittled EEC and EFTA talks as 'always a bore and a nuisance'. The badges of conventional greatness – missiles, East–West summits, Anglo–American conclaves, one foot high white fur hats Macmillan mode – were sexier than Brussels agricultural quotas and pig meat.[33] Ennui explains why in the 1950s politicians and planners were slow to pick up on the desire for greater integration and increasing distrust of Britain. Meeting continental economists in 1953, Robert Hall, director of the Cabinet Office economic section, observed 'a strong desire for integration, a common market'. Suez dissolved Britain's residual moral primacy. 'Scandinavian opinion', declared the Swedish ambassador in London, 'has never been more shocked by a British Government action'. In 1958 European students at the LSE rebuked Britain for refusing to join the EEC, 'We don't trust you because ... you want to be a great Imperial power still'.[34]

The government's approach to negotiations helped scupper the bid. Insistence by a Johnny-come-lately on bespoke terms for British agriculture, Commonwealth trade and EFTA partners was fundamentally flawed. 'Forcing the Six to provide satisfactory terms for New Zealand, for Australia, for India and for Africa had become an impossible task before 1961,' notes the official history. The misjudgement guaranteed protracted wrangling at the expense of the European ideals Britain claimed to espouse. Macmillan's mix of cajolery and bullying towards de Gaulle betrayed naïvety and arrogance. There was no plan B and no back channel to the Élysée. Nor did the premier reach out to Labour Party leader Hugh Gaitskell in order to build a bipartisan approach.[35]

Ministers made a pig's ear of marketing the bid. Assuming talks lasting weeks rather than months, No. 10 damped down expectations and protected its negotiating hand. The sprint became a marathon, but Macmillan resisted engagement with the public. The failure to sell Europe to the country and the unconscionable slowness of the multilateral Brussels game gave the Labour Party and anti-common market lobbies time to mobilize. Support for the bid peaked at 53 per cent in December 1961 before plummeting in 1962. Domestic dissensions confirmed the reservations of the Six about the UK's readiness for Europe.

Contradictions wrong-footed the application. The contrast between Treaty of Rome aspirations and the Brussels sausage factory was a turnoff for the nation. Efforts to secure an American replacement for Blue Streak, Heath warned, meant that 'at the same time as we are trying to negotiate our entry ... we are giving every indication of wishing to carry out policies which are anathema to the two most important members of the Community. This can only increase the mistrust and suspicion felt towards us'.[36]

In the summer of 1962 pro-Europe groups accused the government of neglecting the case for membership. A leading public relations specialist warned: 'To date the government has shown a marked lack of ability – one might say responsibility – over even attempting to explain the intricacies of this complicated problem [EEC entry] to the inhabitants of Coronation Street and their neighbours, a pamphlet and the weekend utterances of ministers are not enough.' Education minister David Eccles alerted Macmillan to voter fatigue: 'The intelligent voter doubts whether we are as a nation fit enough to enter the Common Market. The doubts are spreading like measles ... the cry goes up, "the Government doesn't tell us anything." Everyone is left in the dark about how the Common Market will affect him ... So we will lose votes because we are not explaining things well.'[37]

Whitehall hierarchs cheered the ministerial Rolls for successfully navigating Brussels road blocks and almost reaching the finishing line. Reality was less flattering. Hubris bred over-confidence: 'we're a match for The French at civil service level ... we'll put de Gaulle in his place. He'll learn to speak English in a year or two.' Uninspired leadership hobbled the UK delegation. Styled 'Mr Europe', Heath 'had no particular liking for the French, nor any conspicuous empathy with foreigners'. In Brussels he played solo, suppressing the voices of colleagues. French foreign minister Couve and his énarques, outranked and outgunned him. Ambassador Pierson Dixon kept his Paris posting and commuted between the two capitals. The intention was to preserve the envoy's rapport with de Gaulle, but the double harness sapped his effectiveness in both cities and contributed to an early death.[38]

Whitehall naïvely assumed a level playing field, but community procedures emphasized applicant status. Sir Eric Rolls's legendary fluency in several languages and ability to lip read in three was wasted. Instead of face-to-face bargaining, the Six withdrew behind closed doors to hammer out a collective response on each issue, leaving the British to kick their heels in ante-rooms. Unacceptable responses triggered a repeat of the whole process. London requested an independent chair and strong secretariat but had to accept a rotating chair and weak secretariat. 'We never succeeded in establishing ... [that] the Conference was a place where seven governments were together seeking solutions', bewailed UK officials.[39]

Too many cooks. Multiple actors and plots crisscrossed. It was Uncle Tom Cobley and all: the Six as a Community and as individual member states, together with Britain, Ireland, Denmark, EFTA states, Commonwealth countries, the United States, the European Commission and visiting missions. Rattled by the 'leisurely pace', Heath recommended a more 'aggressive' stance. Gossip and disinformation overwhelmed UK officials: 'It was impossible to circulate a document or make a statement ... unless we were ready to see its substance published at once.' Something safely said on one front, exploded on another.[40]

Without an effective nerve centre and triage the delegation drifted. Commonwealth governments pressed trading interests regardless of relative importance. Under instructions the delegation put forward proposals 'on questions ranging from the trivial to the essential irrespective of the prospects of negotiability'. At weekends senior officials – 'flying knights' – scurried back to London. The commuting made it difficult to take the temperature – 'it was seldom possible ... to make a considered assessment of the current position and decide what fresh instructions were needed'. London did not welcome feedback – severely restricting circulation of the team's forecasts of what might be obtainable. The forecasts 'appeared to have no direct impact on ministerial and official opinion ... or on our instructions'.[41]

Macmillan made no effort to break out of the cage, and lead negotiator Heath was determined to play hardball. As talks got bogged down he sounded off about the need 'to stand up to the French and outwit and outmanoeuvre them'. Strangely, in a city jam-packed with players there were no behind-the-scenes initiatives, despite plenty of potential go-betweens. Bernard Clappier, director of external economic policy at the French Treasury, and Jean François Deniau, leading the Community delegation, proffered advice – one of three senior Eurocrats to resign after the veto. Rolls's friendship with Marjolin, French representative on the European Commission, supplied another conduit. A rigidly hierarchical delegation lacked the resilience for informal probes. On many issues instructions precluded it from taking the initiative.[42]

There is no consensus on the débâcle of 14 January 1963. Explanations of the motive and timing of the veto are 'varied, complex and conflicting'. Was it an expression of settled French policy or an angry swipe provoked by the Anglo–American Nassau agreement about Polaris missiles on 21 December 1962? Allegedly, de Gaulle felt betrayed because a week earlier at Rambouillet on 15–16 December Macmillan had not fully briefed him. For want of a nail? 'All might have been so different', claimed a French diplomat, if the premier had stayed awake instead of snoozing over his Armagnac while de Gaulle rambled on after lunch. Nice anecdote but implausible. Before the encounter the general had decided on a veto – how, when and where was the question. What he said at Rambouillet reads like a dry-run for the 14 January press conference. Nassau was pretext, not cause.[43]

The official history of Britain's European policy asserts that French internal developments drove the veto decision.[44] Opposed on principle to UK membership de Gaulle waited until he felt strong enough to risk a unilateral veto. The simplistic argument conveniently lets British decision-makers off the hook. Certainly, France's internal consolidation mattered. Through 1962 the nation rebounded economically and politically: completion of CAP; Algerian independence; referendum approving the president's election by universal suffrage; and a large Gaullist victory in November legislative elections. But turbulence remained – the general had a narrow escape from an OAS ambush at Petit-Clamart on 22 August. By early autumn external forces dominated the general's decision-making. A triumphal state visit to West Germany in early September made the French president anxious to finalize a Paris–Bonn axis and speed détente with the Soviet Union and eastern Europe. American President John F. Kennedy's minimalist style of consultation with NATO allies in the October Cuban Missile Crisis reinforced the resolve to build an independent nuclear force.

De Gaulle's perceptions of UK intentions decisively swayed his decision-making. Macmillan's tacit 'Non' to the general's overtures binned hopes of partnership. At the Château de Champs summit on 3 June 1962 the general made a final throw of the dice – inviting military and political collaboration. The prime minister again dodged a direct response, and made it clear that cooperation would have to await admission to the Community. The snub alarmed British officials when they checked the official record a few days later: 'De Gaulle could very easily have interpreted this, if not as a refusal to agree to talks ... at least as an attempt to put them off indefinitely.' Precisely. Macmillan's rebuff persuaded the general that he had nothing to gain by prolonging negotiations.[45]

Macmillan's increasingly beleaguered home base had already given the general second thoughts about the desirability of alliance. An avalanche of woes hit No. 10: faltering economic performance, by-election defeats (especially Orpington in March 1962), sex and spy scandals, Conservative party rifts, and resistance to EEC membership culminating in the Labour's Party's condemnation of the bid at its October conference. The sixties countercultural revolution strengthened perceptions of a country in disarray. Labour looked set to win the next general election in 1964. Given Macmillan's growing unpopularity and refusal to make an offer, the general deliberated how to end the talks – regaling ministers in December 1962 with excerpts from Edith Piaf's song *Ne pleurez pas, Milord* (Don't weep, My Lord), including the refrain *Allez-vous en, Milord* (Clear off, My Lord). Macmillan was now an unwanted ally.

Why wait so long to pull the plug? The narrative lacks a convincing explanation of the delay. Brussels supplies an answer. The stately dialogues of president and premier against the backdrop of historic chateaux captured media attention, and turned the horse-trading over Canadian pig meat quotas and New Zealand butter into a dull side show. In reality, the Brussels Leviathan determined the denouement. As the largest multilateral exercise since the Marshall Plan era of the late 1940s the British, Danish and Irish applications marked a seismic moment in European affairs. The negotiation was one of the most complex in the history of international economic relations. How to escape Leviathan? The seemingly endless talks ensnared London and Paris in a multi-dimensional chess game which they could influence, but not control. France's foot-dragging initially paid off, enabling completion of CAP and consolidation of French hegemony in the Community. By late 1962 slow strangulation tactics had served their purpose. With no prospect of a British deal the general wanted out.

The intractability of the Brussels monster swallowed up time and resources, preventing him moving forward. On 12 December Wormser, senior economic adviser, warned of a crisis looming in the coming weeks. Strengthening domestic opposition to membership would compel Macmillan to demand more concessions or withdraw. France, concluded Wormser, should act quickly to protect its interests.[46] For de Gaulle, the alert conjured up unpleasant scenarios: a limpet-like Macmillan launching a formal application, locking France into the Brussels maze; a UK withdrawal saddling France with the blame; deadlock with recriminations on all sides – destabilizing the Community. The scenarios menaced France's standing with Community partners, global publics and French opinion. A veto seemed the lesser evil, offering an emergency exit and opportunity for France to defend the decision. But there was no quick fix. To rush into a veto without a credible pretext and adequate preparation risked breaking up the Community and becoming the fall guy.

Two things rescued the general from the quandary – his press conference machine and the Nassau meeting. Nassau supplied a plausible pretext and the conference a superb propaganda weapon for blaming the Anglo-Saxons and posing as Europe's true champion. The Anglo–American agreement on Polaris missiles, claimed de Gaulle, contradicted Macmillan's avowals of European loyalty. The semi-annual regal-like press conference, the regime's heavy artillery, gathered the political elite and a global television audience – an unrivalled opportunity to sell France's case. The elaborately choreographed performance required lengthy preparation – the president took weeks to memorize script and responses to questions submitted in advance. Hence the delay of nearly a month between Nassau and the veto.

An old-fashioned power struggle triumphed over partnership. De Gaulle won – but not hands down. Shunting the bid aside merely postponed the issue. The contrast between the Six's surging economic clout and UK doldrums guaranteed a second bid. In the meantime, the contest continued – as farce. In March 1963 Heath – to avoid meeting French ambassador Courcel – excused himself from the England–France rugby match at Twickenham. Assured the ambassador had refused an invitation he went, and bumped into Courcel. England won the game. After toasting 'The Queen' the English captain proposed a toast to the 'President of France' – turning to Heath with the mikes on: 'I wasn't going to mention that bastard's name'.[47]

Heath commanded the *Death to the French* brigade: 'so bitterly anti-French as to be ... almost unbalanced in his hatred of de Gaulle', noted Macmillan. Cancellation of a visit by Princess Margaret left Parisians unfazed. The Quai seemed unperturbed when the BBC provocatively televised an interview at a London Chinese restaurant with former foreign minister and OAS chief Bidault, fleeing an angry general. Paris protested the anti-French salvos but held its fire, anticipating a second try in the near future – including efforts to mobilize Community partners against France. The general's 'I want her naked' remarks put Britain on notice that the next round would mean taking off American and Commonwealth clothes.[48]

An avoidable veto? Maybe. The thumbs down is usually regarded as an inescapable expression of French antipathy caused by clashing national ambitions – an Anglo-American Europe vs. a French-led European Europe. This interpretation ignores the shades of grey in the bruising encounter – the general's friendliness, Macmillan's missteps and the Brussels Godzilla. Though the premier recognized the need for 'a personal deal with de Gaulle ... what he says, counts – and nothing else', the American alliance acted like a ball and chain, inhibiting a pact. The years 1958–60 – prime-time for rapprochement – were squandered in ill-conceived moves: corralling the French into the FTA, searching for a Six/Seven accommodation, and applying for Community membership without first getting the French on board. As well as stoking cross-channel distrust, the initiatives altered continental perceptions of Britain. 'The whole experience since 1959', concluded a Whitehall mandarin, 'has been that those in Europe who would like us to join have recognized more and more that Europe can be a going concern without us. Any proposition that we should like to join *if* certain conditions could be fulfilled will get us nowhere.'[49]

The Dictionary of National Biography lauded Macmillan for coordinating 'with skill, cunning, and a certain degree of deception Britain's retreat from world power status... He was sometimes unwilling to do more than hint to his party and his nation the direction in which he was leading, but this was perhaps because he saw that the Britons of his day could not and would not face the facts'. The complacency is telling. On Europe, the premier's condescension, ineptitude, and inability to engage with the nation, proved disastrous. True, membership bids gave citizenry a voice in external policy-making – via polls, parties, pressure groups and the 1975 referendum – but political masters imposed narrow limits, presenting voters 'with the answer rather than the question' – pre-empting advance debate.[50]

The American poet William Carlos Williams wrote of 'the rare occurrence of the expected'. That leaders would draw a line under the interwar *mesentente* and make a fresh start was a reasonable post-war expectation. Diminishing power made collaboration a potential life-saver for post-imperial neighbours. Bungling the application blighted Community development and the cross-channel relationship for over a decade, leaving a large legacy of UK Euroscepticism. Macmillan provided his own epitaph – telling de Gaulle, 'Britain had done some very silly things in the past. A really close Anglo–French alliance would have prevented many mistakes'.[51]

10

Another Harold

The Wizard, a popular comic, featured the adventures of Wilson the Wonder Athlete, a homespun, elixir-drinking superman who emerged from the Yorkshire moors to break athletic records, including a three-minute mile, and become the first to climb Everest. The political wizardry of Labour prime minister Harold Wilson broke all records. The Yorkshire born premier earned kudos for defying the general's veto and keeping Britain's EEC membership application on the table. Economist Uwe Kitzinger praised him as 'a major help to the European cause ... Harold Wilson was almost certainly one of those few men but for whom Britain could not have entered the Community'. Political scientist Gillian Peele commended the premier's skill in maintaining 'commitment to eventual membership'.[1]

Is the Labour leader ripe for rehabilitation? Not quite. Wilson condemned the Macmillan government's 'inept handling of Anglo–French relations' while displaying equal ineptness.[2] This chapter advances three arguments. First, Wilson's failure was primarily self-inflicted, not the work of a Gallic marplot. Britain needed French sponsorship but offered no incentives. Rather than woo the gatekeeper, policy-makers tried to outflank him. Second, demonizing the general has obscured his friendliness and efforts to reach out. Third, the Wilson government's refusal to negotiate a new cross-channel relationship delayed entry into Europe until 1973. Downing Street's disinclination to prepare party and public drained away support for membership. The Labour government of 1966–70 left Whitehall unprepared for an effective post-entry presence in Brussels. Labour's European policy seeded Euroscepticism and Brexit.

When historian Robert Paxton left the University of California Berkeley in 1966 students gave him a dartboard with General de Gaulle for bull's eye. 'The French President was seen as an old man, harbouring the resentments of twenty five years earlier,' wrote Wilson's press secretary, 'taking slow, deliberate and repeated revenge for the affronts dealt to him when he was wartime irritant to Churchill and Roosevelt'. A blue-ribbon diplomat complained, 'It is France alone who prevents Britain joining in talks on the political development of Europe'. Actions seemed to confirm the general's villainy: the blackballing of entry bids, and withdrawal from NATO's military command in March 1966. Within months of the general's resignation the Community's Hague summit in December 1969 authorized enlargement negotiations leading to Britain's accession in January 1973 – proof, it seemed, of an old man's stubbornness.[3]

Labour's talk of opening moves betrayed inexperience and the absence of hard thinking about a reconciliation with France. Apart from affirming a desire for a better understanding, the government had no proposals. The 100 days began ominously with the government scoring an own goal, angering France and Britain's EFTA trading partners. Pleading financial necessity Wilson sought cancellation of the Anglo-French agreement of 1962 on the supersonic airliner Concord – Whitehall spelling without an 'e' – and illegally slapped a 15 per cent surcharge on imports – a hefty blow for the smaller EFTA economies. Aviation Minister Roy Jenkins flew to Paris to negotiate Concord's cancellation. Warned by the FO to expect an 'atmosphere of cold enmity', Jenkins found his opposite number 'friendly throughout'. It was Britain's ambassador who caused displeasure by serving a lightly corked wine at lunch. The Concorde agreement's status as a full-blown treaty gave the French the upper hand and Wilson surrendered.[4]

Talk of bridge-building and fresh starts in Europe grabbed headlines, but ran into trouble – which bridges? which starts? A UK negotiator found the process of establishing closer EFTA/EEC links 'a peculiarly dispiriting one' – since EFTA was a free trade area and the EEC a customs union, there were 'no common policies' to facilitate bridge-building. Discussions perforce focused on cooperation in 'highly technical areas such as patents and customs facilitation'.[5]

The emphasis on rapprochement evoked a warm response from the French president. Winston Churchill's funeral on 30 January 1965 brought Wilson and the general together for the first time. The tall, monarchical-like seventy-five-year-old, master of his nation's history and high culture, speaking a pure classical French, towered over the demotic, pipe smoking forty-nine-year-old, with Yorkshire accent and soft spots for Gilbert and Sullivan opera and singer Vera Lynn. During a fifty-minute icebreaker at the French embassy the prime minister insisted so much on what prevented Britain joining the Community that he 'implicitly accepted de Gaulle's version' of the breakdown of the Macmillan bid. Ignorance of Community governance earned him a mini tutorial from the maestro – 'there was no supreme authority which took decisions. Each of the six governments was master in its own house'.[6]

De Gaulle blessed the warmer relationship, assuring his London ambassador that the two countries 'will walk together'. An Élysée press conference confirmed the new direction: 'there are no mountains between England and France.' True, information minister Peyrefitte recorded the general lambasting Wilson: 'a madcap ... wants to make mischief ... he beats on every drum ... they have only wimps leading them, starting with the socialists. And they are under America's heel'. But de Gaulle expressed confidence in the UK's future – Britons had too much energy and vitality to accept an American empire. Revival would come though 'no one can say when'. Actions speak louder than words. Rather than exploit UK troubles the president instructed: 'above all, don't say anything which might seem to overwhelm them. You can see that they are down on their luck. When we were in a worse state after the collapse they still supported us.' To be sure, tactical reasons in part motivated benevolence. The 'empty chair' crisis within the Community from July 1965 made a friendly Britain desirable, and Wilson's denial of interest in Community membership reassured the Élysée. Affability had limits – the general refused support for a beleaguered pound in September 1965.[7]

The sequel to the conversation at Churchill's funeral was a full-dress Paris summit on 2–3 April 1965, the first top-level get-together since the Macmillan–de Gaulle encounter at Rambouillet in December 1962. The conference was a damp squib. The run-up to the event revealed ingrained distrust on both sides, and unwillingness to rethink the relationship. FO anxieties about French ascendance and Britain's isolation eclipsed earlier expressions of friendship. The anti-French, 'faintly paranoid' views of foreign secretary Michael Stewart and minions excluded a lovefest. Stewart, having replaced Patrick Gordon Walker – Wilson's first choice – wanted to show his mettle, and warned of 'our increasing and dangerous isolation from Europe'. In the face of the Community's more dominating and assertive stance Britain had to hold on to 'those organizations which we had, with EFTA as our principal instrument of economic policy in Europe, the OECD as the economic arm of the Atlantic alliance and NATO ... as the military arm'.[8]

Within weeks Stewart returned to the charge. The Community's growing strength might well push the Commonwealth and United States into dealing separately with the Six, bypassing the United Kingdom: 'this is the time to resume our rightful place on the European stage and set about helping Europe towards a better relationship with the United States within the Atlantic Alliance.' The Paris embassy added its ha'penny – 'the mere fact' of Wilson going to Paris would be interpreted as a success for France. 'The principal French objective is to show to the world ... that Britain's exclusion is now accepted by the British as a permanent feature of the landscape.' The embassy belittled expressions of Élysée goodwill, discounting as classic de Gaulle a 'friendly and relaxed' general's 'little speech about his respect and liking for the British people'.[9]

French distrust matched British suspicions. Wormser, director of economic and financial affairs at the Quai, pulled no punches. After trying to scapegoat France for the failure of the 1961 bid Britain had adopted a more nuanced approach, combining a strong presence in European institutions like the Council of Europe with efforts to reinvigorate EFTA. Notwithstanding the friendly words exchanged at Churchill's funeral and signs of renewed public interest in the Community, Britain, warned Wormser, looked 'to find a way of meddling in the affairs of the Six, doubtless to paralyse them'. It consistently sought to minimize cooperation between the Six while highlighting similar arrangements among the Seven EFTA states as well as denying the importance of Franco–German cooperation by organizing Franco–British and Anglo–German consultations.[10]

At the conference's opening session on 2 April de Gaulle offered a cue, asking 'whether the Prime Minister wished to talk about Europe – the Common Market was making progress.' Wilson batted away the suggestion, staying with East–West relations and Vietnam; Stewart, closeted separately with foreign minister Couve, provided easier prey. Did Britain intend to enter the Common Market? queried Couve. Unrehearsed, the foreign secretary improvised disastrously. A blame game erupted about responsibilities for the 1963 veto. Stewart insisted that the French had changed their tune – now singling out Britain's agricultural policy after previously citing the special relationship as the chief obstacle. Overnight, the premier got his lines together and took the lead, enquiring 'How de Gaulle viewed developments in Europe, both in the Common Market and more widely. In his view it was important to make the point that the Six were not the whole of Europe'. Wilson fenced off the question of British membership: 'Britain would always be prepared to talk about joining on terms which would reconcile her national and Commonwealth interests ... it could not be said that that situation obtained today.'[11]

France's ambassador in London recalled the premier saying, 'Personally, the Common Market is of no interest to me. What we must do is set up Anglo–French cooperation'. But No. 10 did not field anything new. Provision for regular consultations at ministerial and senior official level, and the creation of cultural hubs, would have energized the connection. Discussions merely refreshed existing projects and revived previous consultations on Africa and the Middle East. Concorde, Channel Tunnel and military aviation projects were legacies of Conservative administrations. Despite agreement on continuing technical collaboration, the absence of an overarching political understanding and permanent liaison turned technological cooperation into a snare. Ballooning costs for the Tunnel and Concorde were a running sore in Whitehall. British purchases of civil and military aircraft from the United States irritated the French. 'Great Britain', complained *Le Monde*, 'only works with France on minor programs'.[12]

De Gaulle left the door ajar for further contacts: 'the briefing about the talks, both from the Élysée and the Quai d'Orsay', acknowledged Wilson, was 'unusually friendly'. The tensions that climaxed in the Community 'empty chair' crisis of July 1965 were already evident, as indeed was France's disappointment with the results of the Franco–German Treaty of 1963. Determined to oppose supranational trends de Gaulle withdrew French representation from the Community's Council of Ministers. West Germany's reassertion of ties to the United States disappointed the Élysée. By contrast, Britain opposed supranationalism and offered a credible counterweight to Germany. With presidential elections for a second term upcoming in December 1965 a Downing Street probe might have paid off. True, the couple differed over European unity – an Atlanticist Europe vs. a Gaullist European Europe, but this did not stop Conservative prime minister Heath and President Georges Pompidou agreeing British entry to the Community in 1971-2. Significantly, during the April talks de Gaulle stressed the couple's agreement on fundamentals, despite differences of approach to international issues.[13]

Friendliness was no flash in the pan. The president remained affable and approachable through 1965. Peyrefitte called for France and Britain to draw closer and 'build a future based on exchanges, cooperation and friendship'. Encouraging noises came from other French government sources. 'Remarks which, in other circumstances, might appear conventional', stressed *Le Monde*, acquired in the Empty Chair crisis 'a new significance'. Britain's official history – without citing evidence – shrugs off the episode: 'there appears to have been little more to this flurry than a desire to signal to France's partners that there were other fish than them in the sea'. Quizzed in July 1965 by former Conservative prime minister Alec Douglas-Home, the general after repeating his mantra – 'we do not think that you are yet ready to accept Common Market rules' – extended an olive branch: 'I'm certain that for all kinds of reasons our two countries ... still have lots of things to do together'.[14]

In November the president warmly greeted Heath, the new Conservative leader. Heath rebutted criticism of Britain's military dependence on American Polaris technology, pointing out that Europe lacked the technical resources to achieve independence. The solution, answered de Gaulle, was for 'England and France to work together ... If England and France decide together to make Europe they will succeed'. The general criticized Germany, wondering whether 'it's possible to conclude European arrangements with Germany since she has provocative and even warlike ambitions towards eastern Europe'. Prime minister Pompidou assured Heath that France would like Britain 'to be in the Community for geographical and human reasons and to act as a counterweight to German industry and because a political Europe would be unthinkable without her ... Germany over the past two years seemed to have changed her thinking, to be less attached to the European Community and to consider herself more and more as a world economic power'.[15]

De Gaulle persevered, despite No. 10's unresponsiveness, informing his cabinet on 24 November that UK relations with continental Europe seemed to be 'ripening in a positive sense' and France looked sympathetically on this evolution. Instantly, the FO – without consulting the Paris embassy – spiked the statement, informing UK missions that it was not based on any London–Paris contacts and seemed designed for domestic and Community consumption. The embassy protested that it was highly unusual for press briefings about cabinet meetings to include verbatim texts and London's trigger-happy response had created a very negative reaction in the French press. The ambassador's request for authority to take up the matter with the French came to nothing.[16]

The friendlier the French the more suspicious Stewart and Co. Officials squelched any suggestion that an understanding might be possible. Alpha diplomat Michael Palliser, soon to become Wilson's private secretary, underscored the 'fundamentally negative character of de Gaulle's policy. He destroys. He builds nothing'. In December 1965 Stewart returned to the warpath: 'French influence in Western Europe will continue to grow and British influence to diminish'. A ruthless, unprincipled de Gaulle endangered British interests. The government, continued Stewart, should announce its willingness in principle to accept the Treaty of Rome. Without an early profession of British intent French nationalism might infect Germany – giving her hope of becoming leader in Europe. Wilson stopped circulation of the paper, finding the message 'hard to swallow'. The foreign secretary renewed the attack in late January 1966 with a forecast of 'General de Gaulle's foreign policy over the next two years'. Anticipating France's departure from NATO within two years the foreign secretary recommended reviewing 'our co-operation with France ... it may, for example, become impossible to reconcile an exclusively bilateral cooperation with her over a range of technological and defence projects ... with our loyalty to NATO'. He concluded grimly, 'we are ... dealing with a regime under the control of a man whose attitude and intentions are ... hostile to our own'.[17]

Two months later, in March 1966, de Gaulle announced France's withdrawal from NATO's integrated military command. The action undermined any prospect of Franco–British agreement. Elections in December 1965 had given the French president a satisfying vote of confidence: 85 per cent turnout; 54.6 per cent votes for another seven-year term. In January 1966 the 'Luxembourg Compromise' resolved the Community's 'Empty Chair' crisis by freezing moves towards greater political integration. Reassured, the president returned to his route map – exiting NATO's integrated command and pursuing détente with the Soviet Union and Communist satellites. The UK joined the international chorus condemning de Gaulle's perceived disloyalty to the Western alliance. Surprisingly, an 'unusually warm' exchange of letters followed. Wilson assured the general of 'the overwhelming desire of the British people, animated by ... respect and affection for France and her achievements, to have the closest possible relations with their French neighbours'. In a handwritten letter the general spoke glowingly of Britain's record – 'constant ally, proven with glory, of France and a great European state', Wilson confided to Stewart a sneaking regard for the general's savvy – his 'assessments of the way things are moving in the world may be more up to date and in tune with the times than our own'.[18]

Armed with a thumping majority in the 31 March 1966 election, Wilson allowed the idea of a second application to gain traction, but the condemnation of de Gaulle for his withdrawal from NATO's military command queered the pitch. Paris perceived London's condemnation as proof of American vassalage and an attempt to isolate France. Most importantly, Wilson implemented Stewart's call for a cap on cross-channel cooperation. Over the next three years Britain severely rationed collaboration. The measure threw away bargaining chips: 'we should not start any new bilateral military projects ... we should continue existing projects on the understanding that we had secure break clauses ... we should do nothing to help French nuclear capability ... adopt an attitude of reserve towards bilateral meetings with the French unless these can be clearly shown to be to our advantage'. In force until June 1969 the guidelines stymied rapprochement, and compromised early entry into Europe.[19]

In early May 1966 'Tommy' Balogh, the prime minister's economic adviser, scouted French views. Over lunch in Paris a French economic policy trinity – Wormser, his deputy Jean Marie Brunet, and the assistant governor of the Bank of France Bernard Clappier, shared their take on a second bid. Far from imposing a veto in 1963 France simply concluded Britain was not yet ready to accept the Treaty of Rome: 'once again it was for London to choose and decide'.[20] No. 10 did nothing – no backchannel contacts, no special envoys.

Misperceptions on both sides of the channel were self-reinforcing. The French feared the worst. In late May Wormser summed up France's stance. What mattered was 'to know whether Britain will be able to accept the rules of the Rome Treaty and the arrangements concluded since 1963 ... one no longer knows for sure whether it is a case of bringing the UK into the common market or, on the contrary, of bringing the Common Market into the Commonwealth and EFTA'. Britain, declared the policy czar, hoped 'once again to scapegoat us and put us in the wrong before the negotiation has even opened ... people are speculating in London on the difficulty the French government will have in "blocking" for a second time a British initiative. The NATO crisis in separating us from our allies facilitates a manoeuvre whose object is clearly to isolate us from the outset ... unless the British make a serious mistake our isolation will increase in the course of negotiations'.[21]

Wormser's pessimism deepened. In mid-June he saw no point in negotiations which 'cannot lead to the British accepting our theses'. Community enlargement 'must by definition lead to a free trade zone, probably global'. Britain had declared its political will to enter the Community 'provided satisfactory conditions are obtained'. In other words, Britain was 'not ready to accept the treaty arrangements ... notably the CAP but asks for the rules to be changed'. The United States, which had lobbied heavily for British membership in 1963, wanted Britain in the Community. An American-backed Britain, concluded Wormser, posed a financial and political threat to France and its partners. As well as transferring British debts and deficits to the Community, Washington hoped that within a few years integration would regain a federalist path.[22]

Through May to June 1966 the cabinet mulled options – await de Gaulle's departure before applying or outflank him through his partners. The cabinet committee on Europe handled much of the discussion. Ministers presented the curious spectacle of attempting to enter a locked room without asking for the key. Approaching the French 'would strengthen the French position when our object is to weaken it. The French would be tempted to force the price up to a level which we could not afford to pay'. Significantly, Wilson's summary of discussions ranked 'Probing – especially President de Gaulle' sixth in a list of eight options. The general's withdrawal from NATO's military command made him seem more than ever an enemy to be circumvented. Brown, deputy prime minister and head of the new department of economic affairs (DEA), emerged as a leading advocate of outflanking the general. Like Stewart, Brown viewed Germany, not France, as the key to Britain's European policy. An Anglo–German partnership with 'a truly European approach to security, defence and foreign policy arrangements ... explicitly based on partnership with the US', he suggested, might outflank de Gaulle by rallying the Five and 'large sections of French opinion'. Wilson demurred: the United States 'would not lift a finger to help in this exercise'.[23]

The visit of French ministers on 6–8 July flopped. At a pre-departure press conference the French delegation reportedly treated Wilson 'with scarcely veiled contempt', playing down Brown's zeal for the Community – he 'does not speak for Britain'. Quai bios acknowledged Wilson as a smart tactician 'who has displayed remarkable skill in dodging traps and in making others carry the heaviest responsibilities'. His 'clumsy and self-effacing' foreign secretary was a mediocrity: 'without preconceived ideas in foreign policy he never risks himself beyond strict orthodoxy and the line decided by the Foreign Office who have found in him their most reliable spokesman'. Brown got more sympathetic profiling: son of a lorry driver, number two in party and government, 'a highly coloured personality, courageous and dynamic, renowned for his impulsiveness and imprudent language'.[24]

The summit turned out 'disastrous'. Wilson offered nothing, and caused offence by cancelling a session and skipping a dinner at the French embassy. There was no meeting of minds. Never short of panache the French delivered a lifemanship class. While the British team nursed voluminous folders, none of the French visitors had a sheet of paper in front of them. The latest economic indicators corroborated French insistence on the UK's unreadiness for membership. A May–June seaman's strike paralysed ports. Sharp raids on sterling detonated one of the worst sterling crises since 1945. Defence secretary Denis Healey's untimely swipe at de Gaulle 'as a bad ally in NATO and a bad partner in the Common Market' clouded proceedings. Premier Pompidou was 'annoyed' by the cancellation of a meeting because of a Commons debate – and 'understandably so', conceded Wilson. UK ministers made no bones about their desire to enter Europe and discussions degenerated into arm wrestling over Community admission terms.[25]

'Pompidou,' complained Heath, 'had come over here with an invitation in his pocket for a state visit of the Queen. But he was so disgusted with his reception by Wilson that the invitation was never extended. He and Couve de Murville returned to France convinced that Wilson does not mean business over joining the Common Market.' Not so. The exchanges convinced the French that Wilson meant business. Terrier-like, the prime minister harried the French leaders – demanding assurances that France would not spring a veto because of the Anglo–American connection: 'at the end of the day would we have to choose between the United States and Europe?'[26]

The ground had shifted since 1961–3 when the French queried Britain's motives in applying for admission; now they emphasized economic infirmities. Declaring eligibility for membership 'essentially economic', Couve and Pompidou performed a goody-goody routine, emphasizing the tough fiscal measures France introduced in 1958 to prepare for Community entry. The talks began and ended in confrontation – Stewart admonished the French for recent nuclear tests in the Pacific in violation of the 1963 Moscow Limited Test Ban Treaty. Undaunted, the general kept a line open. A few days later at a Bastille Day reception he assured Reilly that the London discussions had helped, adding delphically, 'It all depended on Britain'. In short, the general wanted real horse-trading.[27]

Why did the prime minister drive up to a closed gate? In early May 1966 the Paris embassy advised, 'It is very unlikely that the French would be willing to start serious negotiations with us for a year at least'. The premier's confidante, Marcia Williams (Lady Falkender) gave the same advice: 'it is improbable that de Gaulle will let us in'. At the London talks in July Pompidou and Couve made it crystal clear they were prepared to use Britain's economic troubles to block entry. A clean bill of financial and economic health, they told the press, was a prerequisite for membership. Pompidou reportedly said that devaluation would be necessary before entry. The remarks accelerated a run on the pound peaking in a mid-July sterling crisis. To be sure, hubris and over-confidence deluded the premier. Like Macmillan, Wilson cherished an inflated opinion of his charm and persuasive powers. More importantly, he had run out of viable alternatives.[28]

How had British policy-makers got themselves into such a bind over Europe? Properly prepared, the July meeting with French ministers might have turned out differently. Both sides blundered. It's easy to spin alibis for the Labour government. Force nine gales pummelled ministers: sterling crisis, death throes of empire – Aden, Rhodesia, Malaysia – Indonesia emergencies. A paper-thin majority of four in the October 1964 election left little or no wiggle room. No. 10 had to deliver quickly on the home front in order to be ready for a second election. After thirteen years in the wilderness Labour's call for a modernized 'white heat' technological Britain revived the millennial mood of 1945 among party faithful.

Crises and emergencies impacted decision-making but the decisive influences were personalities, misperceptions and Whitehall dysfunctionality. Fixated on world power, Wilson overlooked the power base under his nose – partnership with France and Germany. 'We are a world power, or we are nothing', the premier proclaimed in his first major speech. Eight months later the nation's frontiers shifted to the Himalayas. *Paris Match* unfairly labelled him as 'vigorously hostile to France'. More accurately, Wilson had little sympathy for France and West-Europeans, though there was a soft spot for Russians and east Europeans. By 1965 the premier had visited Russia twelve times since the war. A remark to *Guardian* editor Alistair Hetherington summed up his attitude to West-Europeans: 'If we couldn't dominate that lot, there wasn't much to be said for us.' Sporting a pipe, Gannex raincoat and cheeky chappie persona, the premier stood for slipperiness. Wilsonism became 'a catch-all term for cunning, duplicity and even deceit'. Efforts to put a good face on everything, including devaluation, drew the comment that as the Titanic's captain 'he would ... have tried to reassure passengers by telling them the ship had only stopped to take on ice'.[29]

The tactician at no point projected a sense of the nation's role over the coming decades. His memoir *The Labour Governments, 1964-1970* stood out 'for its complete lack ... of any analysis of basic national problems'. Home secretary Roy Jenkins observed, 'I'd give anything for evidence that we have a long-term plan for any part of this Government's policy'. A chronic time waster, the premier talked endlessly without coming to a decision, staying up late 'gossiping obsessively with his "kitchen cabinet"' and spending disproportionate amounts of personal time on Rhodesia and Vietnam. Wilson preferred golf to reflection – at No. 10 he fell asleep 'within seconds of putting out the light'. There were no signs of the decline that marred the government of 1974-6 when he regularly tanked up on brandies before Prime Minister's Questions. None the less, quasi paranoiac suspicions of colleagues, journalists and the BBC evoked Captain Queeg of The USS Caine.[30]

An independent-minded foreign secretary would have probed de Gaulle's professions of goodwill. The musical chairs routine of three foreign secretaries in four years warped policy-making. Determined 'to run' the Foreign Office 'through his menials', Wilson selected two 'donnish, quiet, acquiescent' colleagues: Patrick Gordon Walker and Michael Stewart. Gordon Walker's ideas included rethinking the US alliance, 'good relations' with France, and an effective FO planning unit as 'part and parcel of policy-making – not separated'. After losing his parliamentary seat in October 1964 and failing to secure re-election, Gordon Walker gave way to Stewart in January 1965 – followed by rogue elephant George Brown.[31]

Stewart's francophobia prevailed over Wilson's more open-minded outlook. No. 10 had no policy unit to counter FO expertise. Stewart had gravitas, but little else – prompting the quip 'once seen, never remembered'. Only the Queen and her corgis disturbed his equanimity. Europeanist officials treated him as their mouthpiece. Visiting the minister in 'a huge mausoleum of a room' – a colleague asked, 'how can you get any new thoughts in here?' Back came the reply, 'Ah, the new thoughts come from the papers' – in other words, from the mandarins. Resigned to fighting a rearguard action, Stewart believed 'Britain was in the second rank but ... we could enhance our influence by active participation in ... international groupings'. A grating voice and lack of fluency put people off – so many pauses: 'it was hard to know whether he had finished what he intended to say or was merely searching for words.' One visitor found himself 'in the position not only of forcing a conversation but of sustaining it'. An unexpected success in 1965 in facing down noisy students at a televised Oxford Union 'teach-in' on Vietnam proved short lived. On a return appearance in 1970 he could not get a hearing. Stewart's Mrs Proudie-like spouse was 'hostile to the Foreign Office in many ways ... sending down little notes to the departments asking aggressive questions about all sorts of things'. She was blamed for the removal of a senior diplomat from the Paris embassy after the diplomat's wife advised her to wear gloves at an official function.³²

'It was plain', Stewart later asserted, 'that de Gaulle would be reluctant to admit Britain ... there was a school of thought which held that ... the road to the EEC lay through Paris so we must first placate de Gaulle ... It seemed to me that this would involve too much surrender to Gaullist views'. Not the most convincing of arguments – in the light of the 1963 veto, how could anyone doubt that 'the road to the EEC lay through Paris'? And why should placating de Gaulle mean surrendering to his views? The minister had nothing more constructive to suggest than a declaration of intent to apply for membership followed by patience and pressure on France's partners. The general was the bad guy. That a pact might benefit the wider interests of both countries as well as easing Britain into the Community escaped Stewart's notice. The Paris summit of April 1965, he wrote in his memoirs, convinced him 'that if the three most powerful nations of Western Europe – Britain, France, Germany – were all in the EEC ... they would have to think ... not of hegemony but of partnership'. Precisely, yet as foreign secretary he vetoed the idea.³³

Edging towards a second bid, ministers fought shy of the 800-pound gorilla. Why the reluctance to seduce the general? True, having imposed a cap on cooperation the government had nothing to offer, but the cap was removable. De Gaulle and President Nasser of Egypt topped the FO hit list. Officials held fast to the image of a hostile and treacherous general. Cosying up to France, it was feared, would blight Britain's reputation with EFTA partners and a supposedly friendly Community Five. Diplomats had scores to settle over the Schuman Plan, Messina and the 1963 veto. Many believed Schuman had deliberately sought to exclude Britain from the ECSC. The French, for their part, feared an attempt to take over and dilute the new thriving Community. But the general was not intransigent. He stayed friendly and made important overtures, despite Wilson's lack of interest in a deal.

'French planning, skill and ruthlessness', warned Con O'Neill, ambassador to the European Communities, had put her in a dominant position within the EEC and there was little to be done for the moment. By the mid-1960s a squad of evangelizing Europeanists dedicated to achieving Community membership nudged FO policymaking, notably John Barnes, Michael Butler, Patrick Hancock, and John Robinson. None had any time for France. Butler was particularly pushy. At a crucial UK delegation strategy review in Brussels in July 1962 Butler, then first secretary at the Paris embassy, intervened vigorously –clearly disagreeing with the uncertainty about French attitudes expressed by his ambassador Pierson Dixon. Accused of Francophobia in the Soames affair of February 1969 officials confessed 'Degaullophobia', claiming for it a 'respectable ancestry' from the Second World War. They resented the 1963 veto and loss of European leadership. The hexagon's surging GDP rubbed salt into the wounds.³⁴

Gallic gamesmanship stoked suspicions.³⁵ Wary of entrapment, policy-makers dismissed seemingly mixed signals. From Paris Reilly pooh-poohed junior minister Jean de Broglie's 'favourable noises' about Britain's renewed interest in entry: 'It looks to me as if there may have been a decision that Ministers should use vaguely encouraging language in public, while in private much is made of the obstacles to British entry'. The brief prepared for Brown as incoming foreign secretary in August 1966 summed up FO attitudes. 'France is at present de Gaulle ... de Gaulle's policy ... is anti-American and by extension "anti-Anglo-Saxon" ... Within the [Western] alliance confident Anglo-French collaboration is highly desirable but at present is not feasible'. At the Congress of the European Movement in the Hague in November 1968 Heath declared there could be no Europe without France. As soon as he sat down his secretary was 'set upon by one of the Foreign Secretary's aides in a towering passion. He honestly believed that we had let the side down.'

To isolate de Gaulle, Europeanists looked to his partners, the 'Friendly Five' – Belgium, Germany, Italy, Netherlands and Luxemburg. But the Five would not gang up against France, despite every encouragement. Survival of the fledgling Community mattered more to them than British membership. FO mandarins blamed the general for duplicitously spinning out talks on Britain's 1961 application while blocking closer integration within the Community. Both Butler and Robinson waged an anti-Gaullist crusade, 'relishing confrontations with the Quai d'Orsay'. Butler as first secretary at the Paris embassy in 1961–5 secretly acquired transcripts of the general's conversations with visiting leaders and circulated them within the diplomatic community. 'It was great fun', he recalled, 'because the General didn't hesitate to say completely conflicting things to two visiting Prime Ministers or Foreign Ministers on two successive days ... it was this activity ... that caused him in 1964 to get Couve to try and get rid of me'.[36]

Changing foreign secretaries in midstream envenomed policy-making. Brown, who succeeded Stewart as foreign secretary from August 1966, shared Wilson's assumptions. The general would not risk exercising a veto twice, and the Five would push him into opening the door. A gaffe-prone foreign secretary – by his own admission unsuitable for diplomacy – clashed with a prime minister who also wanted to play foreign secretary. Alcohol and a tug of war with Downing Street discredited Brown and undermined the country's credibility. A whirlwind twenty-month incumbency unfolded like a tragic comedy. A high-octane temperament plus alcohol brought tantrums, abuse, sulks and resignation threats. Subordinates never knew what to expect – a pat on the back or a kick in the pants. Interviewed after the assassination of President John F. Kennedy, Brown claimed the President for a close personal friend. 'Pissed as a coot', commented one viewer.

A feisty Europeanist with a will of his own, Brown seemed indifferent to a Franco-British deal. Rather than sweet-talking de Gaulle, Brown preferred the spouses of French ministers and diplomats – inviting Madame Couve to sleep with him; putting his hand on the knee of Claude Pompidou, and asking for her phone number. Quick as a flash, Martine de Courcel responded to an improper suggestion, 'That's the first time that's been said to me with the soup'. The foreign secretary treated his staff like dirt. Returning late to Britain's Brussels embassy Brown asked for a fire and a large whisky and soda:

> Roddie [Sir Roderick Barclay, ambassador] got up and ... poured George a whisky and soda. George said, 'Fire, I want a fire.' The Ambassador said, 'I'm terribly sorry Secretary of State, but it's getting on for midnight, all the servants have gone ...' 'Where's your wife?' asked George.' Well, she's in bed as she normally is at this time'. 'Get her up'.[37]

One of the few prepared to bawl out Brown was his private secretary, Donald Maitland. The diminutive 5ft 4 Scot riposted during one row, 'You do not imagine. Foreign Secretary, that a person of my stature has got where he is today by kow-towing to bullies?'.

More damaging than the bullying, clowning and bibulousness was the FO–No. 10 vendetta that triggered the foreign secretary's resignation in March 1968. The premier's letter acknowledging Brown's resignation went through seventeen drafts. No. 10 systematically undermined the foreign secretary: accessing secret papers before he saw them; using junior FO minister Lord Chalfont as an 'unofficial minder' – privy to information withheld from the foreign secretary; enlisting Washington's help in educating Brown on the need for a continuing British presence east of Suez. Suspicions of these shenanigans may explain Brown's extreme rudeness to his junior minister and to French foreign minister Couve. The foreign secretary summoned Chalfont to his side, saying loudly, 'Here you speak this man's silly language. What's he on about?' Chalfont duly interpreted. Couve got up and said, icily, in English, 'That was a most interesting conversation. Thank you very much'. To which Brown riposted, 'Oh! The bugger, he speaks English all the time'.[38]

Whitehall dysfunctionality compounded the ministerial shortcomings. Huge and difficult jigsaw puzzles were in vogue. A visitor to Sandringham found the Queen doing 'an enormous, incredibly difficult jigsaw'. Making sense of the international jigsaw overstretched policy-makers. No. 10 and the FO had little grasp of Community culture. Stewart understood the Luxembourg Compromise of January 1966 ending the 'empty chair crisis' to mean individual members had a right of veto in the event of a majority vote in conflict with perceived national interests. It was, in fact, an agreement to disagree – eighteen years later Britain was voted down trying to exercise the Compromise as a veto.[39]

The misunderstanding pointed up the need for a thorough overhaul of the machine. Labour's reforms of government overheated a rickety engine. Wilson acknowledged that the introduction of a Prices and Incomes Board and Department of Economic Affairs 'involved fundamental changes in the Government machinery such as we have not seen in peacetime in the past generation'. 'I thought the whole discussion amateurish', noted an adviser at a conference chaired by the prime minister in December 1964; 'It showed up very clearly the difficulty of conducting a technical argument without prepared papers by experts and in a meeting at which Ministers were largely out of their depth'.[40] Skimping on reflection undermined coherence. The decisions to withdraw from east of Suez and to apply to the EEC were taken separately. Excess paper clogged up the system. The prime minister contributed hugely to the paper mountain. Officials bemoaned hasty and superficial scrutiny of issues. Defeatism ruled. After the devaluation of November 1967 a mandarin likened the atmosphere in the Treasury to the French general staff's headquarters at Sedan in 1870, 'so pervasive was the ... defeatism'.[41]

By mid-1966 Wilson appeared ready to seek the nation's future in Europe rather than on the Himalayas. Why and when did he settle on a bid? The premier's opportunism makes it much easier to answer the why than the when. Amid cabinet and party dissension over Europe, Wilson moved crabwise towards an entry bid. Labour's March 1966 election victory and the mid-July sterling crisis are frequently cited as decision dates. Attempting to establish a specific 'conversion' date misses the point – Wilson the opportunist never regarded the decision as final. The Community's 'empty chair crisis' of 1965–6 and France's departure from NATO's command structure in March 1966 nudged him along. De Gaulle's success in resisting a supranational Europe calmed concerns that joining would endanger sovereignty. London perceived France's exit from NATO military command as preluding full withdrawal. Both events suggested that, once inside the Community, Britain, it seemed, would have ample leverage to wrest the initiative from France.

The premier's prevarication – part personality, part sticking plaster to keep cabinet and party together, curbed the selling of membership, at home and abroad. As late as November 1966 the cabinet secretary confessed 'he really didn't know where the P.M. stood on Europe'. 'Collapsing alternatives' impelled Wilson, not a Damascene conversion. A Micawber-like premier pinned hopes on a European dynamo. A rapidly contracting menu forced membership upfront as a fix for economy and society. From late 1965 several streams pumped up interest in Europe. Labour's scepticism towards European integration sprang from faith in an independent world role. Retreat from power forced reassessment. Prospects appeared bleak – disappointing economic performance, exclusion from a fast growing economic bloc, Commonwealth in tatters and a prime minister looking more and more like 'head prefect to Lyndon B. Johnson's headmaster'. Crucially, by the early summer of 1966 ministers knew they could not deliver on the promise that the National Plan would produce a 25 per cent increase in output for 1964–70. The bad news increased the attraction of a second bid that would demonstrate commitment to growth and deprive the Conservative opposition of the European ball. Brown argued that 'a vigorous and speeded up policy towards Europe could provide the means by which we might work our way out of this box' – slow economic growth and lack of room to manoeuvre internationally and at home.[42]

Economic arguments carried the day – the high growth rate of the Six would repower a faltering economy. By mid-1966 the inevitability of devaluation tightened Europe's pull. Linking devaluation to entry terms would de-fang it. Forecasts that mandatory sanctions against Rhodesia would hurt the British economy brought agreement that 'an attempt to enter Europe would give a boost to economic morale'. Electoral considerations weighed. Surging pro-Europe polls indicated that if Labour hesitated the Conservatives would play the Europe card at the next election. Industry and Whitehall canvassed Europe aggressively. Paradoxically, the economic case for joining made entry problematical. An economy and currency on the skids stiffened French opposition to entry while releasing a crude Francophobia. Chancellor James Callaghan talked of 'a wicked French plot to bring down the dollar by bringing down the pound first and making France the financial capital of the world'.[43]

Did Uncle Sam strong-arm Wilson into a second bid? Historian David M. McCourt asserts American influence determined the timing of Wilson's second bid.[44] Washington of course wanted Britain in Europe, but there was no bullying. Wilson, like Macmillan, realized that staying out threatened the special relationship, but the main driver was the UK economy and the urgency of regaining momentum. Anxieties about the Community's impact on the Anglo–American alliance influenced choices. Whitehall feared that Germany's economic muscle within a burgeoning Community would jeopardize the transatlantic partnership. Joining would confirm Britain as America's European portal; staying out might tempt Washington to favour West Germany. 'The United States was paying increasing regard to West Germany', Brown alerted colleagues. Without British entry, 'West Germany's influence on the United States would more or less replace our own'. The assumption that going into Europe would preserve the relationship went unchallenged.[45]

President Kennedy's cheerleading for Macmillan enabled de Gaulle to denounce Britain as America's Trojan Horse. After the 1963 veto Washington adopted a 'softly softly' approach. The Vietnam War increasingly pulled the United States away from Europe. The fluidity of American policy towards Europe in mid-decade offered British leaders enough wiggle room had they opted for London–Paris rapprochement. American diplomacy became more engaged *after* Wilson decided to apply, but did not directly influence decisions in the spring and summer of 1966.

11

Bash on Regardless

'Bash on regardless', urged Brown following France's second veto in November 1967.[1] As well as bashing on, ministers lashed out at the messengers – firing their Paris ambassador and hounding officials for giving poor advice. In chess parlance policymakers were in zugzwang. The management of diplomacy had similarities to the '*Carry On*' series of British comedy films of the period. Having got into a hole, carry on digging! 'France lost a general and Britain an alibi,' remarked Britain's ambassador Christopher Soames after de Gaulle's resignation in April 1969. The narratives have largely accepted Whitehall's alibi of a hostile, immovable general. In reality, de Gaulle attempted a rapprochement. In a conversation with Soames in February 1969 he proposed secret bilateral talks on Europe. Wilson shot down the overture. Nevertheless, former minister Douglas Jay hailed a 'wonderfully far-sighted offer'. The initiative deserved testing.

After prevaricating for months Wilson inched closer to a second bid in October 1966. Ministers and officials assembled at Chequers on 22 October for a full discussion of joining the Community. Of the choices presented, Going it Alone (GITA), North Atlantic Free Trade Area (NAFTA) and European Community (EC), Europe won hands down. As for wooing the French, not a whisper. Determined to keep a united cabinet, Wilson did not press for a straightforward decision to apply, suggesting instead that he and the foreign secretary should be authorized to conduct a probe of the Six in order to assess support for an application – 'a typically Wilsonian ploy for gaining time and putting off debate', a colleague recalled.[2] The Paris embassy offered cold comfort: East–West rapprochement absorbed the general, advised Reilly, and he would not welcome a new bid: 'We can expect no helping hand ... On the contrary, the French are likely to do all they can to spread amongst the Five doubts and suspicions about our "real intentions".'[3]

Confirmation of Reilly's warning came in early December. Conservative MP Christopher Soames, son-in-law of Winston Churchill, sounded Couve and housing minister Edgard Pisani: 'French government's desire to see Britain in the Common Market ... no greater today than it was in 1963. Should Britain accept the Rome Treaty asking only for reasonable transitional arrangements for New Zealand,' concluded Soames, 'their next line of defence would be the problems that flow from sterling ... you will find them arguing about our presence ... in Singapore and the Persian Gulf in regard to the load on our balance of payments'. Wilson acknowledged, 'Much of what you say coincides with our own impressions'. Hailed as God's gift to British diplomacy,

Palliser, the prime minister's foreign policy secretary, had nothing better to propose than 'making life thoroughly difficult for the General by explaining to all and sundry how thoroughly willing we are to go in and thereby forcing de Gaulle to find much more explicit reasons for keeping us out'.[4]

The foreign secretary upstaged the premier, and zipped ahead on a personal mini probe, meeting Couve on 14 December and de Gaulle two days later. Brilliant at his best, in his cups a public nuisance – Brown made a fool of himself at a NATO Council dinner in Paris. 'A chinless Mr Punch in spectacles', observed the Quai secretary general, who 'to the great embarrassment of FO officials ... interrupted repeatedly ... with bizarre theories on the future of the world and of England, referring every instant to his personal position', and insulting 'in front of us his ambassador [Reilly] and permanent secretary' [Gore Booth], claiming that the French ambassador [Courcel], 'London's most unpopular diplomat', ridiculed him.[5]

Brown's talks with Couve and de Gaulle scored high in banalities. Conversation opened like a children's game: Brown: first tell me what you want, then I'll tell you what I'll do: Couve: first you must tell us what you want. Brown: you must tell us how you are going to respond when we come in January. De Gaulle: you say you want to join – what do you want to do? Brown: I ask you in return what you want us to do. Unwisely, the foreign secretary confessed desperation to enter the Community: 'if we fail we'll have to rethink all our world position. So we must get in first with a minimum of conditions'. Ignoring his country's economic tailspin, the foreign secretary insisted UK entry would enrich the Community: 'entering the Common Market we will bring it a great advantage for we are the centre of the sterling zone; I mean, if we enter with a strong pound and

Figure 11.1 Probing the Dutch in the Hague, foreign secretary Brown and premier Wilson, 27 February 1967- note the body language.

a stable economy.' The general pithily summarized: 'there is the Common Market and for us there is no problem, for you there is one; you want to get in and that's your problem.'⁶ In his autobiography Brown drew the inescapable conclusion, 'it was very clear that de Gaulle was adamantly against us'. At the time no record of the talks was circulated and the foreign secretary prevaricated: 'It was difficult to form any conclusion about his [De Gaulle's] attitude towards our entry into the EEC ... we need not ... take it for granted that there would be French objection to our entry'.⁷ The foreign secretary's bull-in-a-china-shop style alienated potential allies. 'Willy, you must get us in, so we can take the lead', he urged West German Chancellor Willy Brandt. 'The British', Brandt observed, 'were not particularly adroit ... we wanted to observe the rules and not have one claim to leadership replaced by another'.⁸

'Not particularly adroit' sums up the main probe of the Six in January–February 1967, starting with Rome and finishing in Luxembourg. The embassy advised leaving Paris to last, but it came second in order to avoid giving substance to French criticism that Britain was intent on dividing France from the Five. Wilson said he would 'free-wheel' in Paris and 'take my own line'.⁹ The grand tour turned the bitchiness of the Wilson–Brown double act into public spectacle. 'It was a rather undignified excursion and it made us look rather stupid', reflected a Paris embassy official, 'Wilson was not well-briefed and George Brown made a clown of himself ... I felt rather embarrassed by them'.¹⁰ The results of the probe were predictable – the Five would not commit themselves to support Britain against France. In Rome students protested, accusing Wilson of colluding with the United States in the Vietnam war; in Brussels the woman translating the prime minister's speech collapsed drunk, leaving Palliser to save the day. Wilson confessed that it would be unrealistic to expect the Italians 'to stand up to de Gaulle in the event of his deciding to veto our application'.

The findings confirmed what London already knew: 'the Five would not be prepared to disrupt the EEC in order to force the French government to agree to our admittance'. Wilson tried to put a brave face on the Paris talks, assuring colleagues that for 'personal relationships' the visit had gone 'well'. However, the best efforts of prime minister and foreign secretary 'did not in any way appear to have changed the view of de Gaulle that he would prefer that we should not join the EEC at present'.¹¹ So much for the policy of 'sucking up to the Five', as one minister put it.¹² Member states had too much to lose from the break-up of the Community. A Brussels reconnaissance in July 1967 forced Palliser to concede that the Five 'all accept implicitly ... Paris as the capital of Europe'.¹³

Undaunted, Wilson accelerated, announcing on 2 May 1967 a decision to proceed with an application. France's tactics differed markedly from 1961–3 when de Gaulle allowed negotiations with the Six to drag on for over fifteen months. At a press conference on 16 May the general applied what the media called a 'velvet veto'. Super optimists denied a rejection since the French president had suggested some form of association with the EC might be more appropriate for Britain. Quai secretary general Alphand confirmed the general intended a veto – the reference to association was purely cosmetic.¹⁴ Wormser, ambassador in Moscow since September 1966, may well have prompted the amber warning. The former economic policy chief recommended swift action on 'the English affair'. The choice lay between nipping the affair in the bud or risking a repeat of lengthy and potentially damaging negotiations ending in an impasse.[15]

'All this is a war of nerves ... Bash on regardless', urged a foreign secretary high on an adrenaline rush.[16] De Gaulle's unambiguous formal veto on 27 November is usually portrayed as proof of his determination to keep Britain out. What provoked the November red light, however, was the premier's manifest unwillingness to pay for admission. Wilson's bravado about not taking no for an answer, coupled with moves to isolate France, convinced the general he had reached the end of the line – London would give nothing. The emphasis in the UK official history on French hostility does the general a serious disservice. The general hinted at a deal and was rebuffed. When ministers visited Paris on 24–5 January 1967 as part of their grand tour the president invited them to study alternatives to membership: association or 'something completely new and different'.[17] Wilson assumed the president had in mind a new relationship between Britain and the Six. Bizarrely, no one asked de Gaulle what he meant. Reilly later sought illumination from Alphand. The secretary general explained that the president meant 'dismantling' the Community 'and making a new agreement to include Britain'. Reilly cavalierly dismissed the idea as quite impractical. Suspicions of de Gaulle blocked exploration of the suggestion. The cabinet rubbished it as a red herring which would compromise Britain's standing among the Five and waste valuable time. Engaging with the French in a wider settlement had no support.

De Gaulle tried again. Given the lack of response to his initiative, he changed tack and instructed his former diplomatic adviser Pierre Maillard to open up discussions. Over lunch with a senior Paris embassy official Maillard, deputy secretary general of the national defence secretariat, emphasized the urgency of both countries working together to create a credible European nuclear deterrent. Defence cooperation would be 'a very important element' in Community membership negotiations. France wanted to work with Britain on rocket development and telecommunication satellites. Most importantly, Maillard confirmed France had encountered difficulties manufacturing an H-bomb. 'The great thing was to be bold,' urged Maillard, 'to put forward our candidature in new and imaginative terms, and to avoid niggling over details, difficulties and special problems'.[18]

Reilly dithered for over a week before taking the bait. 'Our information', he informed the FO, 'is that the French do not yet know how to make a thermonuclear bomb ... the General might be tempted if we could offer to tell him ... as soon as we are safely in the E.E.C, with his help.' He urged a Wilson–de Gaulle summit. Predictably, the FO was not well pleased by the idea of a thermonuclear bribe: 'It is essential that any European defence arrangements should be within the framework of the Atlantic alliance and should not weaken the commitment of the American nuclear deterrent to the defence of Europe, on which our security rests. Nor must we weaken our own links with the Americans in respect of nuclear know-how.' The FO sat on Reilly's letter for three weeks – arousing the suspicions of Wilson's secretary Palliser. 'I cannot avoid the feeling', he wrote, 'that in certain important matters the Foreign Office are being less than frank with us'.[19]

Would the thermonuclear card have delivered the keys to Brussels? Perhaps, but Wilson muffed it. In early June he instructed Solly Zuckerman, the government's chief scientific adviser, to meet French experts. Zuckerman was to find out 'what the French want from us' and 'to make their mouths water with possibilities', while making clear 'what degrees of freedom we had to exchange information'. The timing for a trade could hardly have been bettered. France's H-bomb schedule was in jeopardy. The general wanted a bomb by 1968, but scientists anticipated a two-year delay because of technical difficulties. China scored first – testing an H-bomb on 17 June 1967. Zuckerman confirmed that a nuclear offer 'might well be the key to the President's attitude about our application to join the EEC'. The stage seemed set for a deal.[20]

Wilson returned to Paris on 18 June – anniversary of the battle of Waterloo and of de Gaulle's broadcast appeal from London in 1940. The location of the talks at the Grand Trianon near the Palace of Versailles presented a perfect backdrop of three centuries of French pride and grandeur.[21] The general lodged his guest in the refurbished Petit Trianon. Squeezing into the back of a small French car for a postprandial drive brought the pair physically closer but no more. The encounter confirmed the limitations of the prime minister's personal diplomacy. After two years of meetings the premier had not fathomed the general's psychology and statecraft. Instead of bearing gifts Wilson chanced his arm and assumed he could get French sponsorship for free. The result was a personal Waterloo. The third of three sessions with the president in six months brought Wilson to the end of the road. Extraordinarily, he adopted a threatening tone. Britain wanted to be in the Community but had other choices – a North Atlantic Free Trade Area which might become quite powerful and aggressive. In the event of a struggle between the United States and France for influence over Germany, Britain as a non-Community member would have to decide its loyalty. The reference to NAFTA was quite disingenuous. The Johnson administration had already expressed disinterest in the idea.

Wilson posed as his own man, not Johnson's poodle – having already squared matters with the White House: 'we might have to make a number of tactical statements and gestures that might seem a bit "non-American" or even "anti-American" for the purpose of proving our Europeanism.'[22] Unimpressed by the premier's disclaimers, the general asked, 'Was it possible for Britain ... to follow any policy that was really distinct from that of the United States whether in Asia, the Middle East or Europe ... This was what France still did not know'. Telling de Gaulle that exclusion from the Community would make Britain more Atlanticist could only be counterproductive. On nuclear issues and missile development it was all jam tomorrow. Wilson's enthusiasm for future technological cooperation in an ETC – first promoted in late 1966, fooled no one. Britain had seriously compromised its track record: regrets over Concorde; misgivings about the Channel Tunnel; reluctance to continue investing in ELDO; cancellation in 1964–6 of several aviation projects, notably the TSR-2, and replacement with US alternatives.

Back in London the prime minister equivocated. De Gaulle 'was now reviewing his whole position ... we should continue to press our application ... it seemed probable that he was now prepared to recognize the inevitability of our membership. If ... we maintained our pressure ... there was a reasonable prospect of our succeeding.'[23] Privately, Wilson admitted: 'He does not want us in and he will use all the delaying tactics he can ... I am not sure that he any longer has the strength to keep us out – a dangerous prophecy, as prophecy always is with the General'.[24] Belatedly, the premier authorized senior scientist Sir William Cook, deputy chief scientific adviser to the Ministry of Defence, to advise the French on their H-bomb project.[25] A year earlier the move might have heralded a breakthrough. In the past, nuclear cooperation initiatives had always stalled because the UK would not jeopardize Anglo–American agreements. Zuckerman now advised that the sharing of Anglo–American nuclear know-how to a third party was not at issue. Since the UK had tested its own H-bomb independently of the United States nothing prevented London from 'informing the French ... about the principles and techniques we had developed on our own'. Cook's assistance put French scientists on track, but Wilson's grudging back to the wall concession came too late.[26]

Threats and bluster multiplied. Downing Street targeted West Germany, de facto leader of the Five. At an EFTA meeting in Lausanne on 26 October 1967 Chalfont, who had Wilson's ear, gave a non-attributable press briefing, spelling out possible responses to a French veto – British military pull-out from Germany, rethinking NATO and abandonment of Franco–British joint programmes. After dinner, he invited journalists back for a second helping – leaving no room for misunderstanding. The media assumed he spoke for Number 10. The resulting storm forced ministers to apologize to Bonn and Washington, denying policy changes.[27] The sterling crisis worsened. Wilson blamed Couve for an October speech attacking the pound 'with the usual superb French sense of timing'.[28] Couve's intervention was a fleabite compared to the impact of UK rail and dock strikes on international confidence. Intense market pressure triggered a 14.3 per cent devaluation on 18 November, clinching France's core argument that Britain had to put its house in order before entry. Convinced he would never get a quid pro quo and unwilling to be trapped again in a quicksand of protracted negotiations, de Gaulle delivered a full-throated Non.

Angry ministers rattled the general's cage. 'We shall not take "No" for an answer' replaced defence of the pound as virility symbol. The huffing and puffing could not conceal the bankruptcy of Britain's international policy: currency woes; exclusion from Europe; failed initiatives in Vietnam and East/West relations; defiant settler regime in Rhodesia; a Nigerian civil war [the Biafran war]. Politicians out of their depth scolded civil servants for faulty assessments of the general's intentions. Brown's bullyboy style destroyed trust between minister and officials. Reilly, for example, became extra cautious, having received 'what amounted to an instruction, to avoid ... being negative in my reports about the prospects for British entry'. Senior officials returned fire. Cabinet office deputy secretary William Nield criticized the implication that 'the responsibility of Ministers and their officials for the adoption of policy and for its success can be clearly separated' as 'a total negation of the concept of collective responsibility'. 'Had he been asked,' wrote Nield, 'he would have advised against starting [the application process] for another six months to a year, not least to allow for careful preparation'.[29]

The official history defends the mandarins: 'Ministers, not officials, determined the timing of Britain's application' and advisers clearly warned of the possibility of a veto. True, ministers rushed their fences. But the conduct of Palliser and other officials in promoting an application that required France's support for its success without recommending a sound strategy to secure that support was, to say the least, dubious. Years later, Palliser explained: 'I always made it clear to Wilson that I was very sceptical of his being able to get General de Gaulle to change his mind. But I do not think that I would ever have told him that there was no hope of success ... To have told him categorically ... would have affected the closeness of our own relationship.' Palliser flouted civil service convention: 'it is the traditional duty of civil servants, while decisions are being formulated, to make available to their political chiefs all the information and experience at their disposal ... without fear or favour, irrespective of whether the advice ... may accord or not with the Minister's initial view'.[30]

'Bash on regardless' meant insisting on Britain's European credentials in the forum of the WEU while ensnaring France in wider talks with WEU members. In practical terms, it amounted to little more than sticking pins in a voodoo doll. Whitehall clutched at the Harmel Plan, former Belgian foreign minister Pierre Harmel's programme for deepening WEU political and military cooperation. In late October 1968 Paris opposed the creation of a study group on the Harmel Plan. When Debré, Couve's successor as foreign minister, suggested bilateral talks on the future of South-East Asia and other areas, London insisted on WEU multilateral contacts before engaging in bilateral exchanges. The media outcry that followed Tony Benn's praise of the first Concorde prototype illustrated the rush to vilify de Gaulle. At the Toulouse rollout in December 1967 Benn announced that the 'British Concord ... would be spelt with an "e" ... for excellence; "E" for England and "e" for "entente concordiale"'. What went down well in France created 'a hell of a row' in the UK. The press accused Benn of capitulating to the general.[31]

Desperate to be seen doing something, Wilson and Brown replaced Reilly with Sir Christopher Soames, Winston Churchill's son-in-law and Conservative party nabob. The ambassador's dismissal marks one of the low points of twentieth-century British overseas policy. The action underlined the inability of ministers and mandarins to formulate effective policies. Rumours of the ambassador's removal circulated as early as November 1966 with a whispering campaign originating – Reilly believed – 'mainly in the Prime Minister's entourage and among party officials'. The foreign secretary considered Reilly a dusty fuddyduddy, and treated him and his wife Rachel appallingly: 'Your job is simply to see that my car is available when I want it. I do everything that is important here'; 'You are not fit to be Ambassadress in Paris' – loud enough for everyone to hear in a formal dinner. Reilly claimed to have had no business meetings with de Gaulle in 1966, alleging that on three separate occasions requests for authority to see de Gaulle were denied: 'once by Stewart and twice by Brown'. The denials severely shook his confidence; 'we felt insecure and something of our zest for the job was lost'.[32]

Summoned home in February 1968, he learnt that Downing Street wanted him out within a month. As a sop to allow completion of a pension year the FO conceded a September separation date. There was no ministerial explanation. A shell-shocked Reilly considered confronting Brown: 'I am not proud of my decision to shirk it'. Permanent secretary Gore Booth had no 'healing word', answering Reilly's request for an explanation of the firing with an unsympathetic and ambiguous letter, which he later admitted to be misleading. The insensitivity reflected the permanent secretary's weak leadership and resolve to stay squeaky clean as his own retirement loomed. Shaming Whitehall, de Gaulle went out of his way to offer Reilly support: 'you have succeeded very well here. I say this as man to man'.[33]

The envoy left Paris in September 1968 with relations 'in a much worse state' than he had found them. The responsibility lay with Downing Street and Whitehall, not the embassy. Apart from beating the British drum and throwing expensive parties, it was unclear how his successor would fill the days. Soames's vacuous instructions did not feature kiss and make-up, 'H.M.G.'s policy in regard to Europe would be to invest, but not assault, the citadel of the Common Market and meanwhile to seek to promote European cooperation in fields such as political, monetary and defence, which are outside the scope of the Treaty of Rome'.[34] In discussions about Soames's role Wilson and Brown acted like innocents abroad. Their naïve optimism about early entry to Europe shocked Soames – Wilson talked of admission by 1970. Premier and foreign secretary clung to their old mantra – pressure from the Five combined with exploiting the WEU for non-EEC issues would bring de Gaulle to heel. Gesture politics ruled. The government wanted the embassy 'opening up to as broad a spectrum as possible of French life'. 'We needed to be seen to be doing something both for the sake of the morale of our friends in the EEC ... and also for political reasons here at home,' declared Brown. Soames pushed the boat out – 'regardless of cost', hiring more footmen and a major domo for the embassy – one of the most magnificent houses in Paris, bought by the Duke of Wellington from Napoleon I's sister Pauline Borghese, and practically on the Élysée's doorstep. 'I have no doubt you will get on famously', former ambassador Lord Gladwyn reassured a French friend, 'since he [Soames] is, among other things, an excellent shot and a considerable judge of champagne'.[35] A tad taller than the general, with patrician credentials and the confidence of No. 10, Soames had an edge on his predecessor. The Churchill connection with its reminder of wartime exile pleased the president – he relished Soames's aristocratic aplomb – downing pheasants at a presidential shoot while keeping up a lively banter. Palliser purred away, commending the new envoy for galvanizing the embassy: 'as I told the PM, the whole place is really humming and one feels this at once'. Lavish parties came at a price. In Wilson's third government of 1974–6 the Berrill inquiry into the FO, accompanied by a general hue and cry of MPs and media, targeted the profligacy of the Paris embassy.[36]

What really set Europe humming was the general's conversation with Soames on 4 February 1969, proposing secret bilateral discussions about the future of European construction and a revived Entente. Ignoring a French request for confidentiality the FCO briefed France's Community partners as well as leaking a doctored version of the conversation – suggesting the general wanted to retool the EEC and NATO with a European 'directory' of France, Britain, West Germany and Italy. Within days the 'Soames affair' turned into an international brawl, pushing the envoy to the brink of resignation. France's commentariat condemned 'perfidious Albion' for sabotaging the general's initiative.

For the FCO, the episode signalled payback time. A pack of 'Euro-fanatics', led by deputy under-secretary Patrick Hancock and John Robinson, chief of the European Integration Department, seized on the overture as a 'devilish trap' in the long stand-off with France. Acceptance would enable the general to accuse Britain of betraying friends and partners; refusal would allow him to say London did not care about Europe's future. Officials proposed the offer should be leaked to the Italian newspaper,

Figure 11.2 Sir Christopher Soames, UK ambassador to France, 22 September 1968. Credit: Keystone Press / Alamy Stock Photo.

Il Messaggero, leaving the Italian government to carry the blame. Nevertheless, some cabinet ministers viewed the offer sympathetically. Barbara Castle, normally an ally of the prime minister, criticized the official response: 'all part of the appalling desire to run to the Five and tell tales out of school to show what good boys we are ... there were some very good points in de Gaulle's ideas'. De Gaulle's resignation in April made it easy to trivialize the affair as a Gaullist eccentricity – 'The absurd Affaire Soames.'[37]

A storm in a teacup? De Gaulle's bid to end the six-year diplomatic war merited exploration, despite its off-piste character. It could have reconfigured the Community and created a real entente. The conversation was part of a full-scale foreign policy reappraisal – monitored by Soames. 'It was no secret', confided de Gaulle's brother-in-law in early November, 'that a review of French foreign policy was in ... progress at the highest level'. Later that month junior foreign minister Jean de Lipkowski talked of changing 'the attitude ... of the old bird at the Élysée'. By the end of November, references to the rethink surfaced in the French press. *Le Monde* editor André Fontaine called for a Franco–British rapprochement and a compromise on 'the strengthening and enlargement' of Europe. France's foreign policy community, signalled Soames, wanted to find ways to end the impasse and were working on de Gaulle.[38]

What provoked the change of gear? May 1968 and its sequelae – the Soviet-led Warsaw Pact invasion of Czechoslovakia in August, a falling franc, flight of capital and declining exports, frightened de Gaulle and badly jolted the regime. The May troubles stopped newspapers, grounded air traffic and affected telephone services. Exposure to ridicule mortified elites. 'We are living through a sort of nightmare', confessed Alphand; 'the English are making fun of us and taking their revenge for the arrogance of certain over-confident Frenchmen'. Wormser in Moscow, deprived of *Le Monde*, had to rely on the British embassy for copies of *The Times*. Returning from Paris, Courcel appeared the worse for wear: 'English had deteriorated; he looked almost dishevelled ... clearly had some of the stuffing knocked out of him by recent events'.[39]

The Warsaw Pact invasion of Czechoslovakia, downplayed by Debré as a 'mishap' [incident de parcours] on the road to détente, was a road closure. A Soviet naval build-up in the Mediterranean, and penetration of Algeria, both heightened anxiety. Nor could Paris count on its West German ally – Bonn refused to revalue the mark in order to support the franc against devaluation. Domestic tensions festered. Anxiety about the deteriorating political and economic climate, especially the danger of France repeating Britain's trajectory, alarmed Debré and the Gaullist clan.[40]

The foreign minister became the moving spirit of the policy reappraisal. Anglophile and an opponent of supranationalism, he canvassed partnership with London. When Soames met him on 30 October 1968 Debré lamented 'this war which is going on between us'. Couve, prime minister since July, admitted relations were such that whatever either government suggested the other suspected an ulterior motive. Debré, noted Soames, canvassed an initiative for several months then sold it 'to the General in such a way that the General would take it up as being his own idea'. France's ambassadors in European capitals backed enlargement – except Rome where the envoy worried about the implications for the status of the French language in the Community.[41]

France's isolation added urgency to de Gaulle's initiative. A week before the Soames–de Gaulle talk, Debré consulted advisers: 'The English question is ... a brake on all progress ... We ... run the risk of cutting ourselves off from Britain. Should France grow weaker ... European policy will be German dominated'. He concluded with a question: assuming the inevitability of British entry, 'what profit can we draw and what initiative should we take in the matter?' Next day during a regular weekly session with the general the foreign minister underlined the danger of France being blackmailed by its partners. The Five might exploit the ongoing CAP negotiations to deliver an ultimatum – accept British entry or we will refuse to renew CAP.[42]

At the meeting with Soames on 4 February the general proposed secret bilateral talks on the reshaping of Europe. Confessing to 'no particular faith' in the Community, he envisaged it becoming 'a looser form of a free trade area'. London and Paris might discuss 'what should take the place of the Common Market as an enlarged European economic association'. The enlarged grouping should have 'a small inner council of a European political association consisting of France, Britain, Germany and Italy'. He was 'anxious' to talk about this and, in reply to questions, conceded NATO would have to be rethought. Had the tiger changed stripes? Yes and no. The proposal for secret talks on a new political partnership reprised the offer made to Wilson and Brown two years earlier. The Soames offer spoke to a change in tactics, not strategy. The general still wanted a French-led European Europe, but Germany's resurgence and France's economic slowdown made a makeweight desirable. De Gaulle was not wedded to the Treaty of Rome. Remaking the Community would balance Germany and satisfy Britain's desire to be a European insider.[43]

The British response to de Gaulle underscored the muddle of policy-making. Stewart accepted the advice of officials that the Five must be informed, starting with West German chancellor Kurt Kiesinger whom Wilson was scheduled to meet in Bonn on 12 February. To describe the mood of the FCO as confrontational would be a serious understatement. Stewart urged the deliberate leaking of the de Gaulle feeler: 'The French will show us more respect if they see us doing this.' The foreign secretary hankered after a German partnership, not French: 'The heart of the matter is this: in Western Europe there are ... only two nations which are both powerful and capable of being resolute in the defence of the West: and these are Germany and ourselves'.[44]

Biographer Philip Ziegler ticked off the prime minister for trying to 'dissociate himself' from the British response while blaming the diplomats for mishandling it. This does Wilson an injustice. His first reaction to the offer was positive: 'We should follow this up ... given encouragement, this could be escalated to higher level meetings – first the foreign secretary then possibly myself'. True, the premier undertook to inform the Germans 'in such a way as to point up the essentially anti-Atlantic nature of the de Gaulle approach'. But Euro-fanatics Hancock and Robinson who accompanied Wilson to Bonn had a hard time convincing him and overcoming a natural vacillation. The conversation with Kiesinger went badly. The speaking notes prepared by the FCO were 'much longer and stronger than the premier expected. He tried to water it down ... it sounded like waffling and became more confusing for Kiesinger in translation ... angry at the muddled meeting, Wilson flew back to London saying he would never have Patrick Hancock travel with him again'. Only then – over a week after the offer – did London authorize Soames to respond to the French.[45]

Out of the loop and twice refused permission to come to London, Soames watched in anger as his report went the rounds. The French felt betrayed. Debré, thicker-skinned than most, assured the general of his readiness to start talks, provided Britain promised secrecy. An angry de Gaulle squashed the idea: 'Poor Soames, he was tricked, like me'. The visit of the new American President Richard M. Nixon at the end of February preoccupied London and Paris – no one wanted to be caught washing dirty linen in public. Debré accused London of deliberately trying to upset Franco–American relations before the president's arrival. At the Élysée Jacques Foccart assumed London leaked the offer in order 'to create an unpleasant atmosphere for the general when Nixon arrived'.[46]

The row epitomized the dangerous casualness of Gaullist policy-making. In his memoirs Élysée secretary general Tricot suggested the president was thinking aloud about possible scenarios, not offering talks. But the general undoubtedly meant business – ministers confirmed the offer. Lipkowski stressed France's desire for bilateral talks, including defence and Anglo–French nuclear collaboration. Debré impressed upon Soames that talks should start as soon as possible. Convinced of the conversation's significance, Soames handed Tricot a copy of his report to London. The secretary general promised to show it to the president, saying 'there was much in it which the General had not reported to him'. Two days later Debré confirmed the general had seen the record and 'there was nothing in it with which he disagreed'. Most likely, de Gaulle used Soames's narrative as a refresher for his own brief 300-word summary – dictated three days after the talk. Although the Quai rightly complained of British leaks deliberately distorting the sense of the conversation, the absence of a full French record meant that the Soames' version became the record by default. The published French diplomatic documents do not include the text which the general dictated to Tricot on 7 February.⁴⁷

De Gaulle's ageing, together with the inadequacies of Élysée record-keeping, warped decision-making and compromised the initiative. The general's pessimism, noted confidant and minister André Malraux, matched his resignation mood in January 1946. The physical and mental slowing down cast doubt on the general's political future. Satraps prepared for his departure. In January 1969 dauphin and former premier Pompidou – 'quite pessimistic about the way France was being governed' – talked of succeeding de Gaulle as chief of state within the coming year. He planned a series of visits at home and abroad to establish his authority in foreign affairs. Within days the ex-prime minister confirmed his candidacy for the presidency, strengthening Whitehall's belief that the general was on the way out – another reason not to rush into talks with him.⁴⁸

Failing powers meant policy-making on the hoof, generating errors of judgement. The seventy-eight-year-old's clumsy handling of the Soames affair confirmed an alarming loss of touch. With the diplomatic war in its sixth year, prudence dictated preliminary soundings before making proposals. The approach to Soames bore the marks of a rushed, improvised move. Though the ambassador's appointment with the general was arranged weeks in advance, Debré did not consult senior advisers about Franco-British relations until 29 January, and claimed to have persuaded the general the next day to take the initiative – only four days before the appointment. No advisers, note-takers or interpreters were present at the conversation. The general briefed Debré and Tricot by phone, but kept them waiting days for a record. Uneasy about the meeting the general telephoned prime minister Couve. The premier cranked up presidential anxiety, saying he 'expected the German Foreign Office had already heard about it from the British'. France's ambassadors to Community partners came off worst. Bereft of guidance for several days they stumbled in front of the media and host governments.⁴⁹

Perfidious Albion? The real perfidy was the waste of time, talent and resources in the pursuit of empty great power ambitions. Singly, Britain and France were on a hiding to nothing. Partnership offered the most promising option. Secret talks could have ended a six-year standoff. Applying standard diplomatic practice would have minimized the perceived risk posed by the general's offer. Recalling Soames for a first-hand report while respecting the request for secrecy would have supplied breathing space. Angry at being locked out of decision-making, the envoy pondered resignation, protesting vehemently, 'Still feel it was the greatest pity that I was not allowed to come home to talk with you [Wilson] and Michael Stewart . . . I believe that there was a real chance . . . of starting something which strong forces in France had every intention of seeing through to fruition'. The next point struck home: 'it was well within the bounds of British diplomatic skill to have covered ourselves with our friends in such a way as to be able to open honourably a dialogue with the French ... As I see it, the General handed me a cup which ... was deliberately smashed to pieces.'[50]

The Soames affair had salutary and lasting consequences. The level of toxicity exposed confirmed the urgency of a modus vivendi. France could not afford continuing isolation. In December 1969, under President Pompidou's leadership, the Community's Hague summit agreed enlargement. In London, second thoughts about the UK's response to the affair fired up a policy debate which had its origins in the autumn of 1968. Stewart recommended the ending of 'the special restrictions on Anglo–French dealings' imposed in 1966.[51]

The couple boxed themselves into a corner. Time mattered for both of them. De Gaulle gained enough of a lead to finalize CAP and consolidate ascendancy in Brussels. Wilson, however, had nothing to tempt the electorate in the June 1970 election. The second Labour government ended with membership undecided. The country paid dearly for late entry. 'The longer the uncertainty as to the fate of our application persisted,' Brown had warned colleagues in November 1967, 'the greater would be the damage to the standing of the Government ... if the delay persisted for some months, the support of our friends abroad and public opinion at home would be lost'. The outcome was a defeat for both nations. The general won the face-off on points – but the issue would not go away. Had he remained in power, pressure from advisers and the Five in the early 1970s would doubtless have forced him to lower the drawbridge. The Russian-led occupation of Prague in August 1968 discredited the search for détente with Moscow, dissolving the vision of a French-inspired European Europe mediating between East and West. West Germany's economic clout and commitment to the United States problematized French leadership. The urgency of finding a counterweight to Bonn provoked the overture to Soames.[52]

Wilson's refusal to take no for an answer has won him praise for keeping enlargement on the agenda and thereby facilitating the negotiations of 1970–2. The argument underwhelms. Ministers kept the application on the table because they ran out of ideas. After the Soames affair, 'Euro-fanatic' Hancock had nothing more constructive to suggest than carrying on 'bashing' the French. Ironically, de Gaulle's suggestion of a wider political organization replacing the Community or working alongside it – greeted with shock horror by Whitehall in February – became avant-garde wisdom two months later. The Treasury advised the new FCO permanent secretary Sir Denis Greenhill that the state of the economy could delay entry for at least another two years and in the meantime domestic support might drain away. Accordingly, Greenhill recommended exploring alternative groupings.[53]

Ennui, indifference and scepticism formed no small part of Wilson's legacy. Heath argued persuasively that Labour's handling of the second bid alienated 'UK public opinion against the Community', destroying the consistently pro-European majority in opinion polls since 1961. By delaying a bid until well into 1967 and making minimal effort to sell it to party and voters, Wilson fuelled distrust of the European project, and left bitter divisions within his party. The indifference and procrastination of Labour and Conservative governments over Europe in the 1960s demoralized Britons.

Interminable negotiation and renegotiation took the shine off membership. Other influences disillusioned voters, too: the top-down elitist nature of the enterprise and the ending of the post-war economic boom. The negative effects of Wilson's legacy were Europe-wide. Post-1967 bashing on, coupled with renegotiation of membership in 1974–5, strengthened Community distrust of Britain's intentions. The 'British Budgetary Question' (BBQ) of the early 1980s – better known in Brussels as the bloody British question – cemented a reputation for sheer cussedness.[54]

Empty great power aspirations do not fully explain the impasse over Europe. Flawed statecraft – the general's reluctance to make the first move – made a huge difference. French initiatives were ill-prepared and badly timed. At the January 1967 meeting in Paris, delphic utterances baffled British interlocutors. With goodwill and timely forethought the general's talk with Soames might yet have changed the plot. British ministers also miscalculated. Assuming a level playing field they saw no necessity to offer France anything. In fact, Wilson, like Macmillan, was a supplicant in search of a sponsor.

The lack of informal pathways and super-domestiques to do the heavy lifting hindered any kind of rapprochement. There are traces of low-level, back-channel contacts which came to naught. Nield, deputy secretary at the Cabinet office, regularly met Jean Wahl, the French embassy's commercial counsellor. Wilson, explained Nield, had no confidence in the foreign secretary and FO and wanted a line to the Élysée. Wahl replied that he could do nothing without informing the ambassador and head of external economic relations at the finance ministry. There is no evidence of any information reaching the Élysée. Stuart Holland, novice Whitehall economist and friend of Pierre Joxe, son of de Gaulle's justice minister Louis Joxe, offered to go to Paris at his own expense to meet his friend's father and plead the case for entry. He met Joxe senior in May 1967 but the justice minister had no influence with the general, and as a rookie official Holland carried no weight.[55]

Might the story have had a happier ending? 'The best way to organize Europe was around an Anglo–French entente', urged US Under-Secretary Eugene Rostow. 'In almost all essential political areas', remarked the Quai's Inspector General, the convergences between the two neighbours were striking – 'like us, [London] has to ensure that in the coming years Germany's relative power in Europe is not excessive'. Partnership at the heart of a reconfigured Community would have empowered both countries. Political elites fought shy of entente, despite a common interest in the containment of Germany and opposition to a supranational Europe. A great power obsession reinforced reluctance to collaborate, and discouraged a radical questioning of options. London and Paris hugely overestimated their ability to exercise a world presence. 'No prospect whatever of de Gaulle letting us in the Common Market', Palliser opined in late 1966, 'unless we are prepared to make changes in our foreign policy and defence policy of such a substantial nature as to be, I believe, out of the question for any foreseeable British government'. Tectonic shifts came anyway. Withdrawal from east of Suez and entry into Europe rewired external policy. Old rivalries die hard, but Soames had the last word – on one subject. At a Paris embassy dinner a French official lit a cigarette. Soames looked 'savagely' at him, saying, 'I wonder if you'd mind putting out that cigarette ... You are about to drink some Haut-Brion '45 ... I think it would be a pity to spoil it by smoking'.[56]

Conclusion

Endgame

Everybody has won and all must have prizes.
Alice's Adventures in Wonderland

Historical landscapes soon get taken for granted. Overviews reinforce the familiar. Tracking broad sweeps of the past, like bullet train travel, blurs way stations. What were once real alternatives can be dismissed as rear-view mirror vision, significant only in the light of what is now known. Brawling over European construction now seems hard-wired into the cross-channel relationship. That's not how it looked in the late 1940s – until 1949–50 a Franco–British Europe looked very much on the cards. In *Fateful Choices*, a study of decisions that changed the world, Ian Kershaw justified staying with the decisions actually made, 'Who knows how it might have turned out had Stalin sided with the Western Powers in 1939? The guessing game is pointless.' But the historical process, as Niall Ferguson reminded him, resembles Borges's image, 'a garden of forking paths'. The course taken was only 'one of the ... number of histories that did not happen but which were, if only briefly, plausible futures for contemporaries.'[1]

A small handful of individuals can make a decisive difference. In the early 1950s French anthropologist Claude Lévi-Strauss revisited Brazil. 'In thinking about Europe as it then was [1930s] and as it is today ... and in watching these young Brazilians in the space of a few years bridge an intellectual gap that one might have expected to hold up development for decades,' he observed, 'I have come ... to realize that those great historical upheavals, which, when one reads about them in the text books appear to be the outcome of anonymous forces ... can also ... be brought about by the vigorous determination of a handful of talented young people.'[2] Franco–British leaders could have crafted a strong partnership. The post-1945 shake-up of the international system unzipped alternatives: customs unions, federations – even a Latin union of Catholic Mediterranean states.

Partnership promised London and Paris a global footprint. Obstacles were surmountable. The technological cool of the supersonic passenger aircraft Concorde demonstrated the viability of close cooperation. Writer J.R.R. Tolkien perversely refused to pay taxes for it, writing across his tax cheque 'Not a penny for Concorde'.[3] A penny for the thoughts of British decision-makers. They refused to woo France. More's the pity. The synergy of association could have delivered far more than a parochial bilateral trade-off. It had the potential to retune the Pax Americana, reinserting Western Europe in world politics, with NATO under a four-power directory of Britain, France,

West Germany and the United States. Upgrading the Paris–Bonn pact of January 1963 into a Paris–Bonn–London triangle would have assuaged anxieties about a resurgent West Germany.

Britain emerged from a six-year life and death struggle in much better fettle than its continental neighbours. Admission in October 1952 to a nuclear club of three, backed by a robust economic performance into the mid-1950s, confirmed pole position in Western Europe. 'With the possible exception of Sweden,' crowed Labour guru Tony Crosland in 1956, 'industrial productivity has risen more in Britain since before the war than in any other European country; while the rise since the war has been almost exactly the same as in the United States ... We stand ... on the threshold of mass abundance'.[4] Macmillan's 'our people never had it so good' stated a self-evident truth. Decolonization proved less traumatic for Britain than for France – conflicts in Cyprus, Kenya, Malawi, Malaysia and Palestine lacked the intensity of protracted back-to-back wars in Indo-China and Algeria.

Why the misfire? Britannia's rule was less secure than it seemed. Flawed assumptions snookered the country's prospects. Periodically a notice appeared in the FO entrance lobby: 'Security Notice: Window Cleaning Today'. Staff locked away papers from the sight of putative KGB agents posing as window cleaners. Policy-makers desperately needed to open windows on the world. 'To see what is in front of one's nose,' George Orwell remarked, 'needs a constant struggle'.[5] The Churchillian precept of maintaining a presence at the intersection of three overlapping circles – North America, Europe and the Commonwealth – became a recipe for overstretch and indecision. The inadequacy of the government machine made policy reviews at best spasmodic. As a result, the assumptions, attitudes and health of prime ministers and foreign secretaries heavily influenced outcomes. Age, alcohol, illness and stress warped decision-making. Forward thinking had low priority. Leaders hunkered down – Attlee re-read Gibbon, Macmillan curled up with a Trollope, and Wilson played golf – only de Gaulle prioritized reflection time in long weekend walks at Colombey-les-Deux-Eglises.

The peculiarities of British policy-making marred responses to geopolitical challenges. Allergic to think tanks, brainstorming and outsiders, the governing elite lived in the Westminster–Whitehall bubble. Tory grandee R.A. Butler likened the civil service to a Rolls-Royce, 'You know it's the best machine in the world'.[6] In the event, the new supercharged Citroën DS upstaged the mid-century Silver Cloud. Mandarins and machine ran on empty. A culture of overwork became an alibi for dodging reflection. Without the capacity for regular appraisal the engine struggled to deliver critical ad hoc reviews like Macmillan's Future Policy Study of 1959–60. Though the idea of national economic planning caught on in the early 1960s – National Economic Development Council (NEDC) and Wilson's National Plan – effective policy units were delayed until the 1970s.

Things were ordered differently in France. 'In its insistence on conducting a global policy by its own lights France stood in growing contrast to ... Great Britain,' observed former American secretary of state Henry Kissinger, 'with every passing year they [British leaders] acted less as if their decisions mattered. They offered advice ... they rarely sought to embody it in a policy of their own'.[7] For US President Richard M. Nixon's first official visit to Europe in February 1969, Wilson paid him an unprecedented

Conclusion 183

honour – participation in a specially convened meeting of the full cabinet; but the leader Nixon most wanted to meet was de Gaulle.

France, the 'sick woman of Europe', recovered. A massive one-time shift of rural population into urban industry, fired by decolonization and a rising birth rate, released energies and resources. Self-promotion as the most civilized and sophisticated country on earth infused confidence; smart statecraft found strength in weakness. 'Power', in the words of economic historian Alan Milward, 'lay not with the mighty in Washington but with the weak in Paris.'[8] De Gaulle saw off threats of civil war, ended the Algerian conflict and asserted leadership of the European Community. The Fifth Republic's international success energized domestic support for Gaullist grandeur.

Enarques outwitted Treasury knights. France's ENA provided a training 'far superior to anything available in Britain'.[9] The verbal skills of graduates dazzled British officials.[10] Alpha ministerial cabinets authored and coordinated policy initiatives. Talent and ideas flowed between civil service, politics and business, ensuring a more flexible and better resourced machine than Whitehall. Civil servant Wilfrid Baumgartner moved from governor of the Bank of France to finance minister to head of the Rhône-Poulenc chemical giant. The suppleness of the French powerhouse enabled mavericks like Monnet to operate across organizational lines.

By contrast, Britain's risk-averse political elite mismanaged bids for Community membership. Success hinged on deal-making with France. The general overcame a legendary reluctance to make the first move, and made friendly overtures. The two Harolds enthused about future cooperation and technological communities, but conceded nothing upfront. De Gaulle waited in vain for a 'Barkis is willin' signal'. The disinclination to sell the Community to the UK electorate cast doubt on the government's sincerity and commitment. In the immediate run-up to the 1967 application, Wilson's entourage did not know which way he would jump. The application signalled a new emphasis on Europe as a base for world power, not a late conversion to Community ideals. The hamster-wheel pursuit of redundant great power ambition in London and Paris militated against partnership and compromise.

The UK's identity crisis hobbled overseas policy-making. 'There is a temptation to sing and dance in rainbow pantaloons,' confessed Yorkshireman Lord Feversham in a House of Lords debate, 'to meditate, copulate and gargle with LSD. It would pass the time until the trustees come up with something to get us out of this grotesque hang-up'.[11] Deep cuts to British Council budgets undermined the country's image. Sixties counterculture drowned out the RP of British Council lecturers. Parsimony inhibited international contacts. When the Mayor of Calais expressed disappointment with youth exchanges between Calais and its twin, Southend-on-Sea, FO officials minuted: 'The crux is money. The French and Germans give millions a year for their youth exchanges. We can with utmost difficulty squeeze £20,000 only from Treasury'.[12]

Mired in an American inspired Cold War propaganda offensive, Britons urgently needed their own act. Ministerial assurances that the country remained a great power with frontiers in the Himalayas exacerbated the crisis of confidence. In *You Only Live Twice* (1964), author Ian Fleming exploited the dissonance between official cheerleaders and post-Suez realities. Tiger Tanaka, head of the Japanese secret service, taunts James Bond about Britain's 'decline': 'we now see a vacuous, aimless horde of seekers after pleasure.' In response, Agent 007 mimics ministerial platitudes: 'but we still climb Everest and beat plenty of the world at sports, and win plenty of Nobel Prizes'.[13]

How to reenergize a country unsure of itself? Language was part of the problem. Whitehallese and posh accents frustrated easy communication across social and regional divides, despite attempts like Sir Ernest Gowers's *Plain Words* (1948) to persuade civil servants to write clear English. The brutalizing and dumbing down of communication as a consequence of the rise of mass politics and the century's savagery compounded a tiredness of language. 'Many of the habits of language in our culture are no longer fresh or creative responses to reality, but stylized gestures', contended literary critic George Steiner.[14] Britannia had no clothes. American expats supplied the main editors of *Encounter*, the country's flagship journal of ideas, and CIA funding kept it afloat. Macmillan's 'our people have never had it so good' offered more of the same – houses and consumer durables; Wilson's 'white heat' of 'scientific revolution' found its monument in London's dreary 1966 Post Office Tower.

The secrecy shrouding decision-making helped strangle a British vision. Lack of information and meaningful participation in policy-making prevented dialogue between government and people. The opacity of government corroded trust, and accelerated loss of nerve. Rulers operated double standards – allowing Eden privileged access to classified material for his Suez memoirs while hounding junior minister Anthony Nutting for exposing Franco–British–Israeli collusion. By narrowly limiting external inputs the SW1 bubble lowered the intellectual level of decision-making as well as impairing focus and the ability to reset goals. Spy and sex scandals, spiced with ministerial mendacity, tainted the close of the Macmillan era. 'Britain is becoming more and more the land of the cover-up', concluded a contemporary analyst.[15]

A paternalist state sealed off external policy as too arcane for ordinary citizens. Foreign secretary Eden's warning to cabinet colleagues in 1952 that the country was in dire straits epitomized paternalism in action. The British people 'faced a difficult choice' between giving up a high standard of living or seeing their country become a second-class power.[16] Facing 'a difficult choice' was a purely rhetorical device – Eden would not have dreamt of consulting the people. Being economical with the truth characterized the governments of the day and still has defenders. 'Telling the whole truth can be… counterproductive', wrote historian Brian Harrison, 'only political bystanders felt free in the 1950s and 1960s to emphasize the UK's stark choices'.[17]

France took the lead in economic growth and prestige, but the couple missed their main targets. 'It's because we are no longer a great power that we need a great policy', the general declared; 'without a great policy we'll be nothing'.[18] Alas, the greatness brand – imperial vintage – was obsolete. Posturing as a global shaker and mover amounted to little more than a virtuoso conjuring trick. France, like Britain, squandered moral capital. Atrocities in Algeria, the Charonne massacre of Algerian demonstrators by Paris police in 1961, supplying arms to prop up South Africa's apartheid regime, and sending troops to support the dictatorship of President Leon M'Ba of Gabon, all belied the 1789 revolutionary tradition. Shouting '*Vive Le Québec libre!*' in French Canada made little sense when the Republic denied autonomy to Breton and Basque minorities. Under an American nuclear shield de Gaulle, noted one of his advisers, poached 'on the edges of the Soviet–American confrontation'.[19]

Gaullist grandeur, like Wilsonian bravado about Himalayan frontiers, had a short shelf life. The Community's rejection of the Fouchet Plan for a French-managed European political union ended the honeymoon years. De Gaulle's opposition to supranational initiatives led to temporary withdrawal from Community affairs – the 'empty chair crisis' of 1965–6. The Community survived, but could not advance. The blackballing of Britain for over a decade soured relations between France and the Five. Deadlock on widening and deepening stifled Europe's voice. France blamed the Five for affirming supranational ideals while encouraging UK entry, despite London's preference for a confederal model. The real contradiction, as a French aide conceded, lay with France because it refused both British entry and supranationalism.

An old man in a hurry overreached himself. Comeuppance came in Paris May 1968 and the Warsaw Pact invasion of Czechoslovakia in August. Events exposed the perils of East–West détente and the brittleness of the Paris–Bonn axis. Bonn became the preferred partner for Washington and Moscow. Germany's mending of relations with Moscow eased the way for Chancellor Willy Brandt's *Ostpolitik* after October 1969. Germans flexed their economic muscle – attempting to dictate a devaluation of the French franc in November 1968. Cold war ringmasters kept the whip hand. NATO emerged strengthened from the crisis caused by France's departure from the military command in March 1966. Moscow would only work with Paris to the extent that it weakened NATO. From 1969 Soviet leader Leonid Brezhnev looked to West Germany, not France. De Gaulle failed to achieve his goals of NATO reform and a European Europe. Whitehall's apoplectic reactions to the Soames affair of February 1969 underscored the seven-year London–Paris impasse.

Britain's quest for European primacy and world distinction earned a double whammy: exclusion from the Community; contraction of influence and economic muscle. Gaullist missteps and Whitehall cack-handedness stalemated negotiations. De Gaulle's olive branch of secret talks on Europe's future miscarried, partly because Wilson and Stewart suspected a snare, partly because the Francophobe FO declared payback time. Fans have lauded Wilson as a 'prime minister who mastered the European question'. Leaving the second application 'on the table' in 1967 ensured that after the general's departure 'it had only to be picked up and dusted off and Labour went into the 1970 election still committed to negotiate, but this time with a real prospect of success'.[20] In reality, the failed bid cost Labour the 1970 election.

Wilson's opportunism diluted popular interest in joining Europe, and put British policy in a bind. Peaking at 70 per cent approval in August 1966, polls plummeted to 22 per cent by March 1970. Government tactics contributed substantially to the downturn. Leaving the application on the table cut both ways. Announcing that Britain would not go away confirmed to voters the government's failure to deliver. Both Harolds played a weak hand weakly – initiating applications without first squaring the doorkeeper. French resistance prompted thinly veiled threats of reprisals, notably Lord Chalfont's bungled press briefing of October 1967. The minister admitted he had 'made a mess of it' – a suitable epitaph for the second Labour government's European policy.[21] To launch bids without first catching the general represented a costly lapse of judgement, a staggering diversion of resources for a country on the skids.

The dragon's departure in April 1969 did not automatically lower the drawbridge. President Pompidou insisted on tight control of timing and conditions – the finalizing of definitive CAP funding arrangements before UK entry. The Élysée warned the Wilson government against repeating its old tactics of egging on the Five against France. A panicky French adviser urged the admission of Spain and Portugal to counter the admission of Britain's Scandinavian and Irish hangers-on. In London, France's ambassador, Courcel, 'as usual . . . put the maximum emphasis on difficulties' and 'was quite emotional about the need for France to "achieve" the Common Market before the next step could be taken'.[22] In December 1969 the Hague summit of the Six announced its priorities – completion, enlargement, deepening.

The Piaf-like 'nothing to regret' verdicts on Wilson's handling of the second entry bid skate over the cumulative cost of Britain's European strategy. The missteps of the two Harolds confirmed continental perceptions of Britain as Europe's awkward squad. The UK negotiating team of 1970–2 noted how 'the massive burden' of the previous two decades weighed on negotiators.[23] True, Conservative premier Edward Heath after his election victory in June 1970 picked up on talks with the Six already arranged by the outgoing administration, but in practice his decision amounted to a separate bid. Whitehall's internal history of the entry negotiation echoed the Heath government's self-congratulatory mood – patience, perseverance and pragmatism paid off – 'under a lucky star'.[24] In fact, the only good fortune was the premier's friendship with Élysée secretary general Michel Jobert – the result of a chance meeting at a Costa del Sol holiday resort in 1964. Personal chemistry helped, but was no magic wand – obsessive attention to dress codes betrayed extreme nervousness on both sides about outcomes. Heath was put out when Jobert, holidaying in Kent, turned up 'in a dark brown suit', despite being told that the prime minister 'would be in seaside clothes'. Arriving at Heathrow 'in a country suit' Pompidou was 'horrified' to find his host in formal dress.[25]

The May 1971 Heath–Pompidou accord on entry failed to revive UK domestic support for membership. 'There will be dancing in the streets, if Mr Heath feels himself unable to continue with the negotiations', declared *The Economist*. 'The British public does not . . . like the French'. Pompidou's insistence on the use of the French language in the enlarged Community was 'an assertion of typical French arrogance'.[26] Massigli – a friend of the Entente through thick and thin – having urged Pompidou in January 1968 to push for British entry, now feared London would imperil the Community by turning the tables on Paris and remaking the rules.[27]

More haste, less speed. The race to reactivate the 1967 application played into the hands of the Six. The UK accepted stiff terms – twice renegotiated within a decade. In retrospect, 1973 seemed 'more like a half-entry'.[28] Gaffes punctuated the final approach to accession. On the eve of Pompidou's first official visit to Britain in March 1972 officials sent immigration forms to the French embassy with instructions that they must be filled in by the president and staff. What looked suspiciously like an attempt to sabotage the visit turned out to be a colossal Whitehall balls-up.[29] Pompidou dutifully completed his form, but Jobert jibbed and found consolation at Chequers. Taking tea, he discovered proof of British decadence – the magnificent porcelain teapot contained tea bags.[30]

Strictly no dancing. Ministers made only a token effort to sell the Community to the people. The high culture 'Fanfare for Europe' formal celebration fell flat. Unmoved by a personal plea from Heath, the French refused to lend the Mona Lisa – though she had travelled to the United States in 1963 – offering instead Georges de la Tour's *Le Tricheur*, a picture of a man cheating at cards. The mood at the European Commission in Brussels was muted. Officials looked back wistfully on the golden pre-enlargement 1960s. The French struck a note of reconciliation, artfully suggesting the British had won the game. '*Voila la vraie affaire Soames*,' quipped Pompidou during the decisive Paris summit of May 1971. Hosting a farewell lunch for Britain's ambassador, the president praised him for overcoming 'opposition' to British entry: 'You have won'.[31] French fans stayed loyal to the Queen. At Heathrow a Frenchman came up to a taxi driver with a magnificent bouquet in his hand, promising to pay double if the driver would give it to the Queen. 'Cor, I couldn't let im and er down, so I just come from the bleeding Palace'.[32]

Everybody had won. But the prizes were unequal. Britain won a Pyrrhic victory at best – top price admission, interminable renegotiations looming and an awkward partner reputation. By contrast, France kept its hegemony, and finalized CAP for its own benefit. The Yaounde Agreements of 1961 and 1969 gave France's former African colonies access to the whole Community. When formal entry talks opened on 30 June 1970 France rammed through an outline Common Fisheries Policy Agreement (CFP). 'By keeping firm control over the timing of developments and the sequence in which solutions of individual problems were reached,' noted Whitehall's internal history, 'the French were able to set up the final package which best suited them, and by doing so to oblige us to pay more on Community finance in return for getting what we wanted on New Zealand'.[33]

Entering the Berlaymont's [the EC's HQ] pearly gates, British officials found a French administration in command. The Commission's French president, François-Xavier Ortoli, directed the ensemble. Jean-Marie Soutou, France's permanent representative to the Community, worried lest 'the extraordinary skill' of the French team should invite retribution.[34] Instructed to use French, British representatives kept their heads down in order to acclimatize. No grace period eased the transition. Brussels inflicted a total culture shock, partly because civil servants were underprepared, partly because many had not wanted to go to Brussels – wrongly assuming they would get less pay. Crash language courses could not deliver the oral and written fluency required for smooth enculturation. Occasionally, a visiting British official speaking French 'of an almost Proustian quality' would catch the French off guard.[35] But these were small victories. French held its own as the Brussels lingua franca and Roy Jenkins's lack of fluency seriously disadvantaged his presidency of the Commission in the late 1970s.[36] Adapting to the jungle-like climate and 'the deviousness and potential bad faith' of co-negotiators took time.[37] In making appointments to the Commission, Whitehall concentrated on inserting people at the top with too few down the line – a mistake which took years to correct.

That so little spadework for entry occurred in the late 1960s suggests Wilson kept options open all the way. Engaging a timely study of the Commission's workings would have demonstrated commitment to the 1967 bid and fortified the 1970–2 talks. Mandarins admitted a 'failure to exert ourselves sufficiently in the run-up to the opening of negotiations in June 1970'.³⁸ The sixties marked a formative growth period for a Community under Franco–German management. In 1961 the Six were learning to walk, and the CAP was unformed. Early entry would have given London a say in rule-making. The absent, as the French say, are always wrong. The British had to put on off-the-peg clothes instead of the bespoke garments worn by France and Germany, and naturally complained about the fit. The vetoes of 1963 and 1967 consolidated France's ascendancy.

Britain's European diplomacy branded it an awkward partner – loath to accept the Community *acquis*. The UK's response to continental integration initiatives since 1950, opined historian Robert Skidelsky, 'might best be described as selective sabotage'.³⁹ The third Wilson government's re-negotiation of membership in 1974–5, followed by prime minister Margaret Thatcher's rebate demand of 1979–84, ratchetted up mainland Europe's distrust. 'The most difficult of all nationalities to deal with were the British,' declared a senior Whitehall-trained official, instancing 'a certain lack of professionalism, i.e. actual knowledge of the treaties'.⁴⁰ London's long courtship of the Five backfired. Wilson's reluctance to evangelize party and public in 1966–7 fuelled Euroscepticism, and eventually Brexit.

The ending of the golden age of the world economy exploded expectations of an entry bonanza. Entry did not equal entente, despite the choreographed cordiality of Heath–Pompidou encounters. The decisive Heath–Pompidou Paris summit in May 1971 neatly closed off alliance. Pompidou made it crystal clear that he envisaged the meeting 'not as a question of creating a new entente cordiale. That had been directed against someone. Clearly France and Britain must have a cordial understanding but their purpose now was to cooperate with others in a common task'.⁴¹ Britain was a rookie in a French-led club. Unsurprisingly, the seven-year diplomatic war hardened both sides. Bickering became an end in itself. Heath criticized the FO's 'anti-French mutterings'.⁴² Policy-makers who had rubbished the France of the 1950s as sick and unreliable now warned of a partner too strong for comfort – forecasting GNP 50 per cent greater than that of Britain by 1980.

The war of words continued. The *Spectator* fulminated against French nuclear tests in the Pacific: 'The reluctance or inability of French politicians to respond to moral arguments and imperatives is one of the few constants in international relations ... many would think that they were born that way ... The French hardly ever win. Their national genius is not to succeed, but to fool people that they used to succeed, will eventually succeed ... The plain historical fact is that the French get things wrong'.⁴³ Conservative prime minister Margaret Thatcher denounced the French for 'trying to take her money and her fish and she would not let them have a penny piece ... France was the kept woman of Europe.'⁴⁴ Pot calling kettle black. The UK conducted many nuclear tests at Australian sites between 1952 and 1963. After forcibly evicting islanders from Indian Ocean island Diego Garcia in 1969, Britain leased it to the United States for the construction of a military base, and refused to allow islanders to return.

The failure of Franco–British partnership spoke to a cross-channel democratic deficit. Ruling elites marginalized cabinets, parliaments and public. 'The calamity of the war, and the impoverishment of the world as a whole,' remarked Orwell in 1945, 'have not been fully brought home to the British people'.⁴⁵ Journalist Malcolm Muggeridge was 'struck once more by the essential unawareness of the ordinary person of what is going on'.⁴⁶ In the Suez crisis, premier Eden, 'a relative amateur' in handling the mass media, 'managed to fashion news and current affairs reporting ... to a remarkable extent'.⁴⁷ 'The ability of British governments to ignore or manipulate public opinion', acknowledged a former Labour minister and director of Chatham House, 'has been at least partly responsible for some of Britain's worst errors'.⁴⁸ The radical protest of the sixties did not topple W.H. Auden's unknown citizen who 'held the proper opinions for the time of year; when there was peace, he was for peace; when there was war, he went'.⁴⁹

Advances in communications technology and the acceleration of international affairs in the sixties vastly expanded news and information. Government responded with more sophisticated management, starving electorates of debate and analysis. On Europe the public waited in vain for a lead. An analysis of Wilson's bid concluded, 'The debate, such as it was, pointed out the key issues of membership without providing the public with the information it needed to evaluate them'.⁵⁰ The political process acted like an anaesthetic. Television had a flattening effect, filling screens with pictures of ministers 'getting on planes, getting off planes, speaking at length to seemingly admiring crowds, and making an allegedly triumphant return'.⁵¹ Grandees sedated voters: 'Lord Elton [Rhodes Trust Secretary] ... gave us ... sugary dissertation on the "British achievement" ... a hymn to the Empire of unadulterated praise, sprinkled freely with allusions to cricket, not a shadow on the picture, not the most indirect allusion to present-day events in Africa'.⁵² For the political class, the information explosion proved a blessing in disguise. 'A surfeit of data,' remarked philosopher and sociologist Jacques Ellul, 'far from permitting people to make judgments and form opinions, prevents them from doing so and actually paralyzes them'.⁵³ Excluded from supposedly arcane matters about the national interest, the passengers on the proverbial Clapham omnibus were stoical, not apathetic.

Barely a handful of the cognoscenti protested the secret state. In a 1961 essay – rejected by the BBC – Marxist historian E.P. Thompson flagged the increasing difficulty of expressing radical dissent. Heterodoxy had an easier time in the Victorian age and formal democratic procedures were 'becoming more and more empty of real content, public life more enervated, and controversy more muffled'.⁵⁴ From the conservative end of the spectrum Max Beloff, Gladstone professor of government at Oxford University, demanded 'a new style of politics appropriate to the kind of issues that now fall to be resolved'. He excoriated politicians 'in a country which professes to be a democracy' for reaching the decision to apply for European Community membership 'without full public debate ... nor is this the only instance ... of a seeming unwillingness to take the public into the confidence of the Government where important issues of foreign policy are concerned'.⁵⁵

In May 1968 Labour technology minister Tony Benn, the only prominent politician to champion the empowering of voters, warned: 'It would be foolish to assume that people will be satisfied for much longer with a system which confines their national political role to the marking of a ballot with a single cross once every five years'.⁵⁶ In a valedictory dispatch, Britain's Paris ambassador Nicholas Henderson called on ministers to explain the Community 'rather than making it the scapegoat for our ills' and to give the public a better sense of Britain's relative economic position in Europe.[57] Did voters want a say in policy-making? No one asked. Poet and writer G.K. Chesterton summed up the relationship pithily: 'Smile at us, pay us, pass us; but do not quite forget. For we are the people of England, that never have spoken yet'.[58]

Timeline, 1944–75

1944   D-Day, 6 June
       Liberation of Paris, 19–25 August
       Provisional Government under General de Gaulle
       Churchill's Moscow visit (percentages agreement) October
       Franco–Soviet Pact, Moscow, 10 December

1945   Yalta Conference, February (France not invited)
       Attlee prime minister, 26 July
       Atomic bomb, Hiroshima, 6 August
       Creation of Commissariat General of Plan, 21 December

1946   Resignation of de Gaulle, 20 January
       US loan to UK, July
       Churchill's Fulton (5 March) and Zurich (19 September) speeches
       Start of Indo-China War, November
       Adoption of Monnet Plan, November

1947   Vincent Auriol, President of Fourth Republic
       UK announces withdrawal from Greece and Turkey, 21 February
       Truman Doctrine, 12 March
       Dunkirk Treaty, 4 March
       French Communist party excluded from government, May
       Marshall's Harvard speech proposes aid for Europe, 5 June

1948   Communist coup in Czechoslovakia, February
       Brussels Pact (Britain, France, Benelux) establishes Western Union, March
       Hague Congress, foundation of European movement, May
       End of Britain's Palestine mandate, May
       Berlin blockade, June
       Malayan Emergency, June

1949   Atlantic Pact (NATO), 4 April
       Council of Europe created at Strasbourg, 5 May
       UK devaluation, 18 September

1950   Schuman Plan for European Coal and Steel Community (ECSC), 9 May
       Korean War, June
       Pleven Plan for European Defence Community (EDC), July

- 1951 Treaty of Paris establishes ECSC, 18 April
        Churchill government, October

- 1952 British A-bomb test, October
        Mau Mau rebellion, Kenya

- 1953 De Gaulle criticizes EDC, February
        René Coty, President of the Republic

- 1954 Geneva Conference, April–July
        Fall of Dien Bien Phu, May
        Geneva accords, June
        Anglo–Egyptian Treaty for evacuation of Suez Canal Base, July
        French parliament rejects EDC, August
        Western European Union (WEU), October
        Algerian War, November

- 1955 Eden prime minister, April
        Messina conference begins talks for an Economic Community, June
        Baghdad Pact, April
        Cyprus Emergency, April

- 1956 Venice conference approves European Economic Community, May
        Nationalization of Suez canal, July
        Cabinet agrees 'Plan G' for a Free Trade Area (FTA), November

- 1957 Macmillan prime minister, January
        Sandys Defence Review, January
        British H-Bomb test, May
        Treaty of Rome establishes EEC and Euratom, March

- 1958 EEC starts, January
        Army revolt in Algeria, May
        De Gaulle prime minister, June
        Full powers voted, June
        France vetoes FTA
        Berlin crisis, November
        De Gaulle elected president, December

- 1959 France enters EEC, January
        President Coty hands over powers to de Gaulle, January
        Michel Debré prime minister, January
        French Mediterranean fleet leaves NATO command, March
        Britain founds European Free Trade Association (EFTA), November

- 1960 New French franc, January
        French A-Bomb, February
        Collapse of Paris 4 Power Summit, May
        Cancellation of Blue Streak missile, February

1961   Macmillan–de Gaulle meeting Rambouillet, January
        Secret Army Organization (OAS) formed, February
        Military revolt in Algiers, April
        France–Algeria peace talks, May
        Conservative government applies for EEC entry, July
        Berlin Wall, August
        De Gaulle escapes Pont-sur-Seine assassination attempt, September
        UK–EEC negotiations begin, October
        Macmillan–de Gaulle summit, Birch Grove, November

1962   EEC agrees Common Agricultural Policy (CAP), January
        OAS attacks in France and Algeria, January–March
        Georges Pompidou prime minister, April
        Collapse of Fouchet Plan for an intergovernmental European union, April
        Macmillan–de Gaulle, Champs, June
        Algerian independence, July
        De Gaulle escapes assassination Petit-Clamart, August
        Cuban missile crisis, October
        Macmillan–de Gaulle Rambouillet, 15–16 December
        Kennedy–Macmillan Nassau meeting, 17–21 December

1963   De Gaulle vetoes UK application, January
        Franco–German Treaty of Cooperation, January
        Indonesia–Malaysia confrontation, January
        Partial Test Ban Treaty, August
        Alec Douglas-Home prime minister, October

1964   Plowden report on overseas representation
        France recognizes Communist China, January
        Chinese nuclear test, October
        First Wilson government, October

1965   Anglo–French summit Paris, April
        Heath Conservative party leader, July
        'Empty chair' crisis EEC, July
        Rhodesian UDI, November
        De Gaulle re-elected, December

1966   'Luxembourg Compromise', January
        France leaves NATO integrated command, March
        Second Wilson government, March
        Anglo–French meeting London, July

1967   Six-Day War, June
        Labour government EEC application, 2 May
        Wilson–de Gaulle Trianon summit, 19 June
        De Gaulle in Quebec, July
        Sterling devaluation, November

De Gaulle vetoes EEC bid, November
UK withdrawal from Aden, November

1968 Announcement of East of Suez withdrawal, January
Foreign Office/Commonwealth Office merger,
Paris events, May–June
Couve de Murville prime minister, July
French H-bomb test, August
Warsaw Pact invasion of Czechoslovakia, August

1969 Duncan Report on overseas representation
Soames affair, February
De Gaulle resigns, April; Pompidou elected, June
French franc devalued, August
Hague EEC summit agrees in principle to open UK entry talks, December

1970 Heath government renews UK application, 30 June

1971 Heath–Pompidou Paris summit, 20–1 May

1972 Treaty of Accession, 22 January

1973 UK joins EEC, 1 January

1974 General election: February
Third Wilson government, 4 March
Death of Pompidou, April; Valery Giscard d'Estaing elected, May
UK renegotiates membership terms, April
General election October: Labour wins majority

1975 Renegotiation concluded, 11 March
UK referendum on European Communities membership, 5 June
Yes (continued membership): 67. 2%; No: 32.8% (64.5% of electorate voted)

APPENDIX 1

British and French Governments, 1944–75

FRANCE

Heads of provisional government

Charles de Gaulle: 3 Jun 44–20 Jan 46
Félix Gouin: 26 Jan 46–12 Jun 46
Georges Bidault: 23 Jun 46–28 Nov 46
Léon Blum: 16 Dec 46–16 Jan 47

Fourth Republic

Presidents
Vincent Auriol: 16 Jan 47–16 Jan 54;
René Coty: 16 Jan 54–8 Jan 59

Prime Ministers
Paul Ramadier: 22 Jan 47–19 Nov 47; Robert Schuman: 24 Nov 47–19 Jul 48
André Marie: 26 Jul 48–28 Aug 48; R. Schuman: 5 Sep 48–7 Sep 48
Henri Queuille: 11 Sep 48–6 Oct 49; G. Bidault: 28 Oct 49–24 Jun 50
H. Queuille: 2 Jul 50–4 Jul 50; René Pleven: 12 Jul 50–28 Feb 51
H. Queuille: 10 Mar 51–10 Jul 51; R. Pleven: 10 Aug 51–7 Jan 52
Edgar Faure: 20 Jan 52–29 Feb 52; Antoine Pinay: 8 Mar 52–23 Dec 52
René Mayer: 8 Jan 53–21 May 53; Joseph Laniel: 27 Jun 53–12 Jun 54
P. Mendès France: 19 Jun 54–5 Feb 55; E. Faure: 23 Feb 55–24 Jan 56; Guy Mollet: 1 Feb 56–21 May 57; Maurice Bourgès-Maunoury: 12 Jun 57–30 Sep 57
Félix Gaillard: 5 Nov 57–15 Apr 58; Pierre Pflimlin: 14 May 58–28 May 58
Charles de Gaulle: 1 Jun 58–8 Jan 59

Fifth Republic

Presidents
Charles de Gaulle: 21 Dec 58–28 Apr 69
Georges Pompidou: 15 Jun 69–2 Apr 74
Valéry Giscard d'Estaing: 19 May 74–26 Apr 81

Prime Ministers
Michel Debré: 8 Jan 59–14 Apr 62
G. Pompidou: 14 Apr 62–11 Jul 68
Maurice Couve de Murville: 11 Jul 68–20 Jun 69
Jacques Chaban-Delmas: 20 Jun 69–5 Jul 72
Pierre Messmer: 5 Jul 72–27 May 74
Jacques Chirac: 27 May 74–25 Aug 76

BRITAIN

Prime Ministers

Coalition government, 1940–45
W. Churchill, 10 May 40–23 May 45

Caretaker government
W. Churchill, 23 May 45–26 Jul 45

Labour governments, 1945–51
C. Attlee, 26 Jul 45–26 Oct 51

Conservative governments, 1951–64
W. Churchill, 26 Oct 51–5 Apr 55
A. Eden, 6 Apr 55–9 Jan 57
H. Macmillan, 10 Jan 57–13 Oct 63
A. Douglas-Home, 18 Oct 63–16 Oct 64

Labour governments, 1964–70
H. Wilson, 16 Oct 64–19 Jun 70

Conservative government
E. Heath, 19 Jun 70–4 Mar 74

Labour government
H. Wilson, 4 Mar 74–5 Apr 76

APPENDIX 2

Foreign Secretaries and Foreign Ministers

BRITAIN
Coalition government, 1940–5
Anthony Eden
Dec 1940–Jul 1945

Labour governments
Ernest Bevin
Jul 1945–Mar 1951
Herbert Morrison
Mar–Oct 1951

Conservative governments
Anthony Eden
Oct 51–Apr 55
Harold Macmillan
Apr–Dec 55
Selwyn Lloyd
Dec 55–Jul 60
Lord Home
July 60–Oct 63
R.A. Butler
Oct 63–Oct 64

Labour governments
Patrick Gordon Walker
Oct 1964–Jan 1965
Michael Stewart
Jan 1965–Aug 1966
George Brown
Aug 1966–Mar 1968
Michael Stewart
Mar 1968–Jun 1970

FRANCE
Provisional government
Georges Bidault
Sep 1944–Dec 1946

Fourth Republic
Léon Blum
Dec 1946–Jan 1947
Georges Bidault
Jan 1947–Jul 1948
Robert Schuman
Jul 1948–Jan 1953
Georges Bidault
Jan 1953–Jun 1954
Pierre Mendès France
Jun 1954–Jan 1955
Edgar Faure
Jan 1955–Feb 1955
Antoine Pinay
Feb 1955–Feb 1956
Christian Pineau
Feb 56–May 58
René Pleven
May 58–Jun 58

Fifth Republic
Maurice Couve de Murville
Jun 58–May 68
Michel Debré
May 68–Jun 69
Maurice Schumann
Jun 1969–Mar 1973

BRITAIN
Conservative government
Alec Douglas-Home
Jun 1970–Mar 1974

Labour government
James Callaghan
Mar 1974–Apr 1976

FRANCE
André Bettencourt
Mar 73–Apr 1973
Michel Jobert
Apr 1973–May 1974
Jean Sauvagnargues
May 1974–Aug 1977

APPENDIX 3

Foreign Office and Quai d'Orsay

Permanent Secretaries, Foreign Office (Foreign and Commonwealth Office 1968–)
Alexander Cadogan, 1938–46
Orme Sargent, 1946–9
William Strang, 1949–3
Ivone Kirkpatrick, 1953–7
Frederick Hoyer Millar, 1957–62
Harold Caccia, 1962–5
Paul Gore-Booth, 1965–9
Denis Greenhill, 1969–73
Thomas Brimelow, 1973–5

Secretary Generals, Quai d'Orsay
Jean Chauvel, 1944–9
Alexandre Parodi, 1949–55
René Massigli, 1955–6
Louis Joxe, 1956–9
Eric de Carbonnel, 1959–65
Hervé Alphand, 1965–72
Geoffroy de Courcel, 1972–6

APPENDIX 4

European Economic Growth, 1950–80

Table 1 Percentage growth in industrial production in selected countries, 1950–6

Federal Republic of Germany (FRG)	100
Italy	63
France	49
Belgium	36
Britain	21

Source: David Sanders, *Losing an Empire, Finding a Role: British Foreign Policy since 1945*, London: Macmillan 1990, 144.

Table 2 Average annual growth of GDP in selected countries, 1950–80

	1950–60	1960–70	1970–80
Belgium	2.0	4.1	3.2
France	3.5	4.6	3.0
FRG	6.6	3.5	2.4
Italy	4.9	4.6	2.1
Netherlands	3.3	4.1	2.3
Britain	2.3	2.3	2.0

Source: Sanders, op. cit., 145

Notes

Abbreviations

AN	Archives Nationales, Paris
BDOHP	British Diplomatic Oral History Programme, Churchill College Cambridge
BLO	Bodleian Library, Oxford
BLPES	British Library of Political and Economic Science, LSE
CAC	Churchill Archives Centre, Churchill College, Cambridge
DBPO	Documents on British Policy Overseas
DDF	Documents Diplomatiques Français
FNSP	Fondation Nationale des Sciences Politiques, Paris
FRUS	Foreign Relations of the United States
HIA	Hoover Institution Archives, Stanford, California
IA	*International Affairs*
MAE	Ministère des affaires étrangères, Paris
OH	*The Official History of Britain and the European Community*, vol. I: Alan S. Milward, *The Rise and Fall of a National Strategy, 1945–1963*, 2002; II, Stephen Wall, *From Rejection to Referendum*, 1963–1975, 2013
RIIA	Royal Institute of International Affairs
TLS	*Times Literary Supplement*
TNA	The National Archives

Acknowledgements

1 Douglas Johnson, ed., *Cross-Channel Currents: 100 Years of the Entente Cordiale*, Routledge 2004; Robert and Isabelle Tombs, *That Sweet Enemy: The French and the British from the Sun King to the Present*, Heinemann 2006; P.M.H. Bell, I, *France and Britain 1900–1940; Entente and Estrangement*, Longman 1996; II, *France and Britain 1940–1994, The Long Separation*, Longman 1997; Laurent Bonnaud, *France-Angleterre, un siècle d'entente cordiale*, L'Harmattan 2004; David Dutton, ed., *Statecraft and Diplomacy in the Twentieth Century: Essays Presented to P.M.H. Bell*, Liverpool University Press 1995; Antoine Capet, ed., *Britain, France and the Entente Cordiale since 1904*, Palgrave 2006; Philippe Chassaigne and Michael Dockrill, eds, *Anglo-French Relations 1898–1998*, Palgrave 2001; François Crouzet, *Britain Ascendant: Studies in British and Franco-British Economic History*, Cambridge University Press 1991; Alan Sharp and Glyn Stone, eds, *Anglo-French Relations in the Twentieth Century*, Routledge 2000; Claire Sanderson, *L'Impossible alliance?: France, Grande-Bretagne et defense de l'Europe, 1945–1958*, Publications Sorbonne 2003; Diana Cooper-Richet and Michel Rapoport, eds, *L'Entente cordiale: Cent ans de relations culturelles franco-britanniques, 1904–2004*, Creaphis 2006; Jacques Viot and Giles Radice, eds, *L'Entente cordiale dans le siècle*, Odile Jacob 2004; Robert Tombs and Emile Chabal, eds, *Britain and France in two world wars: Truth, myth and memory*, Bloomsbury 2013.

2 *L'Ame des Peuples*, Paris: Hachette 1950, 46
3 Herve Alphand, *L'Etonnement d'etre: Journal 1939-1973*, Paris: Fayard 1977, 184

Preface

1 Perry Anderson, 'Degringolade', *London Review of Books*, 2 September 2004.
2 Stefan Collini, 'The Unexpected Professor review – The Puzzle of John Carey,' *Guardian*, Thursday 27 February 2014.
3 Douglas Jay, *Change and Fortune: A Political Record*, London 1980, 137.
4 Jean-Luc Barré, *Devenir De Gaulle, 1939-1943*, Paris 2003; Charles de Gaulle, *Memoires*: introduction par Jean-Louis Cremieux-Brilhac, Paris 2000.
5 Evelyn Shuckburgh, *Descent to Suez, Diaries 1951-1956*, 1986, 12.
6 Georges Mallaby, *From My Level: Unwritten Minutes*, London 1965, 152, 158.
7 Maurice Vaissé, *La Grandeur: Politique étrangère du General de Gaulle, 1958-1969*, Paris 1998, 9-10.
8 Journal de l'Elysée, 1, *Tous les soirs avec de Gaulle (1965-1967)*, Paris 1997, 769.
9 Roger Broad, ed., Britain and Europe, ICBH witness seminar, London 2002, 75, 78.
10 David Hannay, *Britain's quest for a role: A diplomatic memoir from Europe to the UN*, London 2012, 68.
11 OH, I, ix.
12 Stephen Clayman, John Heritage, *The News Interview: Journalists and Public Figures on the Air*, Cambridge 2002, 31.
13 Margaret Gowing, *Independence and Deterrence: Britain and Atomic Energy, 1945-1952*, 1, *Policy Making*, 1974, 415.
14 *The Journey not the Arrival Matters: An Autobiography of the Years 1939-1969*, 1969, 32-3.
15 BLO, Reilly, MS.Eng c.6924.
16 Michael Foot, *Aneurin Bevan, A Biography*, II, 1973, 656.
17 Matthew Cobb, *The Resistance: The French against the Nazis*, 2009, 324, n. 42.
18 Julian Barnes, *Nothing to be Frightened Of*, 2009, 5.
19 *Force of Circumstance*, Penguin 1978, 284.
20 *La Nausee*, Gallimard Paris 1962, 11.
21 TNA CAB 129/52, Questions of procedure for ministers.
22 Ferdinand Mount, *Cold Cream: My early life and other mistakes*, 2008, 311.
23 Edward Heath, *The Course of My Life*, Coronet 1998, 177.
24 John Campbell, *Roy Jenkins*, 2014, 506.
25 *Spycatcher*, Stoddart, London 1987, 136-40.
26 *Downhill All The Way*, 1967, 9-10.
27 *The Captive Mind*, Penguin, 1985, epigraph.

Introduction

1 James Owen (ed.), *The Times, Great Letters*, London 2017, 262; Martin Gilbert, *Winston S Churchill, Road to Victory 1941-1945*, London, Heinemann 1986, 1060; Journal du Septennat 1947-1954, II 1948, Paris, Armand Colin 1974, 187; Peter Catterall, ed., *The Macmillan Diaries*, II, London, Pan Books, 2012, 475.
2 TNA FO371/177874, Tickell to Palliser, 20 February 1964.

3   Frank Giles, 'De Gaulle: Yes or No?', *The Sunday Times*, 13 November 1966.
4   *Britain Ascendant: Comparative Studies in Franco-British economic history*, Cambridge 1990, 3, 5.
5   John R. Gillingham, *Coal, Steel, and the Rebirth of Europe, 1945–1955*, Cambridge 1991, 121.
6   TNA PREM 15/372, Record of conversation between the prime minister and the president of the French Republic, Thursday 20 May 1971.
7   *The Robert Hall Diaries, 1947–53*, ed. Alec Cairncross, 1989, 5.
8   Robert Skidelsky, *John Maynard Keynes*, 3, *Fighting for Britain, 1937–1946*, Papermac 2000, 386.
9   Geoffrey Warner, *In the Midst of Events: Foreign Office Diaries and Papers of Kenneth G. Younger*, 7 July 1949, 2005.
10 Peter Catterall, ed., *The Macmillan Diaries I: The Cabinet Years 1950–1957*, Macmillan 2003, 456.
11 *Britain and World Power since 1945: Constructing a nation's role in international politics*, University of Michigan Press, Ann Arbor, 2014.
12 James Cable, *The Geneva Conference of 1954 on Indochina*, 1986, 3.
13 TNA CAB 129/84, 5 January 1957.
14 Kristan Stoddart, *The Sword and the Shield*, 2014, 14.
15 Ernst B. Haas, *The Uniting of Europe*, Stanford, 1958, 4.
16 TJT and EPT, *There is a spirit in europe: A Memoir of Frank Thompson*, Gollancz, 1947, 86.
17 John Bew, *Citizen Clem, A biography of Attlee*, 2016, 368–9.
18 CAC, KNAT/1/15 Diary, 16 May 1946.
19 TNA PREM 13/1484, Palliser to Wilson, July 1967.
20 Sir William Hayter, *The Diplomacy of the Great Powers*, London 1960, 33.
21 Reilly to London, 9 February 1967, Michael Boehm Lasse, 'Our Man in Paris: The British Embassy in Paris and the second UK application to join the EEC, 1966–7', *Journal of European Integration History*, 10, 2, 2004, 52.
22 Jean Guehenno, *Journal des années noires (1940–1944)*, Paris 1947, 9.
23 'Reflections on the foreign policy of France', *IA*, October 1945, 443.
24 BLO, Reilly, MS. Eng. c 6925.
25 Niall Ferguson, *Kissinger, 1923–1968: The Idealist*, Allen Lane, 2015, 719
26 http://hansard.millbanksystems.com/commons/1995/nov/01/channel-tunnel-rail-link-bill
27 *A Life at the Centre*, Papermac, 1994, 194–5.
28 Richard Overy, *The Morbid Age: Britain between the wars*, 2009.
29 *The Making of the English Working Class*, 1963, 12.
30 *Grand Inquisitor*, Pan Books 1990, 118.
31 *The Remains of the Day*, 1989, 187.
32 Michael Blackwell, *Clinging to Grandeur*, 1993, 13.
33 David Marquand, *Britain since1918: The strange career of British democracy*, 2008, 400.
34 Alistair Horne, *Macmillan*, II, 1989, 319.
35 FRUS 1961–1963,XIII, Washington DC 1994, no 39.
36 TNA PREM 13/324, De Gaulle–Wilson, 2 April 1965.
37 TNA FCO 30/414, Lipkowsky to Chalfont, 6 February 1969.
38 *Strange Defeat*, New York 1968, 176.
39 A.J.P. Taylor, *A Personal History*, Coronet, 1983, 246.
40 Robert Rhodes James, *Anthony Eden*, 1986, 353.

41 David Vital, *The Making of British Foreign Policy*, 1968, 110–11.
42 Perry Anderson, *The New Old World*, New York 2009, 77.
43 James J. Sheehan, *Where have all the soldiers gone*, Boston 2008, xvi.
44 Soames to Stewart, 21 March 1969, TNA FCO 30/418.
45 Richard Crossman, *The Diaries of a Cabinet Minister*, 3, 379.
46 TNA FCO 30/418, Soames to Wilson, 11 March 1969.

1 Anglo-Saxon Attitudes

1 Maurice Vaïsse, ed., *8 Mai 1945: La Victoire en Europe*, Lyon 1985, 275.
2 David Dilks, ed., *The Diaries of Sir Alexander Cadogan, 1938–1945*, 1971, 775.
3 *Daily Express*, 31 May 1940.
4 Robert Dillon, *History on British Television*, Manchester 2010, 1.
5 Mark Pottle, ed., *Champion Redoubable, The Diaries and Letters of Violet Bonham Carter*, Weidenfeld, 1998, 369.
6 Mount, *Cold Cream*, 254.
7 John Carey, *The Unexpected Professor*, 2014, 150–1.
8 Ben Pimlott, ed., *The Political Diaries of Hugh Dalton*, 1986, 361.
9 Christopher Mayhew, *Time to Explain*, 1987, 99.
10 Peter Calvocoressi, *Threading My Way*, 1994, 76.
11 *Out of the Wilderness, Diaries 1963–67*, Arrow 1987, 512.
12 *No Discouragement: An Autobiography*, 1996, 153.
13 Alec Guinness, *My Name Escapes Me*, 1996, 49.
14 John Saville, *The Politics of Continuity*, 1993, 229, n. 9.
15 Bryan Magee, *Growing up in a War*, 2007, 233.
16 Simon Leys, 'The Intimate Orwell', *The New York Review of Books*, 26 May 2011, 42.
17 Arthur Miller, *Timebends: A Life*, 1987, 432.
18 Robin Day, *Grand Inquisitor*, Pan 1989, 72.
19 Linda Colley, *Forging the Nation 1707–1837*, 1996, 30.
20 Michael Blackwell, *Clinging to Grandeur*, 1993, 61.
21 Pat Kirkham, David Thoms, eds, *War Culture*, 1995, 50.
22 George Garnet, 'Riotous', *TLS*, 8 June 2007; *The History of the University of Oxford*, VIII, ed., Brian Harrison, Oxford 1994, 221.
23 Peter Clarke, *Hope and Glory: Britain 1900–1990*, 1996, 401.
24 John Julius Norwich, *Christmas Crackers*, 1980, 265.
25 Blackwell, *Clinging to Grandeur*, 52.
26 Vaïsse, *8 Mai 1945*, 280.
27 David Marquand, *The Political Quarterly*, 64,2, 1993, 211.
28 Perry Anderson, *English Questions*, 1992, 49.
29 George Mikes, *How to be an alien*, 1946, 11.
30 Hugo Young, *This Blessed Plot*, Papermac 1999, 8.
31 Kenneth Dover, *Marginal Comment*, 1994, 29.
32 BLO, Attlee MS. Eng.c.4794, 15 September 1955; *As It Happened*, 1956, 251.
33 E.P. Thompson, *Beyond the Frontier: The politics of a failed mission*, Stanford, California 1997, 63.
34 Jonathan Haslam, *Vices of Integrity: E.H. Carr, 1892–1992*, 1999, 17.
35 David Cannadine, 'James Bond and the Decline of England', *Encounter*, September 1979, 47, 52.

36 John Dickie, *Inside the Foreign Office*, 1992, 1.
37 James R. Vaughan, 'A certain idea of Britain', *Contemporary British History*, 19, 2, 2005, 154.
38 Uwe Kitzinger, *The European Common Market and Community*, New York 1967, 180–2.
39 Richard Hoggart, *An Imagined Life*, v 3, 1992, 149.
40 D.C. Watt, *IA*, 38, 1, January 1962, 71.
41 Margaret Gowing, 'Reflections on Atomic Energy History', The Rede Lecture, University of Cambridge, 1978, 14.
42 Alastair Hetherington, *Guardian Years*, 1981, 24.
43 M.R.D. Foot, *Memories of an SOE Historian*, 2008, 76.
44 Edward Harrison, *The Young Kim Philby*, Exeter 2012, 5.
45 *Contemporary History in Europe*, ed., Donald Cameron Watt, 1969, 11.
46 Anderson, op. cit., 1.
47 Harrison, *History of the University of Oxford*, 8, 221–3, 623–5.
48 Brunello Vigezzi, *The British Committee on the Theory of International Politics (1954–1985) The Rediscovery of History*, Milan 2005, 113–5, 146–7.
49 Mary Warnock, *A Memoir: People and Places*, 2000, 115.
50 Julia Stapleton, *Sir Arthur Bryant and National History in Twentieth Century Britain*, New York 2005, 7.
51 Nicola Lacey, *A Life of H.A.L. Hart*: Oxford 2004, 141.
52 Alexander Werth, *France 1940–1955*, Readers Union 1957, xii.
53 *The Years*, Harvest/ Harcourt Brace, New York 1965, 221–2.
54 'The Intellectuals', *Encounter*, 19, April 1955.
55 'Simone Weil', *New York Review of Books*, February 1963, 22.
56 'Outward Looking', *TLS* 1 July 2016.
57 Blackwell, op. cit., 65.
58 Anthony Hartley, *A State of England*, 1963, 56, n. 2.
59 Vigezzi, op. cit., 38.
60 HIA, Vaizey Papers, Box 9, Vaizey to Gaitskell 28 August 1962.
61 *In My Way*, 1971, 209–10.
62 *The Spirit of British Administration and Some European Comparisons*, 1959, 148.
63 Michael Charlton, *The Price of Victory*, BBC Publications, London 1983, 194–5.
64 Ibid. 182.

2 Vive la France

1 Michael Kelly, *The Cultural and Intellectual Rebuilding of France after the Second World War*, 2004, 185.
2 Robert Gildea, 'Historians in harness', *TLS* 30 July 2004, 10.
3 Werth, *France 1940–1955*, xix.
4 Ian Buruma, *Voltaire's Coconuts*, 1999, 4–5.
5 *Capitalism and the State in Modern France*, Cambridge 1981, 280.
6 Joseph Becker, Franz Knipping, eds, *Power in Europe?: Great Britain, France, Italy and Germany in a postwar world, 1945–1950*, Berlin/New York 1986, 266.
7 *The Need for Roots*, London 1952, 189.
8 Andrew Shennan, *Rethinking France*, Oxford 1997, 289.
9 David Chuter, *Humanity's Soldier*, Providence RI 1996, 192.

10 Becker, *Power in Europe?* 47, 171–2.
11 Matthew Cobb, *Eleven Days in August*, 2013, 362.
12 *Discours et Messages*, 1, Paris 1970, 440.
13 *La France a sauvé l'Europe*, 1, Paris 1947, 30–1.
14 Joseph Kessel, *Army of Shadows*, New York 1944, vi.
15 *Notebooks 1942–1951*, trans and annotated Justin O'Brien, New York 1966, 4–5.
16 André François Poncet, *Souvenirs d'une ambassade à Berlin*, Paris 1946, 314.
17 *Memoires politiques*, Paris 1967, 292.
18 *Lettres, Notes et Carnets* (hereafter *LNC*), 10, Janvier 1964–Juin 1966, Paris 1988, 156–7.
19 Alain Peyrefitte, *C'Etait de Gaulle*, Paris 1994, 347; *War Memoirs: The Call to Honour*, Collins London 1955, 168.
20 *The Mandarins: A Novel*, World Publishing Cleveland, New York 1956, 552.
21 *La Decadence, 1932–1939*, Paris 1979, 368.
22 *A Personal History*, Coronet 1984, 306.
23 Gabrielle Hecht, *The Radiance of France* Cambridge MA 1998, 2, 21, 39.
24 Hecht, op. cit., 39.
25 Robert Gilpin, *France in the age of the scientific state*, Princeton NJ 1968, 3.
26 Andrew Knapp, *The Uncertain Foundation: France at the Liberation*, 2007, 11; Bernard Barbiche, Christian Sorrel (eds), *La France et le Concile Vatican II*, Lang Brussels, 2013; Sylvie Bernay, *L'Eglise de France face à la persecution des Juifs 1940–1944*, Paris CNRS 2012.
27 Jacques and Raissa Maritain, *Oeuvres complètes*, VIII, Fribourg 1989, 1100.
28 Alfred Grosser, *La IV Republique et sa politique exterieure*, Paris 1961, 27.
29 *Memoires*, Paris 1983, 361.
30 *Fast Cars, Clean Bodies*, Cambridge MA 1995, 7.
31 Herman Lebovics, *Bringing the Empire Back Home*, Durham Duke University Press 2004, 180.
32 Carole Seymour Jones, *A Dangerous Liaison: Simone de Beauvoir and Jean-Paul Sartre*, 2008, 409.
33 Charles Drazin, *The Faber Book of French Cinema*, 2011, 244–7.
34 Pascal Ory, *La Culture comme Aventure*, Paris 2008.
35 'Union Sucrée', *London Review of Books*, 26, 18, 23 September 2004.
36 For alleged provincialism of the French academy, see H.Stuart Hughes, *The Obstructed Path: French social thought in the years of desperation 1930–1960*, New York 1969, 7
37 Margaret Gowing, *Independence and Deterrence, Britain and Atomic Energy*, 1, 1974, 9.
38 Antony Beevor, Artemis Cooper, *Paris after the Liberation*, London 1994, 318–19.
39 Adamthwaite, *Grandeur and Misery*, London 1995, 4.
40 *Bourgeois Politics in France 1945–1951*, Cambridge 1995, 275, 267.
41 Pascal Griset, *Georges Pompidou et la modernité*, Brussels 2006, 16.

3 Strangers

1 *Barchester Towers*, Penguin 2003, xxi.
2 Robert Toulemon, *La Construction europeenne*, Paris 1994, 32.
3 CAC, DUFC 4/5, Duff Cooper to Harvey, 7 February 1947.
4 Knopf NY 1944, 76.
5 *La Simple Vérité, 1940–1945*, Paris 1960, 130.
6 P.M.H. Bell, *France and Britain 1940–1994*, Longman 1997, 61–2.

7   Aurélie Luneau, *Je Vous Ecris de France*, Points 2016.
8   *Duff Cooper Diaries*, ed., John Julius Norwich, 320.
9   Jean Chauvel, *Commentaire*, 2, Paris 1972, 161.
10 Jacques Dumaine, *Quai d'Orsay*, Juillard Paris 1955, 185.
11 Ibid., 289.
12 *Journal du Septennat 1947-1954*, ed. Pierre Nora, 4, 1950, Colin Paris 1970, 475.
13 Bryan Guinness, *Personal Patchwork*, Cygnet London 1987, 128-9.
14 BLO, Macmillan MS. dep.c.11/2, Macmillan to Lady Dorothy, 22 August 1949; dep.c.8, 1951.
15 L'Ame des Peuples, 46.
16 Richard Ollard, *A Man of Contradictions: A life of A.L. Rowse*, 1999, 108.
17 Clark, *The Other Half*, 1977, 119.
18 Magee, *Growing up in a war*, 352.
19 Carey, *The Unexpected Professor*, 68.
20 BLO, Instructions, op. cit., 25.
21 *The Times*, Friday 30 December 2016.
22 Thomas K. Robb and Michael Seibold, 'Spying on Friends: British assessments of French security, 1945-1950', *International History Review*, 36, 1, 117-18.
23 Keith Kyle, *Suez*, 1991, 176; DDF 1956, 3, no 321.
24 Charles Mott-Radclyffe, *Foreign Body in the Eye*, Leo Cooper 1975, 90.
25 *Duff Cooper Diaries*, 377.
26 Ibid., 384-6.
27 Mark Pottle, ed., *Daring to Hope: The Diaries and Letters of Violet Bonham Carter*, 2000, 134.
28 Lloyd A. Free, ed., *French Motivations in the Suez Crisis*, Princeton NJ 1956, 98.
29 Paul Claudel, *Theatre*, II, Pleiade Paris 1956, 427.
30 Tony Judt, *Postwar*, Penguin NY 2005, 100.
31 *Journal du Septennat*, VI, 1952, Paris 1978, 289.
32 Dumaine, Quai d'Orsay, 78-9.
33 George Mallaby, *From My Level*, Hutchinson 1965, 57.
34 *Strange Defeat*, W. W. Norton NY 1968, 70.
35 *The Diaries of Cynthia Gladwyn*, ed. Miles Jebb, 1995, 167.
36 TNA PREM 11/1849, 25 November 1957; 30 October 1955.
37 Alistair Horne, *Macmillan*, I, 1988, 348-9.
38 Haslam, *Vices of Integrity*, 92.
39 *The War Diary of Oliver Harvey*, ed. John Harvey, 1978, 244.
40 Lord Gladwyn, *The Memoirs of Lord Gladwyn*, 1972, 130-1.
41 David Dilks, ed. *Retreat From Power*, 2, 1981, 9.
42 Anthony Eden, *The Eden Memoirs: The Reckoning*, Cassell 1965, 444.
43 Harvey, *Diary*, 365.
44 John Charmley, 'Duff Cooper and Western European Union, 1944-47', *Review of International Studies*, 85, 11, 53-64.
45 Ibid.
46 DBPO, Series I, I, no 102; DBPO, I, 3, no 3.
47 Raymond Aron, *Chroniques de guerre*, ed. Christian Bachelier, Gallimard Paris 1990, 1000.
48 Alphand, L'Etonnement d'être, 171.
49 HIA, Kojève Papers, 'Esquisse d'une doctrine de la politique française 1945', Hoover.
50 *La France libre*, 15 January 1944, cited René Massigli, *Une Comédie des erreurs, 1943-1956*, Plon Paris 1978, 45.

51 Gerard Bossuat, *Faire l'Europe sans Défaire la France*, Lang Brussels 2005, 244.
52 Philip M Kaiser, *Journeying Far and Wide*, Scribner NY 1992, 224.
53 *A Different Kind of Weather*, 2015, 67.
54 TNA GEN 551/2, FO memorandum 21 September 1956; William Clark, *From Three Worlds,* 1986, 192.
55 *DDF* 1956, 3, no 123.
56 Donald Cameron Watt, 'Contemporary History', *Journal of the Society of Archivists*, October 1969, 512.
57 Donald Cameron Watt, letter in author's possession.
58 Obituary, *Times*, 27 May 2017.
59 Penguin, 1958, 11–13.
60 Werth, *France*, xviii.
61 *Politics in Post-war France*, 1954, 1.
62 *The State of France*, 1955, 451, 456.
63 *In My Way*, 131–3.
64 *The Paris Embassy*, Rogelia Pastor-Castro, John W. Young, eds, 2013, 48–50; *DBPO*, II, 1, no 136.
65 *FNSP*, CM7, Jebb to Couve, 15 June 1960.
66 Sean Greenwood, 'Not the "General Will" but the Will of the General', *Contemporary British History*, 18, 3, 177–88.
67 TNA PREM 11/4807, 11 September 1964.
68 *Times* obituary 15 December 1992.
69 Henderson, *Mandarin, The diaries of Nicholas Henderson*, Weidenfeld 1994, 163; *OH*, II, 489.
70 RIIA, Study Groups 9/50a, WEU, 28 March 1955; 9/55 Anglo–French, Woodhouse to Vernant, 13 May 1958.
71 Dorothy Pickles, *The Uneasy Entente*, RIIA, 1966.
72 *Gladwyn Memoirs*, 269.
73 Sean Greenwood, *Titan at the Foreign Office*, Martinus Nijhoff, 2008, xv.
74 *The Paris Embassy*, 75.
75 *OH, II*, 364.
76 BLO, MSS. Eng.c 4794, Clem to Tom, 8 August 1955.
77 Agnès Tachin, *Amie et rivale : La Grande-Bretagne dans l'imaginaire français a l'époque gaullienne,* Lang 2009; *OH* II, 127; unpublished Reilly memoir.
78 CAC, SOAM 49/3: *OH* II, 96.

4 New Look

1 Jean Doise, Maurice Vaïsse, *Diplomatie et Outil militaire, 1871–1969*, 1987, 341.
2 Edgar S. Furniss, *France, Troubled Ally*, Harper 1960, vii.
3 Matthew Cobb, *The Resistance*, Pocket Books 2009, 104.
4 Gerard Bossuat, *L'Europe des français*, publications de la Sorbonne Paris 1996, 16.
5 William I. Hitchcock, *France Restored*, 1998, 204; Michael Creswell, *A Question of Balance*, 2006. For a critique of Creswell, see Jeffrey G. Giauque, 'France's Fourth Republic and the Rearmament of Germany', *Diplomatic History*, 32, 1, 139–42.
6 Claude Mauriac, *The Other De Gaulle*, 1973, 277.
7 Jacques Fauvet, *La IV Republique*, 1959, 191–2.
8 Chauvel, *Commentaire*, 2, 154; Dumaine, 193.

9   René Massigli, *Sur Quelques Maladies de l'Etat*, 1958, 9, 11.
10 Alphand, *L'Etonnement d'être*, 184.
11 Armand Berard, *Un Ambassadeur se souvient*, 2, 1978, 35.
12 Marie-Claude Smouts, *La France à l'ONU*, 1979, 180.
13 Jacques Dalloz, *Georges Bidault*, 1992, 102.
14 *Italian Journey*, Penguin 1970, 102.
15 *War Memoirs*, 1, Collins 1955, 109.
16 Tony Judt, 'The French Difference', *New York Review of Books*, 12 April 2001, 18.
17 *Tristes tropiques*, trans John and Doreen Weightman, 1973, 405.
18 Eugen Weber, 'Of Stereotypes and of the French', *Journal of Contemporary History*, 25, 2. 1990, 173.
19 John Morley, *The Life of William Ewart Gladstone*, 1, 1903, 402.
20 Dumaine, 77.
21 Raymond Poidevin, *Robert Schuman*, 1986, 201.
22 Charles Ritchie, *Diplomatic Passport*, 1982, 6.
23 Ben Rogers, *A.J. Ayer: A Life*, 1999, 195.
24 Consultative Assembly, Algiers, *New York Herald Tribune*, 27 January 1944.
25 *Duff Cooper Diaries*, 374.
26 Harold Nicolson diaries and letters 1945–1962, 1968, 76.
27 *Daring to Hope*: 2000, 6.
28 *La France à sauve l'Europe*, I, 1947, epigraph.
29 Arthur Marwick, ed, *Total War and Social Change*, 1988, 87.
30 *Mémoires politiques*, 1967, 252.
31 Magee, *Growing up in a war*, 352–3.
32 Josef Becker, ed, *Power in Europe?*, 403.
33 Ennio Di Nolfo, ed, *Power in Europe?* II, de Gruyter, Berlin/New York 1992, 465.
34 Monnet, *Memoires*, 1976, 306.
35 David Marquand, *The Unprincipled Society*, 1988, 106.
36 Stanley Hoffmann, *France: Change and Tradition*, 1963, 161–4.
37 Edgar Morin, *Commune en France, La Metamorphose de Plozevet*, 1968.
38 Colette Barbier, 'The French decision to develop a military nuclear programme in the 1950s,' *Diplomacy and Statecraft*, 4, 1, 1993, 107.
39 Alec Cairncross, *The Wilson Years: A Treasury Diary*, Historians Press 1997, 100.
40 Henri Mendras, Alistair Cole, *Social change in Modern France*, Cambridge 1991, 197.
41 BDOHP, Sir Michael Palliser interview 28 April 1999.
42 Gerard Bossuat, 'The French administrative elite and the unification of western Europe', Anne Deighton (ed.), *Building Postwar Europe*, St Martin's 1995, 30.
43 Tony Benn, *Against The Tide*, 1989, 613.
44 Alphand, *L'Etonnement*, 183.
45 Auriol, *Journal du Septennat*, 1, 116.
46 *Journaux de voyage*, Gallimard 1978.
47 Raphaele Ulrich-Pier, *René Massigli*, II, 2006, 1437–9.
48 Poidevin, *Schuman*, 271.
49 Massigli, *Une Comédie des erreurs*, Plon 1978, 340.
50 Alphand, *L'Etonnement*, 273–4.
51 J-B Duroselle, 'L'Elaboration de la politique étrangère française', *Revue française de science politique*, Juillet–Septembre 1956, 516–18.
52 *DBPO*, 2, I, no 393.

53 John Young, William Hayter, 'The Foreign Office, the Quai d'Orsay and the case of the Russian bomb, June, 1953', *Intelligence and National Security*, 1, 1986, 3, 451–3.
54 Dumaine, 436.
55 William Hayter, *The Diplomacy of the Great Powers*, 1960, 40.
56 Cairncross, *The Wilson Years*, 16.
57 AN, Fonds Christian Pineau, dossier Europe 580AP/1–32, Massigli to Pineau, 7 February 1977.
58 Dumaine, 197.
59 Shuckburgh, *Descent to Suez*, 169.
60 *In the Midst of Events: The Foreign Office diaries and papers of Kenneth Younger*, Geoffrey Warner, ed., 2005, 13.
61 Massigli, *Comédie*, 187.
62 Becker, *Power in Europe?*, 405.
63 *The French and the Republic*, trans Jean Jacques Demorest, Cornell University Press, 1958, 204.
64 Becker, *Power in Europe?* 400, 406.
65 *Mémoires politiques*, 321–3.
66 *Lieutenant in Algeria*, Hutchinson 1958, 57.
67 Hitchcock, 204–5.
68 Jean-Rémy Bezias, *Georges Bidault et la politique étrangère de la France*, 2006, 481.

5 De Gaulle Redux

1 Marcia Williams, *Inside Number 10*, 1972, 192.
2 Maurice Larkin, *France since the Popular Front*, Oxford 1988, 120.
3 David Chuter, *Humanity's Soldier*, 1996, 202.
4 Ibid., 212.
5 Pierre-Henri Teitgen, *Faites Entrer Le Temoin Suivant*, Rennes, Ouest-France 1988, 175.
6 Andre Malraux, *Felled Oaks*, Rinehart and Winston 1971, 56.
7 Jean Lacouture, *De Gaulle, The Ruler*, Harvill 1991, 359.
8 Lacouture, op. cit., 513.
9 Jean Mauriac, *Le Général et le Journaliste*, Fayard 2008, 124.
10 BLO, Reilly unpublished memoir.
11 Hoffmann, *France: Change and Tradition*, 352.
12 N. Piers Ludlow, *The European Community and the crises of the 1960s*, Routledge 2006, 201.
13 Antony Beevor and Artemis Cooper, *Paris after the liberation*, 1994, 470; Julian Jackson and Matthew Cobb, 'Magical Incantation', *TLS* 12 December 2014, 14–15.
14 Horne, *Macmillan*, II, 1986, 264.
15 Alain Peyrefitte, *C'était de Gaulle,* I, 283–4.
16 *De Gaulle*, trans Richard Howard, Doubleday 1966, 229.
17 BLO, Reilly unpublished memoir.
18 *As I saw it*, W.W. Norton, 1990, 271.
19 TNA PREM 13/909, Peart–Faure meeting 28 October 1966.
20 Maurice Vaïsse, *Grandeur,* 293; Peyrefitte, *C'était de Gaulle*, I, 351.
21 *Witness to History*, Norton 1973, 502.
22 Jerome Perrier, *Michel Debré*, Ellipses 2010, 250.

23 Tricot, *Memoires*, Promeneur 1994, 215–16.
24 *LNC*, 10, 67.
25 Martin Harrison, Jack Hayward, eds, *De Gaulle to Mitterrand*, Hurst 1993, 208.
26 Ibid., 208.
27 Philip Nord, *France's New Deal*, Princeton 2010, 354.
28 Raymond Kuhn, *The Media in France*, Routledge 1995, 255, n. 27.
29 Henri Mendras, Alistair Cole, *Social Change*, 344.
30 French national assembly 26 May 1964, https://en.wikipedia.org #cf wiki #cf Radiodiffusion-Télévision_Française
31 *C'était de Gaulle*, I, 101.
32 HIA, Jacques Leprette Papers, Boxes 119/121, Note pour le Ministre, 20 janvier 1966.
33 Jean-Claude Michaud, *Alain Peyrefitte*, Fallois 2002, 148.
34 FNSP, 2DE29, Debré to de Gaulle, September 1959.
35 Pottle, ed., *Daring to Hope*, 328–30.
36 Michaud, op. cit., 144.
37 Jean K. Chalaby, *The De Gaulle Presidency and the Media*, Palgrave 2002, 8.
38 Alastair Hetherington, *Guardian Years*, Chatto and Windus, 1981, 186.
39 *Britain's Entry into the European Communities*, David Hannay (ed.), Cass, 2000, 357; Hugo Young, *This Blessed Plot*, Papermac 1999, 312.
40 *Journaux de voyage*, Gallimard 1978, 92.
41 Herman Lebovics, *Mona Lisa's Escort*, Cornell, 1999, 24.
42 Bernard Wasserstein, *Barbarism and Civilization: A History of Europe in our Time*, Oxford OUP, 2007, 778.
43 Brian Angus McKenzie, *Remaking France: Americanization, Public Diplomacy, and the Marshal Plan*, Berghahn, 2005, 231–2.
44 Jean Guéhenno, *Voyages: Tournée Americaine, Tournée Africaine*, Gallimard 1952, 45.
45 TNA FO/371/158170, Lee to Barclay, 27 February 1961; Henri Froment-Meurice, *Vu du Quai*, Fayard 1998, 303; Paul Gore Booth, *With Great Truth and Respect*, Constable 1974, 239; Gore-Booth Obituary, *The Times*, 18 April 1985.
46 BLO, MS Eng c 6924, Reilly unpublished memoir, Wormser-Harpham conversation, 10 October 1963.
47 *Une politique étrangère*, Plon 1971, 9.
48 Ritchie, *Diplomatic Passport*, 121–2.
49 Balliol College, Oxford, Harold Nicholson Diaries.
50 Jacques Baeyens, *Au Bout du Quai*, Fayard 1975, 143–4; Albert Chambon, *Que font donc ces diplomates*, Pedone 1983, 118–19; Froment-Meurice, *Vu du Quai*, 196–9.
51 TNA PREM 13/1484, Brown–Couve talk, UN 23 September 1967.
52 Vaïsse, *Grandeur*, 331.
53 *L'Etonnement*, 479.
54 Catbird Press 1993, 1.
55 Hayter, *Diplomacy of the Great Powers*, 35.
56 BLO, Reilly unpublished memoir.
57 Vaïsse, *Grandeur*, 356.
58 Sudhir Hazareesingh, *Political Traditions in Modern France*, Oxford 1994, 278.
59 George H. Gallup, ed., *The Gallup International Public Opinion Polls, France*, I, Random House, 1977; Vaïsse, *Grandeur*, 353–4.
60 *Gallup France*, 446.
61 Chalaby, op. cit., 101.
62 Gerard Noiriel, *Workers in French Society in the 19th and 20th Centuries*, Berg 1990, 200.

63 Edward A. Kolodziej, *Making and Marketing Arms*, Princeton 1987, 400.
64 Smouts, *La France à l'ONU*, 180.
65 Philippe de Gaulle, *De Gaulle, Mon Père: Entretiens avec Michel Tauriac*, Plon 2004, 393.
66 *FNSP*, Fonds Michel Debré, 5DE 1-4.
67 Hoffmann, *France: Change and Tradition*, 352.
68 Tony Benn, *Out of the Wilderness*, Arrow 1987, 502.

6 Unmerrie England

1 *The Diary of Hugh Gaitskell 1945–1956*, Philip M. Williams (ed.), Cape 1983, 16; Harold Nicolson, *Diaries and Letters 1945–1962*, Nigel Nicolson (ed.), Collins 1968, 75.
2 BLO, Macmillan, MS.Eng. c.4778, Letter to Ava, Lady Waverle, 31 July 1947.
3 HIA, Muggeridge Papers, diaries Box 1, 28 March 1950; 14 September 1950.
4 Pottle, ed., *Daring to Hope*, 68; Judt, *Postwar*, 162; Paul Addison, *Literary Review*, May 2007, 40; Gowing, *Independence and Deterrence*, 1, 221.
5 *Distilling the Frenzy*, Biteback 2012; *The Times*, Wednesday 3 June 1953, 'And After?'.
6 Doubleday, 1954, 19, 231.
7 Ritchie, *Diplomatic Passport*, 6.
8 HIA, Victor Hoo Papers, box 1, International Meetings, Hoo to UN Secretary General, 2 October 1946.
9 *Gaitskell Diary*, 176, 224; Geoffrey Warner, ed., *In the Midst of Events: The Foreign Office Diaries and Papers of Kenneth Younger*, Routledge 2005, 38; *Parliament and Politics in the Age of Churchill and Attlee: The Headlam Diaries 1935–1951*, ed. Stuart Ball, Camden Fifth series,14, OUP, 1999, 601, 613.
10 John Colville, *Fringes of Power, Downing Street Diaries*, 2, Sceptre 1987, 306–7.
11 Pimlott, *The Political Diary of Hugh Dalton*,360; *Corridors of Power*, Macmillan 1964, 281.
12 *Diaries of A.L. Rowse*, ed. Richard Ollard, I, Penguin 2003, 279; Wm. Roger Louis, 'American anti-colonialism', *IA*, 61, 3, 1985, 412; *Freya Stark Letters*, VII, Michael Russell 1952–59, ed. Caroline Moorehead, 1982, 158; D.J. Enright, *Academic Year*, Secker and Warburg 1955, 136.
13 Wm. Roger Louis, op. cit., 396; TNA PREM 11/636, Hankey to Churchill, 4 June 1954; Shuckburgh, *Descent to Suez*, 63.
14 Kenneth O. Morgan, *The People's Peace*, Oxford 1990, 144; *A State of England*, Hutchinson 1963, 15, 233; Lawrence Goldman, *The Life of R.H.Tawney*, Bloomsbury 2013, 296–7; Doris Lessing, *A Small Personal Voice*, ed. Paul Schlueter, Vintage 1975, 48.
15 *The Time of My Life*, Michael Joseph 1989, 121; J.F.C. Harrison, *Scholarship Boy*, Rivers Oram 1995, 155.
16 Francis Spufford, 'Operation Backfire', *London Review of Books*, 28 October 1999, 24.
17 Peter Mandler, *The English National Character*, Yale 2006, 224, 227.
18 *The Challenge of Affluence*, OUP 2006, 1.
19 David Reynolds, *Britannia Overruled*, 2nd edn, Routledge 2000, 309; Imperial War Museum, Tizard Papers, HIT465, undated note.
20 Christopher Mayhew, 'British foreign policy since 1945', *IA*, 26, 4 (1950), 478; *The Listener*, 11 November 1954, 788.

21 J.H. Huizinga, *Confessions of a European in England*, Heinemann 1958, 282–8; Horne, *Macmillan*, II, 16.
22 Anthony Sampson, *Anatomy of Britain*, Hodder and Stoughton 1962, 37; 'The Pulse of Britain', *The Times*, 28 July 1962.
23 Sampson, *Anatomy*, 572; Hugh Purcell, *A Very Private Celebrity: The nine lives of John Freeman*, Biteback 2015, 59.
24 Shuckburgh, *Descent*, 163.
25 David Vital, *The Making of British Foreign Policy*, Praeger 1968, 73; *Memoirs, 1950–1963*, II, Little, Brown 1972, 235; George H. Gallop, ed., *The Gallup International Public Opinion Polls: Great Britain 1, 1937–1964*, Random House New York, 1977, 258, 269, 279; 'British attitudes to the EEC', *Journal of Common Market Studies*, 1966, 5, 1, 49–61; Richard L. Merritt and Donald J. Puchala, eds, *Western European Perspectives on International Affairs: Public Opinion Studies and Evaluations*; Praeger 1968, 283; Roger Jowell and Gerald Hoinville, eds, *Britain into Europe: Public opinion and the EEC 1961–75*, Croom Helm 1976, 18–36.
26 Nicolson, *Diaries*, 102; Kenneth Younger, 'Public Opinion and British Foreign Policy', *IA*, January 1964, 32.
27 'History, Morals and Politics', *IA*, January 1958, 2; John Dickie, *Inside the Foreign Office*, Chapmans 1992, 241; Anthony Adamthwaite, 'Nation shall speak peace unto nation', *Contemporary Record*, 7, 3, 569.
28 Asa Briggs, *The History of Broadcasting in the United Kingdom*, IV, OUP 1995, 562.
29 Briggs, op. cit., 564; *The Listener*, 18 May 1978, 626; Briggs, 563.
30 Briggs, op. cit., 647.
31 *Grand Inquisitor*, Weidenfeld 1989, 82; Christopher Driver, *The Disarmers*, Hodder and Stoughton 1964, 37; Adam Sisman, *A.J.P. Taylor: A Biography*, Sinclair Stevenson 1994, 171.
32 John Jenks, *British Propaganda and News Media in the Cold War*, Edinburgh, University Press 2006, 49.
33 Geoffrey Cox, *See It Happen*, Bodley Head 1983, 50–1; *Office without Power*, Hutchinson 1988, 43.
34 *British Foreign Policy, 1945–1956*, Michael Dockrill and John W. Young, eds, Palgrave 1989, 16; Richard Hoggart, *The Uses of Literacy*, Transaction 1957, 227, 230.
35 *Soft Power: The means to success in world politics*, Public Affairs 2004, x; TNA PREM 11/691.
36 D.J. Enright, *Memoirs of a Mendicant Professor*, Chatto and Windus 1969, 96.
37 F. Donaldson, *The British Council, The First 50 Years*, Jonathan Cape 1984, 191.
38 Donaldson, 170; TNA PREM 11/627, Tewson to Monckton, 28 November 1952.
39 BLO, MS. Selborne, Selborne to Lord Salisbury and Eden, 4 July 1956; Peter Hennessy and Mark Laity, 'Suez: what the papers say', *Contemporary Record*, April 1987, 8.
40 Blackwell, *Clinging to Grandeur*, 99; Huizinga, *Confessions*, 86; TNA CAB 128/53.
41 Brotherton Library, University of Leeds, Faye and Geoffrey Elliott collection, 4,79, John Cairncross to Collie Barclay, 22 December 1945.
42 BLO, prime ministerial papers, letter to Macmillan, 17 August 1957; BLO, Gore-Booth Mss Eng c 4516, letter to Paul Gore-Booth, 24 August 1959.
43 BLO, CRD2/34/1, Conservative Party Foreign Affairs Committee, 30 November 1955; Clarissa Eden, *A Memoir*, ed. Cate Haste, Weidenfeld 2007, 240.
44 OUP, 1965, 600.
45 *Crisis in the Civil Service*, ed. Hugh Thomas, Anthony Blond 1968, 7.
46 E.D.R. Harrison, 'J.C.Masterman and the Security Service, 1940–1972', *Intelligence and National Security*, 24, 6, 804.

7 Running on Empty

1. *The Complete War Memoirs of Charles de Gaulle*, Carroll and Graph 1998, 163; Dickie, *Inside the Foreign Office*, 222.
2. *The Diaries of Sir Alexander Cadogan*, David Dilks, ed., Cassell 1971, 782; Oliver Lyttelton, *The Memoirs of Lord Chandos*, Bodley Head 1962, 343.
3. Shuckburgh, *Descent to Suez*, 67, 180; Paul Johnson, *Oxford Book of Political Anecdotes* OUP 1986; Marcia Williams, *Inside Number 10*, 181.
4. Adamthwaite, 'Overstretched and Overstrung: Eden, the Foreign Office and the Making of Policy, 1951–1955', *IA*, 64, 2, 245; DBPO, Series II, I, x; *The Diary of Hugh Gaitskell, 1945–1956*, Philip M. Williams, ed., 1983, 176; Geoffrey Moorhouse, *The Diplomats*, Cape 1977, 369.
5. *Freya Stark Letters*, 254.
6. *Experiences*, OUP 1969, 51.
7. *Diaries of Sir Alexander Cadogan*, 790; Benn, *Office without Power*, 43–4.
8. *Gaitskell Diary*, 117; Hetherington, *Guardian Years*, 25.
9. Harold Macmillan, *Tides of Fortune, 1945–1955*, Macmillan 1969, 567.
10. *The Pebbled Shore: The Memoirs of Elizabeth Longford*, Weidenfeld 1986, 257–8.
11. Nicholas Henderson, *The Private Office*, Littlehampton book services 1984, 116; Christopher Mayhew, *Time to Explain*, Hutchinson 1987, 102–3; Mallaby, *From My Level*, 58.
12. *Gaitskell Diary*, ed. Philip M. Williams, 117.
13. Sir Roderick Barclay, *Ernest Bevin and the Foreign Office, 1932–1969*, 1975, 38–9.
14. Shuckburgh, *Descent to Suez*, 36.
15. Selwyn Lloyd, *Suez, 1956*, Cape 1978, 4; Shuckburgh, *Descent to Suez*, 317, 327, 337; CAC, SELO 3, personal diary, February 1960.
16. *Dalton Diary*, ed., Ben Pimlott, 480; *Double Diploma: The Life of Sir Pierson Dixon*, ed. Piers Dixon, Hutchinson 1968, 234; *Time to Explain*, 107.
17. *Harvey Diaries*, 385.
18. *Dalton Diary*, 482.
19. For this paragraph see Anthony Adamthwaite, 'Introduction: The Foreign Office and Policy-Making', John W. Young, ed., *The Foreign Policy of Churchill's Peacetime Administration, 1951–1955*, Continuum 1988, 13–14; Catterall, *Macmillan Diaries*, I, 325.
20. Dixon, *Double Diploma*, 240–1; Lord Strang, *Home and Abroad*, Andre Deutsch 1956, 280; Warner, *Younger Diary*, 13.
21. C.M. Woodhouse, *Something Ventured*, Harper Collins 1982, 161; Sampson, *Anatomy of Britain*, 632.
22. *Younger Diary*, 89; Edward Boyle and Anthony Crosland, *The Politics of Education*, Penguin 1971, 108; *Dalton Memoirs*, 155; Mallaby, *From My Level*, 57.
23. Hennessy, *The Prime Minister: The Office and its holders since 1945*, 2000, 123; *The Castle Diaries 1964–1970*, Weidenfeld 1984, 241–2; Hennessy, *The Hidden Wiring*, Phoenix 1996, 169.
24. Healey, *The Time of My Life*, 327.
25. Hennessy, *Prime Minister* 164–5; BLPES, Meade diary,1/4, 21 February 1949; TNA CAB 128/15; BLO, MS Woolton 3, the machinery of government, 25 January 1954; Hennessy, *The Hidden Wiring*, 169; Evans Diary, 129.
26. *The Spirit of British Administration*, 132.
27. George Mallaby, *Each in his Office*, Leo Cooper 1972, 59; Jasper Rootham, *Demi-Paradise*, Chatto and Windus 1960, 157.

28 R.V. Jones, Letter to *The Times*, Wednesday 17 December 1980; Isaiah Berlin, *Letters 1928-1946*, ed., Henry Hardy, CUP 2004, 459; *Cadogan Diaries*, 301.
29 Rodney Lowe, *The Official History of the British Civil Service*, I, Routledge 2011, 78, 127, 381, 383.
30 Richard Davenport Hines, *An English Affair*, Harper 2013, 224.
31 Douglas Hurd, *Memoirs*, Little Brown 2003, 151-2; Brian Harrison, *Seeking a Role: The United Kingdom 1951-1970*, OUP 2009, 103.
32 TNA FO366/1462, Gore-Booth minute, July 1945; TNA FO800/492, Attlee to Bevin 25 May 1947; TNA FO/800463, Office circular June 1948; *The Inner Circle: The Memoirs of Ivone Kirkpatrick*, Macmillan 1959, 267; Cecil Parrott, *The Serpent and the Nightingale*, Faber 1977, 214; Jennifer Tratt, *The Macmillan Government and Europe*, Palgrave 1996, 145.
33 DNB, 2004; Warner, *Younger Diary*, 93, Geoffrey McDermott, *The Eden legacy and the decline of British diplomacy*, Frewin, 1969, 105; DNB, 1981; Hurd, *Memoirs*, 151-2; *Times* obituary, 3 July 1984.
34 Douglas Jay, *Change and Fortune*, Ebury 1980, 315.
35 Gore-Booth, *With Great Truth*, 348.
36 TNA FO/800,492, Parliamentary Labour Party, 27 March 1946; Christopher Mayhew, 'British foreign policy since 1945', *IA* October 1950, 477.
37 BLO, Gore-Booth MS.Eng.c.4564, PUS final monthly letter January 1969; BDOHP, interview with Michael Palliser 28 April 1999; interview with Sir Crispin Tickell, 23 July 1998.
38 TNA CAB 128/42; 'The Diary of Michael Stewart as British Foreign Secretary, April-May 1968', ed. John W. Young, *Contemporary British History*, 19, 4, 503.
39 *Time of My Life*, 122; RIIA Archives 2/1/11, 3/6/FORb, *Observer*, 31 October 1954, *Manchester Guardian*, 8 March 1954.
40 Peter J. Beck, *Using History, Making British Policy*, Palgrave 2006, 3, 13-14.
41 Ibid., 241.
42 Huizinga, *Confessions of a European*, 84; CAC, KNAT/1/15, Knatchbull-Hugessen diary, 16 May 1946; John Kent, *British Imperial Strategy and the Origins of the Cold War*, LUP 1993, 217.
43 29 March 1947, Hennessy, *Distilling the Frenzy*, 8-9; DBPO, Series 1, 3, xxv.
44 John W. Young, *The Labour Governments 1964-1970*, 2 International Policy, MUP 2003, 56.

8 Unshakable, Constant, Effective

1 Martin Gilbert, *Winston S. Churchill*, VII, Heinemann 1989, 1060; Valentine Lawford, *Bound for Diplomacy*, 324, John Murray 1963; Knapp, ed., *The Uncertain Foundation: France at the Liberation 1944-47*, Palgrave 2007, 207.
2 'Reflections on the foreign policy of France', *IA*, 21, 4, 443; Hollis and Carter 1960, 3; Diane Kunz, 'British Post-War Sterling Crises', Wm Roger Louis, ed., *Adventures with Britannia*, Tauris 1995, 125; Official History, I, 3; John W. Young, *Britain and European Unity, 1945-1999*, 2nd edn, Macmillan 2000, 49.
3 Edwin Muir, *An Autobiography*, Hogarth 1954, 256; Nicolson Diary, 1945-1962, 98.
4 DBPO, I, I, 102.
5 TNA FO371/66546; V.H. Rothwell, Britain and the Cold War, Cape 1982, 435.
6 The English Way, OUP 1946, 304; A. Nutting, *Europe will not wait*, Hollis & Carter, 1960, 3.

7   Raphaele Ulrich-Pier, René Massigli, II, 1208–9.
8   Andrew Roberts, *The Storm of War*, Penguin 2010, 488; L. Woodward, *British Foreign Policy in the Second World War*, III, HMSO 1971, 102; R. Pastor-Castro and J.W. Young, eds, *The Paris Embassy*, 26–7; Duff Cooper Diaries, 345, 359.
9   Hayter, *A Double Life*, 87; Dumaine, 469–70; Steel to Lloyd, 27 July 1957,TNA PREM 11/184.
10 Claude Mauriac diary, 21–2.
11 War Memoirs, 163, 222; Jean-Rémy Bézias, *Georges Bidault et la politique étrangère de la France*, L'Harmattan 2006, 220.
12 Chauvel, *Commentaire*, II, 63.
13 Ibid., 66–7.
14 Smouts, *La France à l'ONU*, 51; Dalloz, Bidault, 446, n. 37.
15 Harvey Diary, 365.
16 S. Greenwood, *The Alternative Alliance, Anglo-French Relations before the coming of NATO, 1944–48*, Minerva 1996, 50.
17 Hugh Dalton, *High Tide and After*, Frederick Muller 1962, 157; Roger Woodhouse, *British Policy Towards France 1945–51*, Macmillan 1995, 19.
18 Dumaine, 57–8; Ritchie Diplomatic Passport, 12; Barclay, *Ernest Bevin*, 28.
19 Greenwood, 307: TNA FO 371/71768, Kirkpatrick to Bevin, 5 October 1948.
20 Rothwell, *Britain and the Cold War*, 435.
21 David Dilks, *Rights, Wrongs and Rivalries*, University of Hull, 1996, 35.
22 Greenwood, 286; Jean Monnet, *Memoires*, Fayard 1976, 463.
23 M. Gowing, *Independence and Deterrent*, Macmillan 1974, I, 9; Christopher Andrew, *The Sword and The Shield*, Ingram 2000, 152.
24 *France: Change and Tradition*, ed. Stanley Hoffmann, Gollancz 1963, 338.
25 For quotations and discussion in this paragraph, see *British Documents on the end of Empire*, Series A, II, *The Labour Government and the end of Empire 1945–1951*, Part II, ed. Ronald Hyman, HMSO 1992; John Kent, 'Bevin's Imperialism and the idea of Euro-Africa, 1945–1949', Michael Dockrill and John Young (eds), *British Foreign Policy 1945–56*, Palgrave 1989, 47–76.
26 *Old Men Forget*, Rupert Hart Davis, 1953, 381.
27 René Massigli, *Une Comédie des Erreurs*, 1943–1956, Plon 1978, 107–8.
28 Geoffrey Warner, 'Ernest Bevin and British foreign policy, 1945–1951', Gordon A. Craig, Francis L. Loewenheim, eds, *The Diplomats, 1939–1979*, Princeton UP 1994, 115; Richard Clarke, 'Anglo-American economic collaboration in war and peace, 1942–1949', ed. Alec Cairncross, Oxford: Clarendon, 1982 208, n. 27.
29 Alan Bullock, *Ernest Bevin Foreign Secretary*, OUP 1985, 659; Dalloz, 295; 'The Choice at Paris', 13 March 1948, *Economist*.
30 Edmund Dell, *The Schuman Plan and the British abdication of leadership in Europe*, OUP 1995, 111; TNA FO371/71768; Alec Cairncross, ed., *The Robert Hall Diaries 1947–53*, Unwin 1989, 121; Warner, 105.
31 FRUS 1947, III, 271; OH, I, 21; DBPO, 2, I, xi.
32 Woodhouse, 131; OH, I, 17; Hall Diary, 57; Edwin Plowden, *An Industrialist in the Treasury*, Andre Deutsch 1989, 74–5.
33 Dell, 132; DBPO, 2, I, 33, n.4; DBPO, 2, I, 31, n.3.
34 Roy Denman, *Missed Chances*, Cassell 1996, 198–9; *Postwar*, Penguin 2005, 162; DBPO, 2, I, 75.
35 Younger Diary, 20; Christopher Lord, *Absent at the Creation*, Dartmouth 1996, 33.
36 Émile Noël obituary, 9 September 1996, *Independent*.

37 François Lafon's biography based on the Mollet papers does not mention the proposal: *Guy Mollet, Itineraire d'un socialiste controverse (1905–1975)*, Fayard 2006.
38 Eden, *The Eden Memoirs: Full Circle*, Cassell 1960, 476; Gilbert, *Churchill*, VIII, *Never Despair*, 1214; William Clark, *From Three Worlds*, Sidgwick 1986, 185–6; Christophe Le Dreau, 'Le project Guy Mollet d'adhesion de la France au Commonwealth. Le rêve d'une paneurope franco-britannique (Septembre 1956)', in Jean-Michel Guieu, Claire Sanderson et al., L'Historien et les relations internationales: Autour de Robert Frank, Publications Sorbonne, 2012.
39 Pineau speech, TNA FO 371/124424.
40 Keith Kyle, *Suez*, Weidenfeld 1991, 237.
41 TNA CAB 130/120; Official History, I, 251–9.
42 Horne, *Macmillan*, I, 432.
43 DDF 1956, 3, 158.
44 DBPO, 2, I, 92; Nick Holt, *The Mammoth Book of the World Cup*, Running Press 2014, 84.
45 Warner, *Bevin*, 128–9; Clark Kerr to Bevin, 20 January 1949, Oxford, Bodleian, Archibald Clark Kerr Papers, box 70.
46 OH, I, 71; Milward response to review of Alan S. Milward, George Brennan, *Britain's Place in the World: A historical enquiry into import controls 1945–60*, Routledge 1996, *Reviews in History*, posted 10.08.2009; *The Last Chronicle of Barset*, Penguin 2002, 664.

9 Supermac

1 *The General Says No*, Penguin Special 1963 147; Macmillan, Haus 2006, 122; *Supermac: The Life of Harold Macmillan,* Chatto 2010, 618.
2 Macmillan, VI, 367.
3 Life, 7 May 1951, 109.
4 *The General Says No*, 19, 102; *OH*, II, Wall 4.
5 Macmillan, V, 112; Horne, *Macmillan*, I, 153, 188–9.
6 BLO, Eccles to Macmillan 9 August 1959; Elizabeth C. Gaskell, *Cranford*, OUP 1963, 59; Macmillan, VI, 368.
7 TNA PREM 11/2315, minute to foreign secretary, 24 June 1958.
8 Catterall, *Macmillan Diaries*, II, 14–15; Horne, *Macmillan*, II, 22.
9 TNA PREM 11/1850, 15 June 1957; TNA PREM 11/1946, 11 July 1957.
10 TNA PREM 11/2315, minute to foreign secretary, 24 June 1958.
11 Catterall, *Macmillan Diaries*, 129; TNA PREM 11/2326. Record of visit to Paris 29–30 June 1958; *DDF* 1958, I, 459.
12 Macmillan, IV, 449; Catterall, *Macmillan Diaries*,131; *Times* 18 November 1958.
13 Horne, *Macmillan*, II, 152, 214; Debré to Macmillan 9 October 1959, 2 DE71, AHC; Macmillan, V, 110.
14 Macmillan, V., 110, 112–13.
15 Catterall, *Macmillan Diaries*, 276–80.
16 Ibid.
17 Ben Pimlott, *The Queen*, Harper Collins 1996, 302.
18 DDF 1960, I, 153.
19 Barclay note, 17 May 1963, TNA FO371/171441.

20 Eric Roll, *Crowded Hours*, 100.
21 *The History of The Times, V, struggles in war and peace*, Times books 1984, 343; Hetherington, *Guardian Years*, 175-6; Michael McManus, *Edward Heath A Singular Life*, Elliott & Thompson 2016, 32-3.
22 *Crowded Hours*, 129.
23 Vaïsse, *Grandeur*, 209.
24 Horne, *Macmillan*, II, 431.
25 For the gaffe see Jean-François Deniau, *Memoires de 7 Vies*, II, Plon 1997, 186-7.
26 Dumaine, *Quai d'Orsay*, 188.
27 CAC, Haley 15/2, Diary,14 June 1961; MAE, Europe, Grande-Bretagne, box 1741, 26 March 1963.
28 Horne, I, 342; Catterall, *Macmillan Diaries*, I, 486, 493; Oxford, Bodleian Libraries, Macmillan to Ava, 30 October 1959, MS.Eng. c. 4778, fols. 1-2.
29 BLO, Macmillan to Ava, 4 December 1958, MS.Eng. c. 4778, fols. 1-2; Harold Evans, Downing Street Diary, Hodder 1981, 151; CAC, Haley 15/2, diary, 12 October 1960, 14 September 1961.
30 BLO, MS. Woolton 3. 24 October 1955; David Childs, *Britain since 1945*, 6 edn Routledge 2006, 46; Ziegler, *Edward Heath: The Authorized Biography*, Harper 2010, 105.
31 Tessa Blackstone, William Plowden, *Inside the Think Tank: Advising the Cabinet 1971-1983*, Heinemann 1988, 7; Evans, *Downing Street Diary*, 197; Peter Hennessy, *The Hidden Wiring: Unearthing the British Constitution*, W&N 1995, 169.
32 BLO, letters to Ava, 7 May 1961, 23 September 1962, MS. Eng c.4779; Harrod to Macmillan, 18 October 1961, CUC HP920; Macmillan VI, 26; Evans, Downing Street Diary, 161; VBC 240; Miles Jebb, ed., *The Diaries of Cynthia Gladwyn*, Constable 1995, 200.
33 Michael Charlton, *The Price of Victory*, BBC 1983, 195; Philip M. Williams, *Hugh Gaitskell: A Political biography*, Cape 1979, 702.
34 Hall Diaries, 279; University of Leeds, Special Collections, Boyle Papers, MS 660/4, Gunnar Hagglof to Edward Boyle following his resignation from Eden government; CAC, Duncan Sandys Papers, DSND 9/6/1, Lady Rhys Williams to Sandys, 9 February 1958.
35 OH, I, 419; CAC, Haley 15/2, 15 January 1963.
36 Ziegler, *Heath*, 127-8.
37 Tim Traverse-Healy notes, 22 June 1962,TNA INF 12/852; BLO, MS. Macmillan dep. c. 311, 30 April 1962.
38 Nuffield College, Oxford, archive, transcript Sir Kenneth Younger interview, December 1961, p. 31; Horne, *Macmillan*, II, 243; Roll, *Crowded Hours*, 115.
39 TNA FO 371/171441, FO comments on Treasury draft of Whitehall History of the Brussels negotiations.
40 Michael McManus, *Edward Heath: A Singular Life*, Elliott & Thompson 2016, 34-5.
41 TNA FO 371/171442, draft of Brussels delegation report on negotiations.
42 Singular Life, 34-5.
43 OH, I, 466; Heath, *The Course of My Life*, 239.
44 Ibid., 481-2.
45 Shuckburgh to Dixon, TNA FO371/166978.
46 DDF 1962, II, 191.
47 *Course of My Life*, 237.
48 Catterall, *Diaries*, 577.

49 Ibid., 324–5; BLPES, Crosland 4/9, Herbert Andrew note, 20 October 1966.
50 H.C.G. Matthew article, *DNB*, OUP 2004.
51 'At Kenneth Burke's Place', 1946, epigraph, Philip Roth, *American Pastoral*, Houghton Mifflin 1997; Record of a conversation, Chateau de Champs, 5.50pm, 2 June 1962 TNA PREM 11/4019.

10 Another Harold

1 *Diplomacy and Persuasion*, Thames and Hudson 1973, 276; Andrew S. Crines, Kevin Hickson, eds, *Harold Wilson*, Biteback 2016, 283.
2 Bristol speech 18 March 1966, Wall, 116.
3 Haines, *Politics of Power*, 74; O'Neill to Stewart 3 May (valedictory) 1966 TNA PREM13/1306.
4 Campbell, *Jenkins*, 246.
5 David Hannay, *Britain's Quest for a Role*, I.B. Tauris 2012, 39.
6 OH, II, 86–7.
7 LNC, 64–66, 122; Vaïsse, 592–3; Peyrefitte, II, 310–11.
8 OH, II, 110, 88.
9 Stewart to Wilson, 3 March 1965, TNA PREM 13/306; Wall, 93–4.
10 Association eventuelle de la Grande Bretagne au Marche Commun, 19 March 1965; La Grande-Bretagne et L'Europe, 24 March 1965, MAE, Serie Europe, Grande Bretagne, 214, 263.
11 TNA PREM 13/324; DDF 1965, I, nos 152–5; Bernard Ledwidge, *De Gaulle*, Littlehampton 1982, 297.
12 Lacouture, 360; Robert Gilpin, *France in the age of the scientific state*, Princeton NJ 1968, 388.
13 Wilson, *Labour Government*, 1964–1970, 1971, 93.
14 OH, II, 104; Vaïsse 596.
15 Vaïsse, 597.
16 Vaïsse, 597; Wall, 108.
17 Palliser to Stewart, 16 November 1965, Vaïsse, ed., *La France et L'Otan*, 1949–1996, Paris, Complexe, 1996, 512–3; Wall, 109–10; Memorandum by the secretary of state for foreign affairs, 'France: General de Gaulle's foreign policy over the next two years', 28 January 1966, TNA CAB 129/124.
18 OH, II, 115.
19 'The international consequences of the policy of General de Gaulle', 5 April 1966, TNA CAB 148/25 OPD.
20 Paris to London embassy, 3 May 1966, 214 Grande Bretagne MAE.
21 Note, 23 May 1966, MAE, cabinet du ministre, 1958–1966, 39.
22 Le Royaume Uni et la CEE, 22 June 1966, MAE cabinet du ministre, 39; Les Etats-Unis et une eventuelle adhesion du Royaume Uni au Marche Commun, 24 June 1966, MAE, cabinet du ministre, 39.
23 OH, II, 118–19, 124; BLO, George Brown, MS. Eng.c.5012, Brown to Wilson, 23 June 1966.
24 Benn, *Out of the Wilderness*, 449; notices biographiques, 20 June 1966, MAE cabinet du ministre 39.
25 Philip Ziegler, *Wilson*, Weidenfeld 1993, 241; Eric Roll, *Crowded Hours*, Faber 1985, 173; Wilson, *Labour Government*, 244, 249.

26 Cecil Harmsworth King, *The Cecil King Diary 1965-1970*, Cape 1972, 82; For the talks, TNA PREM 13/907; DDF 1966, II, 101, 107, 108.
27 Reilly to Hood, 14 July 1966, TNA PREM 13/1506; Wall, 128.
28 Reilly to London, 3 June 1966, TNA PREM 13/892; Williams to Wilson, 13 September 1966, TNA PREM 13/908; Ziegler, Wilson, 236.
29 Agnès Tachin, *Amie et Rivale: La Grande Bretagne dans l'imaginaire français à l époque gaullienne*, Lang 2010, 336, n. 34; Helen Parr, *Britain's Policy towards the European Community*, Routledge 2006, 103; Paul Routledge, *Wilson,* Haus 2006, 2; *Ambassador to Sixties London: Diaries of David Bruce*, Republic of Letters 2009, 353.
30 Obituary, *The Times*, 25 May 1995; Campbell, *Jenkins*, 291-2; Campbell, 327, 330; Wilson, *Labour Government*, 406.
31 Richard Crossman, *The Diaries of a Cabinet Minister*, I, Cape 1975, 295; Patrick Gordon Walker, *Political Diaries*, ed. Robert Pearce, Historians' Press 1991, 298-301.
32 Bruce Diaries, 378; Benn, *Office Without Power*, 166; John W. Young, *Britain and European Unity*, Macmillan 2000, 82; Dickie, *Inside the Foreign Office*, 93; Bruce, 192; Lord Greenhill of Harrow 14 February 1996, BDOHP, DOHP 3.
33 *Life and Labour*, Sidgwick 1980, 163, 162.
34 TNA/PREM 13/306, O'Neill, 3 May 1965; Donald Maitland, *Diverse Times, Sundry Places*, Brighton, Alpha Press 1996, 117; TNA FCO/33/538, 'Allegations of Francophobia in the Foreign Office,' 28 April 1969.
35 OH II ,123; TNA/PREM 13/907, Reilly to O'Neill, 29 June 1966; BLO, George Brown MS. Eng. c. 5012, "Anglo-French Relations" August 1966; Douglas Hurd, *An End to Promises*, London, Collins 1979, 59
36 Robinson obituary, *Independent*, 5 February 1998; Vaïsse, 593; Butler interview, 1 October 1997, BDOHP.
37 Richard Davenport-Hines, *An English Affair*, Harper 2013, 224; George Paterson, *Tired and Emotional*, Chatto 1993, 159; obituary Claude Pompidou, *Daily Telegraph*, 5 July 2007; unpublished Reilly memoir; Paterson, 215. Robert Harris, *Good and Faithful Servant,* London, Faber, 1991, 77; Donald Maitland, *Diverse Times, Sundry Places, Brighton, Alpha, 1996*, 146-152.
38 John W. Young, *Twentieth Century Diplomacy*, CUP 2008, 25-6; Alun Chalfont, *The Shadow of My Hand*, W&N 2000, 118; Sir John Killick interview 2002, BDOHP.
39 Crossman, *Diaries*, II, 195; Wall, 3-4.
40 BLO, Harold Wilson, Ms. Eng.c 1595, Wilson to Sir Lawrence Helsby, 21 October 1964; Alec Cairncross, *The Wilson Years, a Treasury Diary*, Historians' Press 1997, 28.
41 Deighton, 396, n. 25; Campbell, *Roy Jenkins*, 309.
42 Cairncross, *Wilson Years*, 173; Robert Lieber's phrase, *Young, Britain and European Unity*, 1993, 96; Roy Jenkins, Harold Wilson, *DNB*, 2004; Jim Tomlinson, *The Labour Governments 1964-1970*, 3, *Economic Policy*, MUP 2004, 75; Undated 'Top Secret' note Economic Policy mss George Brown 5012, Bodleian.
43 King Diary, 82-3.
44 *Britain and World Power since 1945*, Ann Arbor 2014, 114-15.
45 TNA/CAB 128/42.

11 Bash on Regardless

1 Brown to Wilson, 18 May 1967, TNA PREM 13/1482.
2 Oliver J. Daddow, ed., *Harold Wilson and European Integration*, Cass 2003, xi.

3   Reilly to Brown, 14 November 1966, TNA PREM 13/910.
4   Soames to Wilson, 14 December 1966; Wilson to Soames, 21 December 1966 TNA PREM 13/922; Palliser to Wright, 21 October 1966, TNA PREM 13/897.
5   Alphand, *L'Etonnement*, 482.
6   DDF 1966, II, 407.
7   *In My Way*, 220; Castle Diaries, 100; cabinet meeting 20 December 1966, TNA CAB 128/41.
8   *My Life in Politics*, Penguin 1993, 420.
9   Young, *The Labour Governments 1964–1970*, 2, *International Policy*, MUP 2003, 149.
10 Sir Crispin Tickell interview 23 July 1998, DOHP 36, BDOHP.
11 TNA CAB 128/42.
12 Castle Diaries, 605.
13 Palliser to Wilson, TNA PREM 13/1484.
14 O'Neill to Brown for prime minister, 18 May 1967, TNA PREM 13/1482.
15 14 April 1967, CM842, AHC.
16 Brown to Wilson, 18 May 1967, TNA PREM 13/1482.
17 TNA PREM 13/1478; DDF 1967, I, 42.
18 Ramsbotham to Campbell, 14 April 1967, TNA PREM 13/1482.
19 Reilly to Mulley, 20 April 1967, TNA PREM 13/1479; Lasse Michael Boehm, 'Our Man in Paris', *Journal of European Integration History*, 10, 2, 54–6.
20 Kristan Stoddart, 'Nuclear Weapons in Britain's Policy towards France, 1960–1974', *Diplomacy and Statecraft*, 18, 4, 725.
21 Records of talks: DDF 1967, I, 319, 320, 322; TNA PREM 13/1731.
22 OH, II, 215.
23 22 June 1967, TNA CAB 128/42.
24 Ziegler, 335.
25 Stoddart, 727; Vincent Nouzille, *Des Secrets Si Bien Gardes*, Fayard 2009, 196.
26 Stoddart, 726.
27 OH, II, 243–4.
28 Wilson, *Labour Government*, 443.
29 OH, II, 266.
30 Parr, *Britain's Policy towards the European Community*, Routledge 2005, 103; 'Duties of Civil Servants', Sir Warren Fisher to the Royal Commission on the Civil Service 1929, cited Sir Llewellyn Woodward, letter to *The Times*, 12 November 1952.
31 Benn Diary, 513–14.
32 Unpublished Reilly memoir.
33 Ibid.
34 Soames to Stewart, 13 November 1968, TNA FCO33/560.
35 Soames record of talks with Wilson and Brown, 28.3.68, SOAM 2/49 CAC; Gladwyn to Prince Jean de Caraman-Chimay, GLAD 1/3/25, CAC.
36 Palliser to Soames, 27 November 1968, SOAM 49/8 CAC.
37 'Euro-fanatics' – John Dickie's term – *Inside the Foreign Office*, 167; Young, *This Blessed Plot*, 203; Castle Diaries, 605; Ziegler, 336.
38 Call on M. Jacques Vendroux, 6 November 1968, TNA FCO 33/560; Soames to Stewart, 13 November 1968 TNA FCO 33/560; Vaisse, 607.
39 Alphand, *L'Etonnement*, 504–5; King Diaries, 199.
40 Debre Tricot correspondence, 5DE-1-4, Debre Papers, AIC.
41 Soames to Stewart, 13 November 1968, TNA FCO 33/560; Soames to Stewart, 8 February 1969, TNA FCO 30/414; Vaisse, 607, n. 219.

42 Jean-Marie Soutou, *Un diplomate engagé*, Fallois 2011, 284–6; Debré, *Gouverner Autrement*,4, Albin Michel 1993, 266.
43 Soames to FCO 5 February 1969,TNA PREM 13/2628.
44 Stewart to Wilson, 11 February 1969, TNA 30/414.
45 Ziegler, 337; Barrington to Maitland, 6 February 1969, TNA PREM 30/414; premier to foreign secretary, 12 February 1969, TNA PREM 30/414; Dickie, 168–9.
46 Paris embassy memo to Soames, 26.2.72, SOAM 49/5; Note pour le ministre, 13 February 1969, 5DE12; Debré to de Gaulle, 13 February 1969, 5DE12; Sanderson, Perfide, 9; DDF 1969, I, 162; *Journal de l'Elysée*, 2, 615.
47 Tricot, 327–8; Chalfont-Lipkowski talk, 6 February 1969, TNA PREM 30/414; Soames to Stewart, 8 February 1969, TNA PREM 30/414; Debré-Soames meeting 8 February 1969, 5AG(1) 172; DDF 1969, 1, prints only a Quai guidance telegram of 22 February 1969 (no. 162). The presidential archive contains three records of the Soames conversation: a brief summary dictated by the general to Tricot dated 7 February; an undated four page note by Tricot. 5AG/1/ 172; the summary in English that Soames gave to Tricot on 6 February. None of these are published in the DDF volume. The Couve de Murville archive contains a copy of the general's dictated summary, CDM9, AHC.
48 Soames to Stewart, 21 March 1969, TNA PREM30/418; FRUS 1969–1976, XLI, 443.
49 Ledwidge, *De Gaulle*, 364–5; Vaïsse, 612; Eric Roussel, *Charles de Gaulle*, Gallimard 2002, 903–4; Bernard Destremau, *Quai d'Orsay*, Plon 1994, 288, and n.i.
50 Soames to Wilson, 11 March 1969, TNA PREM 30/418.
51 Daniel Edwin Furby, 'The revival and success of Britain's second application for membership of the European Community, 1968–1971', PhD thesis, University of London 2010.
52 Cabinet meeting 30 November 1967, TNA CAB129/134.
53 Soames to Wilson, 11 March 1969, TNA PREM 30/418; Wall, 329.
54 *The Course of My Life*, 358–9; Matthias Haeussler, 'A Pyrrhic Victory: Harold Wilson, Helmut Schmidt, and the British Renegotiation of EC Membership, 1974–5', *International History Review*, 37, 4, 768–89.
55 For Wahl see Lawrence Badel, Le role tenu par le poste d'expansion economique de Londres dans le processus d'adhesion du Royaume Uni au marche commun 1966–71, in Raymond Poidevin, René Girault, eds, Le rôle des ministères des Finances et des ministères de l'Économie dans la construction européenne (1957–1978) I, Comite pour l'histoire economique et financiere 2002, 229–71; for Holland see Andrew Blick, *People Who Live in the Dark*, Politico's 2003, 105–6; Helen Parr, *Britain's Policy Towards the European Community: Harold Wilson and Britain's World Role, 1964–1967*, Routledge 2005, 43.
56 Meeting with Wilson and Callaghan, 21 November 1966, TNA PREM 13/910; Soutou, dilomate engagé, 286, n. I; Palliser to Wright, 21 October 1966, TNA PREM 13/897; Palliser interview 28 April 1999, BDOHP.

Conclusion

1 Niall Ferguson 'What might have happened?', *The Times Literary Supplement*, 19 September 2007; Jorma Kalela, *Making History: The historian and uses of the past*, Palgrave 2012, 89.
2 Claude Lévi-Strauss, *Tristes tropiques*, trans John and Doreen Weighton, NY 1973, 104–5.

3   Nigel Cawthorne, *A Brief Guide to J.R.R. Tolkien*, Constable and Robinson London 2012.
4   'The Future of Socialism', Leo Pliatzky, *Getting and Spending*, London 1982, 44.
5   *In Front of your Nose*, Tribune, 22 March 1946, *Collected Essays, Journalism and Letters of George Orwell*, IV, 1945–1950, eds Sonia Orwell, Ian Angus, Penguin 1970, 154.
6   Anthony Sampson, *Anatomy of Britain*, London 1962, 227–8.
7   Henry Kissinger, *The White House Years*, London 1979, 421.
8   Alan Milward, *The Rise and Fall of a National Strategy 1945–1963*, London 2002, 24.
9   Denis Healey, *The Time of my Life*, Penguin London 1990, 405.
10   Broad, ed., *Britain and Europe*, 86.
11   Uwe Kitzinger, *The Second Try: Labour and the EEC*, London 1968, 18–19.
12   Soames to London, 6 November 1968, TNA FCO 33/560.
13   David Cannadine, 'James Bond and the decline of England', *Encounter*, September 1979, 54.
14   *The Death of Tragedy*, London 1961, 314.
15   D.C. Watt, 'Persuasion in Politics', *Government and Opposition*, 1968 3, 1, 13.
16   British Overseas Obligations, 18 June 1952, TNA CAB 129/53.
17   *Seeking A Role: The United Kingdom, 1951–1970*, Oxford 2009, 533.
18   Jean Lacouture, *De Gaulle*, 3, *Le Souverain 1959–1970*, Paris 1986, 285.
19   Jean-Marie Soutou, *Un Diplomate Engagé*, Paris 2011, 308.
20   John Campbell, *Roy Jenkins: A Well-Rounded Life*, London 2014, 285.
21   *The Cecil King Diary 1965–1970*, London 1972, 153.
22   Greenhill–Courcel talk 13 October 1969 TNA PREM 13/2645.
23   David Hannay, *Britain's Quest for a Role*, London 2013, 61.
24   Sir David Hannay, ed., Britain's entry into the European Community, Report by Sir Con O'Neill on the Negotiations of 1970–1972, London 2000, 341.
25   Edward Heath, *The Course of My Life*, Coronet London 1998, 365.
26   *Economist*, 22 May 1971.
27   Raphaele Ulrich-pier, René Massigli (1888–1988) *Une vie de diplomate*, II, Paris 2006, 1448.
28   Brian Harrison, *Finding a Role?*, Oxford 2010, 1.
29   OH, II, 432–3.
30   Michel Jobert, *Mémoires d'avenir*, Paris 1974, 203.
31   Kitzinger, *Diplomacy and Persuasion*, p. 125; Ewart-Biggs to Greenhill 9 November 1972, Soames Papers, 49/7, Churchill College, Cambridge.
32   Laurens van der Post, letter to *The Times* 31 March 1973, *Great Letters*, ed., James Owen, Harper Collins, Glasgow 2017, 278.
33   Sir Con O'Neill, Britain's entry into the European Community, David Hannay, ed., 330–1.
34   Soutou, op. cit., 495.
35   BDOHP, Palliser interview, 28 April 1999.
36   Campbell, *Jenkins*, 484.
37   Peter Pooley, UK representative EEC, Broad, *Britain and Europe*, 25.
38   Hannay, *Britain's Quest*, 61.
39   *Interests and Obsessions*, London 1993, 342–3.
40   Sir William Nicholl, deputy UK representative EEC 1977–82, Broad, *Britain and Europe*, 28.
41   Record of conversation between Heath and Pompidou, 20 May 1971, TNA PREM 15/372.
42   OH, II, 2, 364.

43 *Spectator*, 1 June 1973.
44 John Campbell, *Roy Jenkins*, Vintage 2014, 529.
45 London Letter 5 June 1945, Collected Essays, Journalism, 3,449.
46 25 January 1949, Muggeridge Papers, Box 1, Hoover Archive, Stanford, California.
47 Tony Shaw, *Eden, Suez and the Mass Media*, London 1996, xi.
48 Kenneth Younger, 'Public opinion and British foreign policy', *IA*, January 1964, 31–2.
49 *The Unknown Citizen* (1940), Oxford Dictionary of Quotations, 4th edn, 1992, 36.
50 Robert Jowell, Gerard Hoinville, eds, *Britain into Europe*, London 1976, 25.
51 Roy Denman, *The Mandarin's Tale*, London 2002, 115.
52 Violet Bonham Carter, *Daring to Hope*, London 2000, 210.
53 Jacques Ellul, *Propaganda: The formation of men's attitudes*, New York 1969, 87.
54 'The Segregation of Dissent', *Writing by Candlelight*, London 1980, 2.
55 *The Future of British Foreign Policy*, London 1968, 112, 137.
56 Jad Adams, 'Tony Benn', *Irrepressible Adventures with Britannia*, ed. Wm. Roger Louis, 2013, 329.
57 March 1979, paras 30–2: http://www.margaretthatcher.org/document/110961
58 *Oxford Dictionary of Quotations*, 4th edn.

Select Bibliography

Only works cited in the text are listed.

Official documents

Britain: The National Archives
France: Archives nationales: de Gaulle, president de la republique, 5 AG 1 (fonds Solférino)
Ministère des Affaires Etrangères
Ministère de l'Economie et des Finances
Assemblee nationale, commission des affaires etrangeres, IV–V Republics

Private papers

Britain

Sir Pierson Dixon (private)

Bodleian Library, Oxford

Sir Patrick Reilly unpublished memoir
Harold Macmillan Archive
George Brown
Harold Wilson
Paul Gore-Booth
Conservative Party Archive
Roundell Palmer, 3rd Earl of Selborne
Walter Monckton

Churchill Archives Centre, Cambridge

Lord Gladwyn
Hughe Knatchbull-Hugessen
Selwyn Lloyd
William Haley
Duncan Sandys
Christopher Soames
Edwin Plowden
Alfred Duff Cooper

British Library of Political and Economic Science

Alastair Hetherington
Anthony Crosland
Violet Rhys-Williams
James Meade

Hoover Institution Archives

Raymond Aron
Victor Hoo
Alexandre Kojève
Jacques Leprette
Malcolm Muggeridge
John Vaizey

Royal Institute of International Affairs (Chatham House) Archives

University of Leeds, Special Collection

Edward Boyle Papers

France

L'office universitaire de recherche socialiste (L'OURS)

Guy Mollet

Archives nationales

Christian Pineau

FNSP

Maurice Couve de Murville
Alexandre Parodi
Michel Debré
Wilfrid Baumgartner

Published documents

Documents on British Policy Overseas
Documents Diplomatiques Français
Foreign Relations of the United States
Britain's Entry into the European Community: Report on the Negotiations of 1970–1972 by Sir Con O'Neill, ed., Sir David Hannay, 2000

British Documents on the End of Empire (HMSO, 1992–2000)

Oral history

British Diplomatic Oral History Programme (BDOHP)
EU Oral History Archives: Voices on Europe programme

Memoirs and diaries

Alphand, H., *L'Etonnement d'être* (1977)
Ball, S., *The Headlam Diaries, 1935–1951* (1999)
Baeyens, J., *Au bout du Quai* (1975)
Benn, T., *Out of the Wilderness: diaries, 1963–7* (1987)
Benn, T., *Office Without Power: Diaries, 1968–72* (1988)
Benn, T., *Against the Tide: Diaries, 1973–6* (1989)
Beauvoir, S. de., *La Force des Choses* (1963)
Berard, A., *Un ambassadeur se souvient, I* (1976)
Bloch, M., *Strange Defeat* (1968)
Bohlen, Charles E., *Witness to History* (1973)
Brandt, W., *My Life in Politics* (1993)
Brown, G., *In My Way* (1971)
Cairncross, A. (ed.), *The Robert Hall Diaries* (1989)
Cairncross, A., *The Wilson Years: A Treasury Diary* (1997)
Calvocoressi, P., *Threading My Way* (1994)
Camus, A., *Journaux de voyage* (1978)
Camus, A., *Notebooks 1942–1951* (1966)
Carey, J., *The Unexpected Professor* (2014)
Castle, B., *The Castle Diaries, 1964–70* (1984)
Catterall, P. (ed.), *The Macmillan Diaries I: The Cabinet Years 1950–57* (2003)
Catterall, P. (ed.), *The Macmillan Diaries II: Prime Minister and After 1957–1966* (2011)
Chalfont, A., *The Shadow of My Hand* (2000)
Chambon, A., *Que font donc ces diplomates?* (1983)
Chauvel, J., *Commentaire*, 3 vols (1971–3)
Clark, K., *The Other Half* (1977)
Colville, J., *Fringes of Power, Downing Street Diaries, 2* (1987)
Cooper, A. Duff, *Old Men Forget* (1954)
Cox, G., *See It Happen* (1983)
Crossman, R., *Diaries of a Cabinet Minister, 3, 1968–70* (1975)
Dalton, H., *High Tide and After* (1962)
Day, R., *Grand Inquisitor* (1989)
Deniau, J.-F., *Mémoires de 7 Vies, II* (1997)
Denman, R., *The Mandarin's Tale* (2002)
Dilks, D. (ed.), *The Diaries of Sir Alexander Cadogan* (1972)
Dixon, P. (ed.), *Double Diploma* (1968)
Dover, K., *Marginal Comment* (1994)
Duff Cooper Diaries, 1915–1951, John Julius Norwich (ed.) (2005)

Dumaine, J., *Quai d'Orsay* (1955)
Eden, A., *Memoirs: The Reckoning* (1965)
Enright, D.J., *Memoirs of a Mendicant Professor* (1969)
Evans, H., *Downing Street Diary* (1981)
Foccart, J., *Journal de l'Elysée, I, 1965–1967* (1997)
Foot, M.R.D., *Memories of an SOE Historian* (2008)
Froment-Meurice, H., *Vu du Quai* (1998)
Gaulle, C. de., *The Complete War Memoirs of Charles de Gaulle* (1998)
Gaulle, P. de., *De Gaulle, Mon Père* (2003)
Gladwyn, Lord, *The Memoirs of Lord Gladwyn* (1972)
Gore-Booth, P., *With Great Truth and Respect* (1974)
Guinness, A., *My Name Escapes Me* (1996)
Guinness, B., *Personal Patchwork* (1987)
Guehenno, J., *Voyages* (1952)
Guehenno, J., *Journal des années noires* (1947)
Haines, J., *The Politics of Power* (1977)
Halsey, A.H., *No Discouragement: An Autobiography* (1996)
Hannay, D., *Britain's Quest for a Role: a diplomatic memoir* (2012)
Hartley, A., *A State of England* (1963)
Harvey, J., *The War Diary of Oliver Harvey* (1978)
Harrison, J.F.C., *Scholarship Boy* (1995)
Hayter, W., *A Double Life* (1974)
Healey, D., *The Times of My Life* (1989)
Heath, E., *The Course of My Life* (1998)
Henderson, N., *Mandarin: diaries* (1994)
Hetherington, A., *Guardian Years* (1981)
Hoggart, R., *An Imagined Life, 3,* (1992)
Holroyd, M., *Basil Street Blues* (2000)
Horne, A., *But What Do You Actually Do?* (2011)
Hurd, D., *An End to Promises* (1979)
Hurd, D., *Memoirs* (2003)
Jay, D., *Change and Fortune* (1980)
Jebb, M., *The Diaries of Cynthia Gladwyn* (1995)
Jenkins, R., *A Life at the Centre* (1991)
Jobert, M., *Mémoires d'avenir* (1974)
King, C., *The Cecil King Diary, 1965–70* (1972)
Kirkpatrick, I., *The Inner Circle* (1959)
Kissinger, H., *The White House Years* (1979)
Lacey, N., *A Life of H.A.L. Hart* (2004)
Lessing, Doris, *A Small Personal Voice* (1974)
Lévi-Strauss, C., *Tristes tropiques* (1973)
Lloyd, S., *Suez, 1956* (1978)
Longford, E., *The Pebbled Shore* (1986)
Macmillan, H., *Tides of Fortune, 1945–55* (1969)
Macmillan, H., *Riding the storm, 1956–9* (1971)
Macmillan, H., *Pointing the Way, 1959–61* (1972)
Macmillan, H., *At the End of the Day, 1961–3* (1974)
Magee, B., *Growing up in a war* (2007)
Maitland, D., *Diverse Times, Sundry Places* (1996)

Mallaby, G., *From My Level* (1965)
Massigli, R., *Une Comédie des Erreurs* (1978)
Mauriac, C., *The Other de Gaulle: diaries 1944–54* (1973)
Mauriac, F., *Mémoires politiques* (1967)
Mauriac, J., *Le Général et le journaliste* (2008)
Mayhew, C., *Time to Explain* (1987)
Miller, A., *Timebends: A Life* (1987)
Monnet, J., *Memoirs* (1978)
Moorehead, C. (ed.), *Freya Stark Letters, vol. 7* (1974)
Mott-Radclyffe, C., *Foreign Body in the Eye* (1975)
Mount, F., *Cold Cream* (2008)
Muir, E., *An Autobiography* (1954)
Murville, Couve de, Maurice *Une politique étrangère* (1971)
Nicolson, N. (ed.), *Harold Nicolson: Diaries and Letters 1945–1962* (1968)
Nora, P. (ed.), *Vincent Auriol, Journal du septennat 1947–1954* (1970–8)
Ollard, R., *Diaries of A.L. Rowse, I* (2003)
Ozouf, M., *Composition française, retour sur une enfance bretonne* (2009)
Peyrefitte, A., *C'Etait De Gaulle, I* (1994)
Parrott, C., *The Serpent and the Nightingale* (1977)
Pimlott, B. (ed.), *The Political Diary of Hugh Dalton, 1918–40, 1945–60* (1986)
Pineau, C., *La Simple Vérité, 1940–1945* (1960)
Pineau, C., *Suez 1956* (1976)
Plowden, E., *An Industrialist in the Treasury* (1989)
Poncet, François A., *Souvenirs d'une ambassade à Berlin* (1946)
Pottle, M., *Daring to Hope: Diaries of Violet Bonham Carter* (2000)
Reynaud, P., *La France à sauvé l'Europe, I* (1947)
Ritchie, C., *Diplomatic Passport* (1981)
Roll, E., *Crowded Hours* (1985)
Roy, R. and Young J.W. (eds), *Ambassador to Sixties London: Diaries of David Bruce* (2009)
Rusk, D., *As I Saw it* (1990)
Servan Schreiber, J., *Lieutenant in Algeria* (1958)
Shuckburgh, E., *Descent to Suez: Diaries 1951–56* (1986)
Soutou, J.-M., *Un Diplomate engagé* (2011)
Stapleton, J., *Sir Arthur Bryant and National History in Twentieth Century Britain* (2005)
Stewart, M., *Life and Labour* (1980)
Strang, Lord., *At Home and Abroad* (1956)
Taylor, A.J.P., *A Personal History* (1983)
Teitgen, P.-H., *Faites entrer le temoin suivant* (1988)
Toynbee, A., *Experiences* (1969)
Tricot, B., *Mémoires* (1994)
Waldegrave, W., *A Different Kind of Weather* (2015)
Warner, G., *In the Midst of Events: Foreign Office Diaries and Papers of Kenneth G. Younger* (2005)
Warnock, M., *A Memoir: People and Places* (2000)
Werth, A., *France, 1940–1955* (1957)
Williams, M., *Inside Number 10* (1982)
Wilson, H., *The Labour Government, 1964–1970* (1971)
Williams, P.M. (ed.), *The Diary of Hugh Gaitskell* (1983)

Woodhouse, C.M., *Something Ventured* (1982)
Woolf, L., *Downhill All The Way* (1967)
Wright, P., *Spycatcher* (1987)

Secondary works

Agulhon, M., *The French Republic 1879–1992* (1993)
Anderson, P., *English Questions* (1992)
The New Old World (2009)
Andrew, C., *The Sword and the Shield* (2000)
Barclay, R., *Ernest Bevin and the Foreign Office* (1975)
Barré, J.-L., *Devenir de Gaulle, 1939–1943* (2003)
Beck, P.J., *Using History, Making British Policy* (2006)
Becker, J. and Knipping, F. (eds), *Power in Europe? France, Great Britain, Germany and Italy in a Post-war World, 1945–50* (1986)
Beckett, F., *Macmillan* (2006)
Beevor, A. and Cooper, A., *Paris after the Liberation* (1994)
Beloff, N., *The General Says No: Britain's exclusion from Europe* (1963)
Bell, P.M.H., *France and Britain 1040–1994* (1997)
Bezias, J.-R., *Georges Bidault et la politique étrangère de la France* (2006)
Bew, J., *Citizen Clem, a biography of Attlee* (2016)
Bachelier, C. (ed.), *Raymond Aron: Chroniques de Guerre* (1990)
Blackstone T. and Plowden W., *Inside the Think Tank: Advising the Cabinet 1971–83* (1988)
Blackwell, M., *Clinging to Grandeur: British Attitudes and Foreign Policy in the Aftermath of the Second World War* (1993)
Bossuat, G., *Faire L'Europe sans Défaire la France* (2005)
L'Europe des Français 1943–1959 (1996)
Briggs, A., *The History of Broadcasting in the United Kingdom, IV* (1995)
Broad, R. (ed.), *Britain and Europe: ICBH Witness Seminar Programme* (2002)
Bullock, A., *Ernest Bevin: Foreign Secretary, 1945–51* (1983)
Buruma, I., *Voltaire's Coconuts* (1999)
Cable, J., *The Geneva Conference of 1954 on Indochina* (1986)
Campbell, J., *Roy Jenkins* (2014)
Campbell, J., *Edward Heath: a biography* (1993)
Chalaby, J.K., *The De Gaulle Presidency and the Media* (2002)
Charlton, M., *The Price of Victory* (1983)
Chuter, D., *Humanity's Soldier* (1996)
Clarke, P., *Hope and Glory: Britain 1900–1990* (1996)
Clayman, S. and Heritage, J., *The News Interview* (2002)
Cobb, M., *Eleven Days in August* (2013)
Colley, L., *Britons: Forging the Nation, 1707–1837* (1996)
Craig, G.A. and Loewenheim, F.L. (eds), *The Diplomats, 1939–1979* (1994)
Creswell, M., *A Question of Balance : how France and the United States created Cold War Europe* (2006)
Crouzet, F., *Britain Ascendant: Comparative Studies in Franco-British Economic History* (1990)
Daddow, O. J. (ed.), *Harold Wilson and European Integration* (2003)
Dalloz, J., *Georges Bidault* (1992)

Deighton, A. (ed.), *Building Postwar Europe* (1995)
Dell, E., *The Schuman Plan and the British Abdication of Leadership in Europe* (1995)
Denman, R., *Missed Chances: Britain and Europe in the Twentieth Century* (1996)
Destremau, B., *Quai d'Orsay derrière la façade* (1994)
Dickie, J., *Inside the Foreign Office* (1992)
Dilks, D., *Rights, Wrongs and Rivalries* (1996)
Dillon, R., *History on British Television* (2010)
Dixon, P., *Double Diploma: the life of Sir Pierson Dixon: don and diplomat* (1968)
Dockrill, M., and Young, J.W. (eds), *British Foreign Policy 1945–56* (1989)
Donaldson, F., *The British Council: The First 50 Years* (1984)
Driver, C., *The Disarmers* (1964)
Dumoulin, M. (ed.), *Wartime Plans for Postwar Europe* (1995)
(ed.), *The European Commission 1958–1972: History and Memories* (2007)
Duroselle, J.-B., *La Décadence, 1932–1939* (1979)
Ellul, J., *Propaganda: the formation of attitudes* (1969)
Fauvet, J., *La IV République* (1959)
Ferguson, N., *Kissinger, The Idealist* (2015)
Foot, M., *Aneurin Bevan: a biography, II* (1973)
Free, Lloyd A. (ed.), *French Motivations in the Suez Crisis* (1956)
Gallup, G.H. (ed.), *The Gallup International Public Opinion Polls, France, I* (1977)
Gilbert, M., *Winston Churchill, VII* (1989)
Gillingham, J.R., *Coal, Steel, and the Rebirth of Europe 1945–1955* (1991)
Goldman, L., *The Life of R.H. Tawney* (2013)
Gowing, M., *Independence and Deterrence: Britain and Atomic Energy, 1945–1952, I, Policy Making* (1974)
Greenwood, S., *The Alternative Alliance: Anglo-French relations before the coming of NATO, 1944–48* (1996)
Greenwood, S., *Titan at the Foreign Office: Gladwyn Jebb and the shaping of the modern world* (2008)
Griset, P., *Georges Pompidou et la modernité* (2006)
Grosser, A., *La IV Republique et sa politique exterieure* (1961)
Guieu, J.-M, Sanderson, C., et al., *L'Historien et les relations internationales: Autour de Robert Frank* (2012)
Haas, E.B., *The Uniting of Europe* (1958)
Hardy, H. (ed.), *Isaiah Berlin: Letters, 1928–1946, I* (2004)
Harris, R., *Good and Faithful Servant* (1991)
Harrison, B., *Seeking a Role: The United Kingdom, 1951–1970* (2009)
Harrison, E., *The Young Kim Philby* (2012)
Harrison, M. and Hayward, J., (eds), *De Gaulle to Mitterand* (1993)
Haslam, J., *The Vices of Integrity: E.H. Carr 1892–1982* (1999)
Hayter, W., *The Diplomacy of the Great Powers* (1960)
Hazareesingh, S., *Political Tradition in Modern France* (1994)
Hecht, G., *The Radiance of France* (1998)
Henderson, *The Private Office* (1984)
Hennessy, P., *The Prime Minister* (2001)
Hennessy, P., *The Hidden Wiring* (1996)
Hennessy, P., *Muddling Through* (1997)
Hennessy, P., *Whitehall* (1990)
Hennessy, P., *Distilling the Frenzy* (2013)

Hines-Davenport, R., *An English Affair* (2013)
Hitchcock, W.I., *France Restored* (1998)
Hoffmann, S. (ed.), *France: Change and Tradition* (1963)
Hoggart, R., *The Uses of Literacy* (1957)
Holland, R., *The Pursuit of Greatness: Britain and the World Role* (1992)
Horne, A., *Macmillan*, Vols I (1894–1956); II (1957–1986) (1988–89)
Huizinga, J.H., *Confessions of a European in England* (1958)
James, R. Rhodes, *Anthony Eden* (1986)
Jenks, J., *British Propaganda and News Media in the Cold War* (2006)
Jones, C.S., *A Dangerous Liaison: Simone de Beauvoir and Jean-Paul Sartre* (2008)
Jowell, R. and Hoinville, G. (eds), *Britain into Europe: public opinion and the EEC, 1961–75* (1976)
Judt, T., *Postwar: A history of Europe since 1945* (2005)
Kelly, M., *The Cultural and Intellectual Rebuilding of France after the Second World War* (2004)
Kent, J., *British Imperial Strategy and the Origins of the Cold War, 1944–49* (1994)
Kirkham, P., Thomas, D. (eds), *War Culture* (1995)
Kitzinger, U., *The Second Try: Labour and the EEC* (1968)
Diplomacy and Persuasion: how Britain joined the Common Market (1973)
Knapp, A. (ed.) *The Uncertain Foundation: France at the Liberation 1944–47* (2007)
Kolodziej, E.A., *Making and Marketing Arms* (1987)
Kuhn, R., *The Media in France* (1995)
Kuisel, R.F., *Capitalism and the State in Modern France* (1981)
Kyle, K., *Suez* (1991)
Lacouture, J., *De Gaulle: The Ruler* (1991)
Lafon, F., *Guy Mollet: itineraire d'un socialiste controverse* (1905–1975) (2006)
Larkin, M., *France since the Popular Front* (1988)
Lawford, V., *Bound for Diplomacy* (1963)
Lebovics, H., *Mona Lisa's Escort* (1999)
Ledwidge, B., *De Gaulle* (1982)
Lord, C., *British Entry to the European Community under the Heath Government of 1970–4* (1993)
Lord, C., *Absent at the creation: Britain and the formation of the European Community 1950–2* (1996)
Louis, Wm. R. (ed.), *Adventures with Britannia* (1995)
Lowe, R., *The Official History of the British Civil Service, I* (2011)
Ludlow, Piers N., *Dealing with Britain: and the first UK application to the EEC* (1997)
Ludlow, Piers N., *The European Community and the crises of the 1960s* (2006)
Luthy, H., *The State of France: a study of contemporary France* (1955)
Lyttelton, O., *The Memoirs of Lord Chandos* (1962)
McCourt, D. M., *Britain and World Power since 1945: constructing a nation's role in international politics* (2014)
McDermott, G., *The Eden Legacy and the decline of British diplomacy* (1969)
McDonald, I., *The history of* The Times*: struggles in war and peace*, vol. 5 (1984)
McKenzie, B.A., *Remaking France: Americanization, public diplomacy, and the Marshall Plan* (2005)
McManus, M., *Edward Heath: A Singular Life* (2016)
Mallaby, G., *Each in his Office* (1972)
Mandler, P., *The English National Character* (2006)

Mangold, P., *The Almost Impossible Ally* (2006)
Marquand, D., *The Unprincipled Society* (1988)
Marquand, D., *Britain since 1918: the strange career of British democracy* (2008)
Marwick, A., *Class: Image and Reality in Britain, France and the USA since 1930* (1980)
Marwick, A. (ed.), *Total War and Social Change* (1988)
Mauriac, F., *De Gaulle* (1966)
Mendras, H. and Cole, A., *Social Change in Modern France* (1991)
Michaud, J.-C., *Alain Peyrefitte* (2002)
Moraze, C., *The French and the Republic* (1958)
Morgan, K., *Britain since 1945:The People's Peace* (1990)
Morin, E., *Commune en France: la metamorphose de Plozevet* (1968)
Noiriel, G., *Workers in French Society in the nineteenth and twentieth centuries* (1990)
Nolfo, Di, E. (ed.), *Power in Europe ? II. Great Britain, France, Germany and Italy and The origins of the EEC, 1952–7* (1992)
Nord, P., *France's New Deal* (2010)
Nouzille, V., *Des Secrets Si Bien Gardes* (2009)
Nutting, A., *Europe Will Not Wait* (1960)
Nye, J.S., *Soft Power: The Means to Success in World Politics* (2005)
Offer, A., *The Challenge of Affluence* (2006)
Ollard, R., *A Man of Contradictions: A Life of A.L. Rowse* (1999)
Ory, P., *La culture comme aventure* (2008)
Overy, R., *The Morbid Age: Britain between the wars* (2009)
Pagedas, C.A., *Anglo-American Strategic Relations and the French Problem* (2000)
Pastor-Castro, R. and Young, J.W. (eds), *The Paris Embassy* (2013)
Paterson, P., *Tired and Emotional: The Life of Lord George Brown* (1993)
Perrier, J., *Michel Debré* (2010)
Pimlott, B., *The Queen* (1996)
Poidevin, R., *Robert Schuman* (1986)
Purcell, H., *A Very Private Celebrity: The Nine Lives of John Freeman* (2015)
Reynolds, D., *Britannia Overruled* (2000)
Roberts, A., *The Storm of War* (2010)
Rogers, B., *A.J. Ayer: A Life* (1999)
Ross, K., *Fast Cars, Clean Bodies: decolonization and the reordering of French Culture* (1995)
Rothwell, V.H., *Britain and the Cold War* (1982)
Roussel, E., *Charles de Gaulle* (2002)
Sampson, A., *Anatomy of Britain* (1962)
Sanderson C., *Perfide Albion? L'affaire Soames et les arcanes de la diplomatie britannique* (2012)
Sanderson C., *L'Impossible Alliance? France, Grande-Bretagne et défense de l'Europe* (2003)
Saville, J., *The Politics of Continuity* (1993)
Shaw, T., *Eden, Suez, and the Mass Media* (1996)
Sheehan, J.J., *Where have all the soldiers gone* (2008)
Shennan, A., *Rethinking France* (1997)
Siegfried, A., *L'Ame des Peuples* (1950)
Sisman, A., *A.J.P. Taylor: A Biography* (1994)
Sisson, C.H., *The Spirit of British Administration and Some European Comparisons* (1959)
Skidelsky, R., *John Maynard Keynes, 3, Fighting for Britain, 1937–1946* (2000)
Smouts, M.-C., *La France à l'ONU* (1980)

Tachin, A., *Amie et Rivale: La Grande-Bretagne dans l'imaginaire français à l'époque gaullienne* (2009)
Thomas, H. (ed.), *Crisis in the Civil Service* (1968)
Thompson, E.P and T.J., *There is a spirit in Europe: a memoir of Frank Thompson* (1947)
Thompson, E.P., *Beyond the Frontier: the politics of a failed mission* (1997)
Thompson, E.P., *The Making of the English Working Class* (1963)
Thorpe, D.R., *Supermac* (2010)
Toulemon, R., *La construction européenne* (1994)
Tratt, J., *The Macmillan Government and Europe* (1996)
Ulrich-Pier, R., *René Massigli (1888–1988): une vie de diplomate, II* (2006)
Vaïsse, M., *La Grandeur: politique étrangère du géneral de Gaulle* (1998)
(ed.), *Mai 1945: La Victoire en Europe* (1985)
Vigezzi, B., *The British Committee on the Theory of International Politics 1954–1985: The Rediscovery of History* (2005)
Vinen, R., *Bourgeois Politics in France: 1945–1951* (1995)
Vital, D., *The Making of British Foreign Policy* (1968)
Wasserstein, B., *Barbarism and Civilization: A History of Europe in Our Time* (2007)
Williams, P.M., *Politics in Post-War France* (1954)
Williams, P.M.,*Hugh Gaitskell: A Political Biography* (1979)
Woodhouse, R., *British Policy Towards France, 1945–51* (1995)
Woodward, L., *British Foreign Policy in the Second World War*, vol. 5 (1971)
Young, H., *This Blessed Plot: Britain and Europe from Churchill to Blair* (1999)
Young, J.W. (ed.), *The Foreign Policy of Churchill's Peacetime Administration, 1951–5* (1988)
Young, J.W. (ed.), *Twentieth Century Diplomacy* (2008)
Young, J.W. (ed.), *Britain and European Unity 1945–1999* (2000)
Young, J.W. (ed.), *The Labour Governments 1964–1970*, 2, *International policy* (2003)
Ziegler, P., *Wilson: The Authorized Life* (1993)
Ziegler, P., *Edward Heath: The Authorized Biography* (2010)

Interviews

Sir Frank Roberts
Sir Guy Millard
Louis Joxe
Etienne Burin des Roziers
Jean Donnedieu de Vabres
Etienne de Crouy-Chanel
Christian Pineau

Index

Page numbers in **bold** refer to figures.

Acheson, Dean, 59, 87
Adenauer, Konrad, 133, **134**
Africa, 102, 127–8
Algerian war, 32, 34, 36, 57–8, 61, 132, 138, 144
Allais, Maurice, 81
Alliance francaise, 81
Alphand, Herve, 45, 83, 84
American Council on Foreign Relations, 113
Americanization, 59, 81
Amis, Kingsley, 88
Anderson, Perry, 21, 35
Anglo–American agreements, 126–7
Anglo–American alliance, 2, 45
Anglo–Franco–American Bermuda conference, 1953, 43
Anglo–Franco–American talks, 139
Anglo–French alliance, 1–2, 4
Anglo–French economic committee, 46, 124
Anglo-French Monnet Plan, 124
Anglo–French union, 45
Anglo–German partnership, 159
Anglo–Soviet relations, 123
Anscombe, Elizabeth, 22
anti-Americanism, 34–5
anti-imperialism, 16
archives
    France, xii–xiii
    missing pieces, xiv
    United Kingdom, xiii–xiv
Aron, Raymond, 5, 32, 33, 34, 55, 60, 119
Asterix, 32
Atlantic Charter, 1941, 4, 43, 101
Atlee, Clement, 15, 17, 18, 20, 46, 97, 104–5, 107, 108, 114
Atomic Agency, 62
Attlee, Clement, 3, 4, 101

Auden, W.H., 87
Auriol, Vincent, 40, 46, 57

Ball, George, 84
Balogh, Tommy, 159
Barnes, Julian, xv
Barraclough, Geoffrey, 93
Barrault, Jean-Louis, 34
Baumgartner, Wilfrid, 183
BBC, 16, 48, 79, 93, 94–5, 96
Beauvoir, Simone de, xv, 25, 29–30, 33, 60, 61
Beckett, Francis, 135
Beloff, Max, 189
Beloff, Nora, 135–6
Benn, Tony, xvii, 15, 87, 189
Berlin, Isaiah, 22, 87–8, 109
Berrill inquiry, 174
Berthelot, Philippe, 67
Bevan, Aneurin, xv, 107
Bevin, Ernest, xii, 1, 2, 8, 23, 41, 59, 66, 91, 101, 104, 105, 106, 112, 119, 124–5, **126**, 127–9, 129–30, 133–4
Bidault, Georges, 8, **56**, 58, 59, 65, 67, 69, 72, **72**, 122, 123–4, 125, 126, **126**
Bilderburg conference, 113
Bishop, Freddie, 111, 141
Blackett, Patrick, 21
Bletchley Park, 20
Bloch, Marc, 7, 25, 42
Bloch-Laine, Francois, 63
Blue Streak, 4–5, 90–1
Blum, Leon, **56**, 125
Board of Trade, 110, 127
Boegner, Jean-Marc, 83
Bohlen, Chips, 75
Bokassa, Jean-Bedel, 75
Bonham Carter, Violet, 78–9
Bonnet, Georges, 29

Bonnet, Henri, 57
Bowen, Elizabeth, 5–6
Brandt, Willy, 185
Bretherton, Russell, 131
Bretton Woods Agreement, 101
Brexit, 6
Briand, Aristide, 26
British Budgetary Question, the, 179
British Commonwealth, 44, 127, 132, 148, 165
British Council, 7, 46, 96, 183
British United Europe Movement, 137
Brook, Norman, xvii, 114
Brown, George, 23, 48, 50, 84, 111–2, **154**, 159
Brunet, Jean-Pierre, 83
Brussels Treaty, 1948, xiii, 40, 66, 128
Bryant, Arthur, 21–2
Butler, Michael, 162–3
Butler, R.A., 23, 163
Butterfield, Herbert, 21

Caccia, Harold, 111
Cadogan, Sir Alexander, 15, 111
Callaghan, James, xvii
Camus, Albert, 33, 34, 65, 81
Carr, E.H., 20–1, 21, 43
Carr, Raymond, 21
Castle, Barbara, 95
Catholic Action, 31
censorship, 78–9, 94
Central Economic Planning Staff, 129
Centre d'Etudes de Politique etrangere, 50
Centre d'etudes sociologiques, 62
Centre national de la recherche scientifique, 62
Cerdan, Marcel, 61
Chalfont, Lord, 164, 185
Chartier, Emile, 27
Chateau de Champs summit, 149
Chatham House, 50, 113, 189
Chauvel, Jean, 49, 83, 122, 123
Chesterton, G.K., 190
China, 170
Christian Democracy, 31
Christian Democrat party, 31
Church of England, 16
Churchill, Winston, 1, 13, 16, 17, 28, 41, 46, 50, 71, 89, 101, 102, **120**,

clinging to office, 105
de Gaulle feud, 122–4
and Eden, 105
Europeanism, 137
Franco-British rapprochement attempt, 1944, 119
funeral, 154
health, 106–7
insensitivity, 43
medaille militaire, 40
'Morning Thoughts', 43–4
obduracy, 122
visit to Moscow, 122
Churchill–Truman summit, 1952, xiv
CIA, 7, 90
cinema, 34, 61
Civil Service, deficiencies, 108–12
Clappier, Bernard, 148
Clark, Kenneth, 40–1
Clemenceau, Georges, xiii
CND, 22, 91
Coal and Steel Community, 64
Cobb, Richard, 21
cocacolonisation, 34
Cold War, 8, 14, 34, 41, 61, 66, 81, 102, 103–4, 121, 128–9, 183–4, 185
Cole, G. D. H., 22
collective memory, xvii
Collège Franco-Britannique, 46
commemoration craze, xvii
Commissariat general du plan, 61
Common Fisheries Policy Agreement, 187
Common Market, 156
communications technology, 189
Communist party, France, 2
Concord, 154
Connolly, Cyril, 88
Cook, William, 172
Coty, Rene, 57
Coudenhove-Kalergi, Richard, 131
Council of Europe, 40, 128, 137
Council of Ministers, 102, 156–7
Courcel, Geoffroy de, 49, 83, 186
Couve de Murville, Maurice, **82**, 83–4, 160, 161, 164, 168
Crosland, Tony, 4
Crossman, Richard, 108
Cuban missile crisis, 108

culture shock, xiv
customs union, 127
Czechoslovakia, invasion of, 175, 185

Dalton, Hugh, 89, 107
Dannes, Roger, **56**
Davies, Terence, 14
Day, Robin, 6, 94
Death on the Nile (film), 80–1
Debre, Michel, 39, 75–6, 78, **82**, 87, 139, 172, 175–6, 177, 178
debt, United Kingdom, 14
decolonization, 32, 34, 57–8, 61, 89–90, 102, 182
defence cooperation, 170, 172, 177
defence spending, 104
Defferre, Gaston, 78
Degaullophobia, 163
democratic deficits, 6
Deniau, Jean Francois, 148
Denmark, 143
Dien Bien Phu, battle of, 57
Dior, Christian, 55
diplomats, attitudes, 48–50
Direction generale des Affaires economiques, financieres et techniques, 66
Dixon, Pierson, 50, 141–2, 147
Documents on British Policy Overseas, 114
Douglas Home, Sir Alec, 15, 145
Druon, Maurice, 44–5
Duff Cooper, Alfred, 39–40, 44, **120**, 125, 128
Dulles, John Foster, 58
Dumaine, Jacques, 67
Duncan enquiry, 113
Dunkirk, Treaty of, 1947, 1, 40, 41, 119, 125–8, **126**, 128
Durbin, Evan, 87
Duroselle, Jean-Baptiste, 30, 127

eastern Europe, 23
Eccles, David, 98, 147
École nationale d'administration, 35–6, 62
economic development, France, 46–7
economic growth, 166, 184
economic integration, 2

economic performance, France, 5
Economic Policy Committee, 129
Economist, 128–9, 186
Eden, Anthony, 8, 15, 44, 50, 98, 102, 184
  and Churchill, 105
  destruction of collusion evidence, xv–xvii
  and Franco-British union proposal, 1956, 132
  health, 106
  resignation, 144
EFTA, 143, 154, 156, 163
Eisenhower, Dwight D., 43
Elizabeth II, Queen, 46, 51, 140
Elton, G.R., 90
English language, advance of, 81
entente cordiale, 1, 2–3, 45, 46, 50
Europe
  British-led, 120–1
  division of, 13
European Coal and Steel Community, 111, 129–31
European Defense Community, 58, 67
European Economic Community
  criticised as rich man's club, 23
  de Gaulle vetos UK membership, 2, 73, 75–6
  de Gaulle's support for, 73
  Macmillan membership application, 142–51
  renewal of UK entry talks, 8–9
  second UK membership bid, 5
  UK accession, 186–8
  Wilson membership applications, 158–66, 167–80
European integration, 23
European Union, foundation myth, 2
Euroscepticism, 6, 151
evidence, destruction of, xv–xvii
Expo 58 Brussels World Fair, 96

Faure, Edgar, 57, 75
Febvre, Lucien, 25
federal Europe, 4
Ferguson, Niall, 181
First World War, 1, 26, 29
Foccart, Jacques, xiii, 177
Fontaine, Andre, 175

Foreign Office, 110–1, 112, 113, 114, 145, 157, 162, 163–4, 188
foreign policy, 103
  France, 29, 66–7, 85
  United Kingdom, 14, 19, 92–4, 108
Fouchet Plan, 143, 185
France
  Allied betrayal, 29–30
  archives, xii–xiii
  attitudes, 25–37
  causes of failure, 182–3
  causes of renewal, 59–61
  church state separation, 26
  Committee for the History of the Second World War, 28
  Communist party, 2
  constitutional compromise, 1946, 69
  contradictions, 35–6
  cultural capital, 32–3, 80–2
  de Gaulle's moral leadership, 74
  decolonization, 32, 34, 57–8, 61
  defence of language, 80–1
  distrust of, 132
  economic and political weakness, 2
  economic axis, 133
  economic development, 46–7
  economic growth, 184
  economic performance, 5
  economic recovery, 55
  elections, 1965, 158
  fault lines, 34
  Fifth Republic, 28, 30, 55, 69, 74, 183
  film industry, 34, 61
  foreign policy, 29, 66–7, 85
  Fourth Republic, 28, 33, 34, 36–7, 46–7, 57, 68
  German claims, 122
  great power status, 3
  historians, 47
  impact of Second World War, 25–31
  informality, xiii
  institutionalized talking down of, 47
  isolation, 175–6
  military pride, 32
  modernization, 27, 30–7, 61–2, 74
  national unity, 30
  need for renewal, 57–9
  nuclear weapons, 170
  options, 1945, 3
  overseas image, 66
  permanent crisis, 47–8
  philosophers, 21
  policy co-ordination, 63
  political elite, 35–6
  political rhetoric, 59
  powers of renewal, 5
  Provisional Government, 30, 31, 33–4
  public finances, 63
  quality of life, 61–2
  reconstruction, 25–36
  record-keeping, xii–xiii
  recovery, 183
  relationship with UK, 119–20, 155–8, 181–90
  religious renewal, 31–2
  renewal, 55–69, **56**
  second UK membership bid, 5
  self-liberating myth, 27–9, 36
  soft power, 7, 32–3, 82
  state machine renewal, 62–8
  state service recruitment, 63
  technological development, 37
  Third Republic, 26
  VE Day, 25
  weakness, 44–5
  Wilson membership application, 159, 160, 161
  withdrawal from NATO, 83, 158, 165
Franco–British alliance, 124
Franco–British Council, 45
Franco–British Europe proposals, 120–3, 128
Franco–British relationship, 39–51, 119, 175, 188–9
  attempt to rebuild, 1945-55, 46–9
  diplomats attitudes, 48–50
  friendships, 43
  goodwill, 39–40
  insensitivity of British leaders, 42
  lack of institutional infrastructure, 46
  language problems, 41
  popular responses, 41–2
  scholarly connections, 47
  stereotypes, 40–1
Franco–British union proposal, 1956, xiii, 131–3
Franco–German entente, 46, 63, 133
Franco-German Treaty, 1963, 156

Frankfurt School, 35
Franks, Sir Oliver, 91
Free French movement, 28, 60
free trade, 127, 134
free trade area, 131, 143
free trade talks, 138-9
Freedom of Information Act (2000), xvii
Freeman, John, 96
French Academy, 33
French Communist party, 58
Friendly Five, 163
Fulton Report, 110

Gaitskell, Hugh, 23, 87-9, 146
Gallagher, Willie, 16
Gasperi, Alcide De, 4
Gaulle, Charles de, 71-9, **72**, 160, 185
   aging, 177-8
   Allied betrayal, 29-30
   assassination attempt, 71
   attitude to UK, 51
   and Bidault, 124
   cabinet meetings, 75
   call for Franco-British alliance, 124
   captures moral high ground, 7
   character, 72-3, 75
   Churchill feud, 122-4
   claim for France's moral leadership, 74
   daily routine, 76
   death, xii
   decision making, 76
   diplomatic flexibility, 73-4
   expressions of friendship, 51
   flight to London, 1940, xv
   free trade talks, 138-9
   German claims, 122
   Healey on, 160
   image of detachment, 77
   legacy, 183
   loss of power, 87
   low opinion of the French, 123
   Macmillan membership application, 142, 142-3, 143-4, 149-50
   May 68 troubles, 75
   media management, 77-9
   meeting with Soames, Feb 1969, 174-5, 176
   meetings with Macmillan, 139-40
   ministerial appointments, 74-5
   obduracy, 122
   policy role, xii
   popular support, 85
   powers, 76
   pragmatism., 143
   Rambouillet summit, 142
   on reconstruction, 27
   resignation, 8, 167, 177
   return to power, 138
   roadshows, 77
   route map, 158
   and second UK membership bid, 5
   second Wilson membership application, 168, 169-70, 170-1, 177
   Second World War, 71-2
   sense of humour, 73
   stabilizes country, 59-60
   staff, 77
   state visit, 1960, 140-1
   status, 5, 71, 73
   Stewart on, 162
   support for EEC, 73
   symbolism, 27
   televised press conferences, 79
   velvet veto, 169
   veto of UK EEC membership, 2, 73, 75-6, 148-9
   war memoirs, xii, 101
   wilderness years, 73
   and Wilson, 154-8, 170-1
   Wilson membership application, 162-3
   withdrawal from NATO, 158
Gaullism, 71
Gay, Francisque, 69
Geneva Conference, 1954, 4
Geneva Conference on Vietnam, 102
geography, 13
geopolitical revolution, 101
Germany, 133, 159, 180
Gilson, Etienne, 31
Gladwyn, Cynthia, 146
global politics, 1
globalization, 66, 81, 84, 85, 94
Glubb, Sir John, 19
Gordon Walker, Patrick, 162
Gore-Booth, Paul, 111-2, 113
Gowing, Margaret, 114
Grandes Ecoles, 62

great power status, 3–4, 14, 180
Greenhill, Sir Denis, 179
Groupe 85, 31
Gruber, Francis, 60
Guehenno, Jean, 5

Hague Congress, 128
Hague Summit, 1969, 186
Halsey, A. H., 15
Hancock, Patrick, 175, 176–7, 179
Harmel Plan, 172
Harrison, Brian, 184
Harrod, Sir Roy, 15
Hart, Herbert, 22
Hartley, Anthony, 90
Harvey, Oliver, 48–9
Healey, Denis, 90, 113, 160
Heath, Edward, 3, 84, 157, 186–7, 188
    Macmillan membership application, 145, 147, 148, 150
    renewal of EEC entry talks, 8–9
    Wilson membership application, 160, 163
Heath–Pompidou Paris summit, 1971, 188
Heath–Pompidou accord, 186
Henderson, Nicholas, 189–90
Hetherington, Alistair, 104, 161
history, 13, 28
    Whig interpretation, 17–8
Hitchcock, William, 68
Hitler, Adolf, 1
Hoggart, Richard, 96
Holland, Stuart, 179–80
Hollywood, 34
Holocaust, the, 36
Horne, Alistair, 47, 135
Hurd, Douglas, 110, 111
Hussein, King of Jordan, 5

identity, 13, 17
India, 3
individualism, 27
Indo-China war, 3, 7, 34, 36, 57, 61
informal meetings, xvii
Information Research Department, 7
Institute for Contemporary British History, 20
institutional infrastructure, lack of, 46
insularity, 19, 21–3

interdependence, 4
international committees, 102
internationalism, 103
Ireland, 143
Ishiguro, Kazuo, 6–7
Israel, xv–xvii, 99

James, Henry, 8
Japan, 65
Jebb, Gladwyn, 49, 50
Jenkins, Roy, xvii, 5, 146, 154, 161, 187
Jobert, Michel, 186
joint economic planning, UK abandons, 129
Joxe, Louis, 74, 179–80
Judt, Tony, 34–5

Kennan, George, 93
Kennedy, John F., 81, 140–1, 166
Kenyon, John, 21, 72
Kershaw, Ian, 181
Kessel, Joseph, 28, 39
Keynes, John Maynard, 3, 124
Khrushchev, Nikita, 140
Kissinger, Henry, 4, 5, 182
Kitzinger, Uwe, 153
Knapp, Andrew, 119
Kojeve, Alexandre, 44–5
Konigswinter conference, 113
Korean War, 102, 104
Korukine, Nicolai, 66

la Tournelle, Guy de, 66
Labour government, 1966–70, 153–66
    bridge building, 154
    Europeanists, 163
    inexperience, 153–4
    National Plan, 165, 182
    reforms, 165
Labour Party, general election victory, 1945, 15
Landes, David, 46
language, 41, 80–1, 103, 184
Laniel, Joseph, 43
Laski, Harold J., 22
Laslett, Peter, 95
Le Club Jean Moulin, 63
Leavis, F. R., 23
Lebanon, 61

Lee, Frank, 82
Lefranc, Pierre, 77
Leger, Alexis, 65, 67
Levin, Bernard, 96
Levi-Strauss, Claude, 59, 181
Limited Test Ban Treaty, 1963 160
Lloyd, Selwyn, 4, 93, 94–5, 105–6, **139**, 145
Lodge, David, 20, 87
London
    Pompidou visits, 1966, 48
    the swinging sixties, 51
Luthy, Herbert, 48
Luxembourg Compromise, 158, 164

McCourt, David M., 3–4, 166
Mack Smith, Denis, 21
Mackenzie, Archie, 98
Macmillan, Harold, 3, 7, 40, 44, 98, 104, 105, 135–51, **137**
    on Anglo–French alliance, 1
    Cuban missile crisis, 108
    on de Gaulle, 74
    electoral triumph, 1959, 139, 141
    epitaph, 151
    Europeanism, 137–8
    failure, 140
    free trade talks, 138–9
    Grand Design, 141–2, 145
    health, 136, 144
    Jebb's influence, 49
    on loss of empire, 87–8
    meetings with de Gaulle, 139–40, **139**
    membership application, 135–6, 142–51
    misjudgement, 141
    never had it so good speech, 182
    self-doubt, 146
    status, 135
    Suez crisis diaries, xv
    taste for reading political autobiographies, xv
Madagascar, 61
Maillard, Pierre, 169–70
Malraux, Andre, 32, 71, 80, 177
Manchester Guardian, 88, 113
Mann, Thomas, 120
Maritain, Jacques, 31
Marshal Aid, 128
Marshall, H. E., 18

Massigli, Rene, 65, 83, 84, 123
Masterman, J. C., 16, 99
Mauriac, Francois, 59, 60–1
May 68 troubles, 75, 81, 86, 175
Mead, Margaret, 41
membership application, Macmillan, 142–51
    causes of failure, 146–51
    domestic critics, 144
    escorts, 143
    FO ministerial team, 145
    French red lines, 143–4
    lack of records, 142–3
    marketing failure, 146–7
    veto, 148–50
membership application, first Wilson, 158–66
membership application, second Wilson, 167–80
    legacy, 179–80
Mendè, Pierre, 48
Merchant, Livingstone, 92–4
Messina, 131, 146, 163
MI5, xvii
Michel, Henri, 28, 47
Middle East, the, 3
Millar, Frederick Hoyer, 111
Milward, Alan, xiv, 119–20, 133, 134, 183
Mimoun, Alain, 68
Ministry of Defence, 115
Mitford, Nancy, 43
Mitterand, Francois, 5, 77
Mollet, Guy, xiii, 1, 41, 57, 64, 131, 131–2, **137**
Molotov, Vyacheslav, 58, 102
Monnerville, Gaston, 32
Monnet, Jean, xiii, 2, 27, 45, 58–9, 63, 73, 126, 129
Moravcsik, Andrew, 73
Moraze, Charles, 68
Morrison, Herbert, 8, 19
Morton, H. V., 18
Moscow, 122
Mouvement republicain populaire, 123
multilateralism, 4, 49, 58, 66, 88–9, 101–3, 112, 132–3

NAFTA, 170–1
Namier, Sir Lewis, 18

Nasser, Gamal Abdel, 131, 163
national characteristics, 40–1
National Economic Development Council, 182
National Health Service, 23
national identity, 17
national wealth, United Kingdom, 14
NATO, 33, 102, 128, 158, 176, 181–2, 185
    French withdrawal, 83, 158, 165
Neale, Sir John, 17
newspapers, 79
Nicholson, Harold, 120
Nicolson, Harold, 87, 114
Nield, William, 172
Nixon, Richard M, 177, 182
Noel, Emile, 83, 131, 132
non-aligned movement, 103
Nora, Pierre, 81
nuclear age, 1
nuclear collaboration, 177
nuclear power, 30, 55, 62, 64
nuclear security, 126–7
nuclear weapons, 32, 88, 104, 170, 182
Nuremberg war crimes trials, 103
Nutting, Anthony, 99, 119
Nye, Joseph S., 96

OAS, 124
Observer, 113, 126
Offer, Avner, 91
official histories, xvii
O'Neill, Con, 163
one-world strategy, 127, 134
options, 1945, 3
ORTF, 78, 79
Ortoli, Francois-Xavier, 187
Orwell, George, 4, 16, 20
Ostpolitik, 185

Pakenham, Frank, 104–5
Palewski, Gaston, 43
Palliser, Michael, 113, 158, 180
Paris, 33, 41
    as capital of Europe, 5
    hosts peace conference, 60
    VE Day, 25
Paris Match, 161
Paris Metro, xii
Paris summit, 1960, 141
Paris summit, 1965, 155
Paris talks, 1967, 168–9
Parodi, Alexandre, 58, 67
patriotism, 16–7
Pax Americana, 3, 87, 181–2
Paxton, Robert, 153
Peele, Gillian, 153
Peri, Gabriel, 55, 68
Petain, Marshal Philippe, 26
Petra, Yvon, 61
Peyrefitte, Alain, xiii, 142, 155
Philip, Andre, 61
Philip, Prince, Duke of Edinburgh, 91–2
philosophy, 21
Pinay, Antoine, 75
Pineau, Christian, 39
Plevin, Rene, 58
Plowden Report on Representational Services Overseas, 101, 112, 113
Plozevet, 62
political cultures, 2
Pompidou, Georges, 3, 9, 37, 48, 75, 77, 78, 157, 160, 161, 178, 186, 188
Poncet, Andre Francois, 64
post-war reconstruction, 4
Profumo scandal, 98
protectionism, 134
public intellectuals, 22
Public Records Act, 1958, 20

Quai d'Orsay
    chaos, 64
    Direction generale des Affaires economiques, financieres et techniques, 66
    loss of autonomy, 84
    organizational crisis, 65
    purges, 65
    recruitment, 110
    renewal, 65–8
    secretary-generals, 67, 83
    soft power, 82
    staff shortage, 64–5
    and Wilson, 156

Ramadier, Paul, 119, 127
Rambouillet summit, 142
Raphael, Frederick, 84
Reilly, Patrick, 50, 163, 167, 170, 172, 173

Reynaud, Paul, 27–8, 73
Ridgway, Matthew B, 58
Robinson, John, 163, 175, 176–7
Roll, Sir Eric, 142
Rome, Treaty of, 73, 158, 159
Roosevelt, Franklin D., 13
Rostow, Eugene, 180
Roussillon, 61–2
Rowse, A.L., 89–90
royal visits, 46
RTF, 77, 78
Rusk, Dean, 75
Russell, Bertrand, 1, 22

Saint-Exupéry, Antoine de, 25
Sampson, Anthony, 109
Sargent, Orme, 111, 125
Sartre, Jean-Paul, xv, 25, 26, 33, 34, 35, 42, 55, 61
scholarly connections, 47
Schonfield, Andrew, 47
Schuman, Robert, 59, 67–8, **134**
Schuman Plan, xiv, 2, 63, 64, 67, 130, 163
Second World War, 1, 14, 71–2
    consequences of, 5–6, 7–8, 13–4
    end in Europe, 13
    peace conference, 60
    VE Day, 18, 25
Servan-Schreiber, Jean-Jacques, 68
Service de liaison interministeriel pour l'information, 78
SGCI, 64, 67
Shuckburgh, Evelyn, 92
Siegfried, Andre, 40
Sisson, C. H., 23
Six/Seven impasse, 139–42
Skidelsky, Robert, 188
Smuts, Jan, 44
Snow, C.P., 22, 90
Soames, Christopher, xiv, 8–9, 51, 87, 167, 167–8, 172–7, **174**, 177, 177–9
Society for the Study of French History, 47
soft power, 7, 32–3, 82, 96–7
Sontag, Susan, 23
sources
    destruction, xv–xvii
    missing pieces, xiv, xv

official histories, xvii
selection and handling, xii–xiiv
uncertainty, xiv–xv
sovereignty, 39
Soviet Union, 13, 34, 79, 88, 96, 122, 125, 127
Spaak, Paul-Henri, xiii, 23, 44, 121
Spectator, 188
Stark, Freya, 102
stereotypes, 40–1
sterling, devaluation, 129, 166, 171
Stewart, Michael, 155, 157–8, 162, 164, 176, 178
Strang, William, 111
Suez crisis, 4, 20, 41, 64, 131, 133
    ambassadors excluded from decision making, 49
    Anglo–French collusion, 104
    destruction of collusion evidence, xv–xvii
    Macmillan diaries, xv
    overriding lesson, 97
    political mendacity, 98–9
    recrimination, 91
Sunday Times, The, 2
supranationalism, 157
Sweden, 182
swinging sixties, the, 51
Syria, 40, 61, 119

Tawney, R. H., 22, 90
Taylor, A.J.P., 20, 21, 30, 98
Taylor, Alan, 92
television, 79
Tewson, Vincent, 97
Thatcher, Margaret, 188
Thomas, Albert, 26
Thomas, Hugh, 98
Thompson, E.P., 6, 189
Thompson, Frank, 4
Thorez, Maurice, **56**
timeline, 191–4
The Times, 17, 114, 124, 142–51, 175
Titfield Thunderbolt, The (film), 8
Tizzard, Sir Henry, 88, 91
Tolkien, J.R.R., 181
Toynbee, Arnold, 103, 144–5
Trautmann, Bert, 50–1
Treasury, 110–1, 127, 133, 179

Trevelyan, G. M., 17
Truman, Harry S., 15, 22, 122
Tunisia, 61

UN Security Council, 1, 33
UN Universal Declaration of Human Rights, 31, 33
UNESCO, 33
United Kingdom, 87–99
  accession to EEC, 186–8
  archives, xiii–xiv
  attitude to foreigners, 19, 23
  attitudes, 13–24
  bankruptcy, 127
  belief in a special destiny, 21–2
  bias against recent history, 47
  bungled self-marketing, 7
  causes of failure, 182, 183–4, 185–6
  censorship, 94
  comparisons with the United States, 90
  competitiveness, 97–8
  cost, 186
  crisis of confidence, 183–4
  culture shock, xiv
  debt, 14
  decision-making, 6
  decolonization, 89–90, 182
  degrading effects of Second World War, 5–6, 7–8
  diplomats attitudes, 48–50
  economic strength, 4
  ennui, 87–90
  European diplomacy, 188
  exclusion from the space age, 90–1
  foreign policy, 14, 19, 92–4, 108
  foreign secretaries, 83
  Freedom of Information Act (2000), xvii
  general election, 1945, 15
  great power obsession, 180
  great power status, 3–4, 14
  historians, 47
  identity crisis, 87, 183
  inequalities, 14–5
  insensitivity of leaders, 42
  insularity, 19, 21–3
  lack of faith, 134
  leadership deficiencies, 104–15
  loss of empire, 87
  loss of influence, 90
  loss of initiative, 97
  Macmillan membership application, 135–6, 142–51
  the monarchy, 16, 91–2
  national interest, 93
  National Plan, 165, 182
  national wealth, 14
  need for a vision, 98
  neglect of history, 114
  nuclear weapons, 104, 182
  official histories, xvii
  one-world strategy, 127
  options, 1945, 3
  overstretch, 182
  permanent secretaries, 83
  policy research, 113
  political elite, 183
  political mendacity, 98–9
  position in Western Europe, 4–5
  post-war economy, 47
  press, 95–6
  primacy, 120
  propaganda, 96–7
  questioning of assumptions, 91–2
  rationing, 88
  record-keeping, xiii
  relationship with France, 119–20, 155–8, 181–90
  relationship with USA, 3, 13, 45–6, 92, 166
  renewal of EEC entry talks, 8–9
  secrecy, 184
  self-satisfaction, 18–9
  social hierarchy, 15–6
  soft power, 96–7
  state apparatus, 19–20
  subaltern position, 3
  US dependency on, 127–8
  Whitehall machine, 108–12
  world trade, 13–4
United Nations, 58, 85–6, 102, 103, 124
United States of America, 8, 90
  Cold War alliance, 66
  dependency on Britain, 127–8
  national characteristics research, 41
  nuclear weapons, 104
  relationship with UK, 3, 13, 45–6, 92, 166

Wilson membership application, 159, 166
United States of Europe, 44
utility pact, 1947, 125

Vaizey, John, 23
Vernant, Jacques, 81
Vichy, 26, 28, 29, 36, 60
Vietnam War, 166
Vinen, Richard, 36–7

Wahl, Jean, 180
Wall, Stephen, 136
Warnock, Mary, 21
Washington telegrams, xii
Weil, Simone, 22–3
Werth, Alexander, 47–8
West Germany, 128, 171, 175
  rearmament, 58, 63
Western Organizations Department, 163
Western Union, 128
WEU, 172
Whitehall
  deficiencies, 108–12
  distrust of French, 132
  dysfunctionality, 161, 164
  opposition to customs union, 127
  permanent secretaries, 111–2
  recruitment, 110
Williams, Marcia, 160–1
Williams, Philip, 48
Williams, William Carlos, 151

Wilson, Harold, 51, 97, 108, 153–66, **154**
  achievement, 153
  attitude to West Europeans, 161
  bridge building, 154
  commitment to eventual membership, 153
  and de Gaulle, 154–8, 170–1
  failure, 153
  first membership application, 158–66
  and the FO, 162
  inexperience, 153–4
  The Labour Governments, 161
  legacy, 179
  National Plan, 182
  opportunism, 165, 185
  Paris talks, 1967, 168–9
  prevarication, 165
  reforms, 165
  refusal to take no, 178
  second membership application, 167–80
witnesses, voices of, xii
Wormser, Olivier, 67, 83, 149, 156, 159, 169, 175
Worsthorne, Peregrine, 146
Wright, Peter, xvii

Yalta Conference, 122
Yaounde Agreements, 187
Younger, Kenneth, 113

Ziegler, Philip, 176–7
Zuckerman, Solly, 170, 171

www.ingramcontent.com/pod-product-compliance
Lightning Source LLC
Chambersburg PA
CBHW072137290426
44111CB00012B/1897